Writing the History of the Humanities

Writing History

The *Writing History* series publishes accessible overviews of particular fields in history, focusing on the practical application of theory in historical writing. Books in the series succinctly explain central concepts to demonstrate the ways in which they have informed effective historical writing. They analyse key historical texts and their producers within their institutional arrangement, and as part of a wider social discourse. The series' holistic approach means students benefit from an enhanced understanding of how to negotiate the contours of successful historical writing.

Series editors: Stefan Berger (Ruhr University Bochum, Germany), Heiko Feldner (Cardiff University, UK) and Kevin Passmore (Cardiff University, UK)

Published:

Writing Medieval History, edited by Nancy F. Partner
Writing Early Modern History, edited by Garthine Walker
Writing Contemporary History, edited by Robert Gildea and Anne Simonin
Writing Gender History (second edition), Laura Lee Downs
Writing Postcolonial History, Rochona Majumdar
Writing the Holocaust, edited by Jean-Marc Dreyfus and Daniel Langton
Writing the History of Memory, edited by Stefan Berger and Bill Niven
Writing Material Culture History, edited by Anne Gerritsen and Giorgio Riello
Writing History (third edition), edited by Stefan Berger, Heiko Feldner and Kevin Passmore
Writing Transnational History, Fiona Paisley
Writing Visual Histories, edited by Florence Grant and Ludmilla Jordanova
Writing Material Culture History (second edition), edited by Anne Gerritsen and Giorgio Riello

Forthcoming:

Writing Queer History, edited by Matt Cook
Writing Gender History (third edition), Laura Lee Downs
Writing Conceptual Histories, edited by Pasi Ihalainen and Jani Marjanen

Writing the History of the Humanities: Questions, Themes, and Approaches

Edited by Herman Paul

BLOOMSBURY ACADEMIC
LONDON • NEW YORK • OXFORD • NEW DELHI • SYDNEY

BLOOMSBURY ACADEMIC
Bloomsbury Publishing Plc
50 Bedford Square, London, WC1B 3DP, UK
1385 Broadway, New York, NY 10018, USA
29 Earlsfort Terrace, Dublin 2, Ireland

BLOOMSBURY, BLOOMSBURY ACADEMIC and the Diana logo are trademarks
of Bloomsbury Publishing Plc

First published in Great Britain 2023

Copyright © Herman Paul, 2023

Herman Paul has asserted his right under the Copyright, Designs and Patents
Act, 1988, to be identified as Editor of this work.

Cover images: Pictures Now/Alamy Stock Photo and (background) kaipong/Adobe Stock.

All rights reserved. No part of this publication may be reproduced or transmitted
in any form or by any means, electronic or mechanical, including photocopying,
recording, or any information storage or retrieval system, without prior permission
in writing from the publishers.

Bloomsbury Publishing Plc does not have any control over, or responsibility
for, any third-party websites referred to or in this book. All internet addresses
given in this book were correct at the time of going to press. The author and
publisher regret any inconvenience caused if addresses have changed or sites
have ceased to exist, but can accept no responsibility for any such changes.

A catalogue record for this book is available from the British Library.

A catalog record for this book is available from the Library of Congress.

ISBN: HB: 978-1-3501-9906-4
       PB: 978-1-3501-9910-1
       ePDF: 978-1-3501-9907-1
       eBook: 978-1-3501-9908-8

Series: Writing History

Typeset by RefineCatch Limited, Bungay, Suffolk

To find out more about our authors and books visit www.bloomsbury.com
and sign up for our newsletters.

Contents

List of Illustrations viii
Notes on Contributors ix
Preface xii

Introduction: What is the History of the Humanities?
    Herman Paul 1

Part I Definitions and Backgrounds

1 **What are the Humanities? A Short History of Concepts and Classifications** Fabian Kraemer   27

2 **From Philology to the Humanities: Fragmentation and Discipline Formation in the United Kingdom and United States** James Turner   47

3 **The Humanities in Crisis: Comparative Perspectives on a Recurring Motif** Hampus Östh Gustafsson   65

Part II Research Practices

4 **Modernizing the Comparative Method: Marx and Darwin** Devin Griffiths   87

5 **Language and the Mapping of the World: Nineteenth-Century Linguistics in Relation to Ethnology and Geography** Floris Solleveld   109

6	"Big"-ness in Action: Notes from a Lexicon *Christian Flow*	131
7	Oral History and the (Digital) Humanities *Julianne Nyhan and Andrew Flinn*	153

Part III Values and Virtues

8	Practical Learning: The Transnational Career of an Epistemic Value in Japan *Michael Facius*	173
9	An Ethos of Criticism: Virtues and Vices in Nineteenth-Century Strasbourg *Herman Paul*	193
10	Producing the Masculine Scholar: Europe in the Nineteenth and Twentieth Centuries *Falko Schnicke*	217
11	Scholarly Activism in Africa: The *General History of Africa* (1964–98) *Larissa Schulte Nordholt*	245

Part IV Teaching Practices

12	The Humanities in the Vocational University: On the Unity of Teaching and Research *Kasper Risbjerg Eskildsen*	267
13	On the Purpose of Humanities Education: A Historical Perspective from the Mid-Twentieth-Century United States *Claire Rydell Arcenas*	287

Part V Visions of the Future

14	The Postcritical Turn: Unraveling the Meaning of "Post" and "Turn" *Herman Paul*	305

15 **Environmental Humanities: Entangled
    Interdisciplinarity** *Kristine Steenbergh*   325

16 **Humanities across Time and Space: Four Challenges for
    a New Discipline** *Rens Bod*   345

Glossary   365
Index   369

Illustrations

Figures

5.1 The Standard Alphabet applied to Armenian, from
     the second edition of Lepsius's *Standard Alphabet* (1863)   117

5.2 Lucy Lloyd's transcription and parallel translation
     of a /Xam fable, using a modified version of the
     Standard Alphabet. Bleek and Lloyd Collection,
     University of Cape Town Libraries   119

5.3 Pedigree chart of human races, from Müller,
     Allgemeine Ethnograpie (1872)   124

10.1 Carl Oesterley, Karl Otfried Müller (1830), oil on canvas,
     74 x 63 cm, private collection. © Photo Stephan Eckardt,
     Archäologisches Institut der Universität Göttingen   228

Table

5.1 Main collections of language material, late eighteenth
     to early twentieth century   113

Contributors

Claire Rydell Arcenas is an Associate Professor of History at the University of Montana. She is the author of *America's Philosopher: John Locke in American Intellectual Life* (University of Chicago Press, 2022).

Rens Bod is Professor of Digital Humanities and History of the Humanities at the University of Amsterdam. He is co-founder of the journal *History of Humanities* and serves as the president of the Society for the History of the Humanities. His books include *A New History of the Humanities* (Oxford University Press, 2013) and *World of Patterns: A Global History of Knowledge* (Johns Hopkins University Press, 2022).

Kasper Risbjerg Eskildsen is Associate Professor of History of Science at Roskilde University. His work focuses on the history of the human sciences as well as the history of higher education in the modern era, from the seventeenth century to today. He is the author of *Modern Historiography in the Making: The German Sense of the Past, 1700–1900* (Bloomsbury, 2022).

Michael Facius is an Associate Professor at the University of Tokyo. He has published on the history of knowledge in Japan from a transnational perspective. His monograph on the history of Chinese knowledge in Japan, *China übersetzen: Globalisierung und chinesisches Wissen in Japan im 19. Jahrhundert* was published in German (Campus Verlag, 2017).

Andrew Flinn is a Reader in Archival Studies and Oral History in the Department of Information Studies at UCL. A long-term member of the UK and Ireland Community Archives and Heritage Group, he writes mainly about public history and community-based heritage.

Christian Flow is Assistant Professor of History at Mississippi State University. His research concerns the history of classical scholarship since the Renaissance. He is at work on a book manuscript entitled *Philological Observation*.

Devin Griffiths is Associate Professor of English and Comparative Literature at the University of Southern California. His is the author of *The Age of Analogy: Science and Literature Between the Darwins* (Johns Hopkins University Press, 2016), and co-editor of *After Darwin: Literature, Theory, and Criticism in the Twenty-First Century* (Cambridge University Press, 2022).

Fabian Kraemer is Assistant Professor (*Assistent*) in the History of Science at the Ludwig Maximilians University in Munich. He is the author of *Ein Zentaur in London: Lektüre und Beobachtung in der frühneuzeitlichen Naturforschung* (2014), which will appear in English translation with Johns Hopkins University Press.

Julianne Nyhan is Chair of Humanities Data Science and Methodology at the Technische Universität Darmstadt and Professor of Digital Humanities at UCL. She has published widely in the area of digital humanities and has a particular interest in oral history and the history of digital humanities.

Hampus Östh Gustafsson is a researcher at the Department of History of Science and Ideas, Uppsala University, currently working on a project on university governance. In 2021, he defended his doctoral thesis on the legitimacy of the humanities in the politics of knowledge in twentieth-century Sweden. Recent publications include articles in *History of Humanities* and *Lychnos*.

Herman Paul is Professor of the History of the Humanities at Leiden University, where he directs a research project on "Scholarly Vices: A Longue Durée History." He is the author, most recently, of *Historians' Virtues: From Antiquity to the Twenty-First Century* (Cambridge University Press, 2022).

Falko Schnicke is Senior Lecturer in Modern History at the Johannes Kepler University Linz. He has written on the history of historiography, the history of biography, and the history of masculinity. Currently, he works on a project in contemporary British history exploring the monarchy's role in foreign policy. Also, he is engaged in a project on nineteenth-century European perceptions of climate change.

Larissa Schulte Nordholt teaches history at Leiden University, where she defended her PhD thesis on "Africanizing African History: Decolonization of Knowledge in UNESCO's *General History of Africa* (1964–1998)" in 2021. Recent articles of her appeared in *History of Humanities* and *History in Africa*.

Floris Solleveld is an FWO Postdoctoral Fellow at KU Leuven, working on a project about ethnolinguistics and geography in the long nineteenth century. He obtained his PhD at Radboud University Nijmegen with a study of transformations in the humanities between *c.* 1750–1850 and held fellowships in Halle (Saale), Gotha, and Amsterdam as well as a visiting position at MPIWG (Berlin).

Kristine Steenbergh is Associate Professor of English Literature at Vrije Universiteit Amsterdam. She specializes in the early modern period, the history of emotions, and the environmental humanities. Her most recent publication is a volume edited with Katherine Ibbett, *Compassion in Early Modern Literature and Culture: Feeling and Practice* (Cambridge University Press, 2021).

James Turner is Cavanaugh Professor of Humanities and Professor of History Emeritus at the University of Notre Dame. His research focuses on British and American intellectual life in the long nineteenth century. His several books cover topics ranging from changing attitudes toward animals to the origins of religious agnosticism to the evolution of humanistic scholarship.

Preface

This volume seeks to provide a state-of-the-art overview of a new scholarly field: the history of the humanities. As recent as twenty years ago, this field did not exist. Back then, nobody identified as a historian of the humanities. But much has changed since then. Conferences on "The Making of the Humanities" began to be organized, a Society for the History of the Humanities was founded, the journal *History of Humanities* saw the light of day, and several universities established chairs in the history of the humanities. Also, in the past decade and a half, a small pile of wide-ranging histories appeared, such as Rens Bod's *A New History of the Humanities: The Search for Principles and Patterns from Antiquity to the Present* (2013), James Turner's *Philology: The Forgotten Origins of the Modern Humanities* (2014), Eric Adler's *The Battle of the Classics: How a Nineteenth-Century Debate Can Save the Humanities Today* (2020), Paul Reitter and Chad Wellmon's *Permanent Crisis: The Humanities in a Disenchanted Age* (2021), and Christopher Celenza's *The Italian Renaissance and the Origins of the Modern Humanities: An Intellectual History, 1400–1800* (2021).

While these books all trace the emergence and development of what we now call the humanities, this volume does something different. It offers an introduction, not to how the humanities developed over time, but to what historians of the humanities currently do—what sort of research they conduct, what questions they ask, what themes they address, what approaches they find helpful, and what sources they use. Also, the volume inquires where this new field comes from and what its somewhat unexpected success reveals about the present state of the humanities. In a sense, therefore, the volume provides a map of the history of the humanities as it is practiced in the early 2020s.

This map is primarily intended for readers who are new to the field. Contributors have been asked to write for an audience of graduate students, emerging researchers, and colleagues from other disciplines who seek to acquaint themselves with the history of the humanities. Also, they have been encouraged to think of their chapters as potential reading material for courses in the history of the humanities. Hopefully, therefore, this volume will find its way onto syllabi and contribute to making the history of the humanities a teachable subject.

In its original design, the volume was even more ambitious than this. It tried to cover almost each and every humanities discipline, while giving long overdue attention to regions other than Europe and North America. Unfortunately, this ambition has only partly been realized, due to the COVID-19 pandemic that affected everyone's plans and schedules. While some authors managed to write their chapters while teaching remotely and homeschooling their children in lockdown, several others had to withdraw. As an editor, I have tried to get my priorities right. Despite my intent of producing a well-balanced volume and my regret about chapters (about photography, for instance) that did not materialize, I have not pressed contributors to deliver if personal circumstances did not allow for it. Obviously, I take responsibility for any imbalances resulting from this.

Besides thanking all the contributors for their hard work in challenging circumstances, I would like to thank Stefan Berger and his co-editors of the *Writing History* series for their enthusiasm about the initial idea, their feedback on a draft proposal, and their encouragement along the way. Anonymous reviewers also contributed substantially to refining the content and structure of the volume. Caroline Schep deserves mention for being a first-class student assistant: she standardized all the references (quite a laborious task) and prepared the index. Also, I am much indebted to Paul King for copy-editing the manuscript with great meticulousness and to Emily Drewe, Abigail Lane, and their colleagues at Bloomsbury for cheerfully shepherding the volume into print. Last but not least, I gratefully acknowledge generous research funding from the Dutch Research Council (NWO).

Introduction: What is the History of the Humanities?

Herman Paul

In 2016, the opening issue of the journal *History of Humanities* proudly announced that a new field of research was in the process of emerging. Although humanities scholars had always engaged with the histories of their own disciplines, what was new and exciting, according to the journal editors, was that they had begun to broaden their horizons. If humanities scholars had been used to studying the history of French linguistics or Chinese historiography in relative isolation from other fields, they now began to raise comparative questions. How had Fernand de Saussure's structuralism resonated in disciplines other than linguistics? To what extent had source critical methods been adopted across the humanities? And how is it to be explained that some humanities fields have been more receptive to postcolonial critique than others? The history of the humanities as envisioned by the journal editors thus appears as something more than an umbrella term for the history of linguistics, the history of historiography, and the history of art history. Typical for the field is its "ambition to write comparative historiographies of the humanities." Historians of the humanities are scholars traversing across fields, through all of the humanities (and beyond), with the aim of understanding what the humanities have been, what they are today, and why they are important.[1]

Arguably, the new field's claim to novelty was a little exaggerated: there had been earlier attempts at writing histories of the humanities. Judging by books like James Jarrett's *The Humanities and Humanistic Education* (1973), authors pondering the state of the humanities had sometimes found it necessary to delve deeply into the past.[2] More rigorous historical studies had been written, too. Robert Proctor's 1988 book *The Great Amnesia*, for example, had traced in some detail how the *studia humanitatis* as practiced by Renaissance humanists like Petrarch had given way to the modern humanities.[3] In Germany, there had even been a journal dedicated to the philosophy and history of the *Geisteswissenschaften*.[4] None of these publications, however, had found more than a niche audience. The German journal had ceased publication in 2000, while Proctor's exercise, in the author's own words, had been a solitary one: "The history of classical scholarship, the history of education, the history of classical political ideas, and the historical evolution of Renaissance individualism are all established areas of research. But no one, to my knowledge, has asked how all these fragments might fit together to form the history of the humanities."[5]

Although it is too early to tell whether *History of Humanities* will have a more enduring impact, the signs are not bad. The Society for the History of the Humanities has about 900 members from across the globe, institutional members not included.[6] Conferences on "The Making of the Humanities," organized on an annual (formerly biennial) basis since 2008, attract hundreds of participants who seem honestly excited about the new lines of research that are opened up by a comparative history of the humanities. Since 2016, the journal *History of Humanities* has published an impressive array of articles that unearth connections, similarities, as well as notable differences between traditions of humanities research and teaching in various parts of the world. So, one may wonder: What does this history of the humanities entail? Why does it attract so much attention? And what does this tell us about the humanities in the early twenty-first century?

The World of the Humanities

Before turning to these questions, we have to address the term "humanities" itself. What are the humanities that historians of the humanities claim to be studying? This question is easier to ask than to answer, given that the term "humanities" denotes "a whole set of commitments, ideals, and sensibilities."[7] While it refers, on the one hand, to such concrete activities as students gathering in a lecture room for a class in English, history, or philosophy, the term also evokes images of methods, aims, or values that set the humanities apart from the sciences in particular. In other words, whereas the humanities are, practically speaking, an umbrella term for university departments, journals, and conferences devoted to the study of history, language, and culture, they also, more abstractly, denote what Simon During calls "a looselylinked conglomeration of practices, interests, comportments, personae, offices, moods, purposes and values."[8] Both the one and the other, moreover, look differently in the United States than they do in Germany, Russia, or China. Although *Geisteswissenschaften* (Germany), *sciences humaines* (France), *scienze umanistiche* (Italy), *humanvidenskaber* (Scandinavia), *gumanitarnye nauki* (Russia), and *renwen shehui kexue* (China) are nowadays routinely translated as *humanities*, these terms all carry their own connotations. This explains why Geoffrey Galt Harpham, looking back on a lecture tour in Turkey about the humanities as practiced in the United States, can report about puzzled gazes and raised eyebrows. To his Turkish audiences, says Harpham, the American-style humanities seemed "a mere provincial prejudice," rooted in "a specifically American or at least Western, modern, and secular version of human being and human flourishing."[9]

What then exactly do people disagree about in talking about the humanities? Without aiming to be comprehensive, we might identify three layers of disagreement. First, there is the issue of what *fields* the humanities encompass. When nineteenth-century Germans coined the term *Geisteswissenschaften*, they understood these "human sciences" to include the emerging disciplines of psychology, sociology, and political science, all of which would later be rubricated under the social sciences.[10] Taking an even broader view, the journal *Die Geisteswissenschaften*, founded in 1913, aimed to cover "the entire domain of philosophy, psychology, mathematics, science of religion, science of history, ethnology, [and] pedagogy."[11] If this list of disciplines corresponds badly with what humanities and *Geisteswissenschaften* are nowadays understood to mean, this is because, as Fabian Kraemer argues in this volume, classifications of disciplines change over time, while at the same time mirroring historically grown conventions of organizing learned societies into classes and universities into faculties or departments.[12]

As a result of this, American-style humanities and European *Geisteswissenschaften* differ, for instance in how they relate to the arts. While the *Geisteswissenschaften* are not usually understood to include creative writing or music performance—poetry and opera only appear as subjects of research in fields like literary studies and musicology—first-order engagement with literature, music, film, or dance has a more accepted place in the American humanities (with English departments offering degrees in creative writing, for example).[13] Such differences in turn have implications for what are regarded as "core disciplines." Since the days of Wilhelm Windelband and Heinrich Rickert, the field of history has often been considered the most representative discipline of the *Geisteswissenschaften*.[14] In the United States, by contrast, it is not uncommon to hear that history is "only partially linked to the modern humanities."[15] If the humanities have a core discipline, it is rather English or literary studies (fields in which, perhaps not coincidentally, engagement with the arts can take both first- and second-order forms).[16]

If classifications of disciplines are a first point of contestation, a second one are the *methods, values, or attitudes* associated with the humanities. Back in the nineteenth century, Windelband spoke about an "idiographic" method that set the *Geisteswissenschaften* apart from the "nomothetic" *Naturwissenschaften*.[17] Similarly, Rickert argued that the "historical cultural sciences" (his preferred term) differed from the natural sciences, not only by studying parts of reality that humans have endowed with value, but also by approaching this value-laden reality with an interest in "the particular and the individual" instead of the recurrent or the general.[18] Although these arguments are more than a century old, versions of them continue to be offered in defense of medical humanities and environmental humanities (two of the so-called "new humanities" that the late twentieth century saw emerge).[19] Characteristic of the humanities, we are told, is a sensitivity to human factors, such as patients' experiences, that is often absent from evidence-based reasoning.[20] Alternatively, it is said that the humanities engage in modes of inquiry that are "less straightforward" than scientific methodologies, if only because they shuttle "back and forth between the whole and its parts, between the past, the present, and the future, and in the case of the environmental humanities, between the environment and culture."[21]

While these arguments may appeal to some humanities scholars, the history of the humanities shows that the dream of methodological monism— one scientific method for everyone—has at times been no less appealing than the methodological pluralism of the neo-Kantians and their heirs. In our days too there are scholars who believe that the future of the humanities lies with the neurosciences. How can the humanities pretend to understand the human mind, asks philosopher Bernhard Lauth, as long as they keep a distance from neurocognitive methods for tracing "physical and chemical processes in the brain"? From Lauth's point of view, the sciences–humanities divide is a nineteenth-century mistake whose correction is long overdue.[22] More practically, there are plenty of humanities scholars whose work in language acquisition, econometric history, text mining, or theoretical philosophy does not fit with the claim that the humanities are methodologically distinct from the sciences. By setting up experiments, analysing large data sets, and engaging in abstract mathematical modeling, they challenge the stereotypical image of a humanist who draws on empathy and erudition in developing a new take on an old poem. In short, both on the level of aspirations and on that of actual research, the methods and stances cultivated in the humanities are too diverse to be reducible to a single formula.

Thirdly, as literary critic Ronald Crane observed long ago, while certain interpretative practices, such as close reading and historical contextualization, are widely shared across the humanities, people have different ideas about the *aims* these practice serve.[23] Do the humanities aim to make their practitioners "more human" by encouraging reflection on such timeless questions as "Who am I? Where have I come from? Where am I going? Why?"[24] Or is transformative self-understanding an archaic goal in societies that expect academics to deliver empirical knowledge? As early as 1963, the German philosopher Joachim Ritter argued that the task of the *Geisteswissenschaften* in post-traditional societies is to keep the past accessible. Not Humboldtian *Bildung*, but the preservation of knowledge about languages and cultures that industrial societies tend to disremember is what defines the *Geisteswissenschaften*.[25] If this argument suggests that the humanities are primarily *curative*, in the sense of taking care of vulnerable cultural resources (historical knowledge, foreign language skills, material objects), others prefer to see the humanities as *critical*: their aim is to challenge stereotypical ideas and dubious heritages. Drawing on various strands of critical theory, "critical humanities" as envisioned by the Indian English scholar D. Venkat Rao make people aware of the continuing impact of colonial legacies, while trying to open up spaces for rethinking the world from non-European, non-hegemonic perspectives.[26] In all these cases, moreover, the question is whether the humanities matter mainly because of their research (the books and articles that scholars write) or because of their teaching (the courses through which they educate new generations). Clearly, there is a plurality of aims that are attributed to the humanities, in addition to a variety of knowledge classification systems and an irreducible diversity of methods.

Two conclusions can be drawn from this. The first is that the term "humanities" is an essentially contested concept, on which scholars can project a broad range of expectations.[27] Although essentialist definitions of the humanities continue to be proposed,[28] the sober reality is that agreement on what the humanities signify is unlikely to be reached. This is, secondly, because the things called "humanities" are not a singular entity, but what Simon During calls a "world": a whole conglomerate of continents and countries, sometimes separated by oceans or mountains, sometimes connected through peninsulas, bridges, tunnels, and airways. Its inhabitants speak different languages, despite a global English that allows for international communication, and participate in economic, political, and legal systems that are products of path-dependent historical trajectories.[29] The implications of this metaphor are clear: if the humanities are a world, any attempt to reduce them to a single language, political view, or national character trait is doomed to fail.

Genealogies of the Humanities

It is here that historians of the humanities come in. For if essentialist definitions are unconvincing, what alternatives do we have? One possible strategy is to define the humanities not *descriptively* (as they currently exist), but *prescriptively* (as they might or should be developed). Especially in the blossoming genre of reflections on "the humanities in the twenty-first century," such proposals for future humanities are frequently made. A recent volume on urban humanities, for instance, claims that "the humanities are not just a retrospective analysis of the remains of the cultural record (the archive, the wisdom of the past, the archaeological artifacts of the past), but can be—and we argue, *should be*—attuned to futurity, the possibility of justice, reparation, and perhaps even redemption."[30] Inspiring as such visionary language may be, it does not help much to understand the humanities as we currently know them.

A more promising strategy, therefore, is to approach the humanities historically. How has this complex conglomerate of things called "humanities" come into being? Can a historical approach help elucidate how fields as different as theoretical linguistics and world art studies have ended up in the same cluster of disciplines? Questions like these are central to several recent monographs on the history of the humanities. Christopher Celenza, for instance, presents his book on the *studia humanitatis* in Renaissance Italy as an exercise in understanding "how the humanities have worked in the past and how their history can illuminate the present."[31] Notably, like James Turner's book, *Philology: The Origins of the Modern Humanities*,[32] the title of

Celenza's study speaks about "the origins of the modern humanities," thereby suggesting that knowledge of Petrarch and Lorenzo Valla may contribute to understanding what the humanities have since become. Likewise, Eric Adler argues that a survey of "the path of the humanities from Roman antiquity to the present" may add much to understanding "what the humanities have been and are today."[33] Even Paul Reitter and Chad Wellmon, whose sensitivity to the variety of projects pursued under the rubric of the humanities makes them wary of grand generalizations, write a history aimed at unraveling the "inherited contradictions, oppositions, and presumptions" of the modern humanities.[34] The history of the humanities is therefore to no small degree a *genealogical enterprise*: it seeks to uncover the historical roots of the humanities so as to shed light on what the humanities currently are.

What lends a certain urgency to this genealogical project is what Rob Moore calls "a weakening of disciplinary identities" in contemporary higher education, paired to the rise of "humanities" as a new, overarching meta-discipline.[35] Increasingly, humanities scholars do not identify as Romanists, Egyptologists, or musicologists, but as practitioners of the "humanities." What this reveals, says Simon During, is that the humanities "are decreasingly being thought about as a set of individual disciplines each with its own history and more as a 'meta-discipline' all of its own. Students and teachers are increasingly just 'in the humanities.'"[36] In some countries, such as the Netherlands, institutional policies strongly contribute to this process. Despite the term "humanities" (*geesteswetenschappen*) not having not much of a history in the Netherlands, Dutch funding agencies and university administrators recently embraced it as a new organizational label.[37] While the universities of Amsterdam, Tilburg, Leiden, and Utrecht merged their formerly independent faculties of philosophy, theology, and arts into new faculties of humanities,[38] a whole infrastructure of graduate schools, core curriculums, honors programs, and research priorities areas in the "humanities" was built. To the extent that these new institutions forced faculty members to cooperate with colleagues and students outside of their own fields, they prompted renewed reflection on academic identities. Philosophers, literary scholars, and area specialists alike began to ask: "What are those humanities to which we have been allocated?"[39]

Clearly, a world in which universities and research agencies alike encourage scholars to see themselves as belonging to the humanities is more hospitable to a history of the humanities than an environment in which mono-disciplinary identities are the norm. Indeed, insofar as scholars wonder what these much-discussed but often ill-defined humanities are, it makes sense for them to turn to a field that aims for "a comparative, interdisciplinary history of the related humanistic disciplines."[40] The more people ask what the humanities are, the greater are the chances for a field that promises answers in the form of genealogies.

Defending the Humanities

If this demand for historical explanations is one factor contributing to the rise of the field called the history of the humanities, another one is the perception of the humanities as being in deep trouble. This "crisis of the humanities" is, of course, not a recent phenomenon. Already in 1964, in a volume with the telling title *Crisis in the Humanities*, the English historian John Plumb asserted that "the humanities are at the cross-roads, at a crisis in their existence."[41] As Claire Rydell Arcenas shows in this volume, very similar things had been said about the American humanities in the early 1940s.[42] One might even argue that perceptions of crisis are as old as the humanities themselves, not because the humanities have always been vulnerable, but because they have a long tradition of presenting themselves as a remedy against crises caused by positivism, materialism, or managerialism (as the case may be). As Reitter and Wellmon argue: "[F]or politically progressive and conservative scholars alike, crisis has played a crucial role in grounding the idea that the humanities have a special mission."[43] Dramatic stories of real or anticipated decline thus served, and continue to serve, as "mobilizing narratives," told with the aim of raising support for threatened humanities disciplines.[44]

Such a historicizing of perceptions of crisis—done in much more detail by Hampus Östh Gustafsson in Chapter 3 of this volume—does, of course, not detract from the reality that pressure on the humanities has reached levels of concern in countries across the globe.[45] At a time when the percentage of humanities graduates in dozens of OECD countries is dropping and faculty members throughout the world see their departments being threatened with closure because of "budgetary reallocations," one can understand why many wonder aloud how much of the humanities will survive in its current academic form.[46] Even if perceptions of crisis are old and the trope of "crisis" can be said to obscure as much as it reveals, the sheer number of books and articles that annually appears on the "crisis" and "future" of the humanities indicates that many scholars are worried.

Historians of the humanities contribute to this "humanist metadiscourse" by offering not only genealogies, but also *diagnoses* and *remedies*.[47] This is most apparent in books that explain historically what has gone wrong with the humanities and what can be done about it. Rens Bod, for instance, argues that the humanities have historically produced their own Keplers, Newtons, and Darwins: great scholars whose discoveries changed the world. If humanities scholars want to regain a position of prominence, says Bod, they should give up their neo-Kantian preoccupation with the particular and become "pattern seekers" like Pāṇini, the ancient Sanskrit scholar whose grammatical rules provided the basis for computer programming, or Valla, whose source critical methods are still indispensable for challenging fake news and alternative facts.[48] With a different word of advice but a largely similar strategy of drawing lessons from the past, Christopher Celenza argues that "we may not have institutionally based humanities for much longer" unless we do what Renaissance humanists so successfully did: combining textual research with moral reflection on the self.[49] Even more programmatic is the subtitle of Eric Adler's book: *How a Nineteenth-Century Debate Can Save the Humanities Today*. Over against skill-based defenses of the humanities, Adler argues that until well into the nineteenth century, it was the content of literary, philosophical, and religious texts that was supposed to enrich students' lives. According to Adler, such a "substance-based apologetic" makes "a more historically informed case for the humanities" than the worn-out argument that reading Plato or Goethe enhances students' critical thinking skills (a case that Adler believes to be all the more persuasive if it manages to emancipate itself from a Eurocentric canon).[50]

Clearly, then, it is not only the question what the humanities *are*, but also the question what will *become* of them in a time of budget cuts, plummeting enrolments, and dwindling public support that contributes to the emergence of the history of the humanities. In Robert Proctor's words: "It is only with the so-called 'crisis of the humanities' that the question of defining and understanding the humanities historically becomes a relevant and useful one."[51]

Two Additional Factors

If a burgeoning interest in the identity, purpose, and future of the humanities does much to explain why the history of the humanities finds receptive audiences throughout the world, there are two additional factors that help explain why this new field emerged only recently (and not, say, in the 1960s). Briefly put, the kind of comparative history to which historians of the humanities are committed would have been hard to imagine without supportive trends in the history of science and even impossible to practice without the technological innovations of a digital age.

First, there was the so-called cultural turn in the history of science (as well as in other humanities fields).[52] While scientific theories, hypotheses, and explanations had long been important research topics for historians of science, the cultural turn in the 1980s and 1990s put different sorts of themes on the agenda. Historians began to examine what kind of self was implied in the pursuit of scientific research, how students were being educated in physics or mathematics, how an "ethos of exactitude" and its accompanying means for error prevention were instilled in budding scientists, and what role college sports (cricket, rugby, football) played in cultivating perseverance and collegiality.[53] Also, inspired by the blossoming field of memory studies, historians of science began to inquire how Newton had been turned into a scientific genius or, more generally, how scientists used historical narratives and commemorative events to articulate where they saw themselves coming from and heading to.[54] Although this cultural turn in some respects "lowered the tone" in a field that used to be strongly committed to reason, truth, and progress,[55] more important for our purposes is that it also broadened the conversation: it drew attention to cultural aspects of *Wissenschaft* on which natural scientists could not claim a monopoly. Humanities scholars therefore joined the conversation with studies on the working habits of nineteenth-century historians and their self-fashioning as "men of virtue."[56]

Around the same time, some historians of science also developed a greater interest in how academics outside of the sciences conducted their work. Lorraine Daston, for instance, not only co-authored a monograph on the scientific virtue of objectivity, but also examined how nineteenth-century humanities scholars appropriated this discourse of objectivity.[57] Burgeoning scholarship on the history of early modern learning also contributed to this rapprochement between the sciences and the humanities, partly by demonstrating that modern labels like "science" failed to do justice to how Newton, Boyle, and their contemporaries studied the world,[58] partly also by raising questions that could be fruitfully applied to the modern humanities, too.[59] In the wake of these developments, moreover, a new field called the history of knowledge emerged, which also contributed its share to challenging conventional demarcations between science and society as well as between producers and consumers of knowledge.[60] Seen in this context, the history of the humanities is not an isolated phenomenon, but part of a broader reconceptualization of what "science" and "knowledge" entail. While supplementing and drawing on the history of science,[61] the history of the humanities also fills a "conspicuous lacuna" in the history of knowledge.[62]

On a more practical note, the comparative ambitions of the history of the humanities would be hard to realize without digital means for tracing and examining sources from different disciplines. Transgressing disciplinary boundaries is not just a matter of asking certain types of questions; it is also a matter of having means for tracing words like "facts" and "postcolonialism" through large corpora of texts.[63] A *History of Humanities* article like "German Thoroughness in Baltimore" (2018) would not have been possible without the search engines and digital repositories of Google Books, archive.org, and hathitrust.org. This is not only because the article draws on periodicals and brochures that only few libraries worldwide possess. More importantly, if these nineteenth-century sources had not been digitized, it would have been impossible to identify them as relevant to a study of "German thoroughness"—a trope that the first generation of Johns Hopkins professors eagerly employed in emphasizing the scientific ambitions of their university.[64]

In a recent interview, Lorraine Daston observes ("I'll try to describe it neutrally") how these digital possibilities lead especially younger scholars to approach historical texts very differently from how her own generation was taught to read sources. "Reading practices, in part because of the web and hyperlinks, are now far more granular," in the sense that scholars don't read books from cover to cover anymore, but follow concepts or images through corpora of texts that no one before the age of Google Books could ever hope to master. This does not necessarily convert these scholars to "distant reading" as promoted by Franco Moretti and others (although *History of Humanities* has featured a digital humanities article relying on a data set of more than 2,400 texts).[65] Even when they use databases like JSTOR and EBSCOhost, most historians of the humanities still engage in analog reading of source texts. The point is rather that comparisons across periods, cultures, or disciplines force historians to give up their traditional habit of contextualizing texts in *oeuvres* and authors' biographies. In Daston's words: "This is a very different form of reading than the close reading techniques taught to the previous generation, and I think it's led to a kind of pulverization of texts, which has its uses."[66]

Although it is too early to tell how such modes of reading will affect the presentation of research findings in an age when the monograph is beginning to lose the privileged status that it long had,[67] one thing is clear: a comparative history of humanities disciplines would have been difficult to envision under pre-digital circumstances. The digital revolution is among the factors that make it feasible for historians of the humanities to engage in transdisciplinary comparisons.

A Heterogeneous Field

If the factors contributing to the emergence of a history of the humanities include such diverse things as a sense of crisis, a weakening of disciplinary identities, new trends in the history of science, and a digital revolution, then it is no surprise to find scholars approaching the field from different directions and, consequently, to see them disagreeing over approaches and methods. What is an appropriate time scale or a relevant geographical unit? Are the humanities a modern phenomenon, dating back no further than the nineteenth century, or does it make sense to treat Sima Qian, in Han-dynasty China, and Ibn-Khaldun, in fourteenth-century North Africa, as humanities scholars *avant la lettre*? Should the humanities be studied globally, if only to challenge long-lasting legacies of Eurocentric thinking? But if so, how does that square with a professional commitment to reading sources in their original languages, or with historians' preference for basing their work, if possible, on archival material? Also, how acceptable, or desirable, is an apologetic tone of voice, given both the challenges that the humanities are facing and a long-standing distrust, among historians at least, of "presentist" modes of history writing?

One only needs to compare Jo Tollebeek's *Men of Character: The Emergence of the Modern Humanities* (2011) to Siraj Ahmed's *Archaeology of Babel: The Colonial Foundations of the Humanities* (2018) to see that scholars answer these questions very differently.[68] Based on archival sources, Tollebeek's short book offers a richly textured double portrait of two Dutch literary scholars around 1900. Inspired by ethnographic studies of science, the author examines their everyday practices of teaching and writing, while attending carefully to the importance of student–teacher relations, informal scholarly gatherings, and near-endless exchanges of letters.[69] In marked contrast to this lovingly written microhistory, Ahmed's study offers a sharply critical analysis of comparative philology and its complicity in the colonial project. Drawing on case studies from across the centuries, Ahmed argues that philology enabled colonial rule by offering a supposedly universally applicable method for ordering and classifying languages, literatures, and law. In practice, however, this method not only reduced complex discursive practices to standardized texts; it also ignored and marginalized all forms of culture that were opposed to textual authority. Insofar as "text-based academics today" continue this privileging of written texts, writes Ahmed, they are "inheritors of a colonial legacy." So unlike Tollebeek, whose aim is to understand in some detail how philologists around 1900 lived their professional lives, Ahmed sees it as "a politically urgent task" to "disentangle the postcolonial humanities from their still-unconsidered and hence unresolved colonial legacy." Unlike *Men of Character*, *Archaeology of Babel* is a political project, motivated by what Ahmed calls "the humanities' own radically democratic . . . ideals."[70]

What these examples illustrate is that the history of the humanities mirrors some of the diversity that is typical of the humanities themselves. To the extent that the field offers scholars from across the humanities a space for reflection on who they are, where they come from, and where they are heading, it opens its doors to methods, approaches, and attitudes that are just as varied as the people who enter the conversation. Accordingly, as long as linguists, media scholars, and philosophers alike present their work on conferences organized by the Society for the History of the Humanities, the field is unlikely to develop anything like a shared understanding of how to write the history of the humanities. Although professional historians may have strong opinions in these matters, the history of the humanities would cease to serve as an interdisciplinary realm of reflection if historians were allowed to impose their professional standards on the field as a whole. Ideally, therefore, the history of the humanities should allow for different kinds of "past-present relations."[71] It should be able to accommodate both contextually sensitive readings and exercises in ideology critique, both work that elucidates where current arrangements come from and interventions that challenge existing traditions.

Admittedly, however, such a heterogeneity of voices within the history of humanities can be puzzling, especially for researchers who newly enter the field. They might wonder: What are the questions that historians of the humanities pursue? What are their main themes and key approaches? Is there a map available of this new field?

Questions, Themes, Approaches

"Mapping" the history of the humanities is exactly what this volume seeks to do. In line with the goal of the series in which it appears, it surveys how historians of the humanities do their work—what questions they raise, what themes they address, and what approaches they adopt. *Writing the History of the Humanities* is, in other words, a multi-voiced exploration of how this writing of the history of the humanities currently takes place, both within and outside of the Society for the History of the Humanities. To that end, a variety of scholars active in the field, including both established figures and early-career researchers, have been invited to explain their preferred way of working as concretely as possible—not with abstract arguments about the historiographical advantages of their favorite approaches, but with examples or case studies that show in some detail how they practice the history of the humanities. Contributors, moreover, have been encouraged to write accessibly, for a target audience of graduate students not yet familiar with the field, to introduce them to current approaches and to win their enthusiasm for this area of scholarship. The "map" provided in this volume is therefore not only a means for orientation, but also an invitation to join the exploration.[72]

Given these aims, the volume should not be mistaken for a history of the humanities *as such*. Readers expecting an overview of how the humanities have developed in different parts of the world are referred to other studies, such as Bod's *A New History of the Humanities* (2013) and James Turner's aforementioned *Philology* (2014). Likewise, readers hoping that this volume will pay long-overdue attention to their favorite discipline (analytical philosophy, Chinese studies, critical media studies, ethnomusicology) will likely be disappointed. Although the essays collected in this volume feature a dazzling variety of scholarly enterprises—from linguistic fieldwork in the Philippines and the editing of medieval music in German-occupied Alsace to anti-colonial activism in Africa and liberal arts teaching in Cold War America—the diversity that this volume seeks to map is not one of fields or subfields, but one of questions, themes, and approaches that are currently shaping the field.[73]

Some of the *questions* singled out in this volume include the following:

1. *How did the humanities, or the Geisteswissenschaften, come into being?* Fabian Kraemer traces the origins of the terms, while James Turner

describes how philology gave birth to modern humanities disciplines such as classics, history, and literary studies.
2. *What did these humanities have in common?* Devin Griffiths examines the uses of comparative methods through a variety of humanities fields. Kasper Risbjerg Eskildsen highlights how influential the ideal of a "unity of teaching and research" has been, to which Falko Schnicke adds that such ideals underlying the humanities were often markedly masculine, both in their formulation and implementation.
3. *What kind of normative commitments did research and teaching practices in the humanities display?* Claire Rydell Arcenas examines how closely liberal arts teaching in the 1950s United States was entangled with the country's Cold War politics, whereas Larissa Schulte Nordholt, writing about historians in Africa at a time of decolonization, shows that the thin line between scholarship and activism was subject to constant negotiation.
4. *What were characteristic attitudes of humanities scholars?* If Schnicke's chapter shows how masculine the academic "self" was envisioned to be, my own chapter on the ethos of late nineteenth-century humanities scholars draws attention to standards of virtue shared by linguists, historians, and Orientalists alike. Also, Eskildsen's chapter on teaching practices makes clear that socialization into academia always implied a cultivation of certain skills and attitudes.

In pursuing these questions, the essays collected in this volume also showcase some of the *themes* on which historians of the humanities find themselves working. The influence of what is sometimes called a "practice turn" is visible in chapters on research practices like collecting linguistic data (Floris Solleveld) and compiling historical dictionaries (Christian Flow). Research methods are discussed by Turner and Griffith, while Julianne Nyhan and Andrew Flinn draw attention to research technologies such as punched cards systems. Concepts like "crisis" (Hampus Östh Gustafsson, Arcenas), *jitsugaku* (Michael Facius), and "postcritique" (Herman Paul) traveled across and beyond the humanities, as did scholarly personae like the "interdisciplinary" researcher (Kristine Steenbergh). Boundary work is a recurring theme in this volume, both with regard to other disciplines (Kraemer) and in relation to colonial history writing (Schulte Nordholt). Also, while historical legacies turn up throughout the volume, they receive special treatment in chapters on masculine values (Schnicke), the "colonial library" (Schulte Nordholt), and Eurocentric modes of history writing (Rens Bod).

In addition, the volume illustrates some methodological *approaches* current among historians of the humanities. Although most contributors write as intellectual historians—prosopographical analyses are absent from this volume, as are statistics about student enrolment or institutionalization of new fields[74]—the scales on which the essays operate vary substantially. While some chapters offer broad overviews, across countries and centuries, others analyse specific case studies in considerable detail. Also, while some contributions focus on individual scholars, other examine institutions, discourses, or scholarly paradigms. These different exercises not only come with different conceptions of agency; they also draw on different types of source material. While most chapters make ample use of published sources (books, journals), Flow's chapter shows the significance of archival study in understanding the day-to-day realities of philological research. Also, Nyhan and Flinn's contribution on the emergence of digital humanities illustrates the potential of oral history in examining the recent past. Finally, in terms of temporal and geographical scope, the volume illustrates that the *Geisteswissenschaften* in nineteenth-century Europe continue to fascinate. Increasingly, however, historians of the humanities are recognizing the need for more "global" accounts, if only to compensate for the lack of attention that the humanities outside of the Euro-American world have received. In this volume, chapters on Sino-Japanese learning (Facius) and African historiography (Schulte Nordholt) testify to the importance of this "global turn."[75]

Given that these questions, themes, and approaches run through all of the chapters that follow, they do not offer a neat threefold structure for the book. The sixteen chapters have therefore been clustered differently, in five parts. *Part I*, on definitions and backgrounds, deals with the age-old demarcation problem (what makes the humanities different?) as well as with the institutionalization of disciplines and the classic threat of "crisis." *Part II* examines research practices varying from linguistic fieldwork and historical lexicography to digital humanities in an age of punched cards. The four chapters that make up *Part III* draw attention to what has been called "the flow of cognitive goods," or the circulation of ideals, principles, or methods across disciplinary boundaries.[76] They do so by studying values and virtues, either discursively (as "traveling concepts") or as markers of an ethos embodied by humanities scholars at particular times and places.[77] *Part IV* offers a much-needed corrective to historians' habit of treating humanities scholars primarily as researchers. Not only does it show that teaching formats were imitated and adopted across geographical and disciplinary boundaries;

it also suggests that the "societal impact" of the humanities is even more evident in their teaching than in their research. *Part V*, finally, is called "Visions of the Future," because it examines the temporalities implied in calls for methodological innovation and interdisciplinary cooperation, but also because it contains a chapter on where the history of the humanities as a field might be heading.[78]

That final chapter, by Rens Bod, brings the volume to a full circle. Although the book aims to provide a state-of-the-art overview that reflects both the strengths and the weaknesses of the history of the humanities as it is currently being practiced, this introduction began by observing how energetically the new field has developed in the past two decades, how much enthusiasm its comparative ambitions elicit, and how eager its contributors try to expand the scope of historical inquiry. If Bod in the final pages of this volume calls for broader perspectives and greater inclusivity, he is not delivering a new message: he is appealing to an urge to transcend geographical and disciplinary boundaries that was, and is, foundational for the history of the humanities as such.[79] This, then, is a volume about scholars crossing borders of time, space, languages, and disciplines in the hope of deepening our understanding of what the humanities were, what they are, and what they might become.[80]

Notes

1. Rens Bod et al., "A New Field: History of Humanities," *History of Humanities* 1, no. 1 (2016): 1–8, at 5.
2. James L. Jarrett, *The Humanities and Humanistic Education* (Reading, MA: Addison-Wesley, 1973), esp. 1–45.
3. Robert E. Proctor, *Education's Great Amnesia: Reconsidering the Humanities from Petrarch to Freud: With a Curriculum for Today's Students* (Bloomington, IN: Indiana University Press, 1988). See also Anthony Grafton and Lisa Jardine, *From Humanism to the Humanities: Education and the Liberal Arts in Fifteenth- and Sixteenth-Century Europe* (Cambridge, MA: Harvard University Press, 1986).
4. On the short-lived history of this *Dilthey-Jahrbuch für Philosophie und Geschichte der Geisteswissenschaften* (1983–2000), see Helmut Johach, "Das Dilthey-Jahrbuch als Ort der Hermeneutik-Forschung," in *Vom Wissen um den Menschen: Philosophie, Geschichte, Materialität*, ed. Julia Gruevska and Kevin Liggieri (Freiburg: Karl Alber, 2018), 330–51.

5. Proctor, *Education's Great Amnesia*, 87.
6. Personal communication by Rens Bod (April 19, 2021).
7. Paul Reitter and Chad Wellmon, *Permanent Crisis: The Humanities in a Disenchanted Age* (Chicago, IL: University of Chicago Press, 2021), 5.
8. Simon During, "The Idea of the Humanities" (2017), online at www.academia.edu/34926361 (accessed March 9, 2022).
9. Geoffrey Galt Harpham, *The Humanities and the Dream of America* (Chicago, IL: University of Chicago Press, 2011), 8. Harpham's observations should not be misunderstood as implying that the Turkish and American humanities had developed independently of each other. See Ali Erken, "The Rockefeller Foundation, John Marshall and the Development of the Humanities in Modern Turkey: 1950–1965," *Disiplinlerarası Çalışmalar Dergisi* 20, no. 38 (2015): 113–45.
10. On the difficulties of accurately translating *Geisteswissenschaften* into English, see Roger Smith, *Being Human: Historical Knowledge and the Creation of Human Nature* (New York: Columbia University Press, 2007), 122–6.
11. Quoted from the subtitle of this short-lived German periodical.
12. See also Fabian Krämer, "Shifting Demarcations: An Introduction," *History of Humanities* 3, no. 1 (2018): 5–14 and Julian Hamann, "Boundary Work between Two Cultures: Demarcating the Modern *Geisteswissenschaften*," ibid., 27–38.
13. In this regard, the journal *History of Humanities* firmly positions itself in the tradition of the *Geisteswissenschaften*: "We do not intend to include historical studies of literature, music, theater, or the visual arts; rather, we aim at the history of the studies carried out on literature, music, theater, and the visual arts." Bod et al., "New Field," 4–5.
14. Wilhelm Windelband, "Geschichte und Naturwissenschaft," in *Das Stiftungsfest der Kaiser-Wilhelms-Universität Strassburg am 1. Mai 1894* (Strasbourg: J. H. Ed. Heitz, 1894), 15–41; Heinrich Rickert, *Kulturwissenschaft und Naturwissenschaft: Ein Vortrag* (Freiburg: J. C. B. Mohr, 1899).
15. Eric Adler, *The Battle of the Classics: How a Nineteenth-Century Debate Can Save the Humanities Today* (Oxford: Oxford University Press, 2020), 206 n. 2.
16. Jarrett, *Humanities and Humanistic Education*, vii.
17. Windelband, "Geschichte und Naturwissenschaft," 26.
18. Rickert, *Kulturwissenschaft und Naturwissenschaft*, 15, 20, 45.
19. Richard E. Miller and Kurt Spellmeyer, *The New Humanities Reader* (Stamford, CT: Cengage Learning, 2015). The slogan "new humanities" has, of course, a history of its own. For some older applications, see Patrick Fuery and Nick Mansfield, *Cultural Studies and the New Humanities: Concepts and Controversies* (Oxford: Oxford University Press, 1997) and Kurt Spellmeyer, *Arts of Living: Reinventing the Humanities for the Twenty-First Century* (Albany, NY: State University of New York Press, 2003), esp. 7–8.

20. Janine Naß, Thomas Efferth, and Anita Wohlmann, "Interviews and Personal Stories: A Humanities Approach in Pharmaceutical Education," *Pharmacy Education* 19, no. 1 (2019): 155–61.
21. Hannes Bergthaller et al., "Mapping Common Ground: Ecocriticism, Environmental History, and the Environmental Humanities," *Environmental Humanities* 5 (2015): 261–76, at 265 (discussed in more detail by Kristine Steenbergh in Chapter 15 of this volume).
22. Bernhard Lauth, "Das Dilemma der Geisteswissenschaften," in *"Ethical Turn"? Geisteswissenschaften in neuer Verantwortung*, ed. Oda Wischmeyer and Christine Lubkoll (Leiden: Brill, 2009), 19–33, at 27, 32.
23. R. S. Crane, "The Idea of the Humanities" (1953), in Crane, *The Idea of the Humanities and Other Essays Critical and Historical*, vol. 1 (Chicago, IL: University of Chicago Press, 1967), 3–15.
24. Charles R. Keller, "Can the Humanities Catch Up?" *The Bulletin of the National Association of Secondary School Principals* 48, no. 291 (1964): 60–8, at 60.
25. Joachim Ritter, "Die Aufgaben der Geisteswissenschaften in der modernen Gesellschaft" (1963), in Ritter, *Subjektivität: Sechs Aufsätze* (Frankfurt am Main: Suhrkamp, 1974), 105–40.
26. D. Venkat Rao, "Introduction: Crossing (the) Legacies," in *Critical Humanities from India: Contexts, Issues, Futures*, ed. D. Venkat Rao (London: Routledge, 2018), 1–25, at 11–12.
27. W. B. Gallie, "Essentially Contested Concepts," *Proceedings of the Aristotelian Society* 56 (1955–6): 167–98.
28. E.g., Willem B. Drees, *What Are the Humanities For?* (Cambridge: Cambridge University Press, 2021), 12.
29. During, "Idea of the Humanities."
30. Dana Cuff et al., *Urban Humanities: New Practices for Reimagining the City* (Cambridge, MA: MIT Press, 2020), 4–5.
31. Christopher S. Celenza, *The Italian Renaissance and the Origins of the Modern Humanities: An Intellectual History, 1400–1800* (Cambridge: Cambridge University Press, 2021), x.
32. James Turner, *Philology: The Forgotten Origins of the Modern Humanities* (Princeton, NJ: Princeton University Press, 2014).
33. Adler, *Battle of the Classics*, 9.
34. Reitter and Wellmon, *Permanent Crisis*, 254.
35. Rob Moore, "Policy-Driven Curriculum Restructuring: Academic Identities in Transition?" in *Realizing Qualitative Research in Higher Education*, ed. Craigh Prichard and Paul Trowler (Aldershot: Ashgate 2003), 121–42.
36. Simon During, "Are the Humanities Modern?" in *Latour and the Humanities*, ed. Rita Felski and Stephen Muecke (Baltimore, MD: Johns Hopkins University Press, 2020), 225–48, at 226.

37. J. Goudsblom, "The Humanities and the Social Sciences," in *The Humanities in the Nineties: A View from the Netherlands*, ed. E. Zürcher and T. Langendorff (Amsterdam: Swets & Zeitlinger, 1990), 23–41, at 24–5: "In some European languages, such as German and Dutch, the word humanities has never become accepted, whether in its Latin or vernacular forms."
38. Job Cohen et al., *Sustainable Humanities: Report from the Committee on the National Plan for the Future of the Humanities* (Amsterdam: Amsterdam University Press, 2009), 52 n. 4.
39. Similarly, funding bodies in Europe structured their grant competitions in such a way that historians found themselves competing with archaeologists, just as anthropologists of religion ended up in a panel with analytical philosophers. See, e.g., Thomas König, "Peer Review in the Social Sciences and Humanities at the European Level: The Experiences of the European Research Council," in *Research Assessments in the Humanities: Towards Criteria and Procedures*, ed. Michael Ochsner, Sven E. Hug, and Hans-Dieter Daniel (Cham: Springer, 2016), 151–63.
40. Rens Bod, "Introduction: Historiography of the Humanities," in *The Making of the Humanities*, vol. 1, ed. Rens Bod, Jaap Maat, and Thijs Weststeijn (Amsterdam: Amsterdam University Press, 2010), 7–14, at 10.
41. J. H. Plumb, "Introduction," in *Crisis in the Humanities*, ed. J. H. Plumb (Harmondsworth: Penguin, 1964), 7–10, at 8.
42. See Chapter 13 in this volume.
43. Reitter and Wellmon, *Permanent Crisis*, 3.
44. Hampus Östh Gustafsson, "Mobilising the Outsider: Crises and Histories of the Humanities in the 1970s Scandinavian Welfare States," in *Histories of Knowledge in Postwar Scandinavia: Actors, Arenas, and Aspirations*, ed. Johan Östling, Niklas Olsen, and David Larsson Heidenblad (London: Routledge, 2020), 208–24, at 218–19.
45. See *The Changing Face of Higher Education: Is There an International Crisis in the Humanities?* ed. Dennis A. Ahlburg (London: Routledge, 2019).
46. Rosário Cauto Costa, "The Place of the Humanities in Today's Knowledge Society," *Palgrave Communications* 5, no. 38 (2019), https://doi.org/10.1057/s41599-019-0245-6
47. "Humanist metadiscourse" is a phrase borrowed from Eric Hayot, *Humanist Reason: A History, an Argument, a Plan* (New York: Columbia University Press, 2021).
48. Rens Bod, *A New History of the Humanities: The Search for Principles and Patterns from Antiquity to the Present*, trans. Lynn Richards (Oxford: Oxford University Press, 2013). See also Rens Bod, "The Case for a History of the Humanities," *Chronicle of Higher Education* 63, no. 25 (2017): B10–B11.
49. Celenza, *Italian Renaissance*, 272.

50. Adler, *Battle of the Classics*, 11, 9.
51. Proctor, *Education's Great Amnesia*, 87.
52. On which see Peter Dear, "Cultural History of Science: An Overview with Reflections," *Science, Technology, and Human Values* 20 (1995): 150–70; Suman Seth, "The History of Physics after the Cultural Turn," *Historical Studies in the Natural Sciences* 41 (2011), 112–22, and John F. M. Clark, "Intellectual History and the History of Science," in *A Companion to Intellectual History*, ed. Richard Whatmore and Brian Young (Chichester: Wiley-Blackwell, 2015), 155–69.
53. See, e.g., Steven Shapin, *A Social History of Truth: Civility and Science in Seventeenth-Century England* (Chicago, IL: University of Chicago Press, 1994); Kathryn M. Olesko, *Physics as a Calling: Discipline and Practice in the Königsberg Seminar for Physics* (Ithaca, NY: Cornell University Press, 1991); Andrew Warwick, *Masters of Theory: Cambridge and the Rise of Mathematical Physics* (Chicago, IL: University of Chicago Press, 2003).
54. Patricia Fara, *Newton: The Making of a Genius* (New York: Columbia University Press, 2002); *Commemorative Practices in Science: Historical Perspectives on the Politics of Collective Memory*, ed. Pnina G. Abir-Am and Clark A. Elliot (Ithaca, NY: Cornell University Press, 1999).
55. Steven Shapin, "Lowering the Tone in the History of Science: A Noble Calling," in Shapin, *Never Pure: Historical Studies of Science as if It Was Produced by People with Bodies, Situated in Time, Space, Culture, and Society, and Struggling for Credibility and Authority* (Baltimore, MD: Johns Hopkins University Press, 2010), 1–14.
56. See, e.g., Jo Tollebeek, *Frederique & Zonen: een antropologie van de moderne geschiedwetenschap* (Amsterdam: Bert Bakker, 2008); Kasper Risbjerg Eskildsen, "Inventing the Archive: Testimony and Virtue in Modern Historiography," *History of the Human Sciences* 26, no. 4 (2013): 8–26; *Epistemic Virtues in the Sciences and the Humanities*, ed. Jeroen van Dongen and Herman Paul (Cham: Springer, 2017); Herman Paul, *Historians' Virtues: From Antiquity to the Twenty-First Century* (Cambridge: Cambridge University Press, 2022).
57. Lorraine Daston and Peter Galison, *Objectivity* (New York: Zone Books, 2007); Lorraine Daston, "Objectivity and Impartiality: Epistemic Virtues in the Humanities," in *The Making of the Humanities*, vol. 3, ed. Rens Bod, Jaap Maat, and Thijs Weststeijn (Amsterdam: Amsterdam University Press, 2014), 27–41.
58. As Daston recalls in a recent interview, it was the work of Anthony Grafton, Ann Blair, and Gianna Pomata that made her see "the history of scholarship as part of our bailiwick." Alexander Bevilacqua and Frederic Clark, *Thinking in the Past Tense: Eight Conversations* (Chicago, IL: University of Chicago Press, 2019), 51.
59. Research on the "persona" of the early modern philosopher, for example, has found resonance among historians of the nineteenth- and twentieth-century

humanities. See *The Philosopher in Early Modern Europe: The Nature of a Contested Identity*, ed. Conal Condren, Stephen Gaukroger, and Ian Hunter (Cambridge: Cambridge University Press, 2006); *Scholarly Personae in the History of Orientalism, 1870-1930*, ed. Christiaan Engberts and Herman Paul (Leiden: Brill, 2019); Paul, *How to Be a Historian*; and *Gender, Embodiment, and the History of the Scholarly Persona: Incarnations and Contestations*, ed. Kirsti Niskanen and Michael J. Barany (Cham: Palgrave Macmillan, 2021).

60. On the history of knowledge, see Lorraine Daston, "The History of Science and the History of Knowledge," *KNOW* 1, no. 1 (2017): 131–54 and the forum section, "What is the History of Knowledge?" *Journal of the History of Knowledge* 1, no. 1 (2020).

61. Rens Bod and Julia Kursell, "Introduction: The Humanities and the Sciences," *Isis* 106, no. 2 (2015): 337–40; Rens Bod, "A Comparative Framework for Studying the Histories of the Humanities and Science," ibid., 367–77.

62. Bod et al., "New Field," 5. Given that, historically speaking, fields like history and philosophy have often been more directly entangled with sociology, psychology, and political science than with chemistry or astronomy, one wonders why historians of the humanities orient themselves more on the history of science than on the history of the human sciences. Wolf Feuerhahn and Olivier Orain, "Pour une histoire inclusive des sciences humaines et sociales," *Revue d'histoire des sciences humaines* 34 (2019): 7–10 are right to argue that a *histoire croisée* of the humanities and the human sciences makes just as much sense as an integrated history of the humanities and the natural sciences. On the history of the human sciences as an emerging field of study (like the history of the humanities), see Roger Smith, "What Is the History of the Human Sciences?" in *The Palgrave Handbook of the History of the Human Sciences*, ed. David McCallum (Cham: Palgrave Macmillan, forthcoming).

63. Sjang L. ten Hagen, "How 'Facts' Shaped Modern Disciplines: The Fluid Concept of Facts and the Common Origins of German Physics and Historiography," *Historical Studies in the Natural Sciences* 49, no. 3 (2019): 300–37; Andrew Sartori, "From Political Reference to Self-Narration: 'Postcolonial' as Periodizer," in *Post-Everything: An Intellectual History of Post-Concepts*, ed. Herman Paul and Adriaan van Veldhuizen (Manchester: Manchester University Press, 2021), 155–71.

64. Herman Paul, "German Thoroughness in Baltimore: Epistemic Virtues and National Stereotypes," *History of Humanities* 3, no. 2 (2018): 327–50.

65. Franco Moretti, *Distant Reading* (London: Verso, 2013); Giovanni Colavizza, "Understanding the History of the Humanities from a Bibliometric Perspective: Expansion, Conjectures, and Traditions in the Last Decades of Venetian Historiography (1950–2013)," *History of Humanities* 3, no. 2 (2018): 377–406.

66. Bevilacqua and Clark, *Thinking in the Past Tense*, 56.
67. Ann Rigney, "When the Monograph is No Longer the Medium: Historical Narrative in an Online Age," *History and Theory* 49, no. 4 (2010): 100–17.
68. Michael O'Brien, "Where Have You Gone, Joseph Scaliger?" *Modern Intellectual History* 13, no. 1 (2016): 261–71 offers another glimpse of historians of the humanities disagreeing about questions that are worth raising and attitudes that scholars should display.
69. Jo Tollebeek, *Men of Character: The Emergence of the Modern Humanities* (Wassenaar: Netherlands Institute for Advanced Study in the Humanities and Social Sciences, 2011).
70. Siraj Ahmed, *Archaeology of Babel: The Colonial Foundation of the Humanities* (Stanford, CA: Stanford University Press, 2018), 10, 7. On the study of language in colonial contexts, see also Joseph Errington, *Linguistics in a Colonial World: A Story of Language, Meaning, and Power* (Malden, MA: Blackwell, 2008).
71. Herman Paul, "Relations to the Past: A Research Agenda for Historical Theorists," *Rethinking History* 19, no. 3 (2015): 450–8.
72. In the spirit of Peter L. Berger, *Invitation to Sociology: A Humanistic Perspective* (Garden City, NY: Anchor Books, 1963).
73. In terms of periods covered, the volume reflects the current state of the field in focusing on the nineteenth and twentieth centuries. There are some signs, however, that students of early modern scholarship also begin to conceive of their work as contributing to the history of the humanities. See, for instance, *Confessionalisation and Erudition in Early Modern Europe: An Episode in the History of the Humanities*, ed. Nicholas Hardy and Dmitri Levitin (Oxford: Oxford University Press, 2019). In Chapter 16 the present volume, Rens Bod also advocates a broad temporal scope, unrestrained by actors' use of "humanities" and related terms.
74. Examples of this type of research are provided by Roger L. Geiger, "Demography and Curriculum: The Humanities in American Higher Education from the 1950s through the 1980s," in *The Humanities and the Dynamics of Inclusion since World War II*, ed. David A. Hollinger (Baltimore, MD: Johns Hopkins University Press, 2006), 50–72.
75. See also the theme issue, "Decentralizing the History of the Humanities," *History of Humanities* 6, no. 2 (2021) and, more broadly, *Global Intellectual History*, ed. Samuel Moyn and Andrew Sartori (New York: Columbia University Press, 2013).
76. Rens Bod et al., "The Flow of Cognitive Goods: A Historiographical Framework for the Study of Epistemic Transfer," *Isis* 110, no. 3 (2019): 483–96.
77. The notion of "traveling concepts," now widely used, originated with Mieke Bal, *Travelling Concepts in the Humanities: A Rough Guide* (Toronto: University of Toronto Press, 2002).

78. Chapter 16 is followed by a glossary that briefly explains some of the more technical (historiographical, methodological) terms used in this volume.
79. If I may add one desideratum to the challenges discussed in Chapter 16, I would mention the need to move beyond the nineteenth-century *Geisteswissenschaften* that feature so prominently both in the pages of *History of Humanities* and in the present volume. In the light of all the scholarship done on Friedrich Schleiermacher, Karl Lachmann, Theodor Mommsen, and their contemporaries, one can only hope that historians of the humanities will devote equal amounts of attention to the second half of the twentieth century—a period that witnessed an unprecedented proliferation and expansion of the humanities across the globe. Additionally, a focus on the more recent past would force historians to look beyond "classic" humanities fields like history, philosophy, and literary studies. It would allow them to trace the emergence of dozens of new fields, from cultural studies, media studies, and African American studies to legal humanities, urban humanities, and medical humanities—even if, for reasons still to be explored, the history of the humanities does not yet resonate much within these fields. Does the term "history" carry connotations that square badly with a critical assessment of past failures and wrongs? Or is "humanities" the problem, given that their complicity in the colonial system has been such that "inhumanities" sometimes seems a more appropriate name? (See Will Bridges, "A Brief History of the Inhumanities," *History of Humanities* 4, no. 1 [2019]: 1–26.) Whatever the causes, more sustained attention to the recent past would contribute substantially to the genealogical project that is the history of the humanities.
80. I would like to thank Rens Bod, Ian Hunter, Angus Nicholls, Roger Smith, and James Turner for their most helpful feedback on a draft of this text. Funding was generously provided by the Dutch Research Council (NWO).

Part I

Definitions and Backgrounds

1
What are the Humanities? A Short History of Concepts and Classifications

Fabian Kraemer

Introduction

"Humanities," like "science," is an odd meta term. It does not stand (*qua* chairs, institutes, societies, journals) for a more or less clearly distinguishable discipline, but for a group of disciplines. It is not always immediately clear why these groups and their associated terms are even needed. It stands to reason that where terms like "humanities," "sciences humaines," "Geisteswissenschaften" and their cognates in other European languages are meaningful, it is a matter of *academic politics*. That is, they are invoked where the distribution of resources (material and immaterial) are at stake—*between* these groups of disciplines, but also between different approaches *within* disciplines and their representatives.

The sociologist of science Thomas F. Gieryn introduced a helpful term for linking the performative speech acts that bring about and negotiate the boundaries between disciplines with tangible interests: "boundary work." Gieryn emphasizes that the dividing lines between academic disciplines are typically drawn with the motivation to achieve strategic goals that affect the status and resources of those who participate in the discussion about them.[1] The concept is useful also because it implies that the boundaries between disciplines and groups of disciplines are not givens but were then, and are now, *worked*. These demarcations have been subject to repeated and at times seemingly incessant efforts at drawing and redrawing them.

More often than not, "boundary work" comes with a claim about the relative intellectual value of the discipline or group of disciplines in question and their methods. If we consider the division of science and the humanities from this perspective, it becomes clear that we are dealing here with "shifting demarcations" rather than a one-off emergence: the historical actors often disagreed, both synchronically and diachronically speaking, on where the dividing line between the two groups of disciplines runs.[2] The names they ought to be given also sometimes became a matter of contention. But *that* academic knowledge roughly falls into two halves was a view widely shared in Europa and North America by the late nineteenth century.

In the early modern period, strictly speaking, neither the natural sciences nor the humanities existed. Scholars were often engaged in more than one field, thereby frequently crossing what would become the boundary between the humanities and natural sciences in the nineteenth century.[3] Methodologically and also career-wise, the boundaries between different academic fields were still relatively permeable. The early modern university was characterized by the *"absence of a monodisciplinary career."*[4] The exclusive responsibility of a professor for one and only one discipline in teaching and research only developed in the course of the eighteenth and nineteenth centuries.[5] If we were to identify a single fault line for the Middle Ages and early modernity that was similarly important and seemingly omnipresent as the "two cultures" of modernity, then it would be that between theology and philosophy.[6]

In the Middle Ages and early modern period the dominant principle that structured the European university was the hierarchical order of its four faculties. But by the eighteenth century, this structural principle did no longer go unchallenged.[7] What began to replace it from the eighteenth century onwards was the emergent "regime of disciplines"[8]. Without the disciplinary differentiation, which continued through the nineteenth century, there would have been no need for disciplinary groupings such as "humanities" or "sciences."

It should not therefore come as a surprise how similarly the English "science," the French "science," and the German "Wissenschaft" were used into, and often through the nineteenth century. Like "Wissenschaft" and the French "science" today, the English term "science" was still used for the *entirety* of subjects taught at university. It was only around the close of the nineteenth century that the meaning of the term narrowed. No sooner than around 1900 did it assume the meaning in which we use it today: science became natural science. Chief among the factors that caused this narrowing down of the meaning of science: the rise of the natural sciences.[9] In the German language with its preference for cumbersome compounds, a different way of distinguishing the two areas of knowledge was chosen: *Wissenschaft* was subdivided into *Natur-* and *Geisteswissenschaft*. In French, an analogous subdivision has come to be used, between "sciences humaines" (also "sciences de l'homme") and "sciences naturelles" (also "sciences de la nature").

The division of academic disciplines into sciences and humanities is not only, as outlined above, *in need of explanation*; it was, and is, also *controversial*. Historical actors frequently disagreed as to whether a discipline should be classified in the humanities or in the natural sciences. Some disciplines were, or are, notorious borderline cases, such as psychology in the late nineteenth and early twentieth centuries. Some have argued that the social sciences constitute a category of their own.[10] Finally, the affiliation of a discipline to one or the other category may also change over time: it is historically variable, up to a certain point. So, thirdly, the classification of academic disciplines is inherently *dynamic*.[11]

With these caveats in mind, we will now turn to the histories of some concepts that proved especially important for the history of the humanities in Europe and the United States. As we shall see, they share several features, including the key role for their development played by that powerful other, the natural sciences. We shall start with a conceptual late-comer, the German "Geisteswissenschaften," and then follow the sources back to the earlier British and French discussions about the "moral sciences" or "sciences morales." It will become clear that while the national and sometimes local contexts are often key to understanding the trajectory of the respective French, British, and German concepts, their histories are in significant ways entangled.

Geisteswissenschaften

Contrary to our intuition, the humanities are not *older* than the natural sciences, but—at least in a very specific, precise sense—*younger* than them. This becomes especially clear in the case of the "Geisteswissenschaften." This is not an argument about the genesis of individual disciplines. Several disciplines that we count among the humanities today look back on a very long history. What was new in the nineteenth century is that they came to be seen by many as a more or less clearly defined group of disciplines that could be subsumed under the rubric *Geisteswissenschaften*. This is also reflected in the history of concepts. The term *Geisteswissenschaften* itself is younger in comparison to its counterpart *Naturwissenschaften*.[12]

The *Geisteswissenschaften* were constructed as both similar *and* different. *Natur-* and the *Geisteswissenschaften* were similar in that they were both understood to be *Wissenschaften*.[13] This was, and is, not trivial. For today's native speakers of English, with its linguistically clear opposition of science and humanities (or arts), without a third term from the same word family able to integrate these categories, it may not come naturally that *science* and *humanities* cannot only be considered as different, but also as similar. As we shall see, however, through the nineteenth century, the term "science" was still used in the broad sense of *Wissenschaft* and thus did not imply the same fundamental division of academic knowledge that it implies today.

The fact that philosophers, philologists, and historians, among others, in German-speaking countries began to see themselves in the course of the nineteenth century as representatives of the *Geisteswissenschaften* (or, alternatively, *Kulturwissenschaften* or *historische Wissenschaften*, for the terminology was controversial), in addition to their disciplinary identity, has to be understood in part as a reactive process and as an expression of a defensive strategy. At first glance, this may seem odd. After all, the model disciplines for the German concept *Wissenschaft* in the nineteenth century were philosophy and classical philology.[14] But two developments in turn put the representatives of the humanities disciplines at a disadvantage. First, naturalists increasingly saw themselves as a coherent group with a common name, common interests, and a shared profession. This sense of community becomes tangible in the foundation of scientific meta-societies such as the Gesellschaft Deutscher Naturforscher und Ärzte (1822), the British Association for the Advancement of Science (1831), the Congrès scientifiques de France (1833), later also the Association Française pour l'Avancement des Sciences (1872), and the American Association for the Advancement of Science (1848), to name but a few. In the nineteenth century, these meta-societies had no counterpart on the humanities side.[15]

This non-simultaneity is reflected in the history of words and specifically in the frequency with which the words *Naturwissenschaften* and *Geisteswissenschaften* were used over the course of the long nineteenth century: the term *Naturwissenschaften* was used much earlier than *Geisteswissenschaften*. It came up with some regularity already around the beginning of the long nineteenth century, and from then on was consistently used more frequently than the latter term. *Geisteswissenschaften* appears in the sources in any significant frequency only after c. 1860. This timing was not incidental. It was during the selfsame period that the institutional set-up of German universities was hotly discussed and the first separate Faculty of Science created (in Tübingen, in 1863).[16]

Let us now turn to the second reason why the *Geisteswissenschaften* project was a reactive and defensive one. From the middle of the century onwards, it was mostly the representatives of scientific disciplines who were granted their own institutes, often in magnificent and imposing buildings, with the laboratories and instruments they needed for their experimental studies and for teaching purposes. The contemporaries could not fail to notice that the stream of state funding for science had begun to change direction.

Thirdly, some sciences, chemistry in particular, were of an increasing importance for the economy of the German territories, which also led to the emergence and growth of labor markets for students of these sciences outside of the *Gymnasium* and university systems.[17] It was this development that led the rector of Friedrich-Wilhelms-Universität zu Berlin, the physicist and chemist Heinrich August Magnus to declare in his rector's address of 1862 that the nineteenth century was the age of the *Naturwissenschaften*, for in the form of modern chemistry they had finally begun to impact life, commerce, and production.[18]

These developments led to an increase of confidence in the methods and epistemology of the sciences, which is the fourth factor: By mid-century, they seemed to be on the rise; they were applied to the writing of history, for instance, and played an increasing role in the notorious borderline discipline of psychology. Wilhelm Dilthey indirectly reacted to this increasing confidence when he defensively claimed the methodological autonomy of the *Geisteswissenschaften*.

The philosopher-historian Wilhelm Dilthey (1833–1911) is mostly remembered for his contrasting pair *to explain* versus *to understand*. According to Dilthey, the sciences *explain* their phenomena, i.e., trace them back to their causes and are thus ultimately capable of discovering laws of nature. The objects of the *Geisteswissenschaften* do not allow for this:

> Since the systems of culture have arisen from the context of the life of the soul, they cannot be made tangible from the outside by concluding a causal connection, like systems of nature, but can only be described and understood from the experienced context of inner experience.[19]

From a history of philosophy point of view, Dilthey's efforts constitute a reaction to and defensive move against the steep rise, even emerging dominance of the sciences.[20] His more immediate targets were the positivist and empiricist philosophers who denounced the autonomy of the *Geisteswissenschaften*.[21]

A further factor affecting the entire German university system is aptly described by Eckel as "inner-disciplinary pluralization"[22] in the humanities and the related "intensifying academic cut-throat competition."[23] In the decades after 1880, numerous new approaches were introduced in various disciplines—such as the history of ideas and cultural history in historiography; or *Gestalt*, holistic, individual, and personality psychology in psychology—and had to assert themselves. In the context of these intense inner-disciplinary competitions, distancing your approach and thus yourself from the sciences gained new relevance because it promised a strategic advantage over your competitors.[24]

Geisteswissenschaften and *Moral Sciences*

While the term *Geisteswissenschaften* was, and is, a predominantly German affair, the history of the inception of the concept is an entangled one, linking the English and German, and indirectly also French, discussions about method in the mid-nineteenth century. It was not Dilthey who coined the term *Geisteswissenschaften*. It is received wisdom among historians of philosophy that the term goes back to a liberal translation—some say, a mistranslation—of the term *moral sciences* in a German translation of John Stuart Mill's (1806–73) *A System of Logic* (1843) by Jacob Heinrich Wilhelm Schiel (1813–89) that is usually dated into the year 1849.[25] Content wise this claim is justified—but the date is wrong.

In the English original the sixth and last book of *A System of Logic* is entitled "On the Logic of the Moral Sciences." It discusses the methodological problems of psychology, sociology, economics, and history. Note that other humanistic disciplines such as philology in particular are left out. With "moral sciences," Mill thus chose a term that had long since been established in French and English for the human sciences. We will return to the history of this term in the next section. From the second edition of Schiel's translation onwards, this title was rendered in German as "Von der Logik der Geisteswissenschaften oder moralischen Wissenschaften."[26] That Schiel chose to add to the term "Geisteswissenschaften" an alternative ("or")— "moralische Wissenschaften"—bears witness to the fact that the former term was not yet established. It could not stand on its own feet, as it were. But what about the first edition of Schiel's translation?

The first, 1849 translation from Schiel's pen, entitled *Die inductive Logik*, makes no use of the term *Geisteswissenschaften*, and for good reasons.[27] In Mill's *A System of Logic*, the "moral sciences" play a marginal role. While the first five books of the work deal with the natural sciences alone, Mill turns to the "moral sciences" only in the sixth book, which reads as an annex. The book is structured by the question whether the moral sciences are conceivable as "sciences" in the sense of the methodic principles presented in the preceding books. The sciences provide the model. Mill's question is: Can this model be applied to the study of moral and social phenomena?[28]

Already marginal and a doubtful case in Mill's work, in Schiel's translation of 1849 the "moral sciences" remain completely unmentioned. In the "Preface of the Translator," Schiel, a disciple of the eminent chemist Justus von Liebig (1803–73), justifies his decision as follows:

> The final part contains the application of the principles set forth in this work to the social and moral science. The transfer of these now lay outside the intention of the translator. Mr. Mill himself considers the translated part [books 2–5; FK] to be the core of his work, and he approved the approach of the translator, who had written to him by letter beforehand.[29]

Even more clearly than Mill, Schiel was primarily interested in the natural sciences, as the last sentence of the preface once again makes clear: "May the translation of Mill's work receive the same applause and recognition in Germany as the original work in England; may it help to promote the study of the natural sciences in a similar way."[30] Only the second edition, which was published in two volumes by the same Heidelberg publishing house in 1862, is a full translation. In the sixth book, which is now included, the term *Geisteswissenschaften* is systematically used for the "moral sciences" of the original.[31] This full version of Schiel's translation was so successful that a new edition was published as soon as in 1868.[32]

When Dilthey sought to provide the *Geisteswissenschaften* with a philosophical foundation, then, the term as such had been circulating for little more than two decades. It became quickly established; it can regularly be found in sources dating into the 1870s.[33] Yet the lemma "Geisteswissenschaften" in the *Deutsches Wörterbuch* of 1897 shows that the term could still be perceived as relatively new in the final years of the century: "GEISTESWISSENSCHAFTEN, *plur. recently in contrast to the natural sciences, i.e., philosophy, history, philology, etc.; cf.* philosophy of mind *and* spirit *and* nature *sp. 2699fol.*"[34]

The (pre-)history of the term can be traced back further into the first half of the century.[35] But it was only "through Dilthey's *Einleitung in die Geisteswissenschaften* (1959 [1883]) that the concept received an important foundation in the theory of science and probably only here did it receive an independent systematic definition."[36] While Schiel's Mill translation played a key role in the history of the concept, the fact that the term and related terms such as "Geisteslehre" and "Geistesphilosophie" can already be found in the work of the idealistic philosopher Hegel and in Schelling's school is significant because it explains in part why the term *Geisteswissenschaften* was an option at all when Schiel was looking for a translation for "moral sciences" and why, in the view of many contemporaries in the nineteenth century, the *Geisteswissenschaften* project was associated with idealistic philosophy and especially with Hegel.

The Mill of the German translation made yet another important contribution to the discourse on the *Geisteswissenschaften*: he classified the *Geisteswissenschaften* as deficient in methodical terms and saw the cure in their remodeling based on the natural sciences. A comment in *System der deductiven und inductiven Logik* leaves no doubt about this: "The Geisteswissenschaften can only be helped up if by applying to them the properly extended and generalized methods of the physical sciences."[37] If someone has to be helped up, he or she has been floored and does not have strength enough to get back on his or her feet. The view that the deficits of the *Geisteswissenschaften* can only be overcome by adopting scientific methods, in Mill's case and in its variations in Buckle and other positivists, was an expression of the growing self-confidence of the representatives of the natural sciences. And it did not fail to trigger resistance among representatives of the disciplines that were so severely criticized. Mill and his translator Schiel thus indirectly contributed to shaping the discourse of the *Geisteswissenschaften*: it usually took on a reactive and defensive character in relation to the rise of the natural sciences.[38]

Dilthey's attempt to provide the *Geisteswissenschaften* with a philosophical foundation is a case in point. His *Introduction to the Geisteswissenschaften* can be considered an Anti-Mill.[39] Its starting point, as we have seen, is the so-called foundational crisis (*Grundlagenkrise*) of the disciplines studying culture and society. This crisis was triggered by the antagonism between the two academic schools that shape much of his argument: the Historical School that was firmly established in Berlin and that Dilthey experienced first-hand with his teachers Tredelenburg, Ranke, and Boekh, on the one hand, and French and English positivists and empiricists—Comte, Mill, and Buckle in particular—on the other hand.[40] It is not surprising, then, that Dilthey chose for his Anti-Mill the German term that had been introduced for this group of disciplines by Mill translator Schiel: *Geisteswissenschaften*.

For the above reasons, the influential German term for the humanities is a nineteenth-century creation. Unlike many European equivalents, it does not go back to the Renaissance—neither etymologically, nor conceptually. Its center of gravity, in Dilthey and others, is the study of culture and society, and its paradigmatic discipline history. In Dilthey the term also included theology, jurisprudence, psychology, (proto-)sociology, economics, and political science. In these regards, too, it differs from concepts such as arts and humanities in particular, which instead center around literature and philology. This is why Rudolf Makreel chose to translate Dilthey's term into English as "human studies" rather than humanities.[41] On the other hand, the outlines of *Geisteswissenschaften* as defined by Dilthey can be seen to overlap to some degree with those the concepts *science(s) de l'homme* and human sciences, respectively.[42]

Since the days of Dilthey, however, the ways in which the term *Geisteswissenschaften* is used have become more varied. Dilthey's agenda is almost forgotten, the paradigmatic role he allotted to the study of history has largely waned, and the social sciences have come to be seen as a separate group of disciplines.[43] So that nowadays the term "Geisteswissenschaften" is more often than not used in the sense of "humanities."

Moral Sciences and *Sciences Morales*

As we have seen, the conceptual histories of the *Geisteswissenschaften* and John Stuart Mill's moral sciences were entangled. As we follow the latter term back to its French origins, another case of entanglement presents itself: In his *System of Logic*, Mill harks back to a French intellectual tradition, which he enrolled in his struggle against his British opponents, scientist and historian of science William Whewell (1794–1866) in particular.[44]

For the first two editions of his *System of Logic* (1843, 1846), Mill chose a quote from the philosopher and father of positivism Auguste Comte (1798–1857) for an epigraph. From the third edition of 1851 onward, a lengthy passage taken from the writings of the eminent enlightenment philosopher Nicolas de Condorcet (1743–94) took its place. The choice of these two authors was hardly coincidental: with Comte and Condorcet, Mill ascribed to the moral sciences the same ability to formulate laws and predict events—in the human realm—that the natural sciences were thought to have for the natural world.

The role of Condorcet is particularly significant in our context. After the dismantling of the academies in the wake of the French Revolution, Condorcet was one of the three scholars who contributed reports to the discussion that lead to the creation of an integrated *Institut national*. Among these he was the only one who suggested the creation of a separate "Classe des sciences morales et politiques."[45] His advice was heeded and the name he had fashioned for the class used when the new institute was established on 3 Brumaire IV (October 25, 1795).

Mill was aware of these goings-on and of Condorcet's role in them. In an article entitled "French News" (1832), he commented on and celebrated the creation of the "Classe des sciences morales et politiques" and its accomplishments since. As Wolf Feuerhahn has amply demonstrated, the affirmative references to Condorcet were part of Mill's attempt to counter a certain conception of "moral sciences" in Britain at the time with one that was more clearly experience based, his main target being William Whewell.[46]

In his *Two Introductory Lectures to Two Courses of Lectures on Moral Philosophy* of 1841, Whewell argued for the (pre-)existence of necessary moral truths in the human mind and thus, for their independence of human experience. Mill on the other hand wanted to see the moral sciences based on the "associative psychology" developed by James and Jeremy Bentham and modeled on the physical sciences. Mill's version of the moral sciences was thus characterized by their structural similarity to the physical sciences.

For Mill this question was as much a political one as it was epistemological. Mill saw Whewell as a representative both of the English academic and class systems. For Whewell's approach to moral truths could be used to legitimize contemporary societal hierarchies. Mill considered the French (and the German) academic systems as more flexible and for this reason also aligned with French philosophy and chose to use the French conception of "moral and political sciences."

And as we have seen, Mill's version of the concept was prominent among the notions against which Dilthey would later on develop his version of the "Geisteswissenschaften." With remarkable success: while some version of the concept "moral science" became dominant in France, the UK, Spain, Italy, and Belgium, it had a hard time in the German-speaking countries, where the alternative "Geisteswissenschaften" largely eclipsed its earlier sibling.[47]

Arts, *Lettres*, *Humanités*, and Humanities

While the *sciences morales*/moral sciences, the German *Geisteswissenschaften* (as well as its most prominent nineteenth-century alternatives, such as *Kulturwissenschaften*, and *historische Wissenschaften*), and the twentieth-century French concepts *sciences humaines* and *sciences de l'homme* no longer reflect the medieval and early modern institutional set-up of the university, this was, and is, the case with "les humanités," "humanities," and "arts." These terms refer to the institutional context of the seven liberal arts, i.e., the core of the curriculum of the Faculty of Arts in the Middle Ages and into the early modern period. The Latin root of the term *humanities* is *humaniora*. In the Renaissance, *ars humanitatis* was the name commonly given to the knowledge borne by the humanists. Both "humanities" and "the arts," which are the most common terms in the US and Britain, respectively, for the group of disciplines at hand derived from this concept. As Raymond Williams writes in his entry on "Humanity" in his seminal *Keywords*,

> [t]here was a persistent sense ranging from courtesy to kindness, and there was also the sense, developing from *umanità* and *humanitas*, of a particular kind of learning. There were C15 and C16 uses of **humanity** as a kind of learning distinct from divinity, and Bacon defined 'three knowledges, Divine

Philosophy, Natural Philosophy and Humane Philosophy, or Humanitie' (*Advancement of Learning*, II, v; 1605). Yet in academic use **Humanity** became equivalent to what we now call *classics*, and especially Latin (there are still residual uses in this sense.) From C18 a French form, **the humanities** (*les humanités*) became steadily more common in academic and related usage, eventually adding modern literature and philosophy to the *classsics*. This usage has remained normal in American English, as distinct from the more common English grouping of THE ARTS (q.v.).[48]

The subject area of this knowledge was not identical with that which many today identify with the humanities, nor with that which Dilthey ascribed to the *Geisteswissenschaften*. The *ars humanitatis* encompassed ancient poetry and prose and was used synonymously with "poetry." The humanists were accordingly also called "poets." Philosophy expressly did *not* belong to the *ars humanitatis*. If a term was sought for the knowledge of the humanists *including* philosophy, contemporaries spoke instead of *bonae artes* or *disciplinae*. We encounter the influential Ciceronian notion *studia humanitis* in both meanings—the narrower one excluding, and the wider one including philosophy.[49]

Two basic meanings are also given by the article "Humaniora or Humanitatis Studia" in Zedler's *Universallexikon*, the largest encyclopedia to be published in Europe in the eighteenth century. But even the narrower of the two includes philosophy. The article sets in with the *humaniora* being defined as synonymous with the liberal arts as a whole and thus as a preparatory course for studies at the three higher faculties. According to this definition, *humaniora* comprise the entirety of the subjects taught at the Faculty of Philosophy. But "usually," the article goes on, the following subjects are meant: "philosophy, history, antiquities, poetry, oratorio, grammar and languages."[50]

One way in which the term "humanity" has frequently been used in the English language, throughout the early modern period and unto our present day, comes close to this second meaning. While it sometimes comprises history and philosophy as well, the study of (esp. ancient) literature lies at its heart, as indicated by the definitions given by the *Oxford English Dictionary*:

> Literary learning or scholarship; secular letters as opposed to theology; esp. the study of ancient Latin and Greek language, literature, and intellectual culture (as grammar, rhetoric, history, and philosophy); classical scholarship. In later singular use, chiefly in Scottish universities: the study of Latin language and literature.[51]

Note that, again, the humanities are, if anything, seen in opposition to theology, not the sciences.

While the first instances given date into the second half of the nineteenth century, the second meaning that the *OED* gives—this time, for "humanities" in the plural—is much younger, and considerably closer to Dilthey's definition of the *Geisteswissenschaften*:

> In *plural* (usually with *the*). The branch of learning concerned with human culture; the academic subjects collectively comprising this branch of learning, as history, literature, ancient and modern languages, law, philosophy, art, and music. Hence also in *singular*: any of these subjects.[52]

It is this younger meaning that allows for the humanities to be seen in opposition to the sciences. But before 1800, and in fact well into the nineteenth century, this was not how these term was generally used.[53]

The French term "humanités" appeared as early as in the eighteenth century. It was frequently used, especially as a term for the propaedeutic curriculum at the *collèges*.[54] Its English version, "humanities," never quite replaced the more common "arts" in British English.[55] It was not before the 1930s and in the US that the modern concept of the humanities emerged. In Princeton in 1930 the Program in the Humanities was established. Almost simultaneously the University of Chicago chose to rename its Faculty of Arts and Letters, the new name being Division of the Humanities. Other universities, including Columbia, Yale, Harvard, and Stanford, soon followed their examples. By mid-century, the term "the humanities" was established for a group of disciplines distinct from the sciences and social sciences. These centered around the study of philosophy, literature, the arts and—not always, but sometimes—history and were seen to constitute a critical enterprise, opposed to mass society and other aspects of modernity, including science.[56]

Still more important than "humanités" for the French context was the concept "lettres." The first usage of this word denoting the study of texts, that is, philosophy, philology, and history given by the *Grand Robert* stems from the *Mémoires d'outre-tombe* of the French writer François-René de Chateaubriand, written in the first half of the nineteenth century and published posthumously in 1849 and 1850.[57] During the Second Empire (1852–70), when *écoles speciales* were renamed *facultés*, some of these were merged into *facultés des lettres* and *facultés des sciences* whereas the faculties for medicine and jurisprudence stayed independent. Unlike the faculties at

German universities, their French counterparts retained their Napoleonic independence: there was no overarching university.[58] In contemporary France, students can obtain a *baccalauréat ès lettres*, become a *docteur ès lettres* and eventually a *professeur de lettres*. Most universities have a *faculté des lettres*. And there is a *Secrétariat d'État aux arts et aux lettres*.[59] Much like "les humanities," "les lettres" are seen in opposition to the sciences as well as social sciences.

Conclusion

Arts, humanities, moral sciences, *humanités, lettres, sciences morales, sciences humaines, sciences de l'homme, Geisteswissenschaften* etcetera: the concepts discussed in this chapter did not all emerge simultaneously. Due to their specific political, institutional, and intellectual environments they came up, were defined, and re-defined around different times. What is more, they sometimes differ(ed) significantly in their paradigmatic disciplines and in the set of disciplines they comprise. But they did and do have a lot in common, and this is not surprising.

As we have seen, the conceptual history of the humanities, here used in a generic sense, has been entangled in at least two ways. First, the relevant concepts did not develop independently of each other. Many of them share the same etymological and intellectual roots in that they go back to the *studia humanitatis* of the Renaissance. Second, it has been entangled, in that the scholars and administrators who developed and institutionalized these concepts often took, and still take, some inspiration, both positive and negative, from discussions in other countries (and languages).

The histories of these concepts are entangled also in a different sense: not with each other, but each of them in their own ways with that of other disciplinary groupings, such as the social sciences and, most importantly, the natural sciences. They were, in this sense, the result of boundary work. The moral sciences as defined by John Stuart Mill were modeled in part on the physical sciences. The *Geisteswissenschaften* were also defined and popularized in the late nineteenth century, by Dilthey and others, in reaction to the rise of the sciences. But they were part of a defensive strategy against their emerging dominance. Similarly, when "the humanities" came to be fashionable in the US in the mid-twentieth century, this happened in part because they were often seen to be opposed to science and other aspects of a modernity that was by many deemed as negative.

Notes

1. Thomas F. Gieryn, *Cultural Boundaries of Science* (Chicago, IL: University of Chicago Press, 1999). For an earlier and less well-known explication of the concept, see Thomas F. Gieryn, "Boundary-Work and the Demarcation of Science from Non-Science: Strains and Interests in Professional Ideologies of Scientists," *American Sociological Review* 48, no. 6 (1983).
2. On the notion of "shifting demarcations," see Fabian Krämer, "Shifting Demarcations: An Introduction," *History of Humanities* 3, no. 1 (2018).
3. Cf. Ann Blair, "Disciplinary Distinctions before the 'Two Cultures,'" *The European Legacy* 13, no. 5 (2008): esp. 578.
4. Rudolf Stichweh, *Zur Entstehung des modernen Systems wissenschaftlicher Disziplinen. Physik in Deutschland 1740-1890* (Frankfurt am Main: Suhrkamp, 1984), 33 (italics in original). Unlike otherwise indicated, all translations are mine.
5. Rudolf Stichweh, "Die soziale Rolle des Professors der philosophischen Fakultät: Ein Fall von Professionalisierung? Deutschland im 18. und 19. Jahrhundert," in *Artisten und Philosophen: Wissenschafts- und Wirkungsgeschichte einer Fakultät vom 13. bis 19. Jahrhundert*, ed. Rainer Christoph Schwinges (Basel: Schwabe, 1999), 341.
6. Blair, "Disciplinary Distinctions," 578.
7. Marian Füssel, "Disziplinierte Wissenschaft? 'Fächergeschichte' als Spezialgebiet der Universitätsgeschichte" (forthcoming).
8. On this term and for a discussion of the sociological and historiographical approaches to the modern system of disciplines, see Johan Heilbron, "Das Regime der Disziplinen: Zu einer historischen Soziologie disziplinärer Wissenschaft," in *Interdisziplinarität als Lernprozess: Erfahrungen mit einem handlungstheoretischen Forschungsprogramm*, ed. Hans Joas and Hans G. Kippenberg (Göttingen: Wallstein, 2005).
9. For the eighteenth century, see Annette Meyer, "Zwei Sprachen—zwei Kulturen? Englische und deutsche Begriffe von Wissenschaft im 18. Jahrhundert," *Jahrbuch für die Europäische Wissenschaftskultur* 2 (2012). For the nineteenth century, see Sydney Ross, "Scientist: The Story of a Word," *Annals of Science* 18 (1962); David Cahan, "Looking at Nineteenth-Century Science: An Introduction," in *From Natural Philosophy to the Sciences: Writing the History of Nineteenth-Century Science*, ed. David Cahan (Chicago, IL: University of Chicago Press, 2003), and Denise Phillips, "Bacon among the

Germans: Stories from When 'Science' Meant '*Wissenschaft*,'" *History of Science* 53, no. 4 (2015).

10. The key reference for this claim is still Wolf Lepenies, *Die drei Kulturen: Soziologie zwischen Literatur und Wissenschaft* (Munich: Hanser, 1985). See also Rudolf Stichweh, "Natur- und Geisteswissenschaften? Eine Korrektur," *Frankfurter Allgemeine Zeitung* (December 2, 2008).

11. On the "dynamism of the disciplines" and its bearing on divisions of academic knowledge into two, see Hans-Jörg Rheinberger, "Culture and Nature in the Prism of Knowledge," *History of Humanities* 1, no. 1 (2016).

12. For an earlier and more general exposition of this thesis, see Krämer, "Shifting Demarcations," 7–9. For a similar argument, albeit with a different dating of the emergence of the humanities, see Julian Hamann, *Die Bildung der Geisteswissenschaften: Zur Genese einer sozialen Konstruktion zwischen Diskurs und Feld* (Konstanz: UVK, 2014).

13. On the entire paragraph, see Julian Hamann, *Bildung der Geisteswissenschaften*; Hamann, "Boundary Work between Two Cultures: Demarcating the Modern *Geisteswissenschaften*," *History of Humanities* 3, no. 1 (2018); and Hamann, "The Making of the 'Geisteswissenschaften': A Case of Boundary Work?" *FIW Working Paper* (2017), online at https://www.fiw.uni-bonn.de/publikationen/FIWWorkingPaper/fiw-working-paper (accessed March 9, 2022). While building on Hamann's research, my thesis is not identical with his. In my opinion, the humanities in the long nineteenth century were not only formed *in view of* other groups of disciplines, including the natural sciences, as Hamann writes, but increasingly *in response to* the rise of the natural sciences. Cf. Hamann, *Bildung der Geisteswissenschaften*, where the "dominance of the natural sciences" (13) is considered but one among several context-specific points of reference for the self-reflexive discourse about the modern humanities. We also arrive at a different dating of the phenomenon: while Hamann dates the emergence of the *Geisteswissenschaften* to the period around 1800 (ibid., 17–21, esp. 20), I argue that the second half of the nineteenth century witnessed the emergence of the concept *Geisteswissenschaften*, while the concept *Naturwissenschaften* is relatively older. Søren Kjørup, *Geisteswissenschaften, humanities, sciences humaines: Eine Einführung*, trans. Elisabeth Bense (Stuttgart: J. B. Metzler, 2001) (not cited by Hamann) argues for the same dating (esp. 18–9).

14. On this, see Mitchell Ash, "Academic Politics in the History of Science: Experimental Psychology in Germany, 1879-1941," *Central European History* 13, no. 3 (1980): 259; R. Steven Turner, "The Growth of Professional Research in Prussia, 1818 to 1848: Causes and Effects," *Historical Studies in the Physical Sciences* 3 (1971): esp. 549; and Fritz Ringer, *The Decline of the German Mandarins: The German Academic Community, 1890-1933* (Cambridge, MA:

Harvard University Press, 1969), 102 and *passim*, esp. 110–1. On the history of philology and its role within the humanities, see James Turner, *Philology: The Forgotten Origins of the Modern Humanities* (Princeton, NJ: Princeton University Press, 2000).

15. For the role played in this context by institutions and communities, cf. Cahan, "Institutions and Communities."
16. This is confirmed by a Google NGram search in the German corpus: https://books.google.com/ngrams/graph?content=Naturwissenschaften%2CGeisteswissenschaften&year_start=1780&year_end=2019&corpus=31&smoothing=1& (May 28, 2021). NGrams created with help of Google NGram Viewer have to be taken *cum grano salis*. NGram Viewer searches printed texts digitized for/by Google and not the totality of texts published in a given language at a given time, not to mention the spoken word. What is more, the outlines of the corpus are not made explicit. Such NGrams only offer a first impression, which is however often insightful.
17. On the "explosion" of the labor market for chemists in Germany after 1860, see Rüdiger vom Bruch, "Mommsen und Harnack: Die Geburt von Big Science aus den Geisteswissenschaften," in *Theodor Mommsen: Wissenschaft und Politik im 19. Jahrhundert*, ed. Alexander Demandt and Andreas Goltz (Berlin: Walter de Gruyter, 2005), 399, and Peter Lundgreen, "Examina und Tätigkeitsfelder für Absolventen der Philosophischen Fakultät: Berufskonstruktion und Professionalisierung im 19. Jahrhundert," in Schwinges, *Artisten und Philosophen*, 325. On the development and importance of the diploma (*Diplom*), the standard academic degree qualifying for the non-academic labor market, in this context from 1899 onwards, see Lundgreen, "Examina und Tätigkeitsfelder," 333–4.
18. Heinrich Gustav Magnus, *Festrede auf der Universität zu Berlin am 3. August 1862* (Berlin: Druckerei der Königlichen Akademie der Wissenschaften, 1862), esp. 10–11.
19. Hans-Ulrich Rüegger, "Verstehen statt Erklären? Zur Logik der Interpretation in den Geisteswissenschaften," *Theologische Zeitung* 64 (2008). Cf. Wilhelm Dilthey, "Ideen über eine beschreibende und zergliedernde Psychologie," in *Wilhelm Diltheys gesammelte Schriften*, ed. Georg Misch (Leipzig: J. B. Teubner, 1924 [1894]), 143–8.
20. Cf., e.g., Helmut Pulte's observation that Dilthey's triple goal to demarcate the *Geisteswissenschaften* from the sciences, to assert them, and to provide them with a foundation in light of the emerging dominance of the sciences is a commonplace in histories of philosophy. Helmut Pulte, "Gegen die Naturalisierung des Humanen: Wilhelm Dilthey im Kontext und als Theoretiker der Naturwissenschaften seiner Zeit," in *Dilthey als Wissenschaftsphilosoph*, ed. Christian Damböck and Hans-Ulrich Lessing (Freiburg: Alber, 2015), 63.

21. Cf. on this point Hans-Ulrich Lessing, "Der Zusammenhang von Leben, Ausdruck und Verstehen. Diltheys späte hermeneutische Grundlegung der Geisteswissenschaften," in *Dilthey und die hermeneutische Wende in der Philosophie: Wirkungsgeschichtliche Aspekte seines Werkes*, ed. Gudrun Kühne-Bertram and Frithjof Rodi (Göttingen: Vandenhoeck & Ruprecht, 2008), 59.
22. Jan Eckel, *Geist der Zeit: Deutsche Geschichtswissenschaften seit 1870* (Göttingen: Vandenhoeck & Ruprecht, 2008), 21.
23. Ibid., 23.
24. Ibid., 20–1. Eckel does not mention the many examples we have for the opposite stance: Some representatives of the disciplines that were then or are now more often than not considered as belonging to the humanities and/or social sciences deliberately incorporated methodical or epistemological elements that were associated with the natural sciences. Before 1880, early sociology and positivist historiography are two cases in point, with the 'positive method' of the French sociologist Auguste Comte (1798–1859) and the *History of Civilization in England* (1857) by Henry Thomas Buckle (1821–62) being the most prominent examples. For the time after 1880, the Leipzig-based cultural historian Karl Lamprecht (1856–1915) may serve as an example: he took much of his methodical inspiration from the psychologist Wilhelm Wundt (1832–1920) rather than from Dilthey.
25. Among many other examples, see Hamann, *Bildung der Geisteswissenschaften*, 18.
26. Cf. Kjørup, *Geisteswissenschaften*, 3-4 and 69. Kjørup does not, however, mention that the chapter is absent from the first, 1849 edition of the translation.
27. The term "Wissenschaft des Geistes" is used once, in the singular and meaning psychology. John Stuart Mill, *Die inductive Logik: Eine Darlegung der philosophischen Principien wissenschaftlicher Forschung, insbesondere der Naturforschung*, trans. J. Schiel (Braunschweig: Friedrich Vieweg und Sohn, 1849), 223.
28. See John Stuart Mill, *A System of Logic, Ratiocinative and Inductive, Being a Connected View of the Principles of Evidence, and the Methods of Scientific Investigation*, vol. 1 (London: John W. Parker, 1843), esp. iv.
29. Mill, *Inductive Logik*, vi.
30. Ibid.
31. John Stuart Mill, *System der deductiven und inductiven Logik: Eine Darlegung der Principien wissenschaftlicher Forschung, insbesondere der Naturforschung*, trans. J. Schiel, 2nd edn, 2 vols (Braunschweig: Friedrich Vieweg und Sohn, 1862–3).
32. John Stuart Mill, *System der deductiven und inductiven Logik: Eine Darlegung der Principien wissenschaftlicher Forschung, insbesondere der Naturforschung*,

trans. J. Schiel, 3rd edn, 2 vols (Braunschweig: Friedrich Vieweg und Sohn, 1868).
33. This statement is based on the systematic scouring of the extant rector's addresses and public academy lectures held at the following institutions throughout the nineteenth century. See Fabian Kraemer, *Before the Two Cultures* (in preparation).
34. N. N., "Geisteswissenschaften," in *Deutsches Wörterbuch*, ed. Jacob and Wilhelm Grimm (Leipzig: S. Hirzel, 1897), col. 2769. The *lemma* "Geistesphilosophie" mentioned in this entry was never published. The same applies to many other *lemmata* to which entries in the *Zedler* refer the reader.
35. Cf. Hamann, *Die Bildung der Geisteswissenschaften*, 18–9.
36. Ibid., 18.
37. Mill, *System der deductiven und inductiven Logik*, 2nd edn, xii (summary of book 6, chapter 1, section 1).
38. For a similar argument, see Kjørup, *Geisteswissenschaften*, 4 and 69.
39. Cf. Hans-Ulrich Lessing, *Wilhelm Dilthey: Eine Einführung* (Cologne: Böhlau, 2011), 36–7.
40. On the *Grundlagenkrise*, see Lessing, *Wilhelm Dilthey*, 35–6.
41. Rudolf Adam Makkreel, *Dilthey: Philosopher of the Human Studies* (Princeton, NJ: Princeton University Press, 1975).
42. For an influential historical application of the concept human sciences, here understood as comprising psychology, sociology, anthropology, economics, and political science, see Roger Smith, *The Norton History of the Human Sciences* (New York: Norton, 1997).
43. See Lepenies' seminal book, *Die drei Kulturen*.
44. The entire section is based in large part on Wolf Feuerhahn, "Moral sciences, Geisteswissenschaften (1750–1900)," *Revue d'histoire des sciences humaines* 37 (2020).
45. See also Sophie-Anne Leterrier, *L'institution des sciences morales: L'Académie des Sciences Morales et Politiques 1795–1850* (Paris: L'Harmattan, 1995), 6; Johan Heilbron, *Naissance de la sociologie* (Marseille: Agone, 2006), 176–7.
46. See also Laura J. Snyder, *Reforming Philosophy: A Victorian Debate on Science and Society* (Chicago, IL: University of Chicago Press, 2006).
47. For this observation, see Feuerhahn, "Moral sciences."
48. Raymond Williams, *Keywords: A Vocabulary of Culture and Society* (Oxford: Oxford University Press, 1976), 122 (emphasis in original).
49. On the contemporary terminology, see Arno Seifert, "Das höhere Schulwesen: Universitäten und Gymnasien," in *Handbuch der deutschen Bildungsgeschichte*, vol. 1, ed. Notker Hammerstein and August Buck (Munich: C. H. Beck, 1996), 226. On the reasons for the success of the humanist project and on the effects that this constellation had on the humanities, see Anthony Grafton and Lisa

Jardine, *From Humanism to the Humanities: Education and the Liberal Arts in Fifteenth- and Sixteenth-Century Europe* (Cambridge, MA: Harvard University Press, 1986), Introduction and 220.
50. N. N., "Humaniora oder Humanitatis Studia," in *Grosses vollständiges Universal-Lexicon aller Wissenschaften und Künste*, ed. Johann Heinrich Zedler (Leipzig: Johann Heinrich Zedler, 1739), col. 1155.
51. N. N., "Humanity, n.," Oxford English Dictionary, online at https://www.oed.com/ (accessed March 9, 2022), 2. a.
52. Ibid., 2. b.
53. On the transformation of the humanities between 1750 and 1850 and, in particular, the changing relationship between the study of literature and philosophy, see Floris Solleveld, "The Transformation of the Humanities. Ideals and Practices of Scholarship Between Enlightenment and Romanticism, 1750–1850" (PhD thesis Radboud Universiteit Nijmegen, 2018).
54. Ibid.
55. Williams, *Keywords*, 122.
56. See Geoffrey Galt Harpham, *The Humanities and the Dream of America* (Chicago, IL: University of Chicago Press, 2011), 14. On the humanities in the mid-twentieth century United States, cf. the chapter by Claire Arcenas in this volume.
57. Grand Robert, "lettre n.f. IV. Au plur. LES LETTRES 3 (Par oppos. aux sciences)"; http://gr.bvdep.com.ezproxy.cul.columbia.edu/ (accessed November 4, 2016).
58. See Louis Liard, *Universités et facultés* (Paris: Armand Colin, 1890), 8 and 10.
59. Grand Robert, "lettre n.f. IV. Au plur. LES LETTRES 3."

2

From Philology to the Humanities: Fragmentation and Discipline Formation in the United Kingdom and United States

James Turner

When we think of the humanities nowadays, we call to mind a cluster of related and sometimes overlapping disciplines, such as literary studies and art history.[1] Yet when we write the history of the humanities, our subject shifts shape maddeningly. What counts as "the humanities" varies country by country, institution by institution. The Russian State University for the Humanities includes economics, a discipline that few in western Europe or the Americas would place among the humanities.[2] In anglophone universities philosophy and history are commonly found among the humanities but may also appear elsewhere on the map of knowledge, the former linked with mathematics or economics, the latter with "social sciences." Other disciplines look hybrid. Cultural/social anthropology seems humanistic in questions and methods, while biological/physical anthropology behaves like a natural science. The two ended up yoked together only by historical accident.

Whatever pieces of knowledge we set among the humanities, we picture them individually as discrete disciplines, each with its own journals, learned societies, and niche in the university faculty. Humanities disciplines may collaborate, as in Harvard's venerable concentration in history and literature, Oxford's century-old degree in philosophy, politics, and economics, or Michigan's more recent joint PhD in anthropology and history. But teachers in these programs belong to the distinct disciplines collaborating in them, and participating in cross-disciplinary studies does not erase anyone's disciplinary identity. However often the humanities work together, they remain disciplines, each standing on its own feet. They have all evolved infrastructure to maintain their distinctiveness and police their borders. Historians publish in the *English Historical Review*, rarely in the *Art Bulletin*. Scholars of the ancient Mediterranean hobnob at the annual meeting of the Society for Classical Studies, where professors of German literature are rarely seen.

It was not always so. Prior to 1700, in many places 1800, the subjects that evolved in the West into the modern humanities mixed in a single scholarly stew. The same person might emend and edit ancient texts; study the origin, development, and grammar of languages; sketch old buildings, inscriptions, or coins; write biographies of famous persons or cities; compile mosaics of historical data or chronicle contemporary events; mimic the presumed elegance of ancient Latin.[3] Various labels—philology and antiquarianism perhaps most common—covered these activities in their own day. All of these studies had origins in antiquity. All would today be divided among anthropology, archaeology, art history, classical studies, history, linguistics, literary studies, or religious studies.

In between, all hung together. Such studies were the undivided pursuits of learned persons fascinated by material, linguistic, and literary products of human beings, as distinct from the non-human phenomena of the natural world. (The same individual might also pursue astronomy along with antiquarianism, but natural science is not our business here.) For instance, the Cambridge University scholar Richard Bentley (1662–1742) rediscovered a lost letter in the ancient Greek alphabet (linguistics, we would say today); he also edited Greek and Roman poets (classics), *Paradise Lost* (English literature), and the New Testament (religious studies)—without ever thinking that he was working in different fields of knowledge. Bentley was far from unique. John Selden (1584–1654) published on the history of tithes in England, the history of titles of honor throughout Europe (prince, admiral, boyar, and the like), ancient Middle Eastern deities, classical Greek inscriptions, Jewish marriage and divorce, and the law of the sea. Selden also pioneered Arabic studies in Britain.[4] Early-modern scholars on the Continent look to us just as polymathic; but again, they thought of themselves as pursuing humane learning, not distinct disciplines. No single label covers all of these interrelated humanistic studies. Probably *philology* makes the best portmanteau term, since comparative and historical methods developed within the study of texts and language migrated out to shape other kinds of research.

The question then becomes, how can historians of the humanities illuminate the path from this integrated, broad-gauged "philology" to the separate modern humanities disciplines? Writing the history of the humanities in the European cultural sphere must begin by answering it. The answer, though broadly similar throughout western and central Europe and lands culturally colonized from there (such as the Americas and Australia), differs in specifics from country to country.

To make the story manageable, I will focus on the origins of the disciplines of classics, literature, and history within higher education during the nineteenth century in the United Kingdom and United States. I choose these three disciplines because of the historic centrality of Latin and Greek in education and because history and literature became the most populous of the humanities disciplines. I select the UK and US for no better reason than my greater familiarity with intellectual activity there. I center on higher education during the nineteenth century because the modern humanities—unlike the "philology" that gave birth to them—developed principally within colleges and universities between 1800 and 1900, especially in the latter half of the century.

It will help to recall first a few features of higher education in the two countries in this period.[5] Semantically, the US had mostly *colleges*, the UK mostly *universities*; for our purposes the distinction hardly matters, and as a rule I will use the terms interchangeably. Within the UK, its three political subdivisions—England (including Wales), Scotland, and Ireland—differed in educational provision. In 1800 England and Wales still had only two universities, the medieval foundations at Oxford and Cambridge, both tied to the Church of England. Ireland had only Trinity College in Dublin, also Anglican, founded in 1592 on the Oxbridge model. (*Oxbridge* has come to refer to the characteristics shared by Oxford and Cambridge.)[6] Scotland had universities in four towns, all dating from the fifteenth and sixteenth centuries. The new, decentralized United States inherited nine colleges from their colonial era and added thirteen more between independence and 1800, widely differing in size and solidity.

Very crudely speaking—ignoring much variation—two broad patterns of instruction dominated during the earlier nineteenth century. In the Oxbridge model, a student's entire education was supervised, and very largely imparted, by a single, non-specialized tutor in a residential college within the university. Almost all these colleges required tutors to be celibate Anglican clergy; and, after several years, they commonly moved into parish work, lured by the chance to marry and to climb the ecclesiastical ladder. In Scotland and the United States, students typically learned different subjects from teachers who taught that subject alone. (By no means all teachers were expert in what they taught.) Scottish and American universities also required a wider range of studies than did Oxford or Cambridge; and Scottish and American professors—not chafing under a requirement of celibacy—were more likely to make a career in higher education.

After 1800, the number of universities expanded. In America new colleges proliferated as white settlement pushed west. By 1850 the country had probably over a hundred colleges. Most were church-related, some state-sponsored, and they varied immensely in size, quality, and financial soundness. The number of universities in the UK grew more slowly, but grew. In 1832 Parliament chartered a third, small Anglican university in Durham. Four years later the University of London was chartered to grant degrees to students of schools in the metropolis, most not associated with the Church of England—notably a London University founded in 1826, which now became University College London. (I will call it by its new name even when referring to the pre-1836 institution.) Beginning in the 1840s, pressure for local access to higher education swelled in Ireland and in English cities outside London. This led before 1900 to ten or so new university-level colleges in such towns as Manchester and Liverpool, Belfast and Galway. (Meanwhile, Scotland's universities grew in size but not number.) In approach to instruction, all these new, non-Church-of-England schools followed the Scottish–American model rather than the Oxbridge one, although Oxford and Cambridge carried more prestige. But they, too, were changing. Starting in 1850 and continuing for three decades, parliamentary interventions pushed Oxford and Cambridge toward curricular modernization, abolition of religious tests, and a faculty structure more nourishing of permanent academic careers. By the late nineteenth century Anglican influence in both the ancient universities was diminished, celibacy was no longer demanded, and university professors and lecturers became more serious supplements to college tutors. The drift toward the Scottish–American model mattered, because specialized, career-oriented faculty provided a potential breeding ground for a disciplinary organization of knowledge.

Another change also mattered greatly. University faculties had always housed some intellectually curious individuals who pushed the boundaries of knowledge, pursuing and publishing research. But such scholars were in 1800 a minority, a tiny one in most schools. Everyone understood that the sole *institutional* mission of universities was teaching. This attitude began to change after 1800, especially after mid-century. In universities throughout the English-speaking world, the idea began to sink in that research and publication might properly form a routine part of a college teacher's work. Often research-oriented faculty had an eye on German universities, where an ideal of professorial research had taken hold decades earlier. A landmark came in 1876 with the founding of Johns Hopkins University in Baltimore, the first self-consciously research-oriented university in the English-speaking world.[7] But other universities—the more ambitious ones—on both sides of the Atlantic also began to expect research from their faculty. The parliamentary modernization of Oxford and Cambridge included funding of research. In the US, beginning in the 1870s, universities even developed programs to train college graduates as research specialists: "graduate education," with a PhD at the end. And it was in these decades of new commitment to research that the humanities disciplines took their modern form in the English-speaking world.

Let us begin to see how to write the history of humanistic discipline-formation by examining how scholarship on ancient Latin and Greek texts developed into the modern discipline of classics. Much of what we learn will also bear on the evolution of history and literature into disciplines.

Study of Latin was the original humanistic learning—*studia humanitatis*, when that term was coined in the fourteenth century. In the sixteenth century pairing Latin with Greek became common in higher education. Connecting ancient manuscripts and other ancient artifacts, such as coins or architectural remains, still mattered a lot to scholars such as Bentley. But among university teachers this interest in a broader "philology" had largely disappeared by 1800. Latin and Greek *language* then still bulked large at universities in the US and UK. Even the greater prestige of mathematics at Cambridge did not spare students drilling in classical languages. Scholarly ambitions in the UK in the earlier nineteenth century often expressed themselves in annotated editions of ancient Greek or Roman authors. (Before mid-century Americans lacked resources to produce such things.) Both teaching and research focused on language—grammar, syntax, style—not on Greece or Rome conceived as cultures distinct from modernity. Even when scholars knew antiquity well, from religious rituals to legal practices, they used that erudition to illuminate a text, rather than using a text to cast light on the culture that produced it. In short, the study of Greek and Latin was far from the modern discipline of classics.

This began to change largely because of Germans. From the late 1600s some learned Europeans began to suspect that the *Iliad* and *Odyssey* reflected an unfamiliar, even primitive lifestyle.[8] German scholars especially drifted toward understanding not just Homer but ancient texts generally, including the Bible, as products of cultures vastly different in values, outlook, and social structure than modern Europe.[9] But how could one recover such long-dead civilizations in their various stages of development? Some German professors insisted that ancient material remains, like art and architecture, be brought to bear alongside ancient texts—in effect reviving an older, integrated philology, though one focused exclusively on the ancient Mediterranean. At the turn of the nineteenth century Friedrich August Wolf named this new holistic study *Altertumswissenschaft*, "the science of antiquity."[10] By early in the century *Altertumswissenschaft* had transformed German classical scholarship into something recognizable as the template of the later British and American humanistic discipline called "classics."

But this anglophone discipline waited in the wings a long while.[11] Most Oxbridge classicists ignored German upstarts and focused, as they long had, on editing and commenting on Greek and Latin texts. Even though no American produced original classical scholarship before mid-century, conditions in American colleges were actually more hospitable to *Altertumswissenschaft*, if only because intellectually inclined Americans in general esteemed German culture more than did denizens of Cambridge and Oxford. Already by the 1820s the best informed American professors regarded German philology as superior to English. Scholars at the new University College London likewise looked more generously on *Altertumswissenschaft*, as did some outside of the universities.

But the structure of higher education in both Oxbridge and the US before 1850 hamstrung classical research along German lines. In Germany, lifelong professorial careers devoted to ancient Greece or Rome fostered the deep learning underlying *Altertumswissenschaft*. In Oxford and Cambridge— where the comparatively few professors were still marginal to instruction— college tutors taught all subjects, generalists not specialists. American professors, though more specialized, labored under heavy loads of classroom hours and student oversight, and they lacked substantial libraries for research. Colleges would have to change before classical scholarship in them broadened beyond what Germans called word-philology.

Altertumswissenschaft therefore edged first into teaching. By the late 1830s even Oxford and Cambridge examiners expected students to know a little of it at second hand. But tutors habitually treated ancient writers, less as ghosts of an alien past, more as fellow Victorians in odd clothing who dispensed useful advice to young men of the ruling classes. A few American professors began to reject the context-free grammar-grinding that constituted American teaching of Latin and Greek in favor of an approach more Germanic. At Harvard in the 1830s the Greek professor, Cornelius Felton, groused that Americans taught classical texts without "transporting ourselves back to the time" when their authors lived. He insisted that understanding "the Greek drama fully" required learning "the spirit of the people and the light in which they regarded it," along with "the architectural construction of the theatre, and the scenic details." But even in Felton's mind classical studies had not congealed into a distinct discipline.[12]

Yet, within several decades, the teaching of Latin and Greek in both countries grew into a new discipline, called classical studies or simply classics. Four principal shifts were involved.

First, a consensus gradually took hold that classical scholars must go beyond texts. Archaeology, art history, and ancient history melted into "classics," not as optional adjuncts or even ancillary subdisciplines (like paleography for historians), but as integral to the new discipline. No later than 1872—probably earlier—the University of Michigan included ancient art in undergraduate instruction in classics, a marker of the growing impact of archaeology. At that time in Oxford and Cambridge, most classical scholars still encountered the ancients almost exclusively in writing and swept their awkward antiquity under the rug. A telling moment came in 1879 when reform of the Cambridge classical tripos (the examination for an honours degree) allowed students to add a new Part II, testing work in philosophy, archaeology, history, comparative philology, or art—if they wished. Not until 1918 was Part II required. In the 1880s Cambridge and Oxford both began teaching classical archaeology, though the subject remained marginal until the early twentieth century. In contrast, by 1880 American classicists were writing about Roman private life, the role of women in Athenian murder trials, travel in the ancient Mediterranean, and the staging of Greek drama. Classics was becoming the study of ancient Greece and Rome, not of ancient Greek and Roman texts, however weighty these remained. (Later, "ancient Mediterranean world" often seemed fitter than "ancient Greece and Rome.") Seen in the longest perspective, this broader "classics" sprang from the re-marriage of antiquarianism and philology—divorced not much more than a century earlier.

Second, the gathering effect of these developments made Greece and Rome less familiar, even alien, undercutting the centrality of Latin and Greek in higher education. Since the Renaissance, classical texts had furnished readers guides for contemporary life. But, more and more, classicists highlighted differences between ancient and modern. Most dramatically, from the late 1880s, the so-called Cambridge Ritualists injected into the Greco-Roman past a huge dose of late-Victorian anthropology.[13] They wrote of human sacrifice, the origin of the Olympic gods in animal-spirits of the underworld, and the fundamental irrationality of Greek and Roman religion. The rites and customs they attributed to Greeks and Romans seemed more apt for New Guinea's highlands than for proper Victorians. Few scholars went so far, but this newly divergent ancient world could no longer plausibly form elite young modern Christians.

Third, the educational hegemony of Latin and Greek began to crumble. In the US pressures for more "modern" education eventually marginalized the ancient languages. After 1869 forward-looking Harvard ceased to require them except for freshmen; in 1884 even freshmen were set free. This revolution left teachers of Latin and Greek looking and feeling more like professors of geology or botany; that is, specialists responsible for a body of field-specific knowledge, rather than general-purpose educators dragging all students through standard texts. As universities started to make faculty research a factor in hiring and salary, many American teachers of Greek and Latin (conceiving themselves now as scholarly specialists) morphed into professors of classics alert to research in their area. More and more of them understood classics as one field among many, not as general education. In the UK different institutional developments produced parallel effects. Starting with University College London and continuing with the institutions of higher education that developed in mid-century, new English and Irish universities dumped the classics-drenched curriculum of Oxford and Cambridge. (Scottish universities had never so highly privileged Latin and Greek.) "Modern" or "practical" subjects such as English literature, history, modern languages, and natural science dominated. Latin and Greek, if at first taught at all, took a subordinate position. The parliamentary duress after 1850 also pushed Oxford and Cambridge to create new paths to honors degrees. As with the expanding subjects in American colleges, these new courses slowly turned classics into one field among many rather than an essential of liberal education—and so eventually turned classicists from general-purpose teachers into specialists.

Fourth, in these new circumstances classics became a modern discipline: an inward-looking, university-based field of study, gauging individual achievement mostly by quality of research. Classicists set up new institutions specific to their discipline, such as professional societies and journals. Its practitioners published increasingly for each other's eyes. By the 1920s they rarely dabbled in studies other than classics (and, if so, saw themselves as dabbling). And they differentiated serious scholarship for specialists from popularizing for general readers. All this reinforced the newly disciplinary character of the field.

Americans got there first, perhaps because the powerful Oxbridge tradition of university studies as gentlemanly attainment inhibited professional discipline-formation in the UK. In 1869 US classicists helped to found the American Philological Association (APA). At first the APA encompassed scholars of language and literature from ancient India to modern Europe. Most of its members—all of its leaders—were research-oriented and university-based. Among its first acts was a yearbook to publish research. Before the yearbook reached its tenth year, articles on classical subjects drowned all others. Latin and Greek scholars thereafter dominated the APA. It promoted a broadened classical studies, cooperating closely with the Archaeological Institute of America from its founding in 1879. APA annual meetings became the place for young scholars to make a mark and (as one early member put it) speed their "much desired migration" to a university higher in the pecking order.[14] By 1900, the APA had become a disciplinary organization solely for American scholars of ancient Greece and Rome, though not until 2013 did it change its name to the more apt Society for Classical Studies. New journals announced the newly professionalized discipline. In 1880 the *American Journal of Philology* appeared, a thoroughly research-oriented enterprise, underwritten by its editor's research-obsessed Johns Hopkins University, aimed solely at professional readers. Like the APA itself, the *AJP* at first enveloped "the whole cycle of philological study" from "Comparative Grammar" to "the Teutonic languages."[15] But Greece and Rome soon dominated its pages. The truth is that philology was no discipline but a set of related scholarly practices. It provided no academic center of gravity. Classics *was* a discipline, at least a discipline a-borning; and its acolytes wrote for each other. More periodicals appeared as the discipline gelled: *Cornell Studies in Classical Philology* (a monograph series) in 1887, *Harvard Studies in Classical Philology* in 1890, *Classical Journal* in 1905,

Classical Philology in 1906. Such publications kept readers abreast of the discipline, reporting conferences, memorializing deceased colleagues, reinforcing the identity of classics as a self-enclosed field.

In the UK serious discipline formation came later, *after* the crucial intellectual developments of the 1880s and 1890s. Both Oxford and Cambridge had philological societies by the 1870s, but neither specialized in classical philology. A quartet consisting of an English classicist at a Scottish university, an archaeologist from the British Museum, a London publisher, and the *chargé d'affaires* at the Greek embassy formed in 1879 a Society for the Promotion of Hellenic Studies; under its aegis, a *Journal of Hellenic Studies* (1880) pushed classical studies beyond texts by highlighting history and archaeology. Yet the classical establishment mostly stayed aloof: fewer than a fifth of the founding members came from universities. A British School was founded at Athens in 1886 as a base for excavations and for training classical archaeologists: it mimicked an American School founded five years before. No national organization for classicists existed before the Classical Association in 1903. And this new association aimed more to defend the place of Latin and Greek in education than to promote research—the motive behind the APA thirty-four years earlier. Creation of the Society for the Promotion of Roman Studies in 1910 added both a sister for the Society for the Promotion of Hellenic Studies and further confusion about the center of gravity of classical scholarship. Similar stories could be told about journals available for classicists to publish in. "Classics" did not jell as a *discipline* in Britain until the 1920s or even 1930s.

But, once the infrastructure was in place in both countries, it defined classics as a discipline devoted to the broad-gauged study of ancient Greek and Roman civilizations: their textual legacy, their material culture, their values, beliefs, and institutions. Any reader of the Classical Association's *Classical Quarterly* will recognize the melding of American and British classical scholarship into a single disciplinary whole. So the oldest mode of philology became one discipline among the humanities. In becoming a discipline, classics absorbed not only classical philology but also related inquiries grouped together before 1800 as antiquarianism: archaeology, numismatics, epigraphy, the study of "art objects" like statues and vases. For this reason, classicists studied evidence perhaps broader in scope than any other humanistic scholars. No other of the humanities exhibited so little of the narrowness in subject matter associated with modern academic disciplines, because no other retained so much continuity with the multiple practices of early-modern philology and its erudite neighbors like antiquarianism and chronology. Yet the discipline's organizations and publications also closed off classics from other emergent humanities disciplines.

One can see the trajectory leading to "classics" in still longer perspective. Renaissance and early-modern philologists and antiquarians pursued an undifferentiated quest for knowledge of older times, collecting and correcting ancient texts and amassing other old artifacts of various sorts: statues, coins, seals, vases, inscriptions. But in anglophone higher education philology narrowed to teaching Latin and Greek and emending Greek and Roman texts. The revolution of the later eighteenth and early nineteenth centuries in German universities brought together once again—and more systematically—philological knowledge derived from texts with antiquarian information derived from other artifacts. When scholars melded manuscripts and material objects to create *Altertumswissenschaft*, their gaze shifted from individual classical texts to the ancient world whence they came. The aim of even textual philology became to understand Greek and Roman antiquity in their completeness. This new undertaking American scholars admired from afar and finally succeeded in joining after 1860, while many English classical philologists resisted until after 1900.

Once domesticated in the anglophone world, holistic study of classical antiquity demanded that researchers stay abreast of such diverse subfields as archaeology, epigraphy, papyrology, art history—and textual philology. This pressure tended to separate classicists from philologists once their near neighbors, such as biblical critics and orientalists. As late as 1800 the same scholar might comment on Attic tragedy, Anglo-Saxon poetry, the Hebrew Bible. Not in 1900. Distance between fields grew greater, boundaries clearer, as stresses of professionalization and specialization in newly research-inclined universities detached the learned into disciplines. Philology fragmented into several of these, most collectively labeled humanities. Classics became one. Classicists today may talk about a remarkable range of things, but they talk routinely only to each other.

Literature and history followed similar paths to disciplinarity, but they had to fight their way into higher education in order to get there. Unlike Greek and Latin texts, post-classical literature and history had traditionally not figured in university curricula. Indeed, modern understandings of literary and historical scholarship were themselves cobbled together, mostly out of pieces of philology, relatively late in the annals of learning.

Look first at history, the less complicated story. Writing about the past is ancient. Historians today invoke Thucydides and Tacitus as ancestors. But "history" now means something more specific, something like nonfictional writing about the past, grounded in evidence examined for its accuracy. The evidence is typically, though not necessarily, adduced in reference notes rather than in the main text. Although developing from fragmentary precedents reaching back as early as Eusebius of Caesarea (*c.* 260–340 CE), this notion of history took hold only within the last two centuries. In 1800 a novel could still without affectation be called a history, and sheer speculation about the past could also qualify. A pivotal moment came in 1776 when Edward Gibbon published the first volume of *Decline and Fall of the Roman Empire*. Gibbon adopted the elegant, broad-gauged narrative of the Enlightenment's so-called philosophical histories—think of Voltaire's 1756 *Essay on the Customs and Spirit of Nations*—but insisted on basing it on sources verified by the rigorous methods honed over the centuries by philologists working on ancient texts. This wedding of philological criticism and writing about the past gave birth to historical scholarship as we now understand it. In the early twentieth century the prominent American historian Andrew McLaughlin still used the old philological term critique as a synonym for historical method.[16]

Gibbon's style of history very gradually pushed aside competing versions of history, as more and more writers about the past adopted his principles during the first half of the nineteenth century.[17] The invention of "prehistory" around 1860 perhaps sealed the victory by corralling the past of non-literate peoples into a separate category, leaving history proper to cover only people who produced written documents to scrutinize (including, say, coins or clay tablets).[18] By the time history became a university subject—more about that shortly—the modern conception of history was firmly in place.

Literary scholarship also developed from philological roots, with a late injection of philosophy.[19] (I will not attempt the hopeless effort to define "literature.") Scholars in modern literature departments engage in one or more of three principal activities: (1) producing editions, usually annotated, of literary works ("editing"); (2) writing the history of literature, whether biographies of authors or accounts of periods, genres, and so forth ("literary history"); (3) assessing qualities of literary works, a job that in recent decades has involved "theory" as well as (evaluative) "criticism." These three types of scholarship had distinct roots in different philological practices. The coming together of editing, literary history, and criticism in the nineteenth century created the modern discipline of literature.

Editing has the most ancient roots. Emending and commenting on editions, with commentary sometimes a separate genre, was a main activity of philologists as early as Hellenistic antiquity. It remained central from the Italian Renaissance onward, sometimes treating Greek and Roman texts, sometimes the Hebrew or Christian Bibles. By the early 1700s readers had come to see certain English authors of bygone eras as "classic," in self-conscious analogy to ancient Greek and Roman writers. Philologists accordingly began to produce editions of writers such as Chaucer, Shakespeare, and Milton. By the later eighteenth century editing English-language writers had become a standard form of scholarship, perhaps most famously Samuel Johnson's 1765 edition of Shakespeare. In the first half of the next century, the range of authors edited expanded, and the care and skill of editors grew.

Perhaps not surprisingly, histories of English-language literature began to appear in these same decades. These included Johnson's *Lives of the Most Eminent English Poets* (1779–81) as well as other histories of poetry and several of the theater. The genre proliferated after 1800 and expanded to include literature in other languages. In 1814 the Scot John Colin Dunlop produced a dull but comprehensive history of fictional prose from the ancient Greeks to the present. The American George Ticknor's three-volume *History of Spanish Literature* (1849) topped anything before it. Ticknor began with the advent of written Castilian in the twelfth century and ended in the early nineteenth. He placed works of poetry and prose in the explanatory context of Spanish history and culture. His book was the most sophisticated, most thoroughly researched literary history yet published in English.

The third element of modern literary studies, evaluative criticism, itself had multiple origins. First, histories of literature often included assessments of the quality of works (shrewd ones in the case of Johnson's *Lives of the Poets*). As magazines developed, book reviewing became more common, and some prolific authors of it became increasingly nuanced, erudite, and, as it were, professional—applying skills that often would have seemed familiar to philological commentators on Greek and Latin three centuries earlier. Second, in Scottish universities during the second quarter of the eighteenth century, classical Latin rhetoric (widespread in education throughout the Middle Ages and Renaissance) began to be applied to English. American colleges soon followed suit. The aim was to form students in "properly" writing and speaking English, but famous authors were used as models, and this new rhetoric provided standards by which to judge the quality of writings. Third, critics in the UK and US borrowed new approaches to literature from Germany. From Johann Gottfried Herder and like-minded thinkers came the idea of situating authors in the historically specific cultures that produced them (a key to Ticknor's version of literary history as well). From post-Kantian German idealist writers came the notion of analysing a literary work in terms of how it resonated with the psychological states of imagined readers: a new kind of "meaning" of a novel or poem (as opposed to analysing a work's formal qualities as the Scottish rhetoricians did). Finally, the old idea of "interpretation" was borrowed from biblical critics, who had for many centuries analysed biblical passages in terms of non-literal senses such as allegory and typology. All of these different streams, most originating in the philology of long ago, flowed together into a modern, multivocal understanding of literary criticism.

Thus, by mid-century, the foundations had been laid for both the modern study of history and the modern study of literature. But the distinct modern disciplines of history and literature did not yet exist.

A prerequisite was the entry of modern (that is, post-classical) history and literature into university studies. Straws in the wind appeared when Harvard appointed the first professor of literature in the US in 1819 (the aforesaid George Ticknor) and University College London the first in the UK in 1828. Oxford and Cambridge had both got regius professors of history in 1724; but, since the subject formed part of no degree program, students had no incentive to listen to their lectures and rarely did. Harvard, again, named the first professor of history in the US in 1838. Starting around 1850 both history and literature appeared in more and more college curricula—history at Queen's College Belfast in 1849, Oxford in 1853, Trinity College Dublin in 1856, Michigan in 1858; literature at Queen's Belfast also in 1849, Pennsylvania's Lafayette College in 1855, King's College London in 1857, Michigan in 1858, the Scottish universities collectively in 1861. By the 1870s history and literature were ubiquitous. But they could not at first be called distinct disciplines. Indeed, when the subjects appeared, colleges commonly hired one professor to teach both. This was true, for instance, at Queen's Belfast, Michigan, and King's College.

But soon—sooner in the US—the two fields divorced and grew into modern disciplines. By the 1890s many literature courses looked in structure much as they do today—focused on reading and analysis of individual works—and quite distinct from history, though often still interested in historical context of literary works. Research became increasingly specialized. Already in 1878, Humphry Ward recruited different experts to edit the individual authors in a planned anthology of English poets, on the ground that scholarship had grown too specialized for a single person to handle large chunks of it competently. In 1883 American professors of literature created the Modern Language Association to be their disciplinary home. Its *Publications*, launched a year later, offered a venue for specialized research. In 1886 the journal *Modern Language Notes* started at Johns Hopkins University (translating "the aspirations of classical philology" into "the study of modern languages").[20] By the 1890s the eminent Edward Dowden of Trinity College Dublin was regularly consulted by universities throughout the British Empire on appointments in English literature; young academic job-seekers got a leg up in his recommendations for publishing in disciplinary journals. Yet not until 1906 did UK scholars found the English Association, and like the parallel Classical Association its members came from schools as well as universities. Still, by the 1920s and 1930s, literary scholars in the UK clustered, as they did a few decades earlier in the US, around disciplinary organizations and journals.

History followed a similar trajectory. During the later 1870s and 1880s graduate training in history became common in major American universities. In 1882 Herbert Baxter Adams began the first historical monograph series in the US; two years later, he led in organizing the American Historical Association (AHA), where professors like him called the shots. The AHA's annual meetings in the college lull between Christmas and New Year soon became the main venue for job-hunting and for publishers to consult with authors. In 1895 two AHA members started the *American Historical Review* to publish disciplinary scholarship. An *English Historical Review* had started a decade earlier, though only by the 1890s did it apply consistent scholarly standards like those of its American cousin. One of its guiding lights, Lord Acton, designed in 1896 an early monument of disciplinary history, the fourteen-volume *Cambridge Modern History*. The Royal Historical Society was founded in 1868 but only slowly evolved, by the 1920s, into a disciplinary group for university-based scholars. Like the English Association, the Historical Association (also founded in 1906) united teachers of history in both secondary schools and universities. In contrast, the Institute of Historical Research in the University of London (1920) became the center of a substantial graduate program and a link connecting research-oriented historians in American universities with British peers.

As in classics, professional journals and societies provided walls within which literary scholars and historical scholars created and nurtured their specific disciplinary identities. Conference organizers and journal editors created feedback loops to correct deviations from orthopraxis—through book reviews, accepting and rejecting papers, vetting manuscripts. Historians now wrote mostly for other historians, literary scholars for other literary scholars—although some of each also translated professional research for readers outside the guild.

All of this amounted to a dramatic transformation of erudition. Over the course of the nineteenth century, learned people took fragments of what was once a mostly undifferentiated, broad-gauged humanistic scholarship and forged from them the new, specialized, and largely self-focused humanities disciplines of classics, literature, and history. The process was rarely self-conscious until near its end, but it was nonetheless decisive. If space allowed, we could trace the same evolution of pieces of early-modern philology into new, specialized humanistic disciplines in other fields that we now group together as "the humanities." To write the history of the modern humanities in the English-speaking world means beginning with this story.

Notes

1. Most of this chapter is adapted from sections of my *Philology: The Forgotten Origins of the Modern Humanities* (Princeton, NJ: Princeton University Press, 2014), especially Ch. 4, 6, 7, 10, and 11. Readers will find there a fuller account and copious documentation. Notes in this chapter include only sources of direct quotations and secondary works in English. Sources in other languages can be found in *Philology*.
2. https://www.rsuh.ru/en/faculties-departments-and-international-centers/faculty-of-economics/ (accessed March 9, 2022).
3. A few outstanding studies of this early-modern world of learning are Ann M. Blair, *Too Much to Know: Managing Scholarly Information before the Modern Age* (New Haven, CT: Yale University Press, 2010); Anthony Grafton, *Joseph Scaliger: A Study in the History of Classical Scholarship*, 2 vols (Oxford: Clarendon Press, 1983–93); and Peter N. Miller, *Peiresc's Europe: Learning and Virtue in the Seventeenth Century* (New Haven, CT: Yale University Press, 2000).
4. Kristine Louise Haugen, *Richard Bentley: Poetry and Enlightenment* (Cambridge, MA: Harvard University Press, 2011); James Henry Monk, *The Life of Richard Bentley, D. D.*, 2nd edn, 2 vols (Osnabruck: Biblio Verlag, 1969 [1833]); G. J. Toomer, *John Selden: A Life in Scholarship*, 2 vols (Oxford: Oxford University Press, 2009).
5. Roger L. Geiger, *The History of American Higher Education: Learning and Culture from the Founding to World War II* (Princeton, NJ: Princeton University Press, 2015) provides a recent, comprehensive overview of the American side of the story. There is no equivalent for the United Kingdom, but

see Robert Anderson, *British Universities Past and Present* (London: Bloomsbury, 2006), and relevant portions of *A History of the University in Europe*, vol. 3, ed. Walter Ruegg (Cambridge: Cambridge University Press, 2004).
6. Oxbridge apparently first appeared in 1850 in William Thackeray's novel *Pendennis* (1850) as the name of a fictional university.
7. Hugh Hawkins, *Pioneer: A History of the Johns Hopkins University, 1874–1889* (Ithaca, NY: Cornell University Press, 1960).
8. Kirsti Simonsuuri, *Homer's Original Genius: Eighteenth-Century Notions of the Early Greek Epic* (Cambridge: Cambridge University Press, 1979).
9. Jonathan Sheehan, *The Enlightenment Bible: Translation, Scholarship, Culture* (Princeton, NJ: Princeton University Press, 2005).
10. Anthony Grafton, Glenn W. Most, and James E. G. Zetzel, "Introduction," in F. A. Wolf, *Prolegomena to Homer* (1795), ed. and trans. Grafton, Most, and Zetzel (Princeton: Princeton University Press, 1985).
11. On classical studies in the UK and US, the starting points are Christopher Stray, *Classics Transformed: Schools, Universities, and Society in England, 1830–1960* (Oxford: Clarendon Press, 1998); Frank M. Turner, *The Greek Heritage in Victorian Britain* (New Haven: Yale University Press, 1981); and Caroline Winterer, *The Culture of Classicism: Ancient Greece and Rome in American Intellectual Life, 1780–1910* (Baltimore, MD: Johns Hopkins University Press, 2002).
12. *The Iliad of Homer, from the Text of Wolf: With English Notes and Flaxman's Illustrative Designs*, ed. C. C. Felton (Boston, MA: Hilliard, Gray, and Company; Cambridge, MA: Brown, Shattuck, and Co., 1833), v; Cornelius C. Felton, *A Lecture on the Classical Learning, Delivered before the Convention of Teachers, and Other Friends of Education, Assembled to Form the American Institute of Instruction, August, 20, 1830* (Boston, MA: Hilliard, Gray, Little, and Wilkins, 1831), 16, 18, 20.
13. Robert Ackerman, *The Myth and Ritual School: J. G. Frazer and the Cambridge Ritualists* (New York: Routledge, 2002).
14. Frank Gardner Moore, "A History of the American Philological Association," *Transactions and Proceedings of the American Philological Association* 50 (1919): 15.
15. B. L. Gildersleeve, "Editorial Note," *American Journal of Philology* 1 (1880): 2.
16. Joseph M. Levine, *The Autonomy of History: Truth and Method from Erasmus to Gibbon* (Chicago, IL: University of Chicago Press, 1999); Karen O'Brien, *Narratives of Enlightenment: Cosmopolitan History from Voltaire to Gibbon* (Cambridge: Cambridge University Press, 1997).
17. G. P. Gooch, *History and Historians in the Nineteenth Century* (Boston, MA: Beacon, 1959 [1913]); Mark Salber Philips, *Society and Sentiment: Genres of Historical Writing in Britain, 1740–1820* (Princeton, NJ: Princeton University

Press, 2000); George H. Callcott, *History in the United States, 1800–1860: Its Practice and Purpose* (Baltimore, MD: Johns Hopkins University Press, 1970).
18. A. Bowdoin Van Riper, *Men Among the Mammoths: Victorian Science and the Discovery of Human Prehistory* (Chicago, IL: University of Chicago Press, 1993).
19. Unlike in the case of history, I omit references to secondary works on the evolution of literary scholarship. There are a great many studies of aspects but no histories of the whole phenomenon.
20. Richard Macksey, "Border Line: One Hundred Years of Scholarship," *MLN* 100 (1985): 915, 917–18.

3

The Humanities in Crisis: Comparative Perspectives on a Recurring Motif

Hampus Östh Gustafsson

Introduction: Crisis at the Heart of the Humanities

Edward Said once stated that "no matter who is writing or speaking, where, when, or to whom, the humanities always seem to be in deep and usually terminal trouble. The word 'crisis' is the inevitable one here."[1] A tiresome cliché or not, this notion of a crisis should not be overlooked in efforts to write the history of the humanities. On the contrary, inquiries into this recurring motif are essential for coming to terms with the present state of the humanities, as the concept of crisis has had a deep impact on how these disciplines are conceived today—often turning into a fundamental part of their self-understanding.[2] Crisis is for instance identified in a lack of funding and a decreasing (although this is disputable) number of humanities degrees in both absolute and relative terms. Regarding their role in society, commentators tend to recognize ideological suspicion and a widespread lack of trust among politicians and a public obsessed with usefulness and the promotion of economistic values hostile to the humanities, not least in the wake of the 2008 financial crisis.[3]

The last decades, however, have seen an overuse of crisis rhetorics—coming as no surprise since "[c]risis sells well."[4] Even if it is occasionally stated that there is no crisis, everyone keeps on talking about it ("Don't mention the crisis!"). There are thus innumerable examples of crisis narratives being employed in anecdotal and ambiguous ways, frequently hitting on apocalyptic notes.[5] British historian Peter Mandler for instance claims that "so much attention has been paid to the 'crisis of the humanities' that few have stopped to ask if there actually is such a crisis."[6] Recent years, however, have seen numerous attempts to decide whether there exists a crisis or not. But how do you settle such a question? Is it even possible—or meaningful—to provide a yes or no answer? In some cases, it is even questioned whether it makes sense at all to talk about a crisis in the humanities as this state seems to constitute their *modus operandi*—and as such a strength, rather than a weakness.[7]

It is clearly not an easy task to disentangle the complex and, by now, global discourse of crisis in the humanities. A particular problem, from an historical point of view, is the inclination to simply equate the crisis with the emergence of an explicit discourse of crisis in the postwar era.[8] Empirical studies need to look deeper into the mechanisms that actually forged such notions. In this chapter, I explore how different discourses of crisis emerged, resurfaced, and intertwined throughout the modern era. By reflecting upon the implications of these processes for the legitimacy of the humanities, my analysis addresses questions of general relevance to the history of knowledge as the humanities (within the Humboldt as well as the Liberal Arts tradition) have been depicted as emblematic to the modern university as such. Classicist Justin Stover recently claimed that: "To talk about the crisis of the humanities is to consider the survival of the university itself. The heart of the university is the arts."[9]

Comparative Components of Crisis: Disentangling a Monolithic Term

The conceptual history of the term crisis is a well-trod area. Reinhart Koselleck points out that crises of different kinds seem inseparable from the general self-conception of modernity. Etymologically deriving from the Greek word *krínō*, crisis used to refer to the decisive point when a disease would either lead to recovery or death according to Hippocratic medicine. But crisis narratives do not only represent such experiences, they clearly possess a performative potential of provoking change. In the modern era, however, the multilayered and ambiguous concept of crisis rather seems to point to a permanent (or at least recurring) state of emergency.[10] While this conceptual shift and complexity might explain some of the ambivalence and recurring character of the crisis discourse of the humanities, it is still necessary to examine some particularly critical phases of debate in order to deal with elements of rupture and continuity in a more nuanced manner.

The most well-known explicit discussions on the humanities and their crisis belong to the postwar period, with British historian J. H. Plumb's edited volume *Crisis in the Humanities* (1964) serving as a milestone (in the wake of the famous *Two Cultures* debate).[11] Older examples of precarious situations may be found, however.[12] The German humanities, for instance, have been described as being in a constant state of crisis. Thus, the literature has not only focused on the crisis of the humanities as a recurring phenomenon, but also as a chronic condition. Some scholars even go as far as equating the state of crisis to the very genesis of the humanities as a disciplinary group at the modern university.[13] While it is important to note these recurring and chronic aspects, humanities historiography needs to be more specific by focusing on transnational and transtemporal comparisons. Over the years, numerous elements have been incorporated into the expression "crisis in the humanities." The attempts to open this "black box" would do well by reasoning more in terms of the plural and raise questions about eventual *crises* in the humanities in order to escape the universalizing connotations of the present discourse. Which actors have experienced crises, who have constructed them, deconstructed them, and so forth?[14]

Just like "crisis," "the humanities" function as a kaleidoscopic concept. But as a plural term that gathers a range of heterogenous disciplines (epistemologically and administratively), the humanities come with a monolithic predisposition that several scholars find problematic.[15] When writing the history of the humanities, however, it is essential to empirically highlight the actual use of concepts such as "the humanities" and "crisis in the humanities." Previous historiography has been limited due to a narrow focus on individual disciplines. Therefore, it is essential to elucidate what happened when the humanities were debated as a larger unit, distinguished from other branches of knowledge, and coupled with the word crisis. In several instances, the crisis rhetoric of the humanities was even invented and encouraged by humanities scholars themselves.

As an empirical object, the humanities crisis may obviously be approached from a wide range of angles. Here, I turn to a Koselleck-influenced conceptual interpretation of crisis as requiring a comparative dimension.[16] A decline or threatening disaster is only perceived in relation to a normative standard, such as a different past or future, or a different situation at another site. In order to disentangle the complex discourse of crisis, I thus focus on three comparative aspects: (a) epistemology, (b) chronology, and (c) geography.[17] These were all central to the formation of crisis narratives and frequently created incentives for a reactive, self-justifying logic, which increasingly has been subject to criticism in recent scholarship.[18]

Distinctive Intellectual Cultures: An Epistemological Aspect

As different forms of historicist world views—whose dominance had secured a solid legitimacy for historically oriented disciplines—were contested from the late nineteenth century onward, a potential crisis of humanities scholarship became difficult to ignore.[19] An entire academic culture, based on a relatively stable set of values, was eventually undermined during the early twentieth century in several Western countries. Representatives of the humanities found themselves struggling to maintain their previously influential social and political positions.[20] As the academic system began to expand rapidly, the humanities typically appeared as being left behind at the "old" faculties of philosophy or liberal arts. They often appeared like a loosely defined culture of knowledge, bound by tradition—in contrast to progressive alternatives like the sciences and social sciences that were "applied" and mobilized politically to a great extent. As the American literary scholar Irving Babbitt put it in 1908: "The humanities need to be defended to-day against the encroachments of physical science, as they once needed to be against the encroachments of theology."[21]

Such tensions have been at the fore in attempts to explain the crisis in the humanities as these subjects are constantly defined in contrast to other intellectual categories. For a long time, a central opposition was, just like Babbitt noted, identified between the humanities and theology, or *studia humanitiatis* vs. *studia divinitatis*. This was followed by competition between the humanities and the sciences in the modern period, today often reflected in the juxtaposition of the so-called STEM (Science, Technology, Engineering, and Mathematics) and HASS (Humanities, Arts, and Social Sciences).[22] As the relationship between these clusters of disciplines has been of an asymmetric character, a positivistic ideal of scientific unity eventually put pressure on the humanities. Attempts to legitimize the humanities have thus frequently been of a reactive character with respect to positivist ideals.[23]

The reactive stance of the humanities has been interpreted as a structural problem deriving from Immanuel Kant's philosophical interventions. Throughout the nineteenth century, humanities scholars were increasingly occupied with the task of justifying their disciplines institutionally as well as intellectually, responding to an experienced need of demonstrating that they conducted another type of enquiry compared to the natural sciences—methodologically distinct, and still scientifically valid.[24] The late nineteenth and early twentieth century thus saw German philosophers striving to construct an epistemological foundation for historical and hermeneutical scholarship. In his *Einleitung in die Geisteswissenschaften* (1883), Wilhelm Dilthey famously attempted to legitimize the humanities as an autonomous unit of *Wissenschaft* "next to the natural sciences," stressing the interpretive task of these subjects by focusing on man's inner experience.[25] Dilthey claimed that a scientific understanding of human affairs required a genuine historical approach, an attitude simultaneously developed by the Southwestern school of German neo-Kantianism. Introducing the terms nomothetic and idiographic, Wilhelm Windelband made a formal distinction between science and historical scholarship regarding their respective focus on generalization and individualization—the two types representing different forms of knowledge.[26] This separation provoked a dilemma that was elaborated by Windelband's former student, Heinrich Rickert, by the turn of the century: could the human (or cultural) sciences really operate according to the requirements of objectivity in a way comparable to the natural sciences if they focused on unique and subjective aspects of history?[27]

This is not the place to delve into the manifold discussions on the so-called crisis of historicism. The alleged threat of relativism, however, that seemed to follow from historicist and hermeneutic approaches—together with the decline of the idea of progress—has been interpreted as an important element of a more general experience of cultural crisis. Even if the crisis of historicism depended just as much on ethical implications, the discussions above exemplify how recurring and dichotomic epistemological comparisons functioned as a crisis-generating mechanism with regard to the humanities.[28] While the epistemological tensions may be necessary for explaining many of the challenges to the humanities during the last century, they are however not sufficient for grasping the specific formations of crisis discourse throughout the twentieth century.

Golden Ages and Narratives of Decline: A Chronological Aspect

Legitimization of scholarship is often conducted through the construction of historical narratives, representing the value of scholarly endeavor as a contribution to temporal projects with moral implications, where the present is related to the past either as a continuity or discontinuity. In the case of the humanities, this temporal legitimization has motivated a wide-spread nostalgic attitude. Narratives of their modern history are typically written in terms of decay, identifying previous periods of upsurge and boom according to a classic dramaturgic scheme. The dire state of the humanities in the present is pictured toward the fond of a past golden age, primarily the Renaissance and the nineteenth century.[29] Such idealized pasts provide contours, counter-examples, and meaning to the narratives of crisis—the question being, however, whether these narratives can motivate a modified course of action for the future.[30]

The Renaissance is often employed as a starting point when histories of the humanities are written. In literary historian R. S. Crane's *The Idea of the Humanities* (1967), the history of the humanities was for instance written "from the Renaissance to the Present."[31] Throughout that period, the valuations of the state of the humanities have varied. Seventeenth-century England has been suggested as a site where the humanities saw an early decline,[32] and in utilitarian eighteenth-century Sweden, the sciences were held in high esteem while the humanities were seen as a peculiar and ornamental cluster of subjects.[33] It is thus possible to distinguish a certain pulsation over time, as the state of the humanities has been narrated with respect to cycles of progress and decline.

The nostalgic narratives that compare the present with the nineteenth century, however, seem to identify a more definite, even if not irreversible, rupture regarding the fate of the humanities. The nineteenth century thus stands out as a golden age in recent crisis literature, at least at sites in continental Europe and Scandinavia with a long-lasting Humboldtian heritage. Even if the nineteenth-century humanities faced challenges too, their influence was cemented at universities and in schools. Carried by the notion of *Bildung* and a "classical paradigm," the humanities often dominated public and political life throughout the century.[34] This past experience was frequently mobilized in the twentieth century, functioning as a historiographic corrective that demonstrated how the state of the humanities could be radically different. Writing the history of the humanities thus turned into a central strategy of legitimization.

In contrast to the situation described above, some other geographical areas have seen golden ages of the humanities primarily identified in the early postwar period (*les trente glorieuses*) with its strong faith in public institutions of higher education. In France, it should come as no surprise that the prestige of the humanities has been seen as peaking with the structuralism of the 1960s and 1970s, followed by a decline from the 1980s when the increasingly global context of research and higher education gave rise to new conditions for humanities scholars. The French model that previously generated a particularly high status for so-called "public intellectuals" à la Sartre was thus undermined as the scholarly focus shifted from the national arena of knowledge to more specialized international contexts.[35] In the US, too, the early postwar period has been described as an era of prosperity for the humanities.[36] Recurring nostalgic references to these years might explain why the Anglo-American discourse on the crisis in the humanities seems particularly focused on enrolment numbers and funding, as their golden age occurred parallel to the great student expansion. This may be contrasted to the situation in Sweden, which saw a formation of a discourse of crisis at the same time as large new cohorts found their way into higher education. In this case, the very expansion—along with the political promotion of democratic-egalitarian ideals—put the humanities under pressure in the midst of the alleged success of the welfare state. The early postwar period was thus not depicted as a period of humanistic prosperity in the Swedish case.[37] The fine ancestry of the humanities was instead derived from the previous century, or at least the early twentieth century.[38]

The importance of temporal comparisons as crisis-generating mechanisms is rendered particularly visible if we turn our attention outside of Europe and North America. In a global comparative volume on the crisis of the humanities, it was recently remarked (although these circumstances seem to have changed radically with the political development in the last couple of years) how difficult it may be to talk about a crisis of the humanities in Brazil due to the relatively late establishment of the national university system. Imagining a humanities golden age in the nineteenth century would not make much sense, according to the authors, who claim that these subjects are rather going through a process of consolidation now. Thus, it is difficult to find a normative point of comparison in the past against which a crisis in the present can be distinguished.[39] Such differences indicate the importance for the history of humanities to seriously incorporate transnational comparisons that are sensitive to distinct geographical conditions and regimes of knowledge.

Transnational Comparisons and Intertwined Discourses of Crisis: A Geographical Aspect

Although the history of the humanities is commonly written with particular regard to Western Renaissance Humanism and Romanticism, similar scholarly practices have, obviously, been conducted in other parts of the world, for instance in the context of the Arabic *studia adabiya*, whose curriculum influenced *studia humanitatis*. From a global comparative point of view, the humanities have been organized in distinctive ways, even if a number of common themes characterized their modern formation, such as the legitimization of nation states and competition with the sciences.[40] It is therefore promising that the new history of the humanities is determined to transcend Western frames, embracing wider transnational and postcolonial perspectives (as indicated by several chapters in this volume).[41]

On several instances, national debates on the humanities became intertwined and began to live their own lives. For instance, Sweden can be seen as a fascinating example of how a discourse of crisis was formed relatively early. This discourse was fueled by narratives of an alleged exceptionalism: the humanities were depicted as extremely badly off in this national case, according to an account established through recurring transnational outlooks. A statistical survey presented by the Research Council for the Humanities in 1973 ignited explicit crisis debates in the following years.[42] Such comparisons over geographical borders—here conducted by historical actors themselves—played a central part in generating the discourse of crisis. Already in the 1980s, the challenges to the humanities in this national context were interpreted as part of a regional and soon even world-wide crisis.

The Swedish narrative of an alarming state of the humanities was forcefully contrasted to the general picture of the country being the welfare state *par excellence* in the 1950s and 1960s. The humanities had been excluded from the grand future visions of the welfare project, based on rational planning—in contrast to favored areas such as technology, medicine, and the social sciences. Failing to form relevant coalitions they were soon described as a marginalized category of knowledge.[43] This national trajectory may be contrasted to the situation of the humanities in Norway, where these disciplines managed to preserve their legitimacy to a greater extent through political alliances in a context where nationalistic claims still retained a relatively progressive character. The Norwegian experience of the Second World War did not seem to call for a re-evaluation of the purpose of scholarship as it did in Sweden (and, obviously, in Germany).[44] The importance of specific political constellations should thus not be neglected. Dramaturgical experiences, such as the evolvement of certain wars, also played a central part as narrative dimensions are central to conceptions of crisis. The turbulent experiences of the 1930s and 1940s clearly had different consequences in various places. In countries that were occupied during war, such as Norway, the Netherlands, Ireland, and South Korea, the humanities have been described as maintaining a relatively strong legitimacy far into the postwar period.[45]

In the victorious USA it was less problematic to associate the humanities with values after the Second World War, in contrast to countries more associated with the academic sphere of continental Europe. The humanities were thus not pushed into breaking with old academic traditions in a similar way. Instead, postwar America perceived education and research in the humanities as essential elements for the construction of a sound democratic world order.[46] This era was thus marked by relative harmony. Not least, "the two cultures" seemed to get along quite well, as highlighted by historian Andrew Jewett.[47] The humanities were heralded as carriers of progress and values essential to the moral formation of young citizens—an idea effectively institutionalized through the system of liberal education.

Context-dependent constellations of knowledge cultures had an evident impact on discourses of crisis. The case of Britain is another illuminating example. In 1964, Plumb noted that the humanities were intimately bound to the educational needs of elites and seemed obsolete in the eyes of the democratic and technological postwar society—causing a "crisis in their existence." Here, social science and economics were included in the humanities crisis as Plumb held these disciplines, too, as "deeply influenced by old assumptions and old educational attitudes," unfitted to "the educational and social needs of the modern world."[48] This may be contrasted to the situation in some social democratic welfare states where the social sciences, together with technology, were typically characterized as emblematic to the new democratic and progressive order. The fact that discourses of crisis in the humanities still developed roughly at the same time in various geographical contexts, despite the manifest differences, indicate the necessity of studying local mechanisms of crisis in detail.[49]

Even if the crisis in the humanities has been described as a chronic modern phenomenon, the 1960s and 1970s (or "1968") are regularly identified as the period when their crisis began as we know it. This is not surprising given that crisis became a general buzz word in Western societies along with the heavy critique of economic growth and technological optimism.[50] In these years, crisis narratives were used as strategies for legitimizing change as they could make experiences of marginalization meaningful. Terry Eagleton suggests that the rise of theory in the 1960s and 1970s should be interpreted as a critical self-reflection of the humanities that came "about when [they were] forced into a new self-consciousness about what [they were] doing."[51] Younger generations of scholars in the humanities mobilized themselves through alliances with critical theory and by actively promoting a discourse of crisis, thus embracing their alleged marginal positions. This way, they managed to articulate a seemingly more independent and less reactive defense of the humanities.[52] Through such specific actions, the crisis of the humanities was discursively consolidated on a broad scale—ever since available as an interpretive prism for debates on the humanities. In the following decades, it is also possible to discern how local or national narratives of crisis thus were accumulated and intertwined, eventually converging into the global, recurring motif so familiar in the present day.

Conclusion: Historicizing a Recurring Motif

According to the "Thomas theorem," situations will be real in their consequences if these situations are defined as real in the first place.[53] Quite often, it is pointed out that any talk of a crisis in the humanities is likely to generate crisis, or at least stimulate a reactive stance.[54] To historicize the crisis, however, is something different. If a comprehensive history of the humanities is to be written, this recurring motif cannot be neglected—and it will probably not go away in any foreseeable future anyway.

My tripartite analysis of discursive mechanisms demonstrates that there has been a multitude of interpretations of the crisis in the humanities. It would thus be a hopeless undertaking to provide a single answer to its causes—if the crisis even exists! To the three variables I have presented, a fourth could be added, namely disciplinary affiliation. The lamentations of a crisis in the humanities have not been equally expressed throughout the wide field of the humanities. Who is the most explicit advocate of crisis obviously varies between countries. In the Anglo-American sphere, literary scholars are beyond doubt the most clamant actors in this regard, which is not always the case in some European countries. Here, one should also keep in mind that the humanities as a wider term is more popular among certain scholars, primarily those representing "traditional" disciplines like classics and history, whose "golden age" most notably has been located in the nineteenth century. Other fields, like analytical philosophy, would possibly identify golden ages at later points in time. There are also some disciplinary formations that may be included in the humanities, such as media studies, which are perhaps not equally affected by (and less interested in) crisis discourse as they tend to be part of broader integrative constellations (dominated by social sciences) and generally appear as more future-oriented. And on top of all this, it is also likely that gender issues have had a profound impact on the formation of a crisis narrative, as the humanities throughout the twentieth century were described as an increasingly feminine area of study, in contrast to STEM subjects that maintained more masculine connotations.[55]

Comparative perspectives have indeed been crucial for the construction of crisis narratives. Since the history of the humanities itself encourages comparative approaches, this new scholarly field provides good opportunities for grappling with the recurring crisis motif and, thereby, enabling a deeper understanding of the ever-changing legitimacy of the humanities. Analyses of how historical actors themselves formulated crisis narratives, with reference to comparative aspects, might contribute to the endeavor of nuancing and deconstructing the monolithic or universalizing inclination that devour current debates. In line with such an approach, local and national trajectories need to be emphasized, even if they later have been fused, in order to illuminate the long and complex tradition of depicting the humanities as in a state of crisis. It is not sufficient to refer to inherent elements of modernity, or to rely on reductionist and polarized accounts, aiming either at the rise of the New Left and critical theory on the one hand, or Thatcherism/Reaganism and New Public Management on the other, if the function of crisis as a recurring trope is to be thoroughly comprehended.[56]

Critical engagement with discourses of crisis also stimulates a well-needed reflection on the rationale of the humanities and their value for society, and for exploring general mechanisms of modern intellectual crises. Such a project might well be aided by a cross-fertilization of history of the humanities and the expanding history of science/knowledge that particularly encourages studies on the wider use and circulation of knowledge in other parts of society, outside of the traditional academic sphere.[57] As society changes, the humanities will also go through transformations—although perhaps not in the same way or at the same pace.[58] The discourse of crisis thus reflects the constant negotiations of the humanities' social contract, and also the ongoing need of temporal synchronization as different areas of knowledge have responded differently to the new rhythms of politics that evolved throughout the modern period.[59]

While it has become a cliché to state that crisis creates opportunities, this insight certainly does have some bearing. Historical analyses of the ways in which crisis narratives produce meaning and fill a performative or mobilizing function can teach us plenty about what it means to be scholars—and citizens—in a world marked by crises. This chapter was written while the world really was stuck in deep crisis. Apart from asking what the concept of crisis does, it is urgent to ask what the humanities do in such times. As philosopher Agnes Callard noted in the spring of 2020, when COVID-19 first struck the world with full force:

> Even in good times, the humanistic academy is mocked as a wheel turning nothing; in an emergency, when doctors, delivery personnel, and other essential workers are scrambling to keep society intact, no one has patience with the wheel's demand to keep turning. What is the role of Aristotle, or the person who studies him, in a crisis?[60]

The recent pandemic—just like our transit into the "Anthropocene"—should have made it clear that broad knowledge on man as a cultural and social being is necessary. Will these new challenges push the recurring crisis of the humanities into new directions, perhaps? History has demonstrated that narratives of crisis promise potential turning points. How to turn—or break—the wheel of the humanities in the twenty-first century is up to us.

Notes

1. Edward W. Said, *Humanism and Democratic Criticism* (New York: Columbia University Press, 2004), 31. For valuable critical comments on this text I would like to thank Herman Paul, Isak Hammar, Mats Persson, and Thor Rydin.
2. Cf. Clifford Siskin and William Warner, "To Halt the Crisis in the Humanities, Higher Ed Should Rethink Its Classification of Knowledge," *Inside Higher Ed* (November 4, 2019).
3. See, e.g., Eleonora Belfiore, "The 'Rhetoric of Gloom' v. the Discourse of Impact in the Humanities: Stuck in a Deadlock?" in *Humanities in the Twenty-First Century: Beyond Utility and Markets*, eds. Eleonora Belfiore and Anna Upchurch (Basingstoke: Palgrave Macmillan, 2013), 35.
4. Umberto Eco, *Travels in Hyper Reality: Essays*, transl. William Weaver (Orlando, FL: Harcourt Brace Jovanovich, 1986 [1973]), 126.
5. Paul Holm, Arne Jarrick, and Dominic Scott, *Humanities World Report 2015* (Basingstoke: Palgrave Macmillan, 2015), 192; Albrecht Koschorke, "Über die angebliche Krise der Geisteswissenschaften," *Aus Politik und Zeitgeschichte* 57, no 46 (2007): 22.
6. Peter Mandler, "Rise of the Humanities," *Aeon* (17 December 2015), online at https://aeon.co/essays/the-humanities-are-booming-only-the-professors-can-t-see-it (accessed March 9, 2022).
7. Sibylle Baumbach, "To Be or Not to Be? Crisis and the Humanities in Germany," in *The Changing Face of Higher Education: Is There an International Crisis in the Humanities?*, ed. Dennis A. Ahlburg (Abingdon: Routledge, 2019), 83; Geoffrey Galt Harpham, *The Humanities and the Dream of America* (Chicago, IL: University of Chicago Press, 2011), 40. See also Stefan Collini, *What are Universities for?* (London: Penguin, 2012), 63, Jonathan Culler, "In Need of a Name? A Response to Geoffrey Harpham," *New Literary History* 36, no. 1 (2005): 37, Frank Donoghue, *The Last Professors: The Corporate University and the Fate of the Humanities* (New York: Fordham University Press, 2008), 1, Geoffrey Galt Harpham, "Beneath and Beyond the 'Crisis in the Humanities,'" *New Literary History* 36, no. 1 (2005): 22, Geoffrey Galt Harpham, "Between Humanity and the Homeland: The Evolution of an Institutional Concept," *American Literary History* 18, no. 2 (2006): 247, and Adam Sitze, Austin Sarat, and Boris Wolfson, "The Humanities in Question," *College Literature* 42, no. 2 (2015): 196.

8. Cf. Paul Jay, *The Humanities "Crisis" and the Future of Literary Studies* (Basingstoke: Palgrave Macmillan, 2014), 1.
9. Justin Stover, "There Is No Case for the Humanities," *Chronicle of Higher Education* 65, no. 26 (2018). Stefan Collini rightly notes that "the humanities form a relatively small part of the modern research university, but they bulk very large in all discussions about the 'idea' or 'future' of universities." See Stefan Collini, "On Not 'Justifying' the Humanities," in *The Humanities in the World*, ed. Anders Engberg-Pedersen (Copenhagen: U Press, 2020), 51.
10. Reinhart Koselleck, "Krise" in *Geschichtliche Grundbegriffe: Historisches Lexikon zur politisch-sozialen Sprache in Deutschland*, eds. Otto Brunner, Werner Conze, and Reinhart Koselleck, vol. 3 (Stuttgart: Klett-Cotta, 1982), 617, 627, 629; Janet Roitman, *Anti-Crisis* (Durham, NC: Duke University Press, 2014), 15–16; Matthew W. Seeger and Timothy L. Sellnow, *Narratives of Crisis: Telling Stories of Ruin and Renewal* (Stanford, CA: Stanford Business Books, 2016), 7–16.
11. *Crisis in the Humanities*, ed. J. H. Plumb (Harmondsworth: Penguin, 1964); C. P. Snow, *The Two Cultures and the Scientific Revolution* (Cambridge: Cambridge University Press, 1961).
12. Many defensive claims for the humanities in Britain today still draw on Victorian key texts from the nineteenth century. See Helen Small, *The Value of the Humanities* (Oxford: Oxford University Press, 2013), 7. In Anglo-American contexts, explicit notions of a crisis have been identified at least since the 1920s. American librarian Wayne Bivens-Tatum found 217 articles in the database JSTOR, searching on "crisis in the humanities"—the first article from 1922, and then rapidly increasing from the 1940s onward. See Wayne Bivens-Tatum, "The 'Crisis' in the Humanities," *Academic Librarian* (2010), online at https://blogs.princeton.edu/librarian/2010/11/the_crisis_in_the_humanities/ (accessed March 9, 2022).
13. Hans Ulrich Gumbrecht, *Die ewige Krise der Geisteswissenschaften—und wo ist ein Ende in Sicht?* (Bonn: Hochschulrektorenkonferenz, 2015); Julian Hamann, "'*Bildung*' in German Human Sciences: The Discursive Transformation of a Concept," *History of the Human Sciences* 24, no. 5 (2011), 49; Julian Hamann, *Die Bildung der Geisteswissenschaften: Zur Genese einer sozialen Konstruktion zwischen Diskurs und Feld* (Konstanz: UVK, 2014), 13–4; Paul Reitter and Chad Wellmon, *Permanent Crisis: The Humanities in a Disenchanted Age* (Chicago, IL: University of Chicago Press, 2021).
14. Cf. Michael Freeden, "Crisis? How Is That a Crisis?! Reflections on an Overburdened Word," *Contributions to the History of Concepts* 12, no. 2 (2017): 15.
15. It has even been suggested that we should get rid of the very word "humanities" in order to be able to think more seriously about the state of

these subjects. See Marjorie Perloff, "Crisis in the Humanities," in *Rethinking the Humanities: Paths and Challenges*, eds. Ricardo Gil Soeiro and Sofia Tavares (Newcastle: Cambridge Scholars Publishing, 2012), 46.
16. Roitman, *Anti-Crisis*.
17. This analytical framework is also applied in the concluding chapter of my PhD thesis, from which some findings in this article have been elaborated. See Hampus Östh Gustafsson, *Folkhemmets styvbarn: Humanioras legitimitet i svensk kunskapspolitik 1935–1980* (Gothenburg: Daidalos, 2020).
18. Zoe Hope Bulaitis, *Value and the Humanities: The Neoliberal University and Our Victorian Inheritance* (Basingstoke: Palgrave Macmillan, 2020), 3, 229, 245; Collini, "On Not 'Justifying' the Humanities"; António Sousa Ribeiro, "The 'Crisis of the Humanities' Reconsidered," in Soeiro and Tavares, *Rethinking the Humanities*, 87; Sitze, Sarat, and Wolfson, "Humanities in Question," 191–2.
19. Gumbrecht, *Ewige Krise*, 10–14.
20. See e.g., Fritz K. Ringer, *The Decline of the German Mandarins: The German Academic Community, 1890–1933* (Hanover, NH: University Press of New England, 1990 [1969]).
21. Irving Babbitt, *Literature and the American College: Essays in Defense of the Humanities* (Boston, MA: Houghton Mifflin, 1908), 31.
22. The general dichotomy has been seen as originating in the antique notion of *ars* and *scientia* and also reflected in the tension between Enlightenment rationalism and the new humanism of Romanticism.
23. One striking example is Odo Marquard's thesis of compensation: that the humanities compensate for the deficits of (the scientifically driven) modernity. See Odo Marquard, *Transzendentaler Idealismus, romantische Naturphilosophie, Psychoanalyse* (Cologne: Dinter, 1987), 1, 292 and also Joachim Ritter, *Die Aufgabe der Geisteswissenschaften in der modernen Gesellschaft* (Münster: Aschendorff, 1963). Cf. Aleida Assman, *Ist die Zeit aus den Fugen? Aufstieg und Fall des Zeitregimes der Moderne* (Munich: Carl Hanser, 2013), 316; Jan Eckel, *Geist der Zeit: Deutsche Geisteswissenschaften seit 1870* (Göttingen: Vandenhoeck & Ruprecht, 2008), 131; Hamann, "'Bildung' in German Human Sciences," 59; Peter Kampits, "Geisteswissenschaften wozu? Die Geisteswissenschaften und der Terror des Nützlichen," in *Krise der Geistes-wissenschaften? Ihre Bedeutung und gesellschaftliche Relevanz heute*, ed. Helmut Reinalter (Weimar: VDG, 2011), 65. A similar narrative lay at the bottom of the *Two Cultures* debate. In C. P. Snow's account, science progressively pointed toward the future while activities associated with culture and the humanities were deemed hopelessly traditional. See Snow, *Two Cultures*, 11, and Guy Ortolano, *The Two Cultures Controversy: Science, Literature and Cultural Politics in Postwar Britain* (Cambridge: Cambridge University Press, 2009), 27, 218.

24. Cf. Gumbrecht, *Ewige Krise*, 10–11; Eric Hayot, *Humanist Reason: A History, an Argument, a Plan* (New York: Columbia University Press, 2021), 22–4; Thorsten Botz-Bornstein, "Science Culture, and the University," in *The Crisis of the Human Sciences: False Objectivity and the Decline of Creativity*, ed. Thorsten Botz-Bornstein (Newcastle: Cambridge Scholars Publishing, 2011), 6. For instance, Gadamer noted that Kant's epistemological distinction between a transcendent, knowing subject and an empirical object of knowledge caused an abandonment of a specific claim to truth characteristic to the academic traditions of history and philology. The separation raised the question whether the human subject, epistemologically bound to its limitations, was capable of generating objective knowledge about itself in a way comparable to how the natural sciences approached the natural world. See Hans-Georg Gadamer, *Wahrheit und Methode: Grundzüge einer philosophischen Hermeneutik* (Tübingen: J. C. B. Mohr, 1960), 38, and also Michiel Leezenberg, *History and Philosophy of the Humanities: An Introduction* (Amsterdam: Amsterdam University Press, 2018), 141–2, 181.
25. Wilhelm Dilthey, *Einleitung in die Geisteswissenschaften: Versuch einer Grundlegung für das Studium der Gesellschaft und der Geschichte* (Leipzig: B. G. Teubner, 1922 [1883]), 4.
26. Wilhelm Windelband, "Geschichte und Naturwissenschaft" (1894), in Windelband, *Präludien: Aufsätze und Reden zur Einführung in die Philosophie*, vol. 2 (Tübingen: J. C. B. Mohr, 1911), 144–5.
27. Heinrich Rickert, *Kulturwissenschaft und Naturwissenschaft* (Tübingen: J. C. B. Mohr, 1921 [1899]), e.g., 155.
28. See, e.g., Herman Paul, "A Collapse of Trust: Reconceptualizing the Crisis of Historicism," *Journal of the Philosophy of History* 2, no. 1 (2008), 63–82.
29. Golden age narratives may be interpreted as part of general critique of modernity, in particular as a reaction toward the postwar euphoria of technological and economic progress—Marquard's aforementioned thesis being a characteristic example.
30. Cf. Helge Jordheim, "Krisetid: Introduksjon til en begrepshistorisk forståelse av krisebegrepet," *Arr—idéhistorisk tidsskrift*, no. 2 (2017); Martin Wiklund, *Historia som domstol: Historisk värdering och retorisk argumentation kring "68"* (Nora: Nya Doxa, 2012), 225.
31. R. S. Crane, *The Idea of the Humanities and Other Essays Critical and Historical*, vol. 1 (Chicago, IL: University of Chicago Press, 1967), 16–170.
32. Paul Yachnin, "The Crisis in the Humanities: What Would Shakespeare Do?" *Humanities* 5, no. 2 (2016).
33. Bo Lindberg, "'De rolige vetenskaperna': Om humaniora före moderniteten," in *Omodernt och tankar i förmodern tid*, eds. Mohammad Fazlhashemi and Eva Österberg (Lund: Nordic Academic Press, 2009), 97–141.

34. See, e.g., Isak Hammar, "A Conflict Among Geniuses: Challenges to the Classical Paradigm in Sweden, 1828–1832," *History of Education* 48, no. 6 (2019): 714–15, 728.
35. Michel Wieviorka, "The Crisis of the Humanities and Social Sciences in France Today," in Ahlburg, *Changing Face*, 80–1.
36. John R. Thelin, *A History of American Higher Education* (Baltimore, MD: Johns Hopkins University Press, 2011 [2004]), 260.
37. Hampus Östh Gustafsson, "The Discursive Marginalisation of the Humanities: Debates on the Humanist Problem in the Early 1960s Swedish Welfare State," *History of Humanities* 3, no. 2 (2018): 351–76.
38. Cf. Svante Nordin, *Humaniora i Sverige: Framväxt—Guldålder—Kris* (Stockholm: Atlantis, 2008). Here, an interesting observation should be made: in several instances, golden age narratives tend to leap circa fifty years back in time—that is, just beyond the generational experience of active scholars.
39. Filipe Campello and Mariana Prandini Assis, "Is There a Crisis in the Humanities in Brazil? Ambivalences and Fragilities of a Late Higher Education System," in Ahlburg, *Changing Face*, 30. See also Keith Breckenridge, "Hopeless Entanglement: The Short History of the Academic Humanities in South Africa," ibid., 180–1.
40. See, e.g., Wang Hui, "The Humanities in China: History and Challenges," *History of Humanities* 5, no. 2 (2020): 309–31; George Makdisi, *The Rise of Humanism in Classical Islam and the Christian West: With Special Reference to Scholasticism* (Edinburgh: Edinburgh University Press, 1990), xx, 89, 292, 332, 348.
41. See, e.g., the theme issue of *History of Humanities* 6, no. 2 (2021) on "Decentralizing the History of Humanities," and also Wiebke Denecke, "Comparative Global Humanities Now," *Journal of World Literature* 6 (2021): 479–508.
42. *Humanistisk och teologisk forskning i Sverige: Nuläge och framtidsperspektiv* (Stockholm: Statens Humanistiska Forskningsråd, 1973). Interestingly, the Swedish debates were also referred to internationally as a unique example of how the humanities had been put under pressure. See Peter Weingart et al., *Die sog. Geisteswissenschaften: Außenansichten: Die Entwicklung der Geisteswissenschaften in der BRD 1954–1987* (Frankfurt am Main: Suhrkamp, 1991), 14–15.
43. Östh Gustafsson, *Folkhemmets styvbarn*.
44. Jesper Eckhardt Larsen, *'ikke af brød alene...' Argumenter for humaniora og universitet i Norge, Danmark, Tyskland og USA 1945–2005* (Copenhagen: Danmarks Pædagogiske Universitet, 2006), 59–63, 76, 142, 304; Fredrik W. Thue and Kim G. Helsvig, *Universitetet i Oslo 1811–2011*, vol. 5 (Oslo: Unipub, 2011), 115.

45. Paul Benneworth, Magnus Gulbrandsen, and Ellen Hazelkorn, *The Impact and Future of Arts and Humanities Research* (London: Palgrave Macmillan, 2016), 105; Martha C. Nussbaum, *Not for Profit: Why Democracy Needs the Humanities* (Princeton, NJ: Princeton University Press, 2010), 151–2.
46. See, e.g., *General Education in a Free Society: Report of the Harvard Committee* (Cambridge, MA: Harvard University Press, 1945.) See also Harpham, "Between Humanity," 252; Andrew Jewett, *Science, Democracy, and the American University: From the Civil War to the Cold War* (Cambridge: Cambridge University Press, 2012), 310, 339, 341.
47. Jewett, *Science, Democracy*, 310. Jewett notes that the social sciences rather were set aside, apprehended as a breeding ground for materialism and socialism.
48. J. H. Plumb, "Introduction," in Plumb, *Crisis in the Humanities*, 7–10. Plumb's crisis rhetoric should not be exaggerated, however. Mandler underlines that while a notion of crisis was indeed developed in the British 1960s, this idea did not have immediate consequences for the state of the humanities. See Peter Mandler, "The Humanities in British Universities since 1945," *The American Historical Review* 120, no. 4 (2015): 1304–8.
49. Germany also saw the humanities struggling. In this case, however, their postwar crisis was not regarded as a complete novelty, rather as a second wave, following the turmoil of the first half of the century. See e.g., Eckel, *Geist der Zeit*, 12–3, 23, 112, Hamann, *Bildung der Geisteswissenschaften*, 255–6, 366, and also Edmund Husserl, *Die Krisis der europäischen Wissenschaften und die transzendentale Phänomenologie: Eine Einleitung in die phänomenologische Philosophie* (Hamburg: Felix Meiner, 2012 [1936]).
50. Elke Seefried, "Reconfiguring the Future? Politics and Time from the 1960s to the 1980s—Introduction," *Journal of Modern European History* 13, no. 2 (2015): 315; Elke Seefried, *Zukünfte: Aufstieg und Krise der Zukunftsforschung 1945–1980* (Oldenburg: Walter de Gruyter, 2015), 14.
51. Terry Eagleton, *After Theory* (London: Allen Lane, 2003), 26–7.
52. Hampus Östh Gustafsson, "Mobilising the Outsider: Crises and Histories of the Humanities in the 1970s Scandinavian Welfare States," in *Histories of Knowledge in Postwar Scandinavia: Actors, Arenas, and Aspirations*, eds. Johan Östling, Niklas Olsen, and David Larsson Heidenblad (London: Routledge, 2020), 208–24.
53. William I. Thomas and Dorothy Swaine Thomas, *The Child in America: Behavior Problems and Programs* (New York: Alfred A. Knopf, 1928), 572. See also Robert K. Merton, "The Thomas Theorem and the Matthew Effect," *Social Forces* 74, no. 2 (1995): 379–422.
54. Cf. Bulaitis, *Value and the Humanities*, 5.

55. See e.g., Ann Marie Rasmussen, "The Crisis in the Humanities: Feminism, Medieval Studies, and the Academy," *Medieval Feminist Forum* 29 (2000), 25–32.
56. A popular belief holds critical theory responsible for the crisis, which is a doubtful interpretation as the humanities already faced a number of structural challenges in the 1960s and 1970s. Cf. Paul Jay, "Critique and Theory in the History of the Modern Humanities," in *The Making of the Humanities: The Modern Humanities*, vol. 3, eds. Rens Bod, Jaap Maat, and Thijs Weststeijn (Amsterdam: Amsterdam University Press, 2014), 655–65.
57. Rens Bod, *A New History of the Humanities: The Search for Principles and Patterns from Antiquity to the Present*, trans. Lynn Richards (Oxford: Oxford University Press, 2013), 358; Rens Bod and Julia Kursell, "Introduction: The Humanities and the Sciences," *Isis* 106, no. 2 (2015): 337; Lorraine Daston and Glenn W. Most, "History of Science and History of Philologies," *Isis* 106, no. 2 (2015): 378–90; Johan Östling et al eds., *Circulation of Knowledge: Explorations in the History of Knowledge* (Lund: Nordic Academic Press, 2018), 16.
58. *Hva skal vi med humaniora? Rapport om de humanistiska fagenes situasjon i Norge*, eds. Helge Jordheim and Tore Rem (Oslo: Fritt Ord, 2014), 15.
59. Cf. Isabelle Stengers, *Another Science is Possible: A Manifesto for Slow Science*, transl. Stephen Muecke (Cambridge: Polity, 2018), 52, 55, and also Helge Jordheim, "Introduction: Multiple Times and the Work of Synchronization," *History and Theory* 53, no. 4 (2014): 498–518.
60. Agnes Callard, "What Do the Humanities Do in a Crisis?" *The New Yorker* (April 11, 2020).

Part II

Research Practices

4

Modernizing the Comparative Method: Marx and Darwin

Devin Griffiths

Introduction

The comparative method has had a profound influence on the institutional and disciplinary formation of the modern humanities. This legacy is evident in the many comparative subdisciplines that have shaped the Western academy, ranging from comparative literature, philology, and linguistics, to comparative religion and mythology, and (in the humanistic social sciences) comparative political science and sociology. Comparison—the analysis of similarity and difference in order to discern shared patterns and common histories—is part of the DNA of modern humanism. But it is also deeply entrenched in the natural sciences, especially, the life sciences. How might we interpret the interdisciplinary interplay of the comparative method, and its implications for the humanities of the future?

This essay examines the interdisciplinary origins of the comparative method in the humanities. In a previous study, I examined the development of the comparative method in the latter nineteenth and twentieth centuries within specific humanist disciplines, namely, philology, linguistics, anthropology, sociology, political science, literature, history, and folklore studies.[1] Comparing disciplines in that study made it possible to track convergent developments in the comparative method within distinct fields of inquiry. However, a multidisciplinary approach runs the risk of obscuring the importance of broadly shared, pre-disciplinary developments in the comparative method, and the substantial interplay and porous boundaries between nascent fields. For this reason, the present essay begins with an account of the genesis, around 1800, of the modern comparative method at the intersection of several scientific and humanistic areas of inquiry. It distinguishes the modern comparative method from earlier modes of analysis, and explores its interdisciplinary Romantic formulation in the writings of Erasmus Darwin and Johann Wolfgang von Goethe. The patterns of progress and development that their comparative analyses revealed laid the groundwork both for major innovations in nineteenth-century linguistics and for essentializing theories of racial distinction. Against this background, the survey will then turn to a more thorough case study of the centrality of comparative analysis to the works of Charles Darwin and Karl Marx, two of the nineteenth-century's most influential and interdisciplinary analysts of living systems and human societies. Perhaps no two writers have had a more profound influence on twentieth- and twenty-first-century academic research, especially in the humanities. Their detailed studies of biological and social evolution had a lasting influence on how humanists would understand the implications of comparative analysis, and the importance of discriminating the distinct forces that produce patterns of similarity. Consideration of their distinct approaches to the comparative method will sharpen the contours of a widely-shared approach to comparative analysis at the interplay of multiple areas of inquiry. This, in turn, can give us a fresh understanding of both the critical heft and limitations of the comparative method in modern humanism.

The Prehistory of Modern Comparatism

Understood generally as a study of the similarities and differences between seemingly distinct cases, the comparative method has a very long history within various humanist and philosophical traditions. To take one major example, Aristotle's method of division, whether of literary genres, modes of rhetoric, or biological taxa, explored the differences between similar examples as relations between higher-order genera and distinct species, with lasting impact on classical philosophy and medieval scholarship.[2]

Anthony Grafton, surveying strategies of comparison, argues that a major consequence of the early modern expansion of trade, imperialism, and publishing, which "transformed the landscape of information in which Europeans lived," was a greater awareness of the variety of cultures and artifacts, and a renewed appreciation for the power of comparison as a method of study.[3] This feel for the expanded complexity of the world, an expansion that prompted a new investment in comparison, emerged in the same period that saw the rise of the *studia humanitas* and was impelled by some of the same forces.[4] And understood as a mode of analogical reasoning, comparative analysis has an even deeper history both within and beyond Europe.[5] As Rens Bod observes, "there has been a continuous humanistic tradition from Antiquity to the present that focuses on the quest for patterns and rules (alongside a parallel tradition that concentrates on the *rejection* of patterns)."[6] Bod and Grafton point out that these longer histories undermine the distinction that is sometimes drawn between the modern comparative method, which emerged in the nineteenth century, and earlier traditions.

But these continuities mask key reformulations in how the comparative method was deployed and understood. Analyses of similarity versus difference, though related, were usually not practiced at the same time (as underlined in Bod's account). In the Western tradition, comparison was generally taken as an analysis of *distinction* within rhetoric, jurisprudence, and the natural sciences. (There is a reason we do not call it Aristotle's method of "addition.") Cicero and Quintilian emphasized comparison's power to draw contrasts between distinct cases and amplify differences, a tradition that persisted well into the early modern period.[7] Henry Peacham's *Art of English Poesie* is representative, identifying comparison as a class of figures, or argumentative structures, that "amplify or diminish" differences.[8] Analogy, by contrast, was a method of finding *similarities* that flourished in biblical exegesis and ontology, particularly after the writings of Augustine and Thomas Aquinas.[9] Over the succeeding millennium, analogy became important to Christian apologetics, and especially to claims that the conserved patterns of nature demonstrated the benevolent order of a divine author. William Paley's *Natural Theology* (1802) marked a culmination of this line of thought, famously tracing analogies between human artifacts (a watch) and the superior, and far more intricate design of living creatures.

Transition to the modern comparative method was marked by the collapse of the distinction between these two styles of reasoning, so that comparison (as the study of contrast) and analogy (as the study of similarity) became closely linked in a range of fields. A hallmark of this transition is the intermingling of the terms *analogy* and *comparison* (in English), *analogie* and *comparaison* (in French), and *Analogie* and *Vergleich* (in German) in the early nineteenth-century, especially in works of philology and comparative anatomy. Though from a modern perspective, early linguistics and biology seem widely different, they in fact influenced each other closely (as we shall see) in the combination of analogy and comparison as a comprehensive method of analysis that would study similarities and differences between phenomena. To my knowledge, this important shift, from the historical distinction between comparison and analogy, to their interrelation in the modern comparative method, has not been generally recognized or explained. One possible reason: just as analogy and comparison were once understood to operate in different domains of rhetoric, exegetics, and natural philosophy, so the respective disciplinary histories of these fields have not considered how their vocabularies evolved over time in relation to each other, and for this reason, have overlooked the consolidation of the modern comparative method.[10]

Romantic Formations of the Comparative Method

Perhaps no two Romantic writers better demonstrate the close interplay of the humanities and sciences in the development of the comparative method than Erasmus Darwin (Charles's grandfather) and Johann Wolfgang von Goethe. Each worked to formulate a new mode of comparative analysis that would carefully analyse the similarities as well as differences between various natural phenomena as well as aspects of human behavior and culture.

Erasmus Darwin was a poet, the author of the first extended account of biological evolution in Britain, and also an important theorist of the comparative method. At the opening of his comprehensive medical treatise, *Zoonomia*, he insists that "a certain similitude on the features of nature ... demonstrates to us, that *the whole is one family of one parent*. On this similitude," he continues, "is founded all rational analogy." However, Darwin cautioned, when it "links together objects, otherwise discordant, by some fanciful similitude ... philosophy and truth recoil from its combinations."[11] This important statement of the comparative method is notable in that it draws together the analysis of similarity (as similitude) and difference (by means of comparison) as dimensions of a robust analogical method, one that asserts the genealogical relation of natural classes. In his *Temple of Nature, or, The Origin of Society* (1803), one of several extremely popular didactic poems, Erasmus Darwin extended this method to the structure of languages and phonology, explaining that "a new distribution of the objects of any science may advance the knowledge of it by developing another analogy of its constituent parts."[12] He firmly believed that the comparative method, as applied to both human society and natural history, illuminated the continuous relation between natural and human societies, as well as their continuous evolutionary progress.

Though famous as a novelist, playwright, and poet, Goethe's application of the comparative method had an even more profound impact on the natural sciences. His botanical and anatomical studies, which involved the close comparative analysis of both plant and animal species, made crucial contributions to plant physiology and comparative anatomy. His investigation of vertebrate skulls, which compared humans to a variety of other species, including elephants and apes, demonstrated in print for the first time that humans, *do*, in fact, possess an intermaxillary bone early in development (the absence of which had been taken by Johann Friedrich Blumenbach and others as proof of the strong anatomical distinction between humans and other animals). For Goethe, these analogies of structure did not illustrate common descent, but rather, the differentiated working out of an "idea" or "archetype" that underlies the development of groups of creatures.[13] This analysis of commonalities in structure would have a profound influence on comparative anatomists like Étienne Geoffroy Saint-Hilaire and Richard Owen, who would also explore the more immediate repetitions of pattern within the structure of individual organisms.[14]

Goethe's studies of plant physiology had an even wider impact. His *Versuch die Metamorphose der Pflanzen* (1790) was the culmination of a decade of comparative study of plant specimens, both during his travels and in his botanical garden at Weimar, and explored the common plan of development that, in Goethe's analysis, underwrites the variety of plant forms. Modern botanists consider it both a founding study of plant morphology, and the first definition of its methodology, comparative morphology.[15] As Goethe acknowledges, he was not the first to combine a search for similarities in plant structure with a careful discrimination of differences, noting, for example, that the basal "node" and the leaves of plants "have often been *compared* and *contrasted*" ("Die *Vergleichung* und

Unterscheidung beyder ist schon öfters ... ausgefürt worden").[16] Goethe emphasized that these operations consisted of a single, unified method, applied systematically to the study of specific groups of organisms: "Here it is crucial that we thoroughly observe and compare the different stages nature goes through in the formation of genera, species, and varieties, as well as in the growth of each individual plant."[17] Goethe also mirrored Erasmus Darwin in asserting that this comparative investigation of plants demonstrated a unified order, but gave a different interpretation of that order, positing shared principles of physiological development, not genealogy. The development of all vegetal life, he argued, was exemplified by the metamorphosis of leaves into various other tissues, through a series of relatively conserved cycles of growth and transformation. For Goethe, the "idea" inherent in plants demonstrated itself in these patterns of structural development, which he analysed in terms of three key stages: expansion, compaction, and "anastomosis" (*Anastomose*), in which the tissues combine and metamorphose into a more advanced form. Goethe insisted that the object of the comparative method is the identification of these interlocking "stages," as a sort of "algebraic formula."[18] In this way, Goethe's developmental morphology fused together a version of organicism—in which all the parts of an organism are part of an interlocking whole—with an immanent vitalism—a regulative developmental drive manifesting itself in nature. This analysis of transformative development influenced much of Goethe's thinking, including his famous proposal that modernity marked a new "epoch of World literature"[19] that would subsume national difference.

Eckart Förster has given an extensive analysis of the impact of Goethe's analysis of plant development on German philosophy, especially on Hegel's analysis of logic and human history. Hegel (like many, Goethe's devotee) received the *Metamorphose* as a revelation. For Goethe, the speculative leap required to recognize anastomosis combined "negation" (*aufheben*) of opposing parts with the abstraction and grasping of a higher unity, and Förster details how Hegel eventually reorganized these cycles of development as the logical categories of a *dialectic* operative in both philosophy and historical development. Growth, compaction, and anastomosis became Hegelian thesis, antithesis, and synthesis (via *aufhebung*) as a higher unity.[20]

For our purposes, the major impact of the *Metamorphose* was to demonstrate for Hegel and others how comparative analysis, both between cultures, institutions, and systems of thought, could reveal an inherent program of development that, despite local variation, was consistent and inevitable. Previous enlightenment authors of universal or "stadial" history, including central figures in the Scottish Enlightenment, had also emphasized a step-wise progression in the sophistication of societies.[21] However, these were premised on deist and mechanistic notions of a divine plan articulated through time. Goethe's more physiological analysis (not withstanding his attribution its central "idea" or "archetype"), provided a more vital and naturalistic account, indicating how successive stages might precipitate from the dynamic growth and contradiction of previous stages, through a process of vital, organic growth.[22] This process was given its ideal reinterpretation by Hegel, who described it as the imminent working out in human history of a unitary "Geist" or spirit that develops organically through cycles of expansion or invention, attendant conflicts, and metamorphoses.

Comparative Linguistics and the Analysis of Race

In drawing a close connection between the comparative analysis of living systems and the aesthetic features of literatures, Erasmus Darwin and Goethe illustrate the intertwined practice of philological and physiological comparison in the early nineteenth century. They also indicate the tendency of comparatists, in working to explain the patterns they discovered, to propose unitary patterns of development or internal principles of coherence and identity. Subsequent comparatists would capitalize on those tendencies to substantiate a belief in the superior development of specific cultures, languages, and races. As we will see, the effort of comparative philologists to analyse the relation between modern dialects walked hand in hand with debates over the biological ranking of human populations.

The major achievements of comparative anatomy in the early nineteenth century provided powerful models for the parallel development of comparative philology. Most histories of comparative philology assign a founding role to Sir William Jones's 1786 discovery of basic etymological and grammatical correlations between Sanskrit, Latin, Greek, and what he labeled "Gothic" and "Celtick." Henry Hoenigswald points out that similarities of pattern within European languages had already "been seen, tabulated, and discussed for centuries,"[23] and comparative grammars had long played an important part in missionary and trade expansion beyond Europe.[24] Even so, the identification of what came to be known as Proto-Indo-European

(PIE) opened up a new chapter in the history of comparative philology, largely through the systematic analysis provided by Friedrich Schlegel in what he described as a new science of "comparative grammar"—developed more or less explicitly from comparative anatomy.

As Ernst Fridryk Konrad Koerner explains, Schlegel's five years of study in Paris, from 1802–7, were determinative.[25] In Paris, he likely would have encountered Jean Baptiste Lamarck's controversial theory of the progressive development of species, which argued for the continuous evolution of the nervous system and the properties of the human mind.[26] And Schlegel certainly met the anatomist George Cuvier, imbibing his lectures on fossil analysis. Cuvier, in explicit contrast to Lamarck, used comparison across classes of animals to argue for basic, lawlike patterns governing the adaptation of animals to different modes of movement and diet—an analysis that, in Cuvier's view, shed light on the climatic conditions under which human civilizations developed.[27]

In *Über die Sprache und Weisheit der Indier* (1808), Schlegel split the difference between these developmental and structural positions, arguing that comparative grammar would expose *both* the genealogy and the "inner structure of languages."[28] The similarity of this formulation to the arguments developed by contemporary anatomists is not accidental. Moreover, Schlegel used this method, controversially, to develop a theory of linguistic polygenesis that discriminated between root "inflected" languages (including Sanskrit, the classical languages, and modern German) which permitted spiritual and intellectual expression, and root-combining or "agglutinative" languages (Chinese and Hebrew), which he characterized as animalistic.[29] Schlegel further suggested that language groups implied a racial or ethnic identity that could be traced back to common "tribes" (*Stamm*).[30] Alexander von Humboldt subsequently popularized and amplified these views, arguing that the Indo-European family of languages possessed a superior and "creative life-principle."[31]

Jacob Grimm underlined the formative connection to comparative anatomy in the first volume of his *Deutsche Grammatik* (1819), speculating that more thorough comparisons drawn between languages would make further discoveries possible, in the same way that comparative anatomy had transformed natural history.[32] Using a close analysis of German dialects, and focusing on phonology rather than philology (shift in sound, rather than orthography or grammar) Grimm and Rasmus Rask used comparative analysis to identify a set of "sound laws" that explained the phonological shifts that could derive modern Germanic dialects from precursors. The most important contemporary outcome of this line of research was August Schleicher's reconstruction of the PIE language family, which combined comparative grammar and phonology with textual stemmatics.[33] In the longer view, the discovery of lawlike patterns that governed linguistic transformations, in particular, the example of Grimm and Rasks's sound laws, would prove even more consequential in shaping, via the work of Ferdinand de Saussure and Claude Levi-Strauss, structural accounts of human culture and behaviors. Such laws discovered, beneath the heartbeat of individual human actions and contingent events, the pulse a longer rhythm, a deeper structure that might explain the evolution of all aspects of human life, from languages to systems of belief and cognition.

These arguments for a deeper structure were closely entwined with discussions of the biological as well as cultural status of races. By mid-century, they were so deeply imbricated that Max Müller would complain that the "science of language and the science of ethnology have both suffered most seriously from being mixed together."[34] A decade later, Ernst Haeckel would cite Goethe explicitly as laying the foundation of a new mode for analysing the entire "natural history of creation"—one that balanced a "conservative species drive" that maintained the integrity of both species and races (*konservativen Specificationstriebes*), with a "progressive" *Bildungstrieb* that ensured continuous development.[35] Using these terms, he elaborated the link between "comparative zoology and comparative philology," adducing regional languages, alongside putative racial phenotypes like hair color and skull shape, to classify all of humanity into twelve distinct species with thirty-six varieties, mapping them onto complex *Stammbaum* or family trees.[36]

The collaborative effort of comparative anatomists and philologists to develop comprehensive theories of racial integrity and differentiation is significant, not only in demonstrating the various and destructive purposes to which the comparative method was turned, but also in illustrating that, when it came to the human, these areas of inquiry were not understood as distinctly *humanistic* and *scientific*, but rather, parts of the humanistic *sciences of the human*. (Here it is important to note that Müller considers ethnology and linguistics to be separate yet equally valid "sciences.") Racial science, which was both *about* the human subject, and about secularizing *how* that subject was interpreted, was simply the most pointed and ultimately disastrous example of a comparative and humanistic science, one that furnished a biological reading of essential racial difference that defended African slavery, and laid the groundwork for eugenic science.[37] At the same time, comparative analysis proved to be a powerful tool for critiquing previous readings of biological form and human behavior. To take one famous example, Franz Boas's study of American immigrants disproved contemporary theories of racial differences in cranial volume by comparing European and American populations from the same ethnic groups.[38] Critics of racial science leaned as heavily on comparative analysis as supporters.

Marx's Anatomy

This critical capacity was key to the way that both Darwin and Marx used the comparative method. It is generally recognized that the hallmark of the modern method, elucidated in both anatomy and philology, is a tension between three basic ways of interpreting the patterns which the method exposed: (1) evidence of higher-order structural rules of transformation (rules that themselves might require further explanation, for example, as a more basic pattern in climatological or environmental shift, or cultural evolution, or inbuilt physiological or intellectual constraints); (2) the genealogical construction of a lineage or tree that would explain relationships historically in terms of descent or divergence over time; (3) a functionalist account that would explain patterns with reference to shared environments or parallel adaptation. The tension between (1) and (2) was especially pronounced. For Cuvier, Schleicher, Bopp, Owen, and Goethe, patterns traced in comparison implied higher-order laws that ruled the development of living creatures and languages. For Erasmus Darwin, Lamarck, Geoffroy, and Haeckel, such patterns provided evidence for a history of progressive development. Throughout the first half of the nineteenth century, there was generally a clear division between a majority of naturalists and linguists who thought comparative analysis was analytical and nomothetic (producing higher-order laws), and a smaller minority who believed it was descriptive and idiographic (describing historical patterns of development).

This balance would fundamentally shift over the course of the nineteenth century, and certainly in the twentieth, in no small part due to the writings of Marx and Darwin. While early practitioners of the comparative method generally emphasized one of these modes over the others, it is striking that Darwin and Marx, in developing their own unique combination of all three modes of comparative analysis, elevated the importance of functionalist accounts (3) for later social theorists. For Darwin, functionalist analysis helped explain how specific traits, in adapting organisms to their environment, would motivate evolution, and eventually, speciation; for Marx, functionalist accounts explained how specific social practices served to intensify the economic and ideological forces of capitalism. But their writings also remind us that the comparative method was equally *synthetic* and *analytic*, with one foot set in the analysis of analogical similarity, the other in contrastual comparison. In addition to developing novel interpretations of the coherence of human societies, or the continuity of biological life, Marx and Darwin deployed extensive comparative analysis to powerfully critique, and ultimately dismantle previous scientific and economic theories.

In some ways, Marx is the more intriguing case, insofar as he worked carefully to balance descriptions of the "laws" that govern specific economic formation—for example, the "iron law of wages" or the "law of value"—with detailed historical accounts of how those economic formations emerge, exploring how that evolution contradicted the precepts of classical economics. Marx's mode of analysis, which is he described as a materialist "dialectic," combined Hegel's dialectic with stadial history and classical economics to produce a highly detailed analysis of contemporary capitalism and its history. One of its central challenges was to explain how socioeconomic systems might exhibit a deep integrity but also inhabit contradictions and undergo changes. His response to this problem—the materialist dialectic—drew explicitly on Hegel's reformulation of Goethe's physiological "algebra." Yet over the course of his major writings, this account of historical transformation gained considerable historical depth, as he incorporated increasingly nuanced comparative analysis. As a result, Marx's account of history evolved from the unilinear and stadial model of progress set out in the *German Ideology* (from tribalism, to slavery, to feudalism, and then capitalism) to the much more ramified analysis given in the *Grundrisse* and in *Capital* of the various paths by which different regions transitioned from prehistoric, tribal societies. Though he maintained that all roads eventually led to the world market, capitalism, and then some form of communism, in this more detailed account it was evident that the courses of those paths might diverge widely.

Considerable attention has been given to Marx's foundational engagement with both German idealism and classical economics, from his early years as a "young Hegelian" to his years of immersion in the blue books and historical records of the British Museum library. But it has been less generally noted how much Marx's mature method relied on comparatism, and the inspiration he drew from contemporary developments in comparative anatomy and philology. References to these "sciences" consistently ground explanations of his method. Marx's *Grundrisse* cited philology and the discovery of the sounds laws to explain how his mode of dialectical and comparative analysis differs from the traditional analysis of previous economists. Classical economists like Smith and Mill, he argued, treat the elements of economic activity—individuals, the elements of production, the way in which the proceeds of production are distributed with a society—as distinct and independent objects. But what they were really doing, Marx posited, is projecting into history the elements of modern economies, for instance, bourgeois property relations. By contrast, Marx's comparative analysis would try to understand how a specific economic category, like production, functions in ways that are both similar and different in each period and for each society. As he put this, "this common element is sifted out by comparison [*Vergleichung*], is itself segmented many times over and splits into different determinations. Some determinations belong to all epochs, others only to a few."[39] In practice, this meant the detailed comparative analysis of distinct modes of production within, for example, Germanic family-based tribal societies, ancient slaveholding economies, and the large-scale agrarian and mercantile societies of Asia.

In order to set out the implications of this method, and explain how the productive arrangement of a given society might have both specific historical constraints (be "determined" by specific features of the particular moment and society) yet also share features of other economies, Marx turned to the relation between languages: "the most developed languages have laws and characteristics in common with the least developed" at the same time that "those things that determine their development, i.e. the elements which are not general and common, must be separated out" so that "their essential difference is not forgotten."[40] Marx here takes philology as a model for the power of the comparative method to examine what is common at both more local and wider scales by way of an enhanced study of what is distinct. In this way, a robust and historical comparative method could guard against taking any given feature of contemporary society—here, individualism—as elementary, rather than an historical feature of specific developments. In doing so, Marx underlines the key finding of modern philology: the discovery of "laws" (like the sound shift laws that shaped the development of modern German) that are *regulative* for a given time but not *timeless*. For Marx, this provided a key piece of evidence that complex social formations—whether languages or means of production—could be analysed as governed by internal rules of coherence that change over time.

Philology does not feature in *Capital*, though in volume one, he notes in passing the sedimentary nature of English.[41] Instead, the model for his comparative method is drawn from comparative anatomy. In the preface to the first edition, he explains that his study views "the economic formation of society ... as a process of natural history," an "organism capable of change" that can be studied in the same fashion that the "microscopic anatomy" examines minute differences in the structure of living bodies—with a close and discriminatory attention to detail.[42] In the postface to the second edition, he approves and provides an extensive extract of a Russian reviewer who summarizes the "value of Marx's book" as showing that "social organisms differ among themselves as fundamentally as plants or animals. Indeed, one and the same phenomenon falls under quite different laws in consequences of the different general structure of these organisms, the variation of their individual organs, and the different conditions in which those organs function."[43]

Marx's response, that the reviewer is simply identifying the "dialectical method," underlines the genealogy of his approach. In his own understanding of the method, the analogy between comparative anatomy and the study of society is substantiated by the fact that organisms and societies develop through a series of organic transformations on the model of Goethe's metamorphic physiology. This is why the language of "organism" and "organ" runs throughout the analysis in *Capital*—it provides an anatomic interrelation that comprehends, through detailed comparative analysis, the distinct ways that different societies articulate themselves in time, as well as the internal and necessary conflicts which precipitate their evolution into more advanced forms. Most important, for Marx, Goethe's metamorphosis suggested how a given capitalist society might precipitate its own evolution into a more just and equitable arrangement.[44] The much-discussed concept of totality needs to be read in this light—as the dynamic form taken by any given socio-economic formation, that is, its operation as a social organism.

Darwin's Words

Like Marx, Charles Darwin cultivated his approach to the comparative method from a variety of sources, including both philology and comparative anatomy. But from the outset, his distinct training in the British empiricist tradition led him to draw different conclusions about the way natural systems operate. Gavin Budge has emphasized the distinction between German *naturphilosophie*, with its Goethean idealist and organicist commitments, and the materialism of British empiricism.[45] Though Darwin took major inspiration from the romantic nature described in Alexander von Humboldt's *Personal Narrative* at the outset of his career, his travels aboard the *H.M.S. Beagle* convinced him that nature, including human nature, was far messier than Humboldt and British natural theologians like William Paley had led him to believe—full of conflict, violence, and death. For this reason, even as he used comparison, like Marx, to critique preconceived interpretations of natural structures, his accounts turned upon radical contingency and uncertainty, rather than inherent organization or forces of vital development.

Darwin also echoed Marx in citing philology as evidence that the comparative method could be used to construct more accurate genealogies. His brother Erasmus Darwin (named after their grandfather) was fascinated with contemporary language studies, and his brother-in-law, Hensleigh Wedgewood, was an accomplished philologist in his own right. The introduction to Wedgwood's *Dictionary of English Etymology* explained that the "germ of science" is the question: "what is the reason of some resemblance or contrast?"[46] The extraordinary success of the effort to classify European languages within PIE, celebrated by Wedgwood, had a clear impact on Darwin.[47] Near the close of the *Origin of Species*, Charles reaches to its example, in a striking parallel to Marx's account, in order to explain the connection between relation and degrees of difference:

> it might be that some very ancient language had altered little, and had given rise to few new languages, whilst others . . . had altered much, and had given rise to many new languages and dialects. The various degrees of difference in the languages from the same stock, would have to be expressed by groups subordinate to groups; but the proper or even only possible arrangement would still be genealogical.[48]

Philology provided Darwin a well-known example of what comparative analysis could achieve in reconstructing phylogenetic histories, and a conceptual model for how methods of classification might be reoriented as genealogical techniques. The model of philology was supplemented, as I have elsewhere argued, by Darwin's extensive reading of historical fiction, conjectural histories that drew together historical reconstructions through elaborate narratives of what might have been.[49] In the fiction of novelists like Walter Scott, Darwin found another model for how existing relationships might be remapped as histories of change and development, exploring the present configuration as the sum of particularized and idiosyncratic individual histories.

Darwin's own extensive experience with the comparative method was deeply disorienting, and providing a practical foundation for his thinking about the method. Before publishing his theory of natural selection, he spent nearly a decade on an exhaustive classification of living and fossil mollusks. Throughout the *Origin of Species*, he refers to that lived experience, as in a passage where he explains that "When a young naturalist commences the study of a group of organisms quite unknown to him, he is at first much perplexed to determine what differences to consider as specific, and what as varieties".[50] Darwin's profound insight was to recognize that this experience of disorientation, common to those learning to classify a new group of organisms, was not simply a product of initial ignorance, but rooted more fundamentally in the idiosyncratic rules that systematists relied upon to discriminate difficult cases. In their effort to sharply distinguish between putatively stable categories—like genus, species, and variety—systematists were drawing hard lines over porous boundaries, separating out and stabilizing objects that were deeply in flux. To put this differently, his own experience of the comparative method critically undermined the confident generalizations of systematists, and he subsequently honed this critical capacity in order to develop a repertoire of examples, drawn from both wild and domestic species, that disproved both the thesis of special creation (that organisms were created independently by God) and the notion that patterns of similarity reflected the expression of shared, ideal archetypes. The *Origin*, and all of his subsequent works, teem with juxtapositions and contrasting examples that could not be explained by traditional means, systematically dismantling the founding assumptions of species classification in order to reconfigure it as a genealogical, and so, critically *historical* science.

While the *Origin* studiously avoids commenting on the evolution of humanity and human customs, *The Descent of Man* confronted these problems directly. Though it now reads as a catalogue of contemporary prejudices concerning cultural distinction and gender roles, its more fundamental and revolutionary innovation was to argue that humans and their societies evolved on the basis of sexual selection, and therefore turned on the idiosyncrasy (rather than universality) of aesthetic judgment. As many have explained, one of Darwin's major objects in that work was to dismantle the theory of polygenesis—the notion that different human races were derived from originally distinct species.[51] But perhaps even more influential in the long run has been Darwin's more basic claim that human history does not show a stately progression, and is instead governed by contingent and often wildly contradictory judgments of value and beauty. The result is to place aesthetics at the heart of human history, while also relativizing, and so fatally undermining, arguments for human exceptionalism or cultural chauvinism. This impact was registered directly by the "Darwinian feminists" who seized on Darwin's account of the evolution of sexual dimorphism and feminine choice to overturn Victorian gender norms.[52] And in the longer run, critical race theorists and trans studies scholars have adapted Darwin in exploring the radical instability and cultural mediation of concepts of race and gender.[53] In this way, Darwin provided humanists a foundational argument for the essential historicity of all aspects of human valuation and distinction.

Conclusion

The critical role of historicization, a way of reading current structures as having a history, and so, insisting on their changefulness, is a crucial link between the way Darwin and Marx deployed the comparative method. Within their distinct applications of the comparative method, we can recognize a largely shared critical orientation that has had a significant effect on the thinking of later humanists. The famous dictum of the Marxist literary historian Fredric Jameson, *always historicize*, is really the insistence that historical juxtaposition is a core critical method for humanists, helping to expose the forces that produce a given cultural form, distinguishing them from other moments and objects, but also disclosing the essential instability of all practices and institutions.[54]

Marx clearly recognized the deep congeniality between his own reading of history and Darwin's account of flux and transformation. Marx's repeated readings of the *Origin of Species* are a key reason for his shift from philology to comparative anatomy as the model for his historical "science"; a friend reported that he "spoke of nothing else for months but Darwin and the enormous significance of his scientific discoveries."[55] Though he disliked Darwin's use of Thomas Malthus's population analysis, Marx was much more generally impressed by Darwin's evolutionary interpretation of natural history, and his use of comparative analysis to explain the transitions between distinct forms of life. In particular, Marx praised the deeply *historical* way that Darwin accounts for differences gleaned through comparative analysis, contrasting this to the "abstract materialism" of other natural scientists who "exclude the historical process."[56]

The genealogy I have sketched out here provides a way of rethinking the genealogy of humanist "critical theory" and "cultural studies" as deeply engaged with the comparative method and its interdisciplinary applications—a development that ran in parallel to, and has ultimately influenced, the development of explicitly "comparative history" in the twentieth century. If some later Marxisms and Darwinisms have taken a dogmatic turn in their reading of history, from Louis Althusser's "scientific Marxism" to the "selfish" account of human behaviors proffered by Richard Dawkins, the more general influence of these nineteenth-century figures can be felt in the critique of essentialist conceptions of social and biological categories, and in considering the shifting motivations that underwrite social behavior.[57] They have also bequeathed distinct habits in the way that humanists interpret patterns of similarity and difference in history. As I have elsewhere noted, most comparative analysis assigns patterns of difference and similarity to distinct axes of explanation.[58] For later Marxists, differences have generally been historical and national in character, marking the differentiation of specific relations between societies and over time, while patterns of similarity delineate similarities of function, particularly with respect to dynamic operations of capitalist economies. For Darwinists, by contrast, differences are often explained functionally—as adaptations to distinct conditions and environments—while patterns of similarity often reflect genealogical connection in time.

Looking forward, it seems that the influence of these two comparatist paradigms will only grow. Some of the most interesting recent work, in light of the climate crisis and anthropogenic climate change, has come from environmental humanists who seek to adapt both Marxist and Darwinian frameworks as a way to think about the interaction between human societies and their environment. "Green" Marxists, like Jason Moore and Andreas Malm, are currently working to reexamine the place of natural resources in Marx's analysis of labor and capital in order to understand the history of carbon economies, while a new wave of environmental anthropology, spearheaded by the work of Anna Tsing and Donna Haraway, looks to ecological science (a field which Darwin founded), to understand the complex interaction of humans and a more-than-human nature.[59] As Haraway observes in recent work, Marx and Darwin continue to inspire "bravery and capacity to tell big-enough stories without determinism, teleology, and plan."[60] In all of these efforts, we might read various dimensions of the expansion of the comparative method as a definitive technique of historical and humanist analysis.

Notes

1. Devin Griffiths, "The Comparative Method and the History of the Modern Humanities," *History of Humanities* 2, no. 2 (2017): 473–505.
2. See Marguerite Deslauriers, "Plato and Aristotle on Division and Definition," *Ancient Philosophy* 10, no. 2 (1990): 203–19; Andrea Falcon, "Aristotle, Speusippus, and the Method of Division," *The Classical Quarterly* 50, no. 2 (2000): 402–14; David C. Mirhady, "The Rhetorica Ad Alexandrum and the Tria Genera Causarum," in *Peripatetic Rhetoric after Aristotle*, ed. William W. Fortenbaugh and David C. Mirhady (New Brunswick, NJ: Transaction, 1994), 54–65; Jaakko Hintikka, "Concepts of Scientific Method from Aristotle to Newton," in *Analyses of Aristotle*, ed. Jaakko Hintikka (Dordrecht: Springer, 2004), 183–92.
3. Anthony Grafton, "Comparisons Compared: A Study in the Early Modern Roots of Cultural History," in *Regimes of Comparatism: Frameworks of Comparison in History, Religion and Anthropology*, ed. Renaud Gagné, Simon Goldhill, and Geoffrey Lloyd (Leiden: Brill, 2018), 19.
4. Augusto Campana, "The Origin of the Word 'Humanist,'" *Journal of the Warburg and Courtauld Institutes* 9 (1946): 60–73.
5. For instance, as a mode of argument in traditional Chinese philosophy, and a style of reasoning in Islamic law. Shu-Hsien Liu, "The Use of Analogy and Symbolism in Traditional Chinese Philosophy," *Journal of Chinese Philosophy* 1, no. 3–4 (1974): 313–38; Yun Xie, "Argument by Analogy in Ancient China," *Argumentation* 33, no. 3 (2019): 323–47; Ahmad Hasan, *Analogical Reasoning in Islamic Jurisprudence: A Study of the Juridical Principle of Qiyas* (New Delhi: Adam, 2009).
6. Rens Bod, *A New History of the Humanities: The Search for Principles and Patterns from Antiquity to the Present*, trans. Lynn Richards (Oxford: Oxford University Press, 2013), 348.
7. Patricia P. Matsen, Philip B. Rollinson, and Marion Sousa, eds., *Readings from Classical Rhetoric* (Carbondale, IL: Southern Illinois University Press, 1990), 183; Quintilian, *Quintilian's Institutes of Oratory: Or, Education of an Orator*, trans. John Selby Watson (London: G. Bell and Sons, 1892), 353.
8. Henry Peacham, *The Garden of Eloquence, Conteyning the Figures of Grammar and Rhetorick* (London: H. Jackson, 1593), 156.

9. Victor Harris, "Allegory to Analogy in the Interpretation of Scripture," *Philological Quarterly* 45 (1966): 1–23.
10. Devin Griffiths, *The Age of Analogy: Science and Literature Between the Darwins* (Baltimore, MD: Johns Hopkins University Press, 2016), 256 n. 6, 257 n. 8.
11. Erasmus Darwin, *Zoonomia or, The Laws of Organic Life*, vol. 1 (Dublin: Dugdale, 1800), 1.
12. Erasmus Darwin, *The Temple of Nature, Or the Origin of Society* (London: J. Johnson, 1803), 93.
13. George A. Wells, "Goethe and the Intermaxillary Bone," *British Journal for the History of Science* 3, no. 4 (1967): 358.
14. J. M. Opitz, "Goethe's Bone and the Beginnings of Morphology," *American Journal of Medical Genetics: Part A* 126, no. 1 (2004): 1–8.
15. Donald R. Kaplan, "The Science of Plant Morphology: Definition, History, and Role in Modern Biology," *American Journal of Botany* 88, no. 10 (2001): 1716.
16. Johann Wolfgang von Goethe, *The Metamorphosis of Plants*, ed. Gordon L. Miller (Cambridge, MA: MIT Press, 2009), 83; Johann Wolfgang von Goethe, *Versuch die Metamorphose der Pflanzen zu erklären* (Gotha: Ettinger, 1790), 61. Emphasis mine.
17. Goethe, *Metamorphosis of Plants*, 92.
18. Ibid., 92.
19. Johann Wolfgang von Goethe and Johann Peter Eckermann, *Conversations with Goethe in the Last Years of His Life*, trans. Margaret Fuller (Boston, MA: Hilliard, Gray, and Company, 1839), 203–4. See discussion in Hendrik Birus, "The Goethean Concept of World Literature and Comparative Literature," *CLCWeb: Comparative Literature and Culture* 2, no. 4 (2000); Haun Saussy, "Exquisite Cadavers Stitched from Fresh Nightmares: Of Memes, Hives and Self Genes," in *Comparative Literature in an Age of Globalization*, ed. Haun Saussy (Baltimore, MD: Johns Hopkins University Press, 2006), 3–42.
20. Eckart Förster, *Kant's Final Synthesis: An Essay on the Opus Postumum* (Cambridge, MA: Harvard University Press, 2002), 261, 294–300.
21. Karen O'Brien, "Between Enlightenment and Stadial History: William Robertson on the History of Europe," *Journal for Eighteenth-Century Studies* 16, no. 1 (1993): 53–64.
22. Arthur Zajonc, "Goethe and the Science of His Time: An Historical Introduction," in *Goethe's Way of Science: A Phenomenology of Nature*, ed. Arthur Zajonc and David Seamon (Albany, NY: State University of New York, 1998), 15–30.
23. Henry M. Hoenigswald, "On the History of the Comparative Method," *Anthropological Linguistics* 35, no. 1 (1993): 60. See also Toon Van Hal's discussion of the role of comparative analysis in the "Scythian theory" of

European language origins. Toon Van Hal, "Linguistics 'Ante Litteram': Compiling and Transmitting Views on the Diversity and Kinship of Languages before the Nineteenth Century," in *The Making of the Humanities*, vol. 2, ed. Rens Bod, Jaap Maat, and Thijs Weststeijn (Amsterdam: Amsterdam University Press, 2012), 37–54.

24. Comparative linguistic study of South Asian languages played an important role in both Christian missionary activity and the expansion of the Dutch East Indian trade, as Thijs Weststeijn and Gerhard F. Strasser explain. Thijs Weststeijn, "'Signs That Signify Themselves': Writing with Images in the Seventeenth Century," in *The Making of the Humanities*, vol. 1, ed. Rens Bod, Jaap Maat, and Thijs Weststeijn (Amsterdam: Amsterdam University Press, 2010), 133–59; Gerhard F. Strasser, "The Impact on the European Humanities of Early Reports from Catholic Missionaries from China, Tibet and Japan between 1600 and 1700," in Bod, Maat, and Weststeijn, *Making of the Humanities*, vol. 2, 185–208.

25. Ernest Fridryk Konrad Koerner, "Friedrich Schegel and the Emergence of Historical-Comparative Grammar," in Koerner, *Practicing Linguistic Historiography: Selected Essays* (Amsterdam: John Benjamins Publishing, 1989), 275–7.

26. Jean-Baptiste de Lamarck, *Philosophie zoologique, ou exposition des considérations relatives à l'histoire naturelle des animaux* (Paris: Dentu, 1809).

27. Gowan Dawson, *Show Me the Bone: Reconstructing Prehistoric Monsters in Nineteenth-Century Britain and America*, (Chicago, IL: University of Chicago Press, 2016); Georges Cuvier, *Recherches sur les ossemens fossiles de quadrupèdes*, vol. 1 (Paris: G. Dufour et E. d'Ocagne, 1821), iv.

28. Friedrich Schlegel, *Über die Sprache und Weisheit der Indier: Ein Beitrag zur Begründung der Alterthumskunde: Nebst metrischen Uebersetzungen indischer Gedichte* (Heidelberg: Mohr und Zimmer, 1808), 28.

29. Friedrich Schlegel and Dorothy M. Figueira, "The Politics of Exoticism and Friedrich Schlegel's 'Metaphorical Pilgrimage to India,'" *Monatshefte* 81, no. 4 (1989): 429.

30. Schlegel, *Über die Sprache*, 41–2, 51.

31. Geoffrey Galt Harpham, "Roots, Races, and the Return to Philology," *Representations* 106, no. 1 (2009): 43.

32. Grimm Jacob, *Deutsche Grammatik*, vol. 1 (Göttingen: Dieterichschen Buchhandlung, 1819), vii.

33. Hoenigswald, "History of the Comparative Method," 62.

34. Friedrich Max Mueller, *Lectures on the Science of Language . . .*, 2nd series (London: Longmans, Green, and Co., 1862), 327.

35. Ernst Haeckel, *Natürliche Schöpfungsgeschichte: Gemeinverständliche wissenschaftliche Vorträge . . .* (Berlin: G. Reimer, 1870), 65.

36. Ernst Haeckel, *The History of Creation; or, The Development of the Earth and its Inhabitants by the Action of Natural Causes*, trans. E. Ray Lankester, vol. 2 (London: King, 1876), 301.
37. B. Ricardo Brown, *Until Darwin, Science, Human Variety and the Origins of Race* (London: Pickering & Chatto, 2010).
38. Franz Boas and Immigration Commission, *Changes in Bodily Form of Descendants of Immigrants* (Washington, DC: Gov. Print. Off., 1910).
39. Karl Marx, *Grundrisse: Foundations of a Critique of Political Economy*, ed. Martin Nicolaus, vol. 1 (New York: Penguin, 1993), 85.
40. Ibid.
41. In what is likely a reference to a famous discussion of dialects at the opening of Walter Scott's *Ivanhoe*, Marx notes that English has two terms for the notion of value: "value" itself and "worth," observing that this "is quite in accordance with the spirit of a language that likes to use a Teutonic word for the actual thing, and a Romance word for its reflection." Ibid., 126 n. 4.
42. Ibid., 90–2.
43. Ibid., 102.
44. It is not clear whether Marx ever studied Goethe's *Metamorphosis* directly, though he was well aware of his literary work. Yet his famous "inversion" of Hegel's dialectic should be seen as restoring Goethe's physiological and vitalist emphasis.
45. Gavin Budge, *Romantic Empiricism: Poetics and the Philosophy of Common Sense, 1780–1830* (Lewisburg, PA: Bucknell University Press, 2007).
46. Hensleigh Wedgwood, *A Dictionary of English Etymology*, vol. 1 (London: Trübner, 1859), ii.
47. Stephen G. Alter, *Darwinism and the Linguistic Image: Language, Race, and Natural Theology in the Nineteenth Century* (Baltimore, MD: Johns Hopkins University Press, 2011).
48. Charles Darwin, *On the Origin of Species by Means of Natural Selection* (London: Murray, 1859), 422.
49. Griffiths, *Age of Analogy*, Ch. 5.
50. Darwin, *Origin of Species*, 50
51. Adrian J. Desmond and James R. Moore, *Darwin's Sacred Cause: How a Hatred of Slavery Shaped Darwin's Views on Human Evolution* (Boston, MA: Houghton Mifflin Harcourt, 2009); Evelleen Richards, *Darwin and the Making of Sexual Selection* (Chicago, IL: University of Chicago Press, 2017).
52. S. Pearl Brilmyer, "Darwinian Feminisms," in *Gender: Matter*, ed. Stacy Alaimo (Farmington Hills, MI: Macmillan, 2017), 19–34.
53. Sylvia Wynter, "The Ceremony Found: Towards the Autopoetic Turn/Overturn, Its Autonomy of Human Agency and Extraterritoriality of (Self-)Cognition," in *Black Knowledges/Black Struggles: Essays in Critical*

Epistemology, ed. Jason R. Ambroise and Sabine Broeck (Liverpool: Liverpool University Press, 2015), 184–245; Eva Hayward, "Spider City Sex," *Women & Performance* 20, no. 3 (2010): 225–51.
54. Fredric Jameson, *The Political Unconscious: Narrative as a Socially Symbolic Act* (Ithaca, NY: Cornell University Press, 1981).
55. Quoted in Ralph Colp, "The Contacts Between Karl Marx and Charles Darwin," *Journal of the History of Ideas* 35, no. 2 (1974): 329–30.
56. Marx, *Capital*, vol. 1, 493 n. 4.
57. Louis Althusser, *Reading Capital* (London: Verso, 2016); Richard Dawkins, *The Selfish Gene* (Oxford: Oxford University Press, 2016).
58. Griffiths, "Comparative Method," 497.
59. Jason W. Moore, *Capitalism in the Web of Life: Ecology and the Accumulation of Capital* (New York: Verso, 2015); Andreas Malm, *Fossil Capital: The Rise of Steam-Power and the Roots of Global Warming* (New York: Verso, 2016); Anna Lowenhaupt Tsing, *The Mushroom at the End of the World: On the Possibility of Life in Capitalist Ruins* (Princeton, NJ: Princeton University Press, 2017); Donna Haraway, *Staying with the Trouble: Making Kin in the Chthulucene* (Durham, NC: Duke University Press, 2016).
60. Haraway, *Staying with the Trouble*, 50.

5

Language and the Mapping of the World: Nineteenth-Century Linguistics in Relation to Ethnology and Geography

Floris Solleveld

Introduction

Banished from Spain, and surrounded by a diaspora of Jesuits exiled from the Spanish dominions, Lorenzo Hervás y Panduro set himself to mapping the languages of the world. He did so as part of a twenty-one-volume encyclopedic treatise, *Idea dell'Universo* (1778–87), of which the section on languages fills volumes XVII–XXI; the other main sections are "the life of man" and "the elements of cosmography." Hervás's linguistic compendium was thus part of a larger anthropological–cosmological project in which educational curricula, human anatomy, the history of the earth and its inhabitants, and an "ecstatic journey" through the heavens (à la Galileo) were followed by a catalogue of all known languages, a comparative vocabulary, and a collection of 300 translations of the Lord's Prayer.

An important part of Hervás's information, especially about Latin America and the Philippines, came from the Jesuit exile community.[1] They not only provided him with rare grammars, vocabularies, translations of

Bible segments, and catechisms printed at missionary presses *in situ*, and with working manuscripts of the same, but also committed to writing their knowledge at his request. Some grammars were reconstructed from memory decades after last contact with native speakers;[2] more stable information came from other exile Jesuit scholars like Francesco Clavigero, author of a history of Mexico, and Felipe Gilij and his *Saggio di Storia Americana* (1780). Underneath its attempted uniformity, Hervás's compendium was an epistemic hodgepodge, and both more and less of an original work than it pretended to be.

In the same years as Hervás, Catherine II of Russia developed an interest in the languages of her empire and beyond, which grew into a standardized survey. A questionnaire with 427 substantives and sixteen numerals was sent out through her dominions and to foreign embassies, and a call published in French and German. Berlin publisher and leading *Aufklärer* Friedrich Nicolai provided her with a list of languages and a bibliography; as an editor she selected the German naturalist Peter Simon Pallas, who had explored large swathes of Siberia in her service, but who showed little enthusiasm for the task.[3] The result, *Linguarum totius orbis vocabularia comparativa* (1786–89), entirely in Cyrillic except for a short Latin foreword, was nothing else than a list of 273 "root words" and the numbers 1–10, 100, 1000 in 200 languages without any attention to grammar, for which one of the rare reviews duly criticized it.[4] The second edition (1790–91), by educational reformer Teodor Janković de Mirievo, added further to the number of words and languages and reshuffled their arrangement without comment. Still, the project gave incontrovertible evidence of the massive linguistic diversity within the Russian Empire and collated the meager bits of available information about the languages of Sub-Saharan Africa, while the questionnaire, relegated by Lafayette to Washington, stimulated language study in North America.[5]

Hervás and Pallas stand out as early compilers of large data collections in the comparative study of languages. As such, their work can be seen as part of the wider geographic, naturalistic, ethnographic, and linguistic "mapping of the world," a process that coincided with European colonial expansion and that depended upon the resources of empire as well as upon the reports of—and materials collected by—explorers, missionaries, and colonial administrators. As part of this process, between the late eighteenth and early twentieth century, hundreds of American, African, Asian, Australian, and Oceanic languages that Western scholars had previously only known fragmentarily if at all were studied and classified within the emerging language sciences. Comparative vocabularies and comparative grammars arranged languages into larger families; language atlases literally put these languages and language families on the map, in different colors; and as these classifications turned into administrative realities, ethnic-linguistic identities were cemented, changed, or even created.[6]

This chapter discusses three interrelated aspects of that process: (1) how linguistic information was reformulated as abstracted and decontextualized *data*; (2) the use of language material as a *specimen* representing a linguistic and ethnic species; and (3) the *intersection* of language study with other disciplines. The aim of this is to show how the language sciences, and by implication the humanities, were part of the larger global history of knowledge. Rather than taking disciplinary formations as a starting point, we look at how information travels, both across the globe and between different areas of expertise. The first section, "Language as data," investigates how various kinds of "data" were linked to different research agendas and epistemologies. The second section, "Language as a specimen," discusses the ambivalences in how non-Western languages and their speakers were perceived through the lens of linguistic collection and comparison. Finally, the third section, "The natural history of language," reassesses the position of linguistics in the history of the humanities and sciences.

Both *data* and *specimen* are terms used regularly by nineteenth-century authors, also in relation to language material. The main difference is that *data* is literally a "given," something that can be modeled, rearranged, and quantified, whereas a *specimen* is something to be preserved, which stands as a *pars pro toto* for a species (language, culture) at large. Though the terms were sometimes used interchangeably, and language materials often served both roles at once, data and specimens require different kinds of interpretation and levels of understanding. Also, the connotations are different: "data" stems from mathematics and experimental physics, "specimen" from natural history (though there is also a wider early modern usage of the term "data" in history and even in theology).[7] In face of rapid language death and cultural destruction, much language gathering was salvage work and was perceived as such; it is in this sense that the term "specimens" was used for Lancelot Threlkeld's *Specimens of a Dialect of the Aborigines of New South Wales* (1834), the first extensive documentation of an Australian Aboriginal language, and for Wilhelm Bleek's and Lucy Lloyd's *Specimens of Bushman Folklore* (1911), a selection from a much larger archive of 138 notebooks filled with oral literature in the by then extinct /

Xam language of the Western Cape.[8] That archive is now registered as UNESCO Memory of the World, and narrowly escaped destruction in the 2021 fire at UCT Library.

The guiding question, throughout this article, is what happens to language as it becomes an object of study. What kinds of transformations does it undergo in being registered, classified, and transmitted? We are talking here both about "language" in the abstract and about concrete languages as means of communication. It is a cliché in the history and philosophy of science that to study something is to change it, and that observation is always theory-laden. But the results of colonial expansion were more than theoretical: many indigenous languages did not survive it, together with the peoples that spoke them and/or their cultures. Unwritten languages were put to writing but rarely used as languages of instruction or administration, and speakers subsumed under larger ethnolinguistic and racial classifications. On the level of method, the study of languages with different sounds and structures than those of Indo-European and Semitic languages gave rise to linguistic typology, morphology, and phonetics. On a material level, mapping languages entailed the production and collection of different kinds of language material—a technical term for basically any form of written, printed, or phonographic registration—as well as the repurposing of various kinds of texts *as* language material.

Such collections of language material, and the resulting overviews, are the most important primary sources about the process of mapping the world's languages. Table 5.1 lists nine major collections of original (manuscript or locally printed) material that have been preserved from the late eighteenth to early twentieth century; other collections have been dispersed, destroyed, or otherwise not preserved.[9] Together with a larger number of catalogues of languages, language atlases, and comparative grammars of non-European languages, they allow us to trace the evolution from late Enlightenment encyclopedic projects like Hervás's and Pallas's via the development of specialized linguistic scholarship to large-scale surveys like George Grierson's *Linguistic Survey of India* (11 in 20 vols, 1903–28) and Franz Boas's *Handbook of American Indian Languages* (2+2 vols, 1911–22, 1933–8). While the aims, means, and methods changed, the intersection of language study with ethnology and geography, but also with philology, natural history, and physical anthropology was a constant feature, as we will see in the following sections.

Table 5.1 Main collections of language material, late eighteenth to early twentieth century

Compiler(s)	Region	Period	Current location
Lorenzo Hervás y Panduro	Global (mainly Latin America)	1770s–1805	Rome: Vatican Archives / Archives of the Jesuit Order
William Marsden	South East Asia	1770s–1836	London: SOAS / King's College
Julius Klaproth	Asia	1800s–1835	Paris: Bibliothèque Nationale / Bibliothèque Mazarine London: British Library
Peter Stephen du Ponceau John Pickering	North America	1810s–1840s	Philadelphia: American Philosophical Society
Wilhelm von Humboldt (1) Eduard Buschmann (2)	Global	1800s–1835 (1) 1835–80 (2)	Berlin: Staatsbibliothek (1,2) Krakow: Jagellionian Library (1)
George Grey (1, 2, 3) Wilhelm Bleek (2, 3) Lucy Lloyd (3)	Australia (1) Polynesia (2) Southern Africa (3)	1837–45 (1) 1845–1860s (2) 1851–78 (3)	Destroyed (1) Auckland: Central City Library (2) Cape Town: National Library / University of Cape Town (3)
Karl Berendt Daniel Garrison Brinton	Central America	1853–76	Philadelphia: Penn Libraries
George Grierson	British India	1880s–1928	London: British Library
Franz Boas	North America	1880s–1942	Philadelphia: American Philosophical Society

Language as Data

As most of the "blank spaces" on European maps were filled, a similar thing happened with languages. Hervás, in the 1780s, counted 300 languages; two decades later, Johann Christoph Adelung and Johann Severin Vater provided samples of almost 500 in *Mithridates, oder allgemeine Sprachenkunde* (4 in 6 vols, 1806–19); in 1826, Adriano Balbi's *Atlas ethnographique du Globe* went to 860. The link to geography was often direct: Sigismund Koelle's *Polyglotta Africana* (1854) contains a language map of West Africa made by Ernst Petermann of the Royal Geographical Society, while Heinrich Barth, who would later scrutinize Koelle's findings in his own *Collection of Vocabularies of Central-African Languages* (1862–6), reported word lists, observations, and coordinates from his West African explorations in his letters to Europe, published in the first issue of *Petermanns geographische Mitteilungen*.[10] Koelle's atlas is a remarkable source because it gives a glimpse of the human stories behind large data collections, and a clear insight into how that data was collected and how languages became points on a map. Koelle's informants in Freetown (Sierra Leone), where he was teaching at the missionary Fourah Bay College, had mainly been brought there by the British Navy from intercepted slave ships in the decades following the 1807 ban on the transatlantic slave trade. Koelle's introduction sums up short accounts of their lives and home region before enslavement, on the basis of which Koelle and Petermann located the 156 different languages (in Koelle's counting) that they originally had spoken.[11]

Most of the compilers of language atlases and other overviews were avowed empiricists, in the sense that they professed to shun theoretical speculation and would rather let the data speak for itself. With the exception of Koelle and Barth, most of them did not get their data from direct observation—what they did instead was to bring it under a common denominator. Johann Christoph Adelung, the Dresden librarian and lexicographer whose works helped define modern standard German before he set to collecting more Lord's Prayers than Hervás, provides the most outspoken example of this anti-theoretical stance, taking his distance from the eighteenth-century debate about the origin of language:

> I have no favourite opinion, no supporting hypothesis, but instead based my judgement directly on what is, without bothering about what could be, or should be. I do not derive all languages from one; Noah's Ark is a closed castle to me, and Babylon's rubble remains at rest.[12]

One hundred and twenty years later, in the introduction to the *Linguistic Survey of India*, George Grierson made the same point in declaring the Survey "a collection of facts not of theories"—while making the important proviso that "The languages had to be arranged in some order or other, and this necessitated grouping, and grouping necessitated the adoption of theories as to relationship."[13] Grouping languages into families and clusters was indeed a judgment that even the most professedly neutral compilers could not avoid making, even when, like Adriano Balbi and Robert Needham Cust, they were self-avowedly not linguistic experts and tended to follow the expert judgment of others.

But there were different kinds of empiricism, with different kinds of related scholarly personalities (*personae*). A crucial distinction is between scholars that compiled their data at a distance like Adelung and Hervás, and those that had worked *in situ*. Hervás was a Newtonian popularizer who sought to reconcile science and faith, and who has been described as a representative of the Spanish "Universalist Enlightenment" (as well as of the Spanish Counter-Enlightenment, on account of his reaction to the French Revolution).[14] Balbi, who arranged 860 languages in a hierarchical series of overview tables, was an erstwhile professor of geography and a pioneer of social statistics, for whom mapping languages was the most unambiguous way of distinguishing different populations. Julius Klaproth, by contrast, was an idiosyncratic autodidact who traveled as far as Irkutsk and Tbilisi and acquired around a dozen languages (including Chinese, Japanese, Uyghur, and Manchu)—and who, accordingly, laid great value on autopsy. Still, to a larger extent than Klaproth was willing to acknowledge, the comparative vocabularies in his grand overview *Asia Polyglotta* (1823) were drawn from Pallas.[15] George Grey, who built both a massive corpus of Maori oral literature and a unique collection of Polynesian and Southern African (Khoisan and Bantu) language material in his capacity as governor of New Zealand (1845–53, 1861–8) and the Cape Colony (1854–61), fits within a category that Martin Müller has called "scholar-administrators," motivated by enlightened values, colonial interests, and career considerations.[16] An acute observer and avid collector with no inclination to systematize, Grey made an odd couple with German philologist Wilhelm Bleek, whom he hired to be his librarian in Cape Town, and who used Grey's collections to identify sound shifts and prefix structures in Bantu languages (a name he coined) as well as to hypothesize wildly about cross-family relations and the origins of language. Bleek and Grey worked together surprisingly well, but in other cases there were conflicts over who was the expert that were also clashes of personality.

The formation of linguistics as a discipline and the mapping of the languages of the world are parallel processes that intersect but do not wholly overlap. Until the end of the nineteenth century, discipline formation in the language sciences centered around high-prestige languages with a rich written corpus: Germanic and Romance languages, Sanskrit, and to a lesser extent, Semitic languages and Chinese. Only few trained linguists and philologists until the rise of the late nineteenth-century "neogrammarians" concerned themselves with low-prestige languages, and of these, most held no chair. As the discipline crystallized and means of notation and analysis became increasingly specialized and arcane, the gap between missionary or colonial language-gatherers and professionals grew, not to mention the gap between a language as known to its speakers and as an object of study. While there are early examples of trained experts engaging in what could be called linguistic fieldwork, beginning with Richard Lepsius on his Egyptian-Nubian expedition of 1842–4,[17] the general division of labor was rather that experts set standards, put their stamp of approval, and used the data for further theorizing.

Accordingly, what kind of data were compiled and what counted as valid evidence was subject to change. In general the data fell into three categories: vocabularies, grammars (or grammatical notes), and sample texts. The Lord's Prayer, with its simple vocabulary and broad liturgical use, was an early standard sample text from Conrad Gessner's *Mithridates de differentiis Linguarum* (1555) to Adelung and Vater's eponymous *Mithridates*; but upon taking over the project after Adelung's death, Vater judged it not the most suitable sample, and continued with it just for the sake of consistency.[18] Comparative vocabularies were the most frequently used type of data, relatively easy to assemble and analyse; they are found not just in linguistic overviews but in travel accounts, chorographies, and reports of botanical expeditions. The broader the lexical and geographical range they covered, however, the more they became unwieldy, like the tables in Klaproth's *Asia Polyglotta* and Koelle's *Polyglotta Africana* covering hundreds of words in hundreds of languages. Grierson's *Survey*, initiated in the 1880s, brought together three types of data for (ideally) each language of British India: (1) a translation of a standard sample text, the fable of the prodigal son; (2) an original text or narrative, if possible in the vernacular alphabet, transliterated and translated; and (3) a list of 241 words and short phrases. With its maps drawn from the Geographic Survey of India paired to statistics from the decennial Census, and its phonetic notation supplemented by audio recordings on wax cylinders, Grierson's *Survey* is the most complete and dense outcome of this genre of linguistic colonial knowledge production; and yet it was by and large coordinated from Grierson's house in Surrey after his retirement from the Indian Civil Service, using the network and resources of his former employer but avoiding official affiliations.[19]

The greatest change in the (re)formulation of linguistic data was in the use of phonetic alphabets and of diagrams mapping sound systems, i.e., which sounds are meaningfully distinguished within a language and which are nearest to it. In both regards, Richard Lepsius's *Standard Alphabet* (1854/63) marks a watershed. It represented a new level of descriptive accuracy not only on account of the number (>200) and taxonomy of sounds identified, but also on account of its application to a growing number of unwritten languages and non-Western (mainly ancient) writing systems.[20] Thus, using it became a token of professionalism. In the second English edition (1863), the presentation of Lepsius's alphabet amounted to a catalogue of languages of the world, with text samples and diagrams of sound systems; by that time, it had already been applied with some modifications by Koelle, Bleek, and Barth, as well as endorsed by most of the Protestant missionary societies.[21] Still, in spite of considerable institutional support, it failed to set a lasting standard, and was eventually eclipsed by successive versions of the International Phonetic Alphabet.

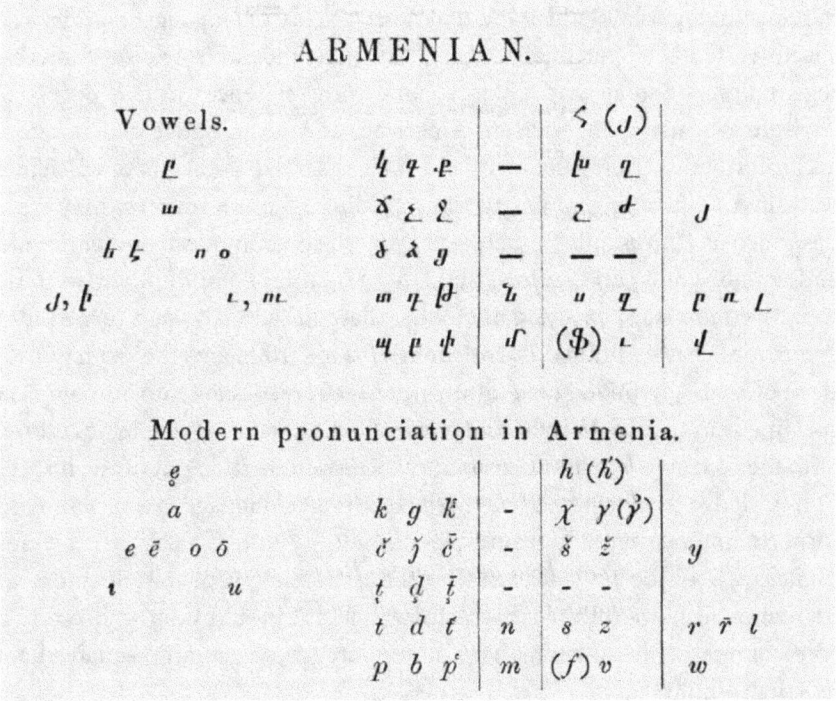

Figure 5.1 The Standard Alphabet applied to Armenian, from the second edition of Lepsius's *Standard Alphabet* (1863).

One could regard ethnolinguistic compilations, and especially comparative vocabularies, as an early example of "big data" in the humanities. What justifies this anachronistic term is not just the size of these collections but also the disconnect between understanding a language and using the data to draw novel conclusions.[22] That this data was distorted by miscommunications, mishearings, and unclear distinctions between languages and dialects was known and factored in. Even so, bulk comparison made patterns of relatedness apparent without further background knowledge—but also proved susceptible to lumping and confirmation bias. The professionalization of linguistic judgment paradoxically both restricted and reinforced these latter tendencies, since the formulation of daring hypotheses and the aspiration to more general validity were part of the logic of scientification.

Language as a Specimen

While the reformulation of language material into data tends to depersonalize it, re-arranging it into tables and diagrams, the use of language material as a specimen tends to personalize it instead. Indigenous histories and myths, registrations of songs and folklore came with references to and page-size portraits of Australian, African, American, and Asian native collaborators and informants. Such references and images served as tokens of epistemic warranty; to further emphasize the reliability of these sources, they were described as ("unusually") intelligent, honest, sober, modest, and either old and wise or young and enthusiastic. There is an inherent duplicity to these narrative templates: by the same token, these individuals were turned into archetypes that embodied the wisdom of their tribe, and the depiction of these old, wise, wrinkled men (always men) rendered them into ethnological specimens in their own right and relics of a disappearing people or culture. Still, the common wisdom that native voices were written out of the history of knowledge is at best half true here. Learning a language is a very intense form of interaction and cannot be achieved (unlike taking someone's photograph or bodily measures) without treating your interlocutors as human beings, even if the reasons for which one would want to do so in a (pre)colonial context—missionary, administrative, or scientific—made them less than wholly so.

These interlocutors were not generic "native speakers." Generally, they were either high-status figures—priests, chiefs, and nobles; or on the contrary, outsiders and uprooted persons; or cultural intermediaries with mixed parentage and/or Western-style education. Some of the intermediaries became investigators of their own environment, like George Hunt, who sent a regular stream of reports and artifacts from Vancouver Island to Franz Boas, or Samuel Ajahi Crowther, the first African Anglican Bishop, who wrote grammars and dictionaries of Yoruba and Nupe after receiving education at Fourah Bay College.[23] Local elites were equally making

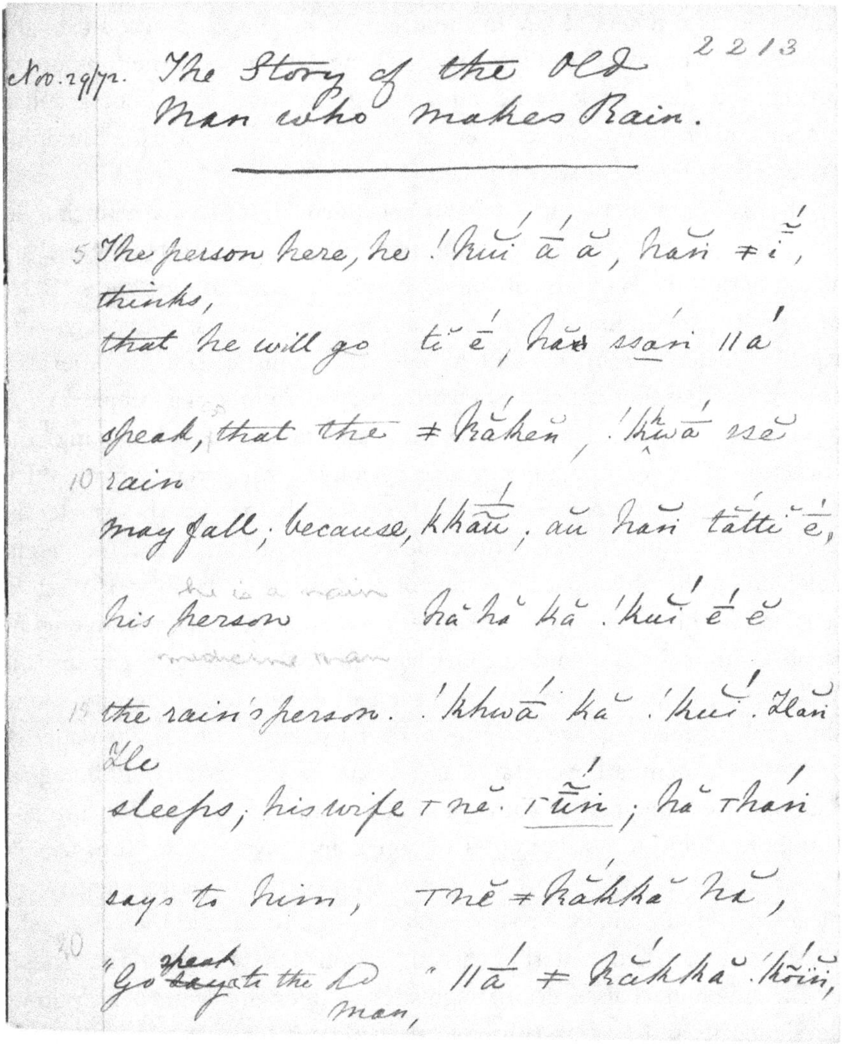

Figure 5.2 Lucy Lloyd's transcription and parallel translation of a /Xam fable, using a modified version of the Standard Alphabet. Bleek and Lloyd Collection, University of Cape Town Libraries.

investigations in return and using Europeans as informants; some traveled to Europe and wrote down their own observations, like the Mughal diplomat I'tisam al-Din, who instructed William Jones in Persian while at Oxford and translated a Persian grammar for him.[24] Finally, some uprooted persons became quite literally living specimens, like the /Xam prisoners that Wilhelm Bleek took into his home, and the Hausa boys, Dorugu and Abbega, that followed Heinrich Barth to England. With Bleek and his *Specimens of Bushman Folklore,* this is manifestly the case as he perceived Khoisan languages as a potential key to the origin of language on account of the perceived "primitivity" of their speakers. The narrators that he took out of prison and gave back some human dignity were also photographed beforehand for Thomas Huxley's empire-wide anthropological photographic project, half-dressed as well as naked.[25]

The distinction between "data" and "specimens" is somewhat artificial—as said, it was not made by nineteenth-century linguists themselves. Vocabularies like Hannah Kilham's *Specimens of African Languages* (1828) or primers like Threlkeld's *Specimens* of the Lake Macquarie language were equally labeled specimens, and so were all linguistic data for Grierson's *Survey,* whether they consisted of word lists, translations of a sample text, or original texts in each language. Still, it is a distinction worth making. The collection of longer texts, samples, and narratives provided information that was not only linguistically richer but also culturally specific. These materials could be edited and studied in the same way as classical texts and fragments, heightening the philological prestige of a language in the eyes of Western scholars. In this regard, figures like Bleek were following the example set by Jacob Grimm for the study of German: compile folklore to capture the *Volksgeist,* edit texts to study the language philologically, identify sound shifts so that the language becomes part of a science with lawlike patterns, and write a comparative grammar to expand its territory. Philological analysis itself entailed a conversion into data, as when Wilhelm von Humboldt subjected six samples of songs and myths from Tonga, New Zealand, and Tahiti to an interlinear commentary so as to identify the meaning and grammatical role of each part of a word, and then devoted a 172-page section to the interlingual comparison of these linguistic particles.[26]

The philological dissection of linguistic specimens made use of techniques developed in and acquired through the study of high-prestige languages, and a typical line of argument for the study of these specimens involved comparisons with such languages, especially Sanskrit. Humboldt started his comparative grammar of Malayo-Polynesian with a commentary on the

Brata Yudha, a twelfth-century Old Javanese adaptation of a section of the Indian epos *Mahabharata* in a courtly language full of Sanskrit loan words; Bleek argued that the study of Bantu and Khoisan languages would be of equal importance to the science of language as the study of Sanskrit; Horatio Hale edited the *Iroquois Book of Rites* and compared it to the Vedas on account of its conservation in oral literature.[27] Clearly, such arguments were double-edged as well, since the comparison to ancient models also reinforced extant linguistic hierarchies and emphasized the archaic nature of oral traditions.

Like botanical specimens that are dried, pressed, and pasted into an album or drawn "true to nature," then, these linguistic specimens were edited and dissected so as to represent language as a living organism. The analogy with botany went further than that. Ever since Friedrich Schlegel's *Über die Sprache und Weisheit der Indier* (1808), which divided all languages into "organic" inflecting ones and "mechanical" agglutinating and isolating ones, German linguists had been obsessed with language as an organism. But this "organism" was described in highly divergent ways: analogous to Cuvier's comparative anatomy (Schlegel), following "organic rules" rather than strict laws (Grimm), as an *energeia* rather than an *ergon* (Humboldt), with references to Kant's third Critique or Schelling's Romantic-Idealist *Naturphilosophie,* or as part of the natural history of mankind (Schleicher). The analogy was more than theoretical. Many specimens had indeed been gathered by botanists, both for the practical reason of gathering information from the local inhabitants, and in order to classify them ethnologically, as Joseph Banks and Reinhold Forster did on Cook's expeditions in the Pacific, and Carl von Martius and Alcide d'Orbigny on their South American explorations in the 1810s to 1820s.[28] Schlegel, moreover, had derived the distinction between inflecting and agglutinating languages from studying missionary grammars procured from Latin America by naturalist/geographer Alexander von Humboldt. The same specimens that were used for philological dissection could also be materials for the natural history of man, as evidence of human descent and migrations.

The Natural History of Language

The intersections of nineteenth-century linguistics with botany, and with ethnology, geography, philology, and physical anthropology, raise questions about its position within the history of the humanities. Then as now, the science of language was and is something of a *Fremdkörper*. Nowadays, it is uneasily located in either the humanities or social sciences, as a data-driven science with a high degree of formalization (as well as, in some fields, laboratories), practiced both in departments of general linguistics and in various "languages and literatures" departments. It has been argued that the shift from botanical analogies to mathematical jargon and computer analogies reflects a shift in scientific hierarchies in the twentieth century, from natural history to STEM.[29]

What is conspicuous in the positioning of nineteenth-century linguistics is not only how knowledge migrates between different disciplines but also how disciplines are defined in interrelation. It is telling that the term *linguistique* was introduced into French by an Italian geographer, Adriano Balbi, in the introduction to his *Atlas ethnographique du Globe*.[30] What domain designations like "linguistics" indicated, initially, was less an institutional domain than an area of expertise; in Balbi's case, the expertise of others to which he deferred. In the same vein, Barth refused to engage in speculation about linguistic affinities from his standpoint as a "geographer and ethnographer," and Boas's first expedition to Baffin Land was conceived as a geographical project.[31]

One could view language atlases and similar overviews as a variety of the scientific "atlases" discussed in Daston and Galison's *Objectivity* (2007): as synoptic presentations of the state of knowledge within a certain field.[32] At the same time, most nineteenth/early twentieth-century compilers of these overviews were not linguists/philologists by training or profession, and those that were consistently extended their judgment to other areas of expertise. Horatio Hale's overview of the languages of Polynesia and the Oregon territory was part of his volume on *Ethnography and Philology* for the report of the United States Exploring Expedition (1838–42); likewise, Friedrich Müller furnished both the linguistic and the ethnographic volumes for the Austrian-Hungarian *Novara* expedition (1857–59), though without having taken part in it. Paradoxically, expert judgment tended to reinforce as well as to flout disciplinary boundaries—asserting them in collecting, correcting, reformulating, and synthesizing earlier work of others while ignoring such arbitrary demarcations for oneself. Moreover, expert judgment was a double-edged sword; it built upon training, observation, and accumulated data but entailed inscrutable authority and far-fetched hypotheses.

The most problematic intersection of different fields, from a moral point of view, is between nineteenth-century ethnolinguistics and scientific racism.

Lepsius, for instance, stands out as one of the authors of the "Hamitic" hypothesis, which traces Berber, Egyptian, and Ethiopian languages to a conquering *Herrenvolk* with presumed origins outside Africa.[33] Such ideas were not simply "a product of their time"; rather, nineteenth-century linguistic scholars were active participants in a debate with conflicting positions, with the common denominator that all presupposed a racial hierarchy that descended from white to black.[34] The attempt to align linguistic genealogies with "hard" biological fact served not only for corroboration but also as a way of going beyond surface phenomena and refuting (or scientifically underpinning) Biblical narratives. Before the advent of Darwinism, the growing insight into the structural differences between language families was used as an argument for polygenism, i.e., the idea that human races have different origins.[35] At the same time, however, skepticism about the specifics of racial theories and the number of distinct "races" were a recurrent feature in linguistic and ethnographic works.[36]

Two shortcomings of linguistic-racial classification were clear to anyone concerned: first, languages and peoples as units never fully overlapped, since people migrated, intermarried, spoke several languages, and adopted the language of dominant groups; and second, skin color was an unreliable designator, since it was a continuum rather than a neat division, and since it was contingent upon climate and other external factors. The second point could also be made with regard to physical proportions. An alternative that now seems comical was suggested by Austrian linguist Friedrich Müller, who instead based his classification of the world's languages upon a distinction between human races by hair types (straight hair, locks, wooly plucks, wooly fleece), presumably a more clear-cut distinction than skin color or skull shape. Although he cited the authority of Geoffroy Saint-Hilaire and Ernst Haeckel on this point, the typology is Müller's own. Figure 5.3 shows how Müller further subdivided these four types into twelve races with up to a hundred independent *Ursprachen*. Separating human races before the advent of language, Müller's purportedly "monogenetic" theory amounted to a second-order polygenism, and was duly criticized by Lepsius, from whom Müller had drawn most of his data, for making too many unnecessary assumptions.[37]

In the early twentieth century, with the birth of cultural anthropology, there is a shift from "race" to "culture" in the study of indigenous languages. The most prominent example of this is Franz Boas, who used anthropometry to destabilize racial classifications and replaced schematic overviews with thick descriptions of individual languages for the *Handbook of American*

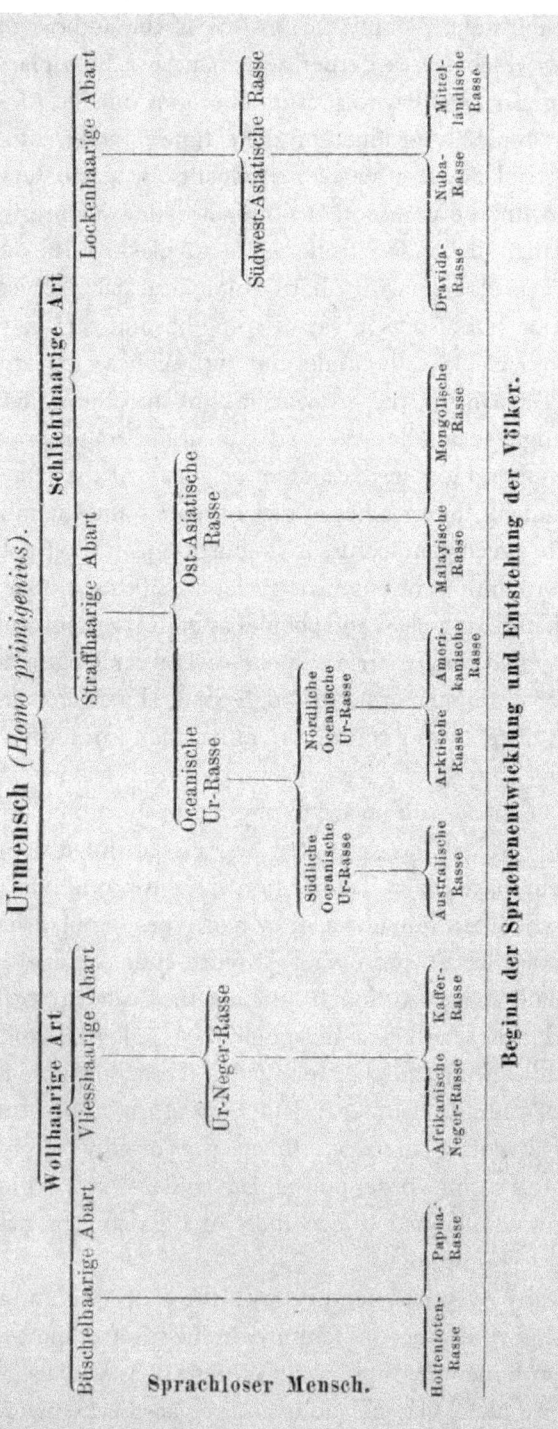

Figure 5.3 Pedigree chart of human races, from Müller, *Allgemeine Ethnograpie* (1872).

Indian Languages.³⁸ In sending out his assistants and PhD students to supply such thick descriptions, Boas established a professional model with fieldwork as a *rite de passage* that still obtains. The rise of linguistic structuralism in the early twentieth century was a further factor in the shift from "race" to "culture." Structuralism emphasized the synchronic description of autonomous "systems of signs" rather than diachronic processes and genealogies; an approach to which questions of race and origins were all but irrelevant and that, in turn, had a formative influence on the further development of cultural anthropology.

These developments did not end racial theories and anthropometry, which faded from scientific discourse only after the Second World War. Nor did they end the process of mapping the world's languages, which continues to this day.³⁹ But they did by and large separate ethnolinguistics from natural history. The study of indigenous languages became a different kind of programme, a form of professional "puzzle-solving" concerned with phonetic and morphosyntactic phenomena, language universals, and systems of meaning. As the only registrations of languages no longer spoken, or of ways in which a language is no longer spoken, some nineteenth-century ethnolinguistic material continues to have actual relevance. Especially in Australia, where half the estimated 250 Aboriginal languages are extinct and most others endangered, nineteenth-century material is used in language revitalization programmes; Koelle's *Polyglotta* is a crucial source about language change in West Africa; and Bleek and Lloyd's *Specimens* have become national literary heritage in post-Apartheid South Africa. The *Linguistic Survey of India* has been used politically by British colonialists, regionalists, secular nationalists, and Hindu nationalists;⁴⁰ the Indian government undertook several attempts to expand and revise it, the last one stalled in 2010.

While less spectacular than nineteenth-century ethnological collections, maps, botanical gardens, and natural history museums, collections of language material belong to the same knowledge infrastructure and should be studied in conjunction with these. They are sources not only about languages but also about imperial history, about global trajectories as well as about local encounters, about colonial domination as much as about indigenous culture and oral history. These different aspects cannot be wholly disentangled and from a historical perspective they shouldn't. The provenance of linguistic and ethnological material teaches us not to treat "knowledge" as a timeless notion or "data" as a given, but to see them as parts of history with a history of their own.

Notes

1. Nicolás Hernán Perrone, "Una mirada a la comunidad de jesuitas americanos expulsos a través de las obras de Lorenzo Hervás y Panduro S.J. (1735–1809)," *História Unisinos* 16, no. 1 (2012): 106–17.
2. Hervás, "Elementi gramaticali della Lingua Betoi" [communicated by Dom Giuseppe Padilla in letters from Pergola, 17 July and 13 September 1783] and "Elementi gramaticali della lingua Yarura" [communicated by Abbate Don Giuseppe Maria Formeri in a letter from Loreto, 6 August 1783]; transcripts in Staatsbibliothek Berlin, Coll.ling.quart 31 ("Grammatiken und Wortverzeichnisse mehrer amerikanischen Sprachen").
3. A description and documents of the genesis and contents of the project are in Friedrich von Adelung, *Catherinens der Grossen Verdienste um die vergleichende Sprachenkunde* (St. Petersburg: Drechsler, 1815); cf. Sylvie Archaimbault, "Peter Simon Pallas (1741–1811), un naturaliste parmi les mots," *Histoire épistemologie langage* 32, no. 1 (2010): 69–91; Folkwart Wendland, *Peter Simon Pallas (1741–1811): Materialien einer Biographie*, vol. 1 (Berlin: Walter de Gruyter 1992), 491–504.
4. Christian Jakob Kraus, [review of] "Vergleichendes Glossarium aller Sprachen und Mundarten," *Allgemeine Literatur-Zeitung* 235–7 (1787): 1–29.
5. Edward Gray, *New World Babel: Languages and Nations in Early America* (Princeton, NJ: Princeton University Press, 1999), 112; Sean Harvey, *Native Tongues: Colonialism and Race from Encounter to the Reservation* (Cambridge, MA: Harvard University Press, 2015), 56ff.
6. For the creation of linguistic identities in colonial Congo, Zimbabwe, Transvaal, and Indonesia, see Joseph Errington, *Linguistics in a Colonial World: A Story of Language, Meaning, and Power* (Basingstoke: Blackwell 2008), 107–46. His information about the language of Dutch and Belgian colonizers is grossly inaccurate, however.
7. Daniel Rosenberg, "Data before the Fact," in *"Raw Data" Is an Oxymoron*, ed. Lisa Gitelman (Cambridge, MA: MIT Press, 2013), 15–40.
8. Of a total of 182 notebooks, also in !kun and other Bushman [San] languages and partly of a later date; entirely digitized at http://lloydbleekcollection.cs.uct.ac.za/ (accessed March 9, 2022; 28 notebooks are by Bleek, 131 by Lloyd, and 32 by Bleek's daughter Dorothea). Cf. Andrew Bank, *Bushmen in a Victorian World: The Remarkable Story of the Bleek-Lloyd Collection of Bushman Folklore* (Cape Town: Double Storey, 2006).
9. Major losses are Thomas Stamford Raffles's collection of Malayan and other South East Asian manuscripts, sunk with a shipload of antiquities, plant and animal specimens, drawings, and live animals off the coast of Sumatra (1824); George Grey's first collection of Australian songs and vocabularies, destroyed

by fire (1848); and Horatio Hale's Polynesian, Melanesian, and Native American notebooks, equally largely (?) consumed by fire after his death (1896)—some notebooks remain in Sydney and in London, Ontario. Julius Klaproth's manuscripts and rare books were auctioned off by his landlady (1835) and are now scattered between London, Paris, and Berlin. Parts of Wilhelm von Humboldt's *Collectanea Linguistica* are registered as "war losses" at the Staatsbibliothek, Berlin. Most recently, the ethnolinguistic collections of the National Museum in Rio de Janeiro went up in flames (2018), including the Amazonian archives of Curt Nimuendajú (compiled 1905–45).

10. August Petermann, "Die Expedition nach Zentral-Afrika," *Petermanns geographische Mitteilungen* 1 (1855): 3–14, 85–9; Floris Solleveld, "Language Gathering and Philological Expertise: Sigismund Koelle, Wilhelm Bleek, and the Languages of Africa," in *Les linguistes allemands du XIXème siècle et leurs interlocuteurs étrangers*, ed. Jacques François (Paris: Société de Linguistique de Paris, 2020), 169–200.

11. Sigismund Koelle, *Polyglotta Africana; or, a Comparative Vocabulary of Nearly Three Hundred Words and Phrases in More than One Hundred Distinct African Languages* (London: Church Missionary House, 1854), 1–24; cf. Judith Irvine, "Subjected Words: African Linguistics and the Colonial Encounter," *Language and Communication* 28 (2008): 323–43.

12. Johann Christoph Adelung and Johann Severin Vater, *Mithridates oder allgemeine Sprachenkunde mit dem Vater Unser als Sprachprobe, in bey nahe fünf hundert Sprachen und Mundarten*, vol. 1 (Berlin: Voss, 1806), xi.

13. George Grierson, *Linguistic Survey of India*, vol. 1 (Calcutta: Govt. Printing House, 1927), 21–2; cf. Javed Majeed, *Colonialism and Knowledge in Grierson's Linguistic Survey of India* (London: Routledge, 2018).

14. Pedro Aullón de Haro and Davide Mombelli, *Introduction to the Spanish Universalist School: Enlightened Culture and Education versus Politics* (Leiden: Brill, 2020), 64–82; Carolina Armenteros, "Eclectic, Conservative, Cosmopolitan: The Linguistics and Anthropology of Lorenzo Hervás y Panduro (1753–1809)," in *Cosmopolitan Conservatisms: Countering Revolution in Transnational Networks, Ideas and Movements (c. 1700-1930)*, ed. Matthijs Lok, Friedemann Pestel, and Juliette Reboul (Leiden: Brill, 2021), 67–85.

15. Floris Solleveld, "Klaproth, Balbi, and the Language Atlas," in *History of Linguistics 2017: Selected papers from the 14th International Conference on the History of the Language Sciences (ICHoLS XIV)*, ed. Émilie Aussant and Jean-Michel Fortis (Amsterdam: John Benjamins, 2020), 81–99.

16. Martin Müller, "Manufacturing Malayness: British Debates on the Malay Nation, Civilisation, Race and Language in the Early Nineteenth Century," *Indonesia and the Malay World* 42, no. 123 (2014): 170–96, at 176.
17. Floris Solleveld, "Lepsius as a Linguist: Fieldwork, Philology, Phonetics, and the 'Hamitic Hypothesis,'" *Language and History* 63, no. 3 (2020): 193–213.
18. *Mithridates*, vol. 2, xvii.
19. Majeed, *Colonialism and Knowledge*, 50ff.
20. For the genesis and reception of the Standard Alphabet, see J. Alan Kemp's introduction to Lepsius, *Standard Alphabet for Reducing Unwritten Languages and Foreign Graphic Systems to a Uniform Orthography in European Letters*, ed. J. Alan Kemp (Amsterdam: John Benjamins, 1981 [1863]), 1*–87* and Solleveld, "Lepsius as a Linguist," 193–8, 207–9.
21. Solleveld, "Language Gathering," 178ff.
22. Cf. Thomas Trautmann, *Languages and Nations: The Dravidian Proof in Colonial Madras* (New Delhi: Yoda, 2006), 21–34.
23. Isaiah Lorado Wilner, "Friends in This World: The Relationship of George Hunt and Franz Boas," in *Franz Boas as a Public Intellectual—Theory, Ethnography, Activism*, ed. R. Darnell et al. (Franz Boas Papers I; Lincoln: University of Nebraska Press, 2015), 163–89; P. E. H. Hair, *The Early Study of Nigerian Languages* (Cambridge: Cambridge University Press, 1967).
24. I'tisam al-Din, *Shigurf Namah-i-velaët; or, Excellent Intelligence concerning Europe: being the travels of Mirza Itesa Modeen in Great Britain and France*, ed./trans. J. Alexander (London: Taylor, 1827); Kapil Raj, "Cartographier l'humanité depuis Calcutta: à propos de la théorie ethnolinguistique de Sir William Jones (1746-1794)," *Littérature* 4 (2016): 21–34, at 21–3.
25. Bank, *Bushmen in a Victorian World*, 103–27.
26. Wilhelm von Humboldt, *Über die Kawi-Sprache auf der Insel Jawa, nebst einer Einleitung über die Verschiedenheit des menschlichen Sprachbaues und ihren Einfluß auf die geistige Entwickelung des Menschengeschlechts*, ed. Joh. Carl Ed. Buschmann, vol. 3 (Berlin: Königliche Akademie der Wissenschaften, 1839), 524–695. (From p. 596 onwards the author is Buschmann, as marked in the text.)
27. Humboldt, *Kawi-Sprache* vol. I, cccxxxviii–cccxli; Bleek, *A Comparative Grammar of the South African Languages*, vol. 1 (London: Trübner, 1862), i–ix; Horatio Hale, *The Iroquois Book of Rites* (Philadelphia, PA: Brinton, 1883), 37.
28. Johann Reinhold Forster, *Observations made during a Voyage round the World* (London: Robinson 1778), 276–84; Alcide d'Orbigny, *Voyage en Amérique méridionale*, vol. 4, part 1 (Paris: Pitois-Levrault, 1839), 145–64; Carl von Martius, *Beiträge zur Ethnographie und Sprachkunde Amerika's zumal Brasiliens*, vol. 2 (Leipzig: Fleischer, 1867). Banks's vocabularies are in the SOAS Library, London, MS 12153 and 12156, originally part of Marsden's collection.

29. John Joseph, *From Whitney to Chomsky: Essays in the History of American Linguistics* (Amsterdam: John Benjamins, 2002), 47.
30. Sylvain Auroux, "The First Uses of the French Word 'Linguistique,'" in *Papers in the History of Linguistics*, ed. Hans Aarsleff, L. G. Kelly, and Hans-Joseph Niederehe (Amsterdam: John Benjamins, 1987), 447–59.
31. Heinrich Barth, *Sammlung and Bearbeitung Central-Afrikanischer Vokabularien / Collection of Vocabularies of Central-African Languages*, vol. 1 (Gotha: Justus Perthes, 1862), xxxii; Franz Boas, *Baffin-Land: Geographische Ergebnisse einer in den Jahren 1883 und 1884 ausgeführten Forschungsreise* (Gotha: Justus Perthes, 1885); cf. Michel Espagne, "Franz Boas et la Pensée géographique," in *Franz Boas: le travail du regard*, ed. Michel Espagne and Isabelle Kalinowski (Paris: Armand Colin, 2013), 77–105.
32. Lorraine Daston and Peter Galison, *Objectivity* (New York: Zone Books, 2007).
33. Peter Rohrbacher, "'Hamitische Wanderungen': Die Prähistorie Afrikas zwischen Fiktion und Realität," in *Vom Wandern der Völker: Migrationserzählungen in den Altertumswissenschaften*, ed. Felix Wiedemann, Kerstin P. Hofmann, and Hans-Joachim Gehrke (Berlin: Topoi, 2017), 249–82; cf. Michael Robinson, *The Lost White Tribe: Explorers. Scientists, and the Theory that Changed a Continent* (Oxford: Oxford University Press, 2016).
34. Markus Messling, *Gebeugter Geist: Rassismus und Erkenntnis in der modernen europäischen Philologie* (Göttingen: Wallstein, 2016).
35. George Stocking, *Victorian Anthropology* (New York: Macmillan, 1987), 68; Gareth Knapman, "Race, Polygenesis and Equality: John Crawfurd and Nineteenth-Century Resistance to Evolution," *History of European Ideas* 42, no. 7 (2016): 909–23.
36. E.g., Julius Klaproth, "Fragments sur les races et sur les langues de l'ancien et du nouveau continent," in *Mémoires relatifs à l'Asie: contenant des recherches historiques, géographiques et philologiques sur les peuples de l'Orient*, vol. 2 (Paris: Dondey-Dupré, 1826), 1–54; Friedrich Max Müller, "The Last Results of the Researches respecting the Non-Iranian and Non-Semitic Languages of Asia and Europe, or the Turanian Family of Languages," in Christian Carl Josias von Bunsen, *Outlines of the Philosophy of Universal History, Applied to Language and Religion*, vol. 1 (London: Longman, Brown, Green, and Longmans, 1854), 263–521, at 349–53; William Dwight Whitney, *Language and the Study of Language: Twelve Lectures on the Principles of Linguistic Science* (London: Trübner, 1867), 370ff.
37. Friedrich Müller, *Grundriß der Sprachwissenschaft*, vol. 1 (Vienna: Hölder, 1876), 71–8; R. Lepsius, *Nubische Grammatik, mit einer Einleitung über die Völker und Sprachen Afrikas* (Berlin: Wilhelm Hertz, 1880), iv–v, lxx–lxxi; cf. Ernst Haeckel, *Natürliche Schöpfungsgeschichte: Gemeinverständliche wissenschaftliche Vorträge* . . . (Berlin: Georg Reimer, 1868), 513ff.

38. Charles King, *Gods of the Upper Air: How a Circle of Renegade Anthropologists Reinvented Race, Sex, and Gender in the Twentieth Century* (New York: Doubleday, 2019), Ch. 5; Martha Hodes, "Utter Confusion and Contradiction: Franz Boas and the Problem of Human Complexion," in *Indigenous Visions: Rediscovering the World of Franz Boas*, ed. Ned Blackhawk and Isaiah Lorado Wilner (New Haven, CT: Yale University Press, 2018), 185–208.
39. See *Atlas of the World's Languages*, ed. Ronald Asher and Christopher Mosely (London: Routledge, 2007 [1993]) and the online databases *Ethnologue* and *Glottolog*.
40. Javed Majeed, *Nation and Region in Grierson's* Linguistic Survey of India (London: Routledge, 2018).

6

"Big"-ness in Action: Notes from a Lexicon

Christian Flow

Introduction

Despite an early affinity for the "exalted image" of "the lone scientist in pursuit of truth," the American physicist and Manhattan Project alumnus Robert R. Wilson, like many of his colleagues, found himself part of a contrary reality.[1] "[M]y search for truth led me deep into the nucleus of the atom," wrote Wilson in an autobiographical sketch in 1970, "and it is almost as hard to reach the nucleus by oneself as it is to get to the moon by oneself."[2] By then he was head of a large government laboratory and "the compleat bureaucrat"—presiding with pleasure over "perhaps the *ne plus ultra* of team research in high energy physics."[3] The work entailed the suspension of Wilson's periodic "fight against team research" and with it the posture of the singly acting scientist. His account's wry coda—*sic transit gloria*—captures its central ambivalence: an appreciation for the moon-shooting and nucleus-splitting power of big collaboration, big apparatus, and big money, coupled with a recurrent suspicion that these trappings of "team research" came at a cost for the scientist's identity, initiative, and creativity.

Such ambivalence was not atypical for those who saw the quick rise of twentieth-century physics from a "parochial establishment" to a pursuit that could help win wars and command lavish spending.[4] By the 1950s and 1960s, practitioners were taking high energy physics alongside efforts like space exploration (see Wilson's reference to the moon) to represent a particular mode of "big" or "large-scale" research—"Big Science"—well-resourced, collaboratively conducted, and subject to some of Wilson's tensions "between the me and the us."⁵ In the decades since, "Big Science" has acquired its own literature, which has been nicely synthesized elsewhere.⁶ I will not retail it at length, but one can speak broadly of three principal, and often intertwined, lines of inquiry. The first is definitional: it looks to distill a set of attributes and implications that can be understood under the label "Big Science" (or "big science" or "large-scale science" or "team research"), as an actors' and/or an analytical category.⁷ The second moves towards a genealogy of Big Science by identifying elements of its profile prior to the post-war context in which it has lately become an object of study.⁸ The third entertains a similar shift away from the particle accelerators and lunar probes, discarding not just chronological but also disciplinary assumptions by examining "big"-ness in a wide array of knowledge-producing operations—including fields like history and philology.⁹

The present contribution is aligned most squarely with the third of these agendas. What I intend here is a short consideration of a remarkable philological project—an unprecedently comprehensive lexicon of the Latin language, begun in the late nineteenth century as a testament to German philological might and still underway in Munich today. Now as then the so-called *Thesaurus linguae Latinae* aims to deliver nothing less than a complete history of each Latin word from its first recorded usage through the sixth century CE, when Latin began to give way to the Romance languages.¹⁰ To that end, it relies on a staggering collection of evidence: an archive of millions of paper slips, each documenting a single instance of a single word. For the literature of several centuries this *Zettelarchiv* is flatly exhaustive—including every appearance of every word of every text.¹¹ It is no exaggeration to say that the lexicographers at the project's Munich Bureau, in working through the slips available for a given word, acquire a more detailed view of its scope and development than any prior researcher. So painstaking is the work, and so ample the task, that after more than 125 years, the lexicon has advanced only as far as N and R: about a third of the alphabet remains to be treated.

Was—*is*—the *Thesaurus* "Big Science"? To be sure, the effort was designated by those involved as a "big undertaking" and it was in line with what contemporary doyens of organized research identified as "big research" (*Grosswissenschaft*) and "big enterprise" (*Grossbetrieb*).¹² It had demanded by 1900 coordinated work from the five principal academies of the German-speaking world, exacted pledges of half a million marks of state money, and erected Bureau of full-time lexicographers. It was identified with a nation's scholarly preeminence, and was projected to take two decades to complete. It is quite possible here to find parallels—division of labor, state funding, publicity imperatives—to characteristics of "big"-ness advanced in other studies. But rather than engage strictly in such a matching exercise, I would like to advance a concept from James Capshew and Karen Rader, who have written of "dramas of scale" in connection with Big Science.[13] My proposal is simply to let "big"-ness here be defined by the drama—the *friction*—created by perceived disparities in scale as reported by scientists and scholars at work. Deborah Coen has called recently for a "history of scaling" that will historicize how such disparities are handled—how differently sized or weighted layers of observation and experience are reconciled—and indeed how they arise: that is, how, in given contexts, components of sensemaking come to appear differently sized in the first place.[14] Working in this line, I will present three instances of scalar friction in evidence at the *Thesaurus*, on the organizational, technological, and temporal planes, considering some of their perpetuating factors and evolving attempts at their resolution. I will close with summary thoughts about where further studies of "Big Humanities" are headed.

Big Organization

What Wilson found to be true of the nucleus—that it was hard to get there alone—applied to any number of scientific objects. That included the history of a long-dead language, a point made in the nineteenth century's final decades by a Basel-born Latinist named Eduard Wölfflin (1831–1908).[15] After ascending to an influential chair in Munich in 1880, Wölfflin took decisive steps to further an ambitious agenda—one based on comprehensive lexicographical investigation. The massive lexicon he had in mind was an operation "much bigger than is typically believed."[16] He painted a dire picture of predecessors: "one hears of philologists who have set up lexical collections for single or several authors, but then burned them in desperation," he wrote, "after realizing halfway through that the task outstripped the powers of an individual."[17] The truth was, he said, that such "huge tasks" could never be laid on the "shoulders" of single actors.[18] One did not unlock the secrets of Latin words alone.

Wölfflin had, by the early 1880s, begun to suggest ways to augment individual efforts. The mode he took up soon after arriving in Munich was a journal, the *Archiv für lateinische Lexikographie*, which he founded in 1883 to prepare for an eventual Latin *Thesaurus*. The journal was to rely on a network of over two hundred volunteers, each responsible for a portion of Latin literature. In response to a semesterly questionnaire, these volunteers would comb their assigned texts for particular words and grammatical phenomena, log them onto standardized paper slips, and send them to Wölfflin's home.[19] The result was meant to be a complete catalogue of the lexical items specified: in theory, if Wölfflin wished to witness every appearance of the word *abhorreo* (included on the third questionnaire), he could do so by consulting the citations his volunteers mailed him.[20] Wölfflin and others used the material to generate articles—published in the *Archiv*— that served as test-runs for the eventual *Thesaurus*. He touted the results: only a year after the journal's founding he credited it with helping "hundreds of philologists" learn its historical-lexicographical methods and "see with different eyes and think differently than before."[21]

Did Wölfflin perceive a friction in the *Archiv*-engineered shift of scale— from a single lexical collector to hundreds? He certainly did, and it is there, rather than per se the number of scholars involved, that we find "big"-ness in action. The fundamental problem was how to render compatible the collections of far-flung contributors. Wölfflin's solution was the regular *Archiv* questionnaire, meant to calibrate his volunteers' efforts.[22] The contributors were to have no choice in the lexical instances they noted: every occurrence of a requested word like *abhorreo* was to be taken up, without exception, so as to avoid the heterogenous material that would result if "one excerptor noted what the other passed over" based on individualistic notions of importance.[23] Still, engaging and aligning volunteers demanded hundreds of letters, not just to hector and instruct, but to maintain the personal connection that kept people involved.[24] Faced with unresponsive contributors, Wölfflin went so far as to note in the *Archiv* their delinquency—leveraging, in short, public shame as an organizational maneuver.[25] Regional politics were part of the challenge: working from the Bavarian *Hauptstadt*, Wölfflin complained of difficulty bringing in participation from Berlin.[26] The notebooks cataloguing his *Archiv* correspondence, as well as the slips and letters he received from contributors, all held at the *Thesaurus*-Bureau, are a rich source for the messy practice of administering "team research," and engaging, dispatch by dispatch, in the "scaling" it demanded.

The *Archiv*'s organizational problems paled in comparison to what would follow a decade later. Wölfflin's journal was run out of his home, initially with a small amount of Bavarian Academy financing. A full-fledged *Thesaurus* required a broader basis. The eventual arrangement, which emerged by 1893, included a new entity—the so-called "Cartel" of academies in Munich, Leipzig, Göttingen, and Vienna—in collaboration with the Berlin Academy. The Cartel and subsequent internationalization efforts have been treated by scholars like Brigitte Schroeder-Gudehus and Martin Gierl, both of whom have made clear the vexing persistence of particularist allegiances.[27] It is impossible to do succinct justice to the cacophony of interests needing to be harmonized to achieve the Cartel-plus-Berlin *Thesaurus* structure.[28] But a look at just a couple of the stakeholders indicates the difficulties. The Basel-born Wölfflin claimed to carry "republican" sentiments from his Swiss hometown and was stationed at the principal Bavarian university: neither fact predisposed him to affection for his Berlin colleagues, whom he found despotic and inflated. The rhetoric of regional rivalry ran like a red-thread through his correspondence, where he sniffed plots to make a *Thesaurus* without him and dredged up old schemes allegedly meant to drive him from his lexicographical labors so as to "pounce on the master-less inheritance with the Prussian Eagle."[29] Wölfflin had lexicographical experience and the ear of the Bavarian regime. But colleagues in Berlin disliked him personally and maligned him professionally.[30] The ancient historian Theodor Mommsen, the weightiest voice in the Berlin Academy, considered it disqualifying for the *Thesaurus* to be "Wölfflinized."[31] And the north, too, spoke the language of regional suspicion: Berlin was concerned that there not be "too much Müniching."[32] In short, the very core of the *Thesaurus*-collaboration simmered with personal and political distrust.

The problems did not end there. Each of the five academies involved needed to have the assent of their members and of the interested ministries, activating layers of complexity that were on full display in Berlin. When Mommsen set out in 1892 to gather support for what would become the Cartel, counsel had to be taken with the Foreign Office.[33] As the collaboration developed, the members of the Berlin Academy—much to Mommsen's chagrin—voted against formal entry, later agreeing instead to work with the Cartel on the *Thesaurus* as an individual case.[34] To help cover the Göttingen and Berlin contributions to the arrangement, the Prussian Ministry of Culture wanted an extraordinary allotment to be placed in the state-budget. This meant a petition to the Finance Ministry, which was hardly a rubber stamp: there were concerns about the project's cost-estimate and Culture's apparent lack of compunction about outstripping the funds already at its disposal.[35] Even in the run-up to the *Thesaurus*, in other words, an enormous amount of friction had to be resolved: organizing academies demanded interpersonal, inter-regional, inter- (and intra-) Academy, inter-ministerial, and international alignment. Robert W. Smith has written of the "coalition building" that was as much a part of the Hubble Space Telescope as its physical components.[36] The same can be said of the *Thesaurus*, which was a multi-front diplomatic exercise before it was words on page or paper slips in waiting. Asked in 1894, with the inter-Academy cooperation secured, how he had managed it, Wölfflin's answer said it all: "As number one on my recipe, I say: 'Take ten years' patience.'"[37]

Big Equipment

The *Thesaurus*' priority in its first years was to collect the lexical material—the trove of example citations—from which the lexicon would be written. A partly mechanized system that allowed copied sections of text to be quickly reproduced for filing helped generate 1.5 million slips by mid-year 1897, 4.5 million by fall 1899 when the collection was centralized in Munich and the A-volume begun.[38] Wölfflin reported the material's impression on a visiting minister, who had walked slowly through the Munich Bureau, turning his head to take in the boxes cataloguing the (ample) works of the Roman orator Cicero.[39] The slips threatened to buckle some of the shelves on which they were placed.[40] In the early days, when they were still arrayed by author and not alphabetically, it took months for an aide simply to extract and arrange the slips for the letter "C."[41] The question of where to house this new tool—one that allowed users to witness centuries of a word's development—was not trivial: there was, after all, no equivalent elsewhere. When it was secured for Munich, Wölfflin wrote to the Bavarian ministry of the "honor and advantage" won thereby, since "numerous scholars will be forced to seek out the Munich university" to use it.[42] Carlos Spoerhase's suggestion that the *Thesaurus* was a "big instrument" in its own right is evocative: like an accelerator or an early computer, it was physically imposing, effectively non-portable (for the collection's safety, slips remained in the *Thesaurus* office), and able to yield singular results to those with access.[43]

That the *Zettelarchiv* might pose a scalar problem was something Wölfflin had noted by the early 1890s, thanks to his *Archiv* experience. In a co-authored memorandum on how the *Thesaurus* might proceed, he pointed to the slips his journal-contributors had collected to document the (very common) preposition *a, ab*. There were seven boxes in all—an enormous quantity, the presence of which posed an "instructive, that is, terrifying example, in that no one can resolve to read through and work on them."[44] The disjuncture, in other words, between the attention-limited, time-bounded will of a human lexicographer and the forbidding mounds of slips was significant—and the challenge of "scaling" between the two acknowledged at the outset. Indeed, one of the first, most consequential debates between the Academy delegates steering the *Thesaurus* had much to do with precisely this: Wölfflin contended in effect that it would be best to collect citations with some discretion, leaving aside "dispensable ballast"—those lexical examples that did not appear useful for future analysis.[45] This would unburden the eventual lexicon-authors by presenting them with a more manageable, "already sifted" material.[46] Wölfflin's Berlin counterpart Hermann Diels saw things differently: he believed allowing excerptors to determine what to collect and what not would yield a "subjectively colored and incomplete, therefore unscientific body of material."[47] He suggested instead a process for generating more resolutely exhaustive collections.[48] Diels' proposed solution for the exacerbated problem of scale on large articles was to insert an intermediary figure—a "pre-processor" (*Vorarbeiter*)—between the collected material and the lexicon-author.[49] The "pre-processor" would assess the slips for each word statistically and select the "most notable," sending on a set of "sifted" items to the lexicographer. In the end, Diels' position prevailed, though without the "pre-processor," leaving the lexicon-authors to fend for themselves amid the looming "slip-towers."[50]

As those towers materialized, Wölfflin continued to emphasize the misalignment between philologists and their paper instruments. Diels had said he considered the *Zettelatom*—the atomized slip, containing a single lexical instance—to be very suitable for the analytical work of the lexicographer.[51] But Wölfflin, who preferred slips that each displayed several citations (as the *Archiv* slips had) lambasted the design in what amounted to an endorsement of a different model of cognition: "the person who is supposed to read through 20 boxes [of slips] on a particle," he wrote, "will already have a brain-sickness by the twelfth or thirteenth."[52] The disregard for the lexicographer's brain-health was symptomatic of what he elsewhere styled a Berlin tendency to show a higher regard for the developing slip apparatus—the equipment—than for the scholars meant to operate it. More than once, Wölfflin rendered spiteful account of the opinion—allegedly voiced by Mommsen—that "were the slip-material (the principal thing) assembled, it didn't much matter what came at the head and what at the tail" of the articles to be written from it.[53] He warned against "instil[ling] the idea that all wisdom stands already on the slips, and that [the lexicographers] have only to press the juice out of the grapes offered to them."[54] It was not, he contended, the slips that were "the highest oracle" in lexicography, but the lexicographer who wielded them.[55] The evident concern to keep the equipment from overpowering or overdetermining the operator is familiar: one finds a parallel sense among Big Scientists of Wilson's generation that actual "thinking" might succumb to a reliance on expensive machines, or that work dictated by the routine of the apparatus could become "just a little dull."[56]

Despite Wölfflin's hand-wringing, the process went forward: the *Thesaurus* had its millions-strong slip-archive. The question of how to make it manageable for the individual lexicographer would become a significant through-line in the lexicon's history. It was suggested early on that the article-writing process could be expedited by having lexicographers physically manipulate the slips into the order of the eventual entry before writing out a manuscript—a strategy that was ultimately discarded.[57] Wölfflin urged that the philologists at work on the *Thesaurus* cultivate a particular mode of attentive "observation" that would allow them to establish more efficiently what was worth noting in the mass of available material.[58] Another tack—at odds with Wölfflin's push to elevate the lexicographer over the slips—was to warn *Thesaurus* lexicographers not to attempt too much of their own analysis: "it must always be borne in mind that the *Thesaurus* only wishes to offer *material*," read an internal instruction from the inter-war period: "to present this cleanly sifted and separated is the only task of the article-author: doing *research* on the basis of this material must be left to the specialized disciplines."[59] The scaling struggle continues to this day: after deciding in 2005, with "P" coming to a close, to take up work on N and R, the *Thesaurus* faced certain words so often attested—some ten boxes of material for the particle *nam*, some 45,000 slips for the negation *non*—that new approaches had to be developed to deal with them.[60] To avoid "sink[ing] in the flood of material" for such "huge words," lexicographers devised a way of drafting their treatments first from a limited sub-sample of citations, then filling in from those remaining, giving only cursory attention to examples liable to deviate little from stylistic norms.[61] The compromise was a solution to a condition one *Thesaurus* editor—in words that would have resonated with Wölfflin a century earlier—pithily diagnosed: "the curse of completeness."[62]

Big Time

Hundreds of feet below a mountain in the Black Forest, a former mine-tunnel now houses unlikely contents.[63] Stored in air-tight stainless-steel cylinders, behind pressure-sealed doors, and beneath enough granite to weather a nuclear blast, is a cache of microfilm-reels that would, if unspooled, extend thousands of miles. Here in the so-called *Barbarastollen* are reproductions of a range of one-of-a-kind archival materials—everything from the coronation document of Otto I, to building plans for the Cologne cathedral, to the text of the Peace of Westphalia, all accorded a secure place in Germany's subterranean cultural "bunker."[64] One item is particularly significant for our purposes: a set of images of the millions of slips that comprise the *Zettelarchiv* of the *Thesaurus*. The composition of the polyester film and the conditions of its storage ensure that the filmed documents can last for hundreds of years.[65] The archive is an emissary to a distant future.

The delivery of the *Thesaurus* slips into the bunker (and unto ages hence) in the 1990s—nearly a century after many of them were created, and while their originals were still in active use by those writing the lexicon—elegantly captures some of the temporal layering characteristic of the lexicon-project, which in fact has provided another of the scalar friction-points constitutive of its "big"-ness.[66] The *Barbarastollen* was hardly the *Thesaurus*' first flirtation with eternity. Wölfflin himself had shown an early interest in handling certain components of philological work in a manner that could stand "for all time."[67] It was an orientation maintained as he built support for his lexicographical program and one that went hand in hand with the totalizing pitch of the preliminary collections he organized for the *Archiv*—a thing done *totally* had staying power. The stance would have been legible to contemporaries, as work by Markus Krajewski and Lorraine Daston has made clear: both the concern for epistemic durability and the sort of exhaustiveness on display in cataloguing-cum-archival projects like the lexicon *Zettelarchiv* were period impulses.[68] In effect, so Daston's argument, the elevation of archival collection—and not just by philologists—was a mode of scaling the patent time-boundedness of human work to the ambitions of eternal up-to-date-ness: the (eventually outmoded) conclusions of the moment could be emended by later recourse to the preserved material on which they were built.[69] Thus at the *Thesaurus* it was precisely the slip-archive, not the printed lexicon written from it, that was promised to be "for all time the center for studies of the Latin language."[70] These were grand words: they kept "for all time" on the agenda, and took some pressure off lexicographers' published work. But, crucially, there were collateral effects: In the first place, by conferring immortality on the archived material one risked devaluing the decidedly mortal scholars working with it, a tendency to which we have seen Wölfflin react above. Secondly, there was a clear friction between celebrating the timelessness of the *Zettelarchiv*, and the fact that it, too, was obviously subject to the vicissitudes of age and fortune—a reality underscored by the need to station a copy in the *Barbarastollen*.

As for the time required to produce the printed lexicon volumes: the *Thesaurus* had originally projected a completion-date around 1914. But by 1902, the third year of production, it was already clear that the project was not keeping pace, necessitating attempts to accelerate the work, with Wölfflin proposing measures such as tying salary-increases to shorter articles.[71] Such conversations presaged things to come. In the early 1930s, speeding up was considered a *Lebensfrage* for the *Thesaurus*.[72] After the Second World War, too, some struck a bleak note: an American involved in arranging support for the lexicon found its protracted time-estimates "very sobering"—he had no confidence that "a stable Europe and a stable world" would endure for the decades of work still projected.[73] Seven decades later, the uncertainty persists: recent correspondence from Munich warns that even after the coronavirus pandemic, "there will not be a simple return to normalcy: the future of the Thesaurus is even with all its successes in no way secure."[74] 2025 will mark yet another reckoning, with a best-case extension of a subsequent quarter-century forecast—and even that contingent on a competitive proposal. Scholars' jobs, a storied international base for Latin-language study, not to mention the prospects of closing in on Z, hang in the balance. The tension at the uneasy juncture between the timing of a career, a long-term project, and a (budgeted) organization is not just palpable; it is existential.

"Big" Future?

Whither work on "Big Humanities"? I offer here a few observations intended not as novel pronouncements but as weather-vane readings synthesizing live (in some cases already for some time) areas for investigation.

First, the "Big Humanities" dialogue is primarily inflected by a particular personage in a particular place and time: namely Theodor Mommsen, whom we have met briefly above, and the nineteenth-century Berlin Academy.[75]

For this there is eminent justification: Mommsen in his own time was known as the "master of scholarly *Grossbetrieb*."[76] A cornerstone of his reputation was his role in establishing the *Corpus Inscriptionum Latinarum* (CIL), which looked to collect the widely scattered Latin inscriptions of the Roman world: the CIL had published some 130,000 of them by 1903, and—like the *Thesaurus*—continues its work today.[77] Regarded as "a first of its kind model of [scholarly] cooperation and *Grossbetrieb*," the project was a harbinger of Mommsen's prowess, unfolded in Berlin, as an organizer of collaborative efforts—including the *Thesaurus*, for which he drafted initial regulations (he had done the same for the Cartel).[78] Because of Mommsen's extraordinary profile, and thanks especially to the work of Stefan Rebenich, we have a good outline of his activity and illuminating depictions of certain of the projects linked to him. There is, in short, a solid foundation from which to analyse characteristics of *Grosswissenschaft* as Mommsen and those around him understood and practiced it.

The story that has emerged is one in which *Big Science* or *Big Scholarship* in the study of antiquity (and/or at the Berlin Academy) has its "beginning" either in 1858, when Mommsen became an ordinary Manhattan Project alum-member, or in 1853, when his leadership of the CIL became assured: the "founding date" of joint humanities research, meanwhile, is set in 1815, coincident with a proposal for collecting Greek inscriptions that identified collaborative projects as an Academy *raison d'être*.[79] Subsequent decades saw both the CIL's realization and the consolidation of Mommsen's influence within the Academy, which by century's end would support a wide array of comparable, comprehensive editorial and collection efforts, aimed at organizing scholarly labor to make available "fundamental" historical and philological sources.[80] There was a common profile to these Academy *Unternehmungen*, as scholars like Petra Hoffmann have shown: division of labor, long time-horizons, supervision by a commission, a distinct material-collection period.[81] And they provided a model that would be emulated by Academy-projects in the sciences.[82] When Mommsen moved to assemble an inter-Academy coalition, it was initially with expansive humanities projects in mind—the *Thesaurus*, a coin catalogue, further inscriptions work.[83] All of which has supported the conclusion that decades before twentieth-century scientists were remarking on "big science," scholars in the humanities were using the same label as they organized expensive, collaborative, long-term projects, and took the lead in devising structures (the Academy *Unternehmung*, the Cartel) to pursue them. This, then, is the so-called "birth of *Big Science* from the humanities."[84]

The argument has an attractive counter-intuitive bent, perhaps encouraging its invocation in ways that are a bit too glib—collapsing a narrative about an advancing style of work in the Berlin Academy with one about scientific developments more broadly.[85] It is a bold leap from the observation that projects cataloguing fixed-star positions or flora and fauna availed themselves of an Academy-infrastructure developed by scholars of antiquity to the assertion that Mommsen's *Großwissenschaft* was "the prototype of all Big Science ever since, whether in the humanities or the sciences" or that it was with Academy-projects at century's end that the natural sciences at large "finally . . . enter[ed] the 'era' of the *Grossbetrieb der Wissenschaften*."[86] In fact, at key points in the development from the CIL to the Cartel, there are of course indications of cues from the natural sciences. Entering the Academy in 1858, Mommsen greeted its ability to move on the CIL as having "delivered one more proof, that *as in the field of the natural sciences* and modern history, so also in that of classical philology, scientific organization delivers results."[87] What precursors did he have in mind? Likewise, decades later, a ministerial letter on Mommsen's inter-Academy ambitions introduced the idea by citing international organizations in areas like geodesy and astronomy. The goal was to *extend* the system to the study of antiquity.[88] And indeed, when Wölfflin began to work out his lexicographical ambitions in the 1870s and 1880s he invoked everything from a "central laboratory," to meteorology, to forestry.[89] He certainly saw a family resemblance between the CIL and his envisioned *Thesaurus*, but he was also inclined to look elsewhere for organizational models and inspiration.

It is difficult to sustain the narrative, then, that the currents of what Mommsen called "big"-ness ran a direct channel downstream from the humanities to the sciences and outwards from there. Let us scramble over quickly to the scientists' side. With the Cartel in the making, the great Berlin physiologist and physicist Hermann von Helmholtz was asked his opinion: he endorsed the idea, while distancing himself from the type of work he believed it to represent ("collective efforts of many collectors and observers").[90] This naturally wasn't because he was hidebound. He was at the time the head of the costly Physikalisch-Technische Reichsanstalt, overseeing some fifty personnel; two decades earlier, Prussia had put over 1.5 million marks towards the largest physics institute in Germany as part of a pledge meant to draw him to Berlin.[91] Institutes of this sort were taken by contemporaries to be the "capitalist counterpart to the big manufacturing enterprises (*Grossbetrieben*)," and one scholar could speak readily of the "world-mastering *Grossbetrieb* of a Mommsen or a Helmholtz."[92] So

Helmholtz's operation, too, was *Grossbetrieb*, and it wasn't learned from Mommsen's inscription collections.

The prescription for Big Humanities enthusiasts is thus to work towards a core narrative of nineteenth-century scholarly "big"-ness that is a bit less originary and a bit more backward-facing, a bit less linear and a bit more "entangled"[93]: one that embraces the crucial insights about the essential role of philologists and historians without relegating scientists to their train or relying on Mommsen as the *terminus post quem*. Useful will be further pursuit of just how much identity humanists saw between their work and the comparanda—industrial, to be sure, but also military and scientific—that surface in their rhetoric. Useful, too—and this will hardly make news—will be continuing to devise detailed studies of ambitious humanities enterprises that adjust the lens anterior to Mommsen or laterally away from Berlin.[94] Our *Thesaurus*-story above hardly writes the "Mommsenians" out of the picture—indeed some in Berlin, much to Wölfflin's dissatisfaction, insisted on regarding Mommsen as the *pater Thesauri*.[95] But precisely because it is a story with a gravitational center in Munich, it stands at an angle to the Berlin paradigm. One sees the perspective of an eager founder looking to achieve something that would not sit in Prussia's shadow, who had to engage in diplomacy on the part of an Academy (Munich) with considerably less discretionary funding than Berlin, who was eager to resist the north on key points (see Wölfflin's tangle with Diels), and who expressed a set of referents and templates (the laboratory, the forestry garden) that direct our eyes beyond the frame of other Academy-projects.

A second point is that collaboration comes in many forms, which remain difficult to taxonomize.[96] Indeed, one of the things that a close look at the *Thesaurus* tells us is that those involved could register significant differences in the organization of projects as apparently isomorphic as collecting inscriptions and collecting Latin words. For the lexicon, Wölfflin (though flexible) inclined towards a model of coordinated work based at a single centralized workplace similar to what eventually prevailed—a Bureau of on-site lexicographers under an editor proceeding through the alphabet together.[97] Mommsen's preference—modeled on the CIL—was to divide the *Thesaurus* into segments of the alphabet to be worked as separate volumes by largely independent individuals under Academy oversight.[98] Each was repulsed by the perceived inclination of the other. Wölfflin thought Mommsen's CIL-adjacent plan would amount to a "race for favor," editor-versus-editor, in Berlin and fail to give the work a "uniform spirit."[99] Mommsen, meanwhile, recoiled at Wölfflin's "perverse" notion of the "leader, and under him the Philologist-*Bureau* working with several horsepower."[100] The devil was in the details in project organization, and, depending on the circumstances, a myriad political and efficiency calculations could attend each permutation. Caution is therefore in order around assertions that, for instance, modern digital humanities projects "share the same form of research organization as the long-term projects of the Prussian Academy of Sciences,"[101] since the forms involved may prove to be more variegated than one initially suspects.

Third, scholars have already generated exciting results by examining not just the leaders of "big" enterprises—chair-holders like Mommsen and Wölfflin—but the less well-known figures toiling inside or in support of them.[102] Contemporary discourse attested the risks such figures faced. One could be straitjacketed by "mechanical" tasks, consigned to the menial service of the "carter," to dulling "factory-work."[103] As studies have indicated, such language speaks to period notions of creativity and the hierarchicalization of academic labor.[104] How much it reveals about what people were in fact doing, and how routinized their work actually was, is less clear. The script grows suspect when one finds Mommsen, for example, apparently on a swivel: describing the work of editing inscriptions in elevated fashion as requiring scholars to "consider and examine the whole of Roman antiquity," but later equating editing to mere cart-hauling: "the carting—which one calls *editing*—everyone can do."[105] Certainly Wölfflin was not inclined to downplay rank-and-file lexicographers: others might see them as "boot-cleaner[s]"—for him, he insisted, they had the noble role "of the artist, the architect, or the painter."[106] But exactly what "boot-cleaning" and what "painting" those on projects like the *Thesaurus* did, and whether they believed their hands to be caked with dirt or with pigments, remains for the historian to show.

A final note: there is further room to probe the relationship between the "official" or initial rhetoric of humanities projects and the shifting realities of behavior under the gun and on the ground. The vexing topic of "completeness" provides an example.[107] Mommsen could speak neatly of "unify[ing] all Latin inscriptions in a collection," even while signaling the far more realistic view that to "visit every little place where there is even the prospect of old inscriptions" was completely impractical.[108] Wölfflin, meanwhile, could move in a decade from extolling "complete lexical material" and "absolute completeness" in his *Archiv* to pushing back in *Thesaurus*-planning against Diels' advocacy for an exhaustive approach.[109] Experience and exigency had a way of tarnishing shiny objectives, or turning them into moving targets.

The same was true of the "archive" that featured in both the *Thesaurus* and the CIL. In Mommsen's oft-quoted formulation, the "groundwork of historical *Wissenschaft*" lay in organizing "the archives of the past."[110] At mid-century, an example of the "organized" archives he had in mind appears to have been the printed CIL volumes themselves, neatly presenting inscriptions. But as Daston shows, there arose another, subtending archive, one consisting of the materials—including the paper impressions of faraway inscriptions known as "squeezes"—from which the CIL was assembled, and from which it could be checked after the fact.[111] It is worth underscoring that the embrace of the latter seems to have been a process and not foreordained. Indeed, when confronted in the 1850s with a mass of such "squeezery," mailed to him by another scholar, Mommsen expressed little enthusiasm.[112] And in a volume published three decades later, the CIL epigrapher, Berlin professor, and former Mommsen acolyte Emil Hübner would note that when he had set about gathering visual examples of inscriptions, the CIL had not laid in many squeezes: "manuscript and printed copies had been collected as fully as possible for preparing the CIL volumes, but only rarely paper or plaster or aluminum impressions, or photographs—and usually only of these inscriptions which presented some difficulty in making out."[113] Clearly, then, there had been no effort from the outset to construct a systematic library of paper impressions. Hübner would go on to collect more than 4,000, which were available for viewing in Berlin, and which he knew could reveal discrepancies with what had been "archived" in the printed CIL.[114]

For its part, the *Thesaurus* could assert by 1900 that its slips would be there perpetually for lexicon-revisions future.[115] But as we have seen that was easier said than done, with the *Barbarastollen* but one step in a long effort, begun in the lexicon's planning stages, to determine the make-up and shape of the archive. Those leading the project tangled not just on how complete the slips should be, but also their appearance, production, and storage. The fault-lines opened on issues like this, expressed in protocols, in letters, and in manuscript memoranda, do not emerge readily in the lexicon's public-facing materials. But digging for them is worthwhile: they show epistemological commitments, scholarly priorities, and politics worked out in real time, in the language of boxes and paper slips. They represent for us "big" humanities in action.

Notes

1. Robert R. Wilson, "My Fight Against Team Research," *Daedalus* 99, no. 4 (1970): 1076–87, at 1076. Citations have been held to a minimum for reasons of space.

2. Ibid.
3. Ibid., 1087.
4. Ibid., 1076. For the growth of physics, see, e.g., Peter Galison, *Image and Logic: A Material Culture of Microphysics* (Chicago, IL: University of Chicago Press, 1997), 239–431.
5. So, e.g., Merle Tuve, "Is Science too Big for the Scientist?" *Saturday Review* (6 June 1959): 48–52; Alvin M. Weinberg, "Impact of Large-Scale Science on the United States," *Science* 134, no. 3473 (1961): 161–4; Wilson's words at "My Fight," 1076.
6. See James H. Capshew and Karen A. Rader, "Big Science: Price to the Present," *Osiris* 7 (1992): 3–25; Carlos Spoerhase, "Big Humanities: 'Größe' und 'Großforschung' als Kategorien geisteswissenschaftlicher Selbstbeobachtung," *Geschichte der Germanistik* 37/38 (2010): 9–27, esp. 9–19; Torsten Kahlert, "'Große Projekte': Mommsens Traum und der Diskurs um Big Science und Großforschung," in *Wissenskulturen: Bedingungen wissenschaftlicher Innovation*, ed. Harald Müller and Florian Eßer (Kassel: Kassel University Press, 2012), 67–86, at 70–9.
7. See Weinberg's "Impact"; Derek J. de Solla Price, *Little Science, Big Science* (New York: Columbia University Press, 1963); *Big Science: The Growth of Large-Scale Research*, ed. Peter Galison and Bruce Hevly (Stanford, CA: Stanford University Press, 1992).
8. Often cited is Lawrence Badash, "The Origins of Big Science: Rutherford at McGill," in *Rutherford and Physics at the Turn of the Century*, ed. Mario Bunge and William R. Shea (New York: Science History Publications, 1979), 23–41, but there is plenty that fits the bill, including, e.g., the *longue durée* reflections in Capshew and Rader, "Big Science," 19–22.
9. See Stefan Rebenich, *Theodor Mommsen und Adolf Harnack: Wissenschaft und Politik im Berlin des ausgehenden 19. Jahrhunderts* (Berlin: Walter de Gruyter, 1997), 55–94; *Theodor Mommsen: Eine Biographie* (Munich: C. H. Beck, 2002), 135–64, and a number of further works by the same author, cited below. Likewise, Rüdiger vom Bruch, "Mommsen und Harnack: Die Geburt von *Big Science* aus den Geisteswissenschaften," in *Theodor Mommsen: Wissenschaft und Politik im 19. Jahrhundert*, ed. Alexander Demandt et al. (Berlin: Walter de Gruyter, 2005), 121–41; Torsten Kahlert, *"Unternehmungen großen Stils": Wissenschaftsorganisation, Objektivität und Historismus im 19. Jahrhundert* (Berlin: be.bra wissenschaft, 2017).
10. On the *Thesaurus*, see esp. *Wie die Blätter am Baum, so wechseln die Wörter: 100 Jahre Thesaurus linguae Latinae*, ed. Dietfried Krömer (Stuttgart: B. G. Teubner 1995). Further publications are listed online at https://www.thesaurus.badw.de/ueber-den-tll/literaturhinweise.html
11. All texts into the second century CE are exhaustively represented. Thereafter, some have been taken into the *Zettelarchiv* in their entirety, but most have been excerpted.

12. For *Thesaurus*-idea as "großes Unternehmen," see, e.g., transcript of Theodor Mommsen to Friedrich Vogel, 22 January 1880, Thesaurus linguae Latinae Archive (= TLLA) ("Je mehr die Realisierung des . . . geplanten grossen Unternehmens"); Eduard Wölfflin, "Vorwort," *Archiv für lateinische Lexikographie* 1:1-12, at 6. For "Großwissenschaft" and "Grossbetrieb," see Rebenich, *Theodor Mommsen und Adolf Harnack*, 55–94; further, *Adolf von Harnack als Zeitgenosse: Reden und Schriften aus den Jahren des Kaiserreichs und der Weimarer Republik*, vol. 2, ed. Kurt Nowak (Berlin: Walter de Gruyter, 1996), 1007, 1009–19.
13. Capshew and Rader, "Big Science," 4, 18–22.
14. See Deborah R. Coen, "Big Is a Thing of the Past: Climate Change and Methodology in the History of Ideas," *Journal of the History of Ideas* 77, no. 2 (2016): 305–21, at 311–14 and Coen, *Climate in Motion: Science, Empire, and the Problem of Scale* (Chicago, IL: University of Chicago Press, 2018), 16–20.
15. On Wölfflin, see Christian Flow, "Philological Observation," *Modern Intellectual History* 19, no. 1 (2022), 187–216.
16. Wölfflin, "Vorwort," 6.
17. Ibid.
18. Ibid.
19. Eduard Wölfflin, "Organisation der Arbeit," *Archiv für lateinische Lexikographie* 1:12–15; first questionnaire at *Archiv für lateinische Lexikographie* 1:15–19.
20. For *abhorreo* see *Archiv für lateinische Lexikographie* 1:462 (no. 85).
21. *Archiv für lateinische Lexikographie* 1:573.
22. Wölfflin, "Organisation," 14: "auch dürfte die einheitliche Fragestellung . . . die Verschiedenheit der HH. Mitarbeiter wesentlich ausgleichen."
23. See Wölfflin on the shortcomings of a prior *Thesaurus* plan: "Vorwort," 4.
24. Wölfflin, "Zwei Gutachten über das Unternehmen eines lateinischen Wörterbuches" (1892), in Krömer, *Wie die Blätter*, 145–56, at 150, 152; Friedrich Vogel, "Zu Eduard Wölfflins hundertstem Geburtstag: Die schwierigen Anfänge des Thesaurus linguae latinae," *Bayerische Blätter für das Gymnasial-Schulwesen* 66 (1930): 345–50, at 346, 349.
25. *Archiv für lateinische Lexikographie* 2:147.
26. See Vogel, "Die schwierigen Anfänge," 348, quoting Wölfflin letter from 27 February 1884. From the (TLLA) original: "Die Folge davon ist, dass Archiv I.1 + 2 nichts aus Berlin enthält. . . . Ein schöner Anfang zu dem *National*werke."
27. B. Schroeder-Gudehus, "Die Akademie auf internationalem Parkett: Die Programmatik der internationalen Zusammenarbeit wissenschaftlicher Akademien und ihr Scheitern im Ersten Weltkrieg," in *Die Königlich Preußische Akademie der Wissenschaften zu Berlin im Kaiserreich*, ed. J. Kocka et al. (Berlin: Akademie Verlag, 1999), 175–95; Martin Gierl, *Geschichte und Organisation: Institutionalisierung als Kommunikationsprozess am Beispiel der Wissenschaftsakademien um 1900* (Göttingen: Vandenhoeck & Ruprecht, 2004), esp. 213–320.

28. See Gierl, *Geschichte*, 215–63.
29. See Wölfflin to Franz Bücheler, October 25, 1891 ("die herrenlose Erbschaft"), November 11, 1893 ("*ganz ohne mich*"), Stadtarchiv und Stadthistorische Bibliothek, Bonn (= SSBB), SN 43.
30. Stefan Rebenich, "'Mommsen ist er niemals näher getreten': Theodor Mommsen und Hermann Diels," in *Hermann Diels (1848–1922) et la science de l'antiquité*, ed. W.M. Calder III and J. Mansfeld (Geneva: Fondation Hardt, 1999), 85–142, at 123–27.
31. Ibid., 124 ("wölfflinisirt").
32. Hermann Diels to Theodor Mommsen, October 13, 1893, Staatsbibliothek zu Berlin, Preußischer Kulturbesitz, NL Mommsen I: Diels, 45v: "so kann man vielleicht verhüten, dass zu stark gemünchnert wird."
33. Gierl, *Geschichte*, 221–23.
34. Ibid., 237–63.
35. See Robert Bosse to Johannes Miquel, August 20, 1894, GSA-PK I. HA Rep. 76 V $_C$ Sekt. 1 Tit. XI Teil VD Nr. 8 Bd. 1. For Finance's stern posture, see correspondence to Bosse of October 14 and December 3, 1894.
36. Robert W. Smith, "The Biggest Kind of Big Science: Astronomers and the Space Telescope," in Galison and Hevly, *Big Science*, 184–211.
37. Eduard Wölfflin to Heinrich Wölfflin, May 18, 1894, Universitätsbibliothek Basel (=UB) NL 95, IV, 1368.
38. See (Beilagen to) protocol of 1897 and report of 1899 Thesaurus Commission meetings, TLLA.
39. Wölfflin to Franz Bücheler, January 8, 1899, SSBB SN 43: 995.
40. TLLA binder: Geschäftsführung I, 144.
41. Friedrich Vollmer, "Vom Thesaurus Linguae Latinae," *Neue Jahrbücher für das klassische Altertum, Geschichte und deutsche Literatur* 17, no. 1 (1904): 46–56, at 49.
42. Wölfflin report of June 7, 1898, Bayerisches Hauptstaatsarchiv, MK 11769, vol. 1.
43. Spoerhase, "Big Humanities," 14.
44. Franz Bücheler and Eduard Wölfflin, "Memorial betr. Thesaurus linguae latinae" (1893), in Krömer, *Wie die Blätter*, 162–76, at 164.
45. Ibid., 163.
46. Ibid.
47. Diels, "Stellungnahme zum Memorial" (1893), in Krömer, *Wie die Blätter*, 177–86, at 177.
48. Ibid., esp. 181–6.
49. Ibid., 184–5.
50. Friedrich Vollmer to Eduard Wölfflin, June 8, 1899, UB NL 93 83: 930 ("vor den Zetteltürmen").
51. Diels, "Stellungnahme," 184.

52. Wölfflin to Franz Bücheler, October 16, 1894, SSBB, SN 43: 999.
53. See, e.g., Wölfflin, "Die Form der Lexikonartikel," May 23, 1896, TLLA, 34–5.
54. Ibid., 25.
55. Ibid., 15.
56. See Weinberg, "Impact," 162; Galison, *Image and Logic*, 422.
57. For slip-manipulation, see TLLA binder: Geschäftsführung I, 147.
58. Flow, "Philological Observation," 207–11.
59. "Entwurf einer Arbeitsinstruktion für die Mitarbeiter des Thesaurus linguae Latinae," TLLA, 2.
60. Hugo Beikircher, "Der Fluch der Vollständigkeit," *Akademie Aktuell* 15 (2005): 62–3.
61. Ibid., 63.
62. Ibid. (see title).
63. On the *Barbarastollen*—officially "Zentraler Bergungsort der Bundesrepublik Deutschland"—I rely on Stephan Krass, "Der Kulturbunker," in *Deutsche Erinnerungsorte*, vol. 3, ed. Etienne François and Hagen Schulze (Munich: C. H. Beck, 2001), 651–9.
64. Ibid., 653.
65. Ibid., 655.
66. The author is currently at work on an article-length treatment of temporality at the *Thesaurus*.
67. See Flow, "Philological Observation," 204.
68. See Markus Krajewski, *World Projects: Global Information Before World War I*, trans. Charles Marcrum II (Minneapolis, MN: University of Minnesota Press, 2014); Lorraine Daston, "The Immortal Archive: Nineteenth-Century Science Imagines the Future," in *Science in the Archives: Pasts, Presents, Futures*, ed. Lorraine Daston (Chicago, IL: University of Chicago Press, 2017), 159–82.
69. Daston, "Immortal Archive."
70. "Denkschrift über den Thesaurus linguae Latinae," November 29, 1913, in TLLA binder: Thesaurus-Geschichte 1893–1948, I, at 2. See further Flow, "Philological Observation," 212–13.
71. See I(9) and II(1) of the 1902 Thesaurus Commission meeting protocol, and Wölfflin's memorandum "Auch der Thesaurus"—with, e.g., suggestion about exercising "[e]ine sanfte Pression" on article-authors at [3]. Both TLLA.
72. See "Bericht der Herren Fraenkel, Norden und Stroux über ihre Vorbesprechung in Naumburg am 14. February 1931," TLLA.
73. Howard Comfort to Heinz Haffter et al., November 21, 1948, TLLA.
74. Michael Hillen and Manfried Flieger to Friends of the Thesaurus, December 2020.
75. So, e.g., treatments like Annette M. Baertschi, "'Big Science' in Classics in the Nineteenth Century and the Academicization of Antiquity," in *The Making of*

the Humanities, vol. 3, ed. Rens Bod, Jaap Maat, and Thijs Weststeijn (Amsterdam: Amsterdam University Press, 2014), 233–49; and Chad Wellmon, "Loyal Workers and Distinguished Scholars: Big Humanities and the Ethics of Knowledge," *Modern Intellectual History* 16, no. 1 (2019): 87–126, are heavily framed by earlier argumentation on Mommsen and the Academy (esp. that of Rebenich and vom Bruch).

76. See Wilhelm von Hartel, "Organisation der wissenschaftlichen Arbeit," *Zeitschrift für die österreichischen Gymnasien* 58 (1907): 1–15, at 10; similarly, Hermann Diels, "Die Organisation der Wissenschaft," in *Die Kultur der Gegenwart*, vol. 1, no. 1, ed. P. Hinneberg (Berlin: B. G. Teubner, 1906), 591–650, at 626.

77. See Stefan Rebenich, "Berlin und die antike Epigraphik," in *Öffentlichkeit—Monument—Text*, ed. Werner Eck et al. (Berlin: Walter de Gruyter, 2014), 7–75.

78. See Hartel, "Organisation," 5. For the Cartel statutes see *Theodor Mommsen und Friedrich Althoff: Briefwechsel 1882–1903*, ed. Stefan Rebenich and Gisa Franke (Munich: Oldenbourg, 2012) no. 457; Mommsen's *Thesaurus* regulations at no. 509.

79. See Stefan Rebenich, "Vom Nutzen und Nachteil der Großwissenschaft: Altertumswissenschaftliche Unternehmungen an der Berliner Akademie und Universität im 19. Jahrhundert," in *Die modernen Väter der Antike: Die Entwicklung der Altertumswissenschaften an Akademie und Universität im Berlin des 19. Jahrhunderts*, ed. Annette M. Baertschi and Colin G. King (Berlin: Walter de Gruyter, 2009), 397–421, at 398 (1858); Rebenich, "Berlin," 19 (1853), 9 (1815).

80. See Stefan Rebenich, "Die Altertumswissenschaften und die Kirchenväterkommission an der Akademie: Theodor Mommsen und Adolf Harnack," in Kocka, *Königlich Preußische Akademie*, 199–233.

81. See Petra Hoffmann, *Weibliche Arbeitswelten in der Wissenschaft: Frauen an der Preußischen Akademie der Wissenschaften zu Berlin 1890–1945* (Bielefeld: transcript, 2011), 55–110.

82. Rebenich, "Altertumswissenschaften," 223; Diels, "Organisation," 626.

83. *Theodor Mommsen und Friedrich Althoff: Briefwechsel*, no. 431.

84. vom Bruch, "Geburt."

85. Kahlert, "'Große Projekte,'" 71–2, 77 for cautionary notes.

86. Lorraine Daston, "Authenticity, Autopsia, and Theodor Mommsen's *Corpus Inscriptionum Latinarum*," in *For the Sake of Learning: Essays in Honor of Anthony Grafton*, ed. Ann Blair and Anja-Silvia Goeing, vol. 2 (Leiden: Brill, 2016), 955–73, at 967–8; Wellmon, "Loyal Workers," 113.

87. See his oft-cited Antrittsrede at Rebenich, *Theodor Mommsen und Adolf Harnack*, 44. Emphasis mine.

88. *Theodor Mommsen und Friedrich Althoff: Briefwechsel*, no. 431. See Gierl, *Geschichte*, 219–20.

89. Flow, "Philological Observation," esp. 195–204, 214–15.
90. *Theodor Mommsen und Friedrich Althoff: Briefwechsel*, no. 447.
91. David Cahan, *An Institute for an Empire: The Physikalisch-Technische Reichsanstalt 1871–1918* (Cambridge: Cambridge University Press, 1989), 21-2, 70-1. For the rise and size of institutes in German physics generally, see the same author's "The Institutional Revolution in German Physics, 1865–1914," *Historical Studies in the Physical Sciences* 15, no. 2 (1985): 1–65.
92. Adolph Wagner, *Die Entwicklung der Universität Berlin 1810–1896* (Berlin: Julius Becker, 1896) at 28–9 ("ein kapitalistisches Seitenstück"); Richard M. Meyer, *Betrieb und Organisation der wissenschaftlichen Arbeit* (Berlin: Leonhard Simion, 1898), 54.
93. See Sjang ten Hagen, "History and Physics Entangled: Disciplinary Intersections in the Long Nineteenth Century" (PhD thesis University of Amsterdam, 2021).
94. See, e.g., Laetitia Boehm, "Langzeitvorhaben als Akademieaufgabe: Geschichtswissenschaft in Berlin und in München," in *Die Preußische Akademie der Wissenschaften zu Berlin 1914–1945*, ed. Wolfram Fischer (Berlin: Akademie Verlag, 2000) 391–434 (Munich as comparandum); Kahlert, *Unternehmungen*, 185–273 (non-Academy project as comparandum; also attempt to de-center Mommsen in CIL account: e.g., 55, 121).
95. Wölfflin to Bücheler, October 3, 1893, SSBB, SN 43 for "Mommsenianer."
96. See, e.g., Capshew and Rader, "Big Science," 22–3.
97. See *Theodor Mommsen und Friedrich Althoff: Briefwechsel* no. 506.
98. See *Theodor Mommsen und Friedrich Althoff: Briefwechsel* no. 509: 7 (lies: 8).
99. Wölfflin's reaction at "Zwei Gutachten," 152 ("eine Seele erhalten"; "ein einheitlicher Geist"); Wölfflin to Bücheler, October 25, 1891, SSBB, SN 43 ("Wettrennen"); Wölfflin to Heinrich Wölfflin, December 20, 1891, TLLA ("Gunst-Wettrennen"). This in response to Mommsen, "Gutachten über das Unternehmen eines lateinischen Wörterbuchs (1891)," in Krömer, *Wie die Blätter*, 139–44, at 140–1.
100. *Theodor Mommsen und Friedrich Althoff: Briefwechsel*, no. 508.
101. Baertschi, "Big Science," 242.
102. Hoffmann, *Weibliche Arbeitswelten*; Horst Fuhrmann, *"Sind eben alles Menschen gewesen": Gelehrtenleben im 19. und 20. Jahrhundert* (Munich: C. H. Beck, 1996), esp. 37–44, 77–115.
103. See Nowak, *Adolf von Harnack*, vol. 2, 1012; Rebenich, "Vom Nutzen," 412–13; Rebenich, *Theodor Mommsen und Adolf Harnack*, 81, 621–2 (Kärrner); further, Katharina Manteufel, "A Three-Story House: Adolf von Harnack and Practices of Academic Mentoring around 1900," *History of Humanities* 1, no. 2 (2016): 355–70, at 365–6.
104. Manteufel, "Three-Story House," 362–9; Rebenich, *Theodor Mommsen und Adolf Harnack*, 80; Diels, "Organisation," 627–8.

105. See CIL 9 (1883): X, and compare Mommsen letter of August 10, 1871, quoted in Lothar Wickert, *Theodor Mommsen: Eine Biographie*, vol. 3 (Frankfurt am Main: Klostermann, 1969), 137–8.
106. Wölfflin to Franz Bücheler, June 25, 1894, SSBB, SN 43.
107. See Kahlert, *Unternehmungen*, 40–9.
108. See Mommsen, "Über Plan und Ausführung eines Corpus Inscriptionum Latinarum," in A. Harnack, *Geschichte der Königlich Preussischen Akademie der Wissenschaften zu Berlin*, vol. 2 (Berlin: Reichsdruckerei, 1900), 522–40, at 523, with the practical take at 527.
109. Wölfflin, "Vorwort," 7–8.
110. Rebenich, *Theodor Mommsen und Adolf Harnack*, 227.
111. Daston, "Immortal Archive," 165–6, 173.
112. Wickert, *Theodor Mommsen*, vol. 3, 273.
113. Emil Hübner, *Exempla scripturae epigraphicae latinae* (Berlin: George Reimer, 1885), xvii.
114. Ibid., xx-xxi.
115. *Thesaurus linguae Latinae*, vol. 1 (Leipzig: B. G. Teubner, 1900), [iii].

7

Oral History and the (Digital) Humanities

Julianne Nyhan and Andrew Flinn

Introduction

The inaugural issue of the journal *History of Humanities* observes: "It is probably impossible to give a definition of the term *humanities* that would cover a category of practices, or objects of study, that remains fixed throughout all periods of intellectual activity across the world."[1] It is likewise with the definition of *digital humanities*, which, according to Ramsey: "can mean anything from media studies to electronic art, from data mining to edutech, from scholarly editing to anarchic blogging, while inviting code junkies, digital artists, standards wonks, transhumanists, game theorists, free culture advocates, archivists, librarians, and edupunks under its capacious canvas."[2] Neither the geographies, taxonomies, nor circumferences of the humanities or digital humanities are fixed, yet substantial commonalities crosscut their diversity, for example, the centrality of modeling as a research strategy,[3] and the centrality of artifacts of cultural heritage as the unit of analysis for both.[4]

Following from this, the jumping-off point of this contribution is that bridging points between the history of the humanities and the history of digital humanities must similarly exist, and that their mapping can enrich understandings of their shared geographies, taxonomies, and circumferences. In the context of the history of digital humanities, recent work has demonstrated that when used with care, oral history can advance rich and pluralized readings of the field, readings that are commensurate with its variegated scope of operation.[5] Examples of this are attested in two books that we have recently worked on. *One Origin of Digital Humanities: Fr Roberto Busa S.J. in His Own Words* (2019) interfolds oral history with archival research to select and contextualize previously out of print or inaccessible writings of Busa, and translate them into English.[6] For instance, an oral history interview with Busa's translator, Philip Barras, captures recollections about Busa not previously on record, and foregrounds how Barras' memories of Busa informed how he translated the articles contained in the volume. These kinds of reflections are not regularly captured in scholarship of this kind.

The second book, *Hidden and Devalued Labour in the Digital Humanities: On the Index Thomisticus Project 1954–67*, again interfolds oral history and extensive archival research to uncover the overlooked labor that underpinned Busa's *Index Thomisticus* project.[7] It not only describes how female keypunch operators worked with electromechanical punched-card machines, but also identifies the factors that served to devalue and ultimately silence these female operators. In doing so, the book draws attention to obscured historical dynamics and processes encoded in the "deep time" of the digital tools, data, and algorithms that digital humanities makes and uses.

Drawing and expanding on these two books, this chapter further explores the contributions that oral history can make to historicizing the digital humanities. After a brief survey of recent scholarship on the history of humanities computing, we highlight some of the promises and pitfalls of oral history. We discuss Stéfan Sinclair and Geoffrey Rockwell's work on forgotten text analysis technologies. Finally, drawing on an oral history interview with the German humanities computing expert Wilhelm Ott, we show how this line of research might be expanded.

The History of Digital Humanities

The source of the branching course now known as digital humanities has been traced to a number of springs, the most high-profile being that of Busa's work on the *Index Thomisticus*, beginning around 1949.[8] The years following the field's emergence are not notable for having produced many works that sought to historicize its emergence and development.[9] Since about 2000, however, a more sustained interest in the history of digital humanities can be noticed, along with a decidedly more pluralized panoply of readings, and ways of reading, its histories.

One of the most influential histories of humanities computing sought to "highlighting landmarks where significant intellectual progress has been made or where work done within humanities computing has been adopted, developed, or drawn on substantially within other disciplines."[10] More recent work has tended to look around, under, over and behind landmarks of progress, and problematize received, andro- and machine-centric histories of the field, to better account for the contributions of those actors and agents who were subsumed by the canonical history.[11] Alternative histories for the field have been proposed and the search for historical precedents and inflections has expanded to spaces and communities beyond the Anglo-American.[12] Some historiographical reflections on the context of, and potential for, histories of digital humanities have also appeared.[13]

A rich pallet of methodological approaches, and theoretical framings have contributed to the gradations and nuance of recent historicizations. The work of Rockwell, Sinclair and Jones, in particular, has utilized media archaeology and humanistic fabrication to recover forgotten technologies that "help us understand opportunities and challenges as they were perceived at the time and on their own terms rather than imposing our prejudices."[14] Parikka indeed characterizes media archaeology as a "way to investigate new media cultures through insights from past new media, often with emphasis on the forgotten, the quirky, the non-obvious apparatuses, practices, and inventions."[15] Sinclair and Rockwell's humanistic modeling of now lost infrastructures and their interactive digital simulation of keypunching;[16] and Jones and colleagues 3D reconstruction of Busa's first laboratory in Gallarate,[17] pose fundamental questions about epistemologies of historical knowledge production, and raise new possibilities for encountering interpretations of that which once was in the digital humanities.

Oral History for Digital Humanities

The research that we have been undertaking has centered on oral history, and sought to situate the emergence and development of digital humanities in wider socio-cultural and political contexts, so as to better account for how human agency shaped the field. This has often been eclipsed by the machine-centric readings, and techno-utopian viewpoint that is a prominent feature of the field's scholarly literature. As with humanistic fabrication, which, as mentioned above, offers the possibility of elaborating and encountering interpretative models of historical artifacts, the oral history interview can also be understood as an interpretative model, in the sense that it does not necessarily claim to represent an "objective" or "authoritative" rendering of the encounters that it recalls. Rather, an oral history interview is self-consciously a refraction of past events through time, narrative, language, and memory, further mediated by factors like the identity and interrelationship of interviewer and interviewee, and their convergence in the physical and exploratory space of the interview.[18]

The oral history work that we have done on the history of digital humanities has especially been taken under the rubric of the "Hidden Histories: Computing and the Humanities, c. 1949–1980" project. This work has demonstrated that when used with care oral history can contribute to a grounded history that exposes overarching processes while acknowledging through personal narratives the agency and creativity of a plurality of individuals, and not just the great men and women of scientific advancement. The book *Computation and the Humanities: Towards an Oral History of Digital Humanities* presents the first oral history account of the history and development of digital humanities.[19] Thirteen oral history interviews and four analytical chapters incrementally unpick shifting, complex, and heterogeneous aspects of the emergence and development of digital humanities and the experiences of those who helped develop it. In the next section, we will turn, then, to a more detailed exploration of some of the advantages that oral history offers when doing this kind of work.

Why Oral History?

Oral history can open new opportunities to foreground rarely-heard or lesser-known voices, to "give back to the people who made and experienced history, through their own words, a central place."[20] Archives are not neutral spaces; the subjectivities of data collection and preservation that they enfold can work in the interests of some and against the interests of others.[21] Minoritized communities, like women, have "comparative lack of archival trace to secure them in the sightlines of history"[22] and it is often difficult to find them in the (analogue) archive "predominantly produced and preserved by men."²³ The oral history interview, then, can seek to redress this, "to reconstruct the world"²⁴ lost to, or excluded from documents, archives, and, as this article suggests, technologies. Oral history has been intertwined, for example, in work that has uncovered the previously unacknowledged role of gender in the history of computing.²⁵

Though multiple individual testimonies may be enfolded into an overarching historical narrative, rich patterns of understanding can arise from the analysis of multiple narratives, as much as the individual narrative: "In contrast to simplified storylines of individuals reduced to a single identity or experience . . . the flexible and expansive form of the interview allows a narrator, in their own words with their own frameworks, to contextualise their experiences within a broader socio-political and historical milieu, and in the process more fully represent the many dimensions of their identity."²⁶ In this way, oral history can allow different lenses, with different resolutions of personal or community experience, for example, or motivation, to be foregrounded. Oral history, then, contributes "to the creation of imaginative frameworks through which the past is felt, as well as thought about."²⁷

Challenges of Oral History

Early criticisms of oral history revolved around the credibility of retrospective personal testimonies, inconsistencies of memory, choice of interviewees, and bias when compared with the contemporaneous record. Equally, the possibility that such a democratizing methodology would undermine the very principles of scholarly rigor troubled historians.²⁸ As has already been demonstrated, however, what was once considered limiting is now considered the strength of (a no less rigorous) oral history methodology: subjectivity and the way in which people remember the past and contextualize their relationship with it, however flawed, is itself a vista of more sociologically meaningful questions than might otherwise be possible through traditional textual sources alone, and when enfolded with archival research.

Nonetheless, there remain considerations of representativeness and particularly for oral histories that are "community" focused, for instance with a community of practice like the digital humanities, there is a need to be broad and inclusive in the choice of interviewees, and with voices both positive and critical. Oral History, after all, should critically embrace difference and dissonance in recollection and interpretation.²⁹ In this vein, we must attend to the memories and perspectives of oral testimonies not as self-contained points of interest but as interconnected by shared narratives, society, culture, ideology.

Further, more practical challenges of this approach are the intersubjective dynamics between interviewer and interviewee, as well as the level of experience and expertise of the interviewer, all of which shape the quality and trajectory of the dialogue. Likewise, whilst not falling into the trap of too simplistic binary distinctions, the "insider" or "outsider" perspective of the interviewer and the kind of relationship this generates can have both advantages and disadvantages.[30] Insider knowledge and familiarity may at once be crucial to accessing certain interviewees and knowing the right questions to ask, but equally it may foreclose the asking of more difficult questions of one's peers or more critical readings of their answers. On the other hand, while an outsider may struggle to acclimate to a particular group/community—and this may be a linguistic, gender, generational, or cultural as well as epistemic challenge—interviewees may indeed speak more freely with a "trusted outsider."[31]

Lastly, loss of such interpersonal context is risked in the archiving and afterlife of recordings, perhaps most glaringly so when a transcript supersedes or outlives the original recording as the authoritative record. These interstices should be mitigated for at the point of creation and documentation of new oral histories, as well as accounted for in using oral testimonies as historical sources. Interlinked with this and extending the parameters of informed consent is the need for an ethics of care with due regard to archiving, copyright, re-use, re-analysis, digitization, access, and publishing of oral history recordings or data.[32] Ultimately a critically and feminist informed approach to oral history must be one that embraces intersubjectivity and the sharing of authority at the heart of its practice.[33] As such, the authors have elsewhere advocated for more radically centering "shared authority" between interviewers and interviewees in such oral history projects as those discussed in this contribution, and to which we now turn.[34]

Case Study: Robert Busa

In the research that we have conducted, oral history has particularly supported ways of going beyond standard written texts, and of encountering and reflecting on different types of evidence and "imaginative frameworks."

In their media-archaeology informed presentation at the Digital Humanities conference 2014, Sinclair and Rockwell explored three forgotten text analysis technologies from before the advent of the World Wide Web, "when humanists and artists were imagining what could be done" in very different text analysis environments to the ones we routinely encounter now. Their three examples were Busa's use of punched cards for data entry; the command language that was designed by John B. Smith for the early text analysis tool ARRAS; and Robert J. Glickman's PRORA text analysis tool, including his observations about how:

> concordances could be printed as cards for 2-ring binders so that they could be taken out and arranged on a table by users. He was combining binder technology with computing to reimagine the concordance text. Today we no longer think about output to paper as important to tools, and yet that is what the early tools were designed to do as they were not interactive. We will use this case study to recover what at the time was one of the most important features of a concording tool – how it could output something that could be published for others to use.[35]

In their case studies of pre-internet text analysis technologies, Sinclair and Rockwell give a further example of when, in 1957, Paul Tasman of IBM, Busa's close collaborator, wrote a rather limpid description of the methodology that was devised for the *Index Thomisticus* project. Tasman's account of the methodology is paraphrased below:

1. The scholar analyses and pre-edits the text (e.g., text by Thomas Aquinas) and marks the phrase;
2. Two keypunch operators input the phrases (twice onto the same card);
3. The checking machine verifies the accuracy of the input;
4. From the phrase card the machine outputs cards which each contain one of the words contained in that phrase along with essential information to allow it to be identified in the text ("word cards"). It also produces a copy of each of the phrase cards;
5. The machine checks the "word cards" and produces "form cards," e.g., by eliminating duplicates and calculating word frequency;
6. The scholar must intervene again now to produce "entry cards" from "form cards." They perform the linguistic operations that the machine cannot i.e., they distinguish between homophones and group inflected word forms under their corresponding lemma;
7. Now the machine is called for again to "interpret" the four groups of cards that have been generated during this process. Tasman describes

the process of interpretation as "the machine will print on the top of each card in letters and consecutive numbers whatever information the card contains 'written' in holes;"[36]

8. The information about the text that is contained on these four sets of cards (i.e., the phrase and word cards, which contain two transcriptions of the text and the form and entry cards, which contain information about the text at the unit and linguistic level) can now be printed for the scholar "on sheets, in brochures or books or on other cards. Valuable tools in philological research like an index verborum or concordance are available without further scholarly effort."[37]

When reflecting on Busa's technical plan, the dance between human and machine that it entailed, Winter perceptively concluded: "Father Busa, with IBM's enabling help, was at the pivot point (or was the pivot point) between handmade scholarly tools and machine-made scholarly tools."[38]

From our oral history interviews, we can extend Rockwell and Sinclair's case studies with a fourth example of a forgotten text analysis technology: a kind of finding device, or a kind of paper-based search engine,[39] that Wilhelm Ott devised to allow readers to navigate the material contained in his publications on the metrical analysis of various Latin poems. This case study further exemplifies the humanistic-machinic pivot point in the history of digital humanities tools.

Case Study: Wilhelm Ott

Having completed his PhD in New Testament theology in 1965 at the University of Wurzburg, Wilhelm Ott took up the position of research officer at the Computing Center of the University of Tübingen in 1966. In 1970 he also became head of the Division for Literary and Documentary Data Processing and it was there that the Tübingen System of Text Processing Programs (TUSTEP) was developed. In addition to his work on TUSTEP, Ott was engaged in other quite high-profile activities in the field of digital humanities (or humanities computing as it was then known). He provided specialized support for many humanities computing projects in Germany, such as Bonifatius Fischer's work on a concordance to the Vulgate. From 1973 until 2004, Ott organized a "colloquium on the application of electronic data processing in the human sciences" (*Kolloquium zur Anwendung der*

EDV in den Geisteswissenschaften) at the University of Tübingen. From an early stage on, he was also engaged in research commercialization. In 1973 he became co-founder of the firm Pagina, which now specializes in XML and other aspects of electronic publication. In recognition of his contributions, in 2007 the Alliance of Digital Humanities Organisations (ADHO) bestowed the Busa award upon him.

In 2015, Ott participated in an oral history interview with Nyhan, during which he recalled the first instruction in computing that he took in the *Deutsches Rechenzentrum* (German Computing Centre) in Darmstadt in 1966. In this interview he recounts that having become somewhat inattentive to the practical tasks that he and other students on the course were asked to complete, he turned his attention to writing a computer program to automate the metrical analysis of dactylic hexameter poetry, a research problem that had been occupying him for a while and that he expected to be amenable to computing. The program worked and his research on the metrical analysis of Latin hexameters would occupy him for the next nineteen years. The output of this work was published incrementally with Niemeyer, between 1970 and 1985.

During the visit to Ott in Tübingen in 2015, Nyhan had the opportunity to peruse his library, and the editions of the metrical analysis that it contained and noticed that some of the editions were accompanied by what appeared to be a small stack of punched cards. In conversation with Ott, she determined that the punched cards functioned as a kind of paper search engine to the material contained in the editions, in the sense that they permitted the material to be searched and navigated in response to user-generated queries posed via the cards.

Up until the 1970s, punched cards were widely used in humanities computing projects—also in Busa's *Index Thomisticus* project. Busa's punched cards, however, served a quite different function from those of Ott. For Busa, they were very much a vehicle for encoded data. The punched cards of the *Index Thomisticus* were routinely transformed to another storage medium (like magnetic tape) so the encoded information could be processed serially, further manipulated and ultimately printed (which, as mentioned above, was de rigueur during the period under discussion).[40] The idea of utilizing the punched cards post-printing to facilitate the interrogation of the published work seems to be a largely forgotten example of a material infrastructure for text search and analysis, in the vein of the forgotten text analysis tools discussed by Sinclair and Rockwell.[41]

In conversation with Nyhan, Ott described how the punched cards worked, while recalling where the inspiration for his approach had come from:

Wilhelm Ott (WO): The problems that I wanted to solve (in addition to providing overviews for the hexameter poetry) I had drawn from the appendix to the commentary of Eduard Norden to the sixth book of the *Aeneid* (1957). He was convinced that metrics were important for interpreting a poem and had a lot of criteria that he looked for: the number of words and the position of the word endings in respect to the verse structure. In the middle of a hexameter there is normally also a caesura (or a pause) and he also looked for where exactly this caesura is on average, or in most verses, and so on.

Therefore, one of the tools I provided, and which I thought it was possible to provide beyond the printed lists, was a tool to allow one to look for combinations of word endings in the verse. I thought that it could be done relatively easily using a punched card. The punched card had eighty columns, with at least ten positions which could easily be numbered vertically. Additional rows twelve and eleven, as they were called, were not used for representing the number of lines, or the number of verses. Therefore, I provided sixteen punched cards, one for each position in the hexameter, as the hexameter consists of six feet, and each foot can have either two or three syllables: two long syllables, or one long syllable and two short syllables (that makes sixteen times three, or eighteen, but the verse end is always a word end, therefore it can be neglected, and the last foot is almost always two syllables only. That meant I had sixteen positions that were interesting).

And so, I provided sixteen punched cards. On each card I made a hole in the respective position. Where, for example, a word ended just after the first syllable in line three of a poem, then in column zero, in row three, I made a hole in the first card, this meant there is a monosyllabic word at the beginning of the verse. And this I did for the sixteen positions in the verse and for every line. Then, if you want to see if, for example, a verse starts with a monosyllable, and ends with a monosyllable, you just take the first and last card and put them together, one above the other, hold them against the light, and where the holes are shining through, there you have the number of the lines of the verses which start and end with a monosyllabic word. It's as easy as this.

Julianne Nyhan (JN): And where did the idea for this come from?

WO: Well, I was accustomed to punched cards. Data entry was on punched cards and some output was on punched cards for further processing. The compiled programmes were also on punched cards. So, for a second run, if you have the same programme but different data, you could just use the binary text of the programme to produce it. I was also aware of some people's work with so-called *Randlochkarten* [edge-punched cards] where one could sort the material by mechanical means . . .

JN: *Randloch* is the hole at the side of the card?

WO: It was cards where the content was written by hand and on the margin of those cards was a perforation, I think it was, and you could cut this to the margin with the help of a special scissors, so that if you got a needle or a nail or something to go through a notched hole and lifted the needle, the respective cards would fall back. This is a mechanical tool I also knew, and I thought such approaches to inspection could aid this problem.[42]

As space does not allow detailed discussion of the *Randlochkarten* referred to by Ott, a brief outline must suffice. *Randlochkarten* seem to have been quite commonly used for manually sorting and managing punched cards. Halmann, for example, when introducing his "multi-sorter for separating edge-punched cards," writes: "In the usual technique of manual sorting of punched cards, a needle is used to separate about 200 cards at a time."[43] Kelly states that in the US they were called McBee Keysort Cards and often used in library settings: "Before the advent of computers [they] were one of the few ways you could sort large databases for more than one term at once. In computer science terms, you could do a 'logical OR' operation."[44]

Various references to the cards can also be found in publications of projects that fell within the interests of Digital humanities and Computational Linguistics. For example, a report written for the European Atomic Energy Community (EURATOM) in 1963 describes "a method developped [sic] . . . for preparing a five-lingual card file by using edge-notched cards . . . The card file is especially useful for translation and terminology services for several languages, where new terminologies in the science and technology field are recorded."[45] A 1974 research report describes their uses in Soviet historiography and mentions three formats of cards in use: "Two such methods are described in the Russian literature to hand: edge-notched cards, the *Sichtlochkarte*, and the dual card which is a special form."[46] The report goes on to describe how and by whom they were used and writes that "In 1962 Edge-punched cards were introduced to the Estonian Academy of Sciences on a large scale so that by 1965 half of the staff used them."[47] Though such cards now appear to be a dead, mostly forgotten technology they offer an interesting case study in the context of the media archaeology of Digital humanities (and beyond) and it would be intriguing to follow other references to their uses in other historical Digital humanities projects.

The Promise of Oral History for Digital Humanities

The case study that is given above of the punched-card based text navigation and analysis tool that was devised by Ott and the case studies by Sinclair and Rockwell referenced previously, especially that of Glickman, alert us to the way that actors other than Busa also pirouetted on the so-called 'pivot point' and that it endured, or was remade, beyond the geographical and temporal confines of the *Index Thomisticus* project.

Ott's combinatorial tool is an exemplification of this: it seems to pivot between genres and technologies, and between the old and the new in an intriguing bricolage. Ott's navigation aid repurposed the punched-card technology that had been used to input the textual content of his metrical analysis for processing so that it could facilitate an engagement with, and command over text that went beyond the fixity of the traditional index and book. Ott did not offer a standard alphabetic index or word frequency table to readers, rather he wanted to allow them to search at a much higher resolution, for "combinations of word endings in the verse." To do so, Ott did not use the computational infrastructures, affordances, and tools that are now considered synonymous with Digital humanities. Rather, he utilized the inherent flexibility and recombinant nature of the shared, paper-based materiality of the book and the punched card to push forward analogue information management and retrieval technologies. The form of the punched cards, with their rows and columns, the possibility of detaching the cards from the fixity of the printed book, and of holding them against the light, so that they could then disrupt the fixity of the printed book, were identified by Ott as having potential to open a multi-layered, embodied, and combinatorial interrogation of printed verse. And in doing so, Ott used a paper-based technology in an innovative way that could supersede the limitations of the newer mainframe-based computing of his day where interactive computing was, for most of those who worked in Humanities departments, still some way off.

Within the context of Ott's work this example of a forgotten text technology gives us an insight into the kinds of access that Ott hoped to provide, even though neither the standard book technologies of the day, nor, indeed, the computational tools of the day could directly facilitate it in their dominant forms.[48] In this way Ott's now forgotten text analysis and navigation tool offer new approach routes to the history of digital humanities and underline again the importance of Sinclair and Rockwell's call for "digital humanities archaeology."[49] That oral history can play an important role in "thickening" such an archaeology is also suggested by Ott's interview, which gave space for Ott to contextualize the development of the tool within his own personal history of encountering quantification, mechanization, and computation in the humanities, in a way that is not routinely captured in the computing and academic literature that accompanies text technologies, again amplifying the thesis of Sinclair and Rockwell.

Conclusion

The case study of Ott's "paper search engine" speaks to the history of digital humanities and points to transversal routes across the history of the humanities and the history of the digital humanities. Considered next to other forgotten technologies, Ott's interview is one example of how oral history can open the possibility of understanding the history of Digital humanities not as a series of revolutionary and triumphalist developments but as a something that was, of course, deeply interconnected with and influenced not only by the issues and ideas of its days but also by its expansive material, informational, and intellectual background.[50] This may seem like an obvious point to make but, as we have argued elsewhere, the history of digital humanities has tended to be overlooked until recently and it has sometimes been portrayed as a development that is unmoored from its longer historical contexts.[51]

The case studies above attest to how Busa, Glickman, Ott, and Smith sought to wrangle the atomic and sub-atomic units of text e.g., individual words and syllables, so that they could be identified, tracked, combined and recombined in various way that could support the creation of new knowledge and result in interpretative purchase. At first glance one might presume that such a perspective was new and that it emanated from computing technology (after all, printed books usually produced fixed representations of their contents and allowed those contents to be accessed through standard paths like alphabetical or thematic indexes, page layout or chapter arrangement).

Yet, the ability to recognize and manipulate atomic units of text far preceded computational technology. For example, it is now quite common for dictionaries to be organized alphabetically. Yet, for the vast majority of their history dictionaries were organized thematically; it was not until after the printing press that complete alphabetization became widespread. MacArthur has argued that this is due to the advent of movable type and the way that the letters of the alphabet existed for the first time as tangible, individual, hard metal objects. As people involved in the printing press began to touch and re-order letters, the advantages of the alphabetical system may have been impressed upon them, and, he contends, gradually an awareness of this system spread from people involved in making fonts to people who thought and theorized about letters and words:

> Where scholars and copyists had previously been unaccustomed to thinking of words and even parts of words alphabetically, printers were now spending a great part of their time doing nothing else. Sheer familiarity with hard physical objects in a very practical craft appears, therefore, to have promoted interest in alphabetical order in other, related but more abstract fields.[52]

The text analysis tools developed by those such as Busa, Glickman, Smith and Ott also sought to model and find patterns in and with the texts and text technologies they attended to. The attention to forgotten technologies, then, can alert us not only to the technology itself, but to the ways text itself has been conceptualized and studied across longer trajectories with a multiplicity of tools in the humanities and digital humanities. Accordingly, oral history has the potential not only to inform histories of digital humanities but to grant insight into the shape that the Humanities has taken, over the *longue durée*.[53]

Notes

1. Rens Bod et al., "A New Field: History of Humanities," *History of Humanities* 1, no. 1 (2016): 2.
2. Stephen Ramsay, "Who's in and Who's Out," in *Defining Digital Humanities: A Reader*, ed. Melissa Terras, Julianne Nyhan, and Edward Vanhoutte (Surrey: Ashgate, 2013), 239.
3. E.g., Willard McCarty, *Humanities Computing* (Basingstoke: Palgrave Macmillan, 2005); Rens Bod, "Modelling in the Humanities: Linking Patterns to Principles," *Historical Social Research*, Supplement 31 (2018): 78–95.
4. E.g., Rens Bod, *A New History of the Humanities: The Search for Principles and Patterns from Antiquity to the Present*, trans. Lynn Richards (Oxford: Oxford

University Press, 2013); Samantha Lutz, "{D1G1TAL HER1TAGE}: From Cultural to Digital Heritage," *Hamburger Journal für Kulturanthropologie* 7 (2018): 3–23.

5. Julianne Nyhan and Andrew Flinn, *Computation and the Humanities: Towards an Oral History of Digital Humanities* (Cham: Springer, 2016), 21–36.
6. *One Origin of Digital Humanities: Fr Roberto Busa in His Own Words*, ed. Julianne Nyhan and Marco Passarotti (Cham: Springer, 2019).
7. Julianne Nyhan, *Hidden and Devalued Labour in the Digital Humanities: On the Index Thomisticus Project 1954–67* (London: Routledge, forthcoming).
8. Julianne Nyhan and Marco Passarotti, "Introduction, or Why Busa Still Matters," in *One Origin of Digital Humanities*, 1–18.
9. Publications tended to be article-length surveys of the history of the application of computing to particular fields of the humanities, like classics and musicology. See, e.g., Walter B. Hewlett and Eleanor Selfridge-Field, "Computing in Musicology, 1966–91," *Computers and the Humanities* 25, no. 6 (1991): 381–92; T. F. Brunner, "Classics and the Computer: The History of a Relationship," in *Accessing Antiquity: The Computerization of Classical Studies*, ed. J. Solomon (Tucson, AZ: University of Arizona Press, 1993), 10–33; histories of the development indexes and concordances, humanities computing's canonical tools (in a series of articles by Burton e.g., Dolores M. Burton, "Automated Concordances and Word Indexes: The Fifties," *Computers and the Humanities* 15, no. 1 (1981): 1–14; and articles on acclaimed scholars like Busa e.g., Thomas Nelson Winter, "Roberto Busa S.J. and the Invention of the Machine-Generated Concordance," *The Classical Bulletin* 75, no. 1 (1999): 3–20.
10. Susan M. Hockey, "The History of Humanities Computing," in *A Companion to Digital Humanities*, ed. Susan Schreibman, Ray Siemens, and John Unsworth (Malden, MA: Blackwell, 2004), 3.
11. E.g., Amy Earhart et al., "Alternate Histories of the Digital Humanities: A Short Paper Panel Proposal" (2017), online at https://dh2017.adho.org/abstracts/115/115.pdf (accessed March 9, 2022); Tom Scheinfeldt, "The Dividends of Difference: Recognizing Digital Humanities Diverse Family Tree's" (April 7, 2014), online at http://foundhistory.org/2014/04/the-dividends-of-difference-recognizing-digital-humanities-diverse-family-trees/ (accessed March 9, 2022).
12. James O'Sullivan, "The Digital Humanities in Ireland," *Digital Studies/Le Champ Numérique* 10, no. 1 (2020); Joris van Zundert and Karina van Dalen-Oskam, "Digital Humanities in the Netherlands," *H-Soz-Kult* (October 28, 2014), online at http://www.hsozkult.de/debate/id/diskussionen-2396 (accessed March 9, 2022).

13. Willard McCarty, "Getting There from Here: Remembering the Future of Digital Humanities Roberto Busa Award Lecture 2013," *Literary and Linguistic Computing* 29, no. 3 (2014): 283–306.
14. Stéfan Sinclair and Geoffrey Rockwell, "Towards an Archaeology of Text Analysis Tools," Presented at Digital Humanities 2014, Lausanne, Switzerland (2014), 357–8.
15. Jussi Parikka, *What Is Media Archaeology?* (Cambridge: Polity Press, 2012), 2.
16. Stéfan Sinclair, "Experiments with Punch Cards," online at http://stefansinclair.name/punchcard/ (accessed March 9, 2022); Geoffrey Rockwell and Stéfan Sinclair, "Tremendous Mechanical Labor: Father Busa's Algorithm," *Digital Humanities Quarterly* 14, no. 3 (2020).
17. Steven Jones et al., "RECALL: Reconstructing the First Humanities Computing Centre" (2017), online at http://www.recaal.org/pages/walkthrough.html (accessed March 9, 2022); Steven Jones, "Reverse Engineering the First Humanities Computing Center," *Digital Humanities Quarterly* 12, no. 2 (2018).
18. Alessandro, Portelli, *Battle of Valle Giulia: Oral History and the Art of Dialogue* (Madison, WI: University of Wisconsin Press, 1997), viii.
19. Nyhan and Flinn, *Computation and the Humanities.*
20. Paul Thompson, *The Voice of the Past: Oral History*, 3rd edn (Oxford: Oxford University Press, 2000), 3.
21. E.g., Terry Cook, "The Archive(s) Is a Foreign Country: Historians, Archivists, and the Changing Archival Landscape," *The American Archivist* 74, no. 2 (2011): 600–32.
22. Antoinette M. Burton, "Finding Women in the Archive: Introduction," *Journal of Women's History* 20, no. 1 (2008): 149.
23. Catherine Bishop, "The Serendipity of Connectivity: Piecing Together Women's Lives in the Digital Archive," *Women's History Review* 26, no. 5 (2017): 767.
24. Valerie J. Korinek, "Locating Lesbians, Finding 'Gay Women,' Writing Queer Histories," in *Beyond Women's Words: Feminisms and the Practices of Oral History in the Twenty-First Century*, ed. Katrina Srigley, Stacey Zembrzycki, and Franca Iacovetta (London: Routledge, 2018), 128.
25. E.g., Janet Abbate, *Recoding Gender: Women's Changing Participation in Computing* (Cambridge, MA: MIT Press, 2012).
26. Sarah K, Loose and Amy Starecheski, "Oral History for Building Social Movements, Then and Now," in Srigley, Zembrzycki, and Iacovetta, *Beyond Women's Words*, 238.
27. Ludmilla J. Jordanova, *History in Practice* (London: Arnold, 2000), 1.
28. Robert Perks and Alistair Thomson, *The Oral History Reader* (Abingdon: Routledge, 2016), 3–6.

29. Linda Shopes, "Oral History and the Study of Communities: Problems, Paradoxes, and Possibilities," *The Journal of American History* 89, 2 (2002): 588–98.
30. Lynn Abrams, *Oral History Theory* (Abingdon: Routledge, 2016), 58–63.
31. See Nyhan and Flinn, *Computation and the Humanities,* 32 (and 21–34 for an extended discussion of challenges to oral history).
32. Anna Sheftel and Stacey Zembrzycki "Slowing Down to Listen in the Digital Age: How New Technology Is Changing Oral History Practice," *The Oral History Review* 44, no. 1 (2017): 94–112.
33. Katrina Srigley, Stacey Zembrzycki, and Franca Iacovetta, "Introduction," in Srigley, Zembrzycki, and Iacovetta, *Beyond Women's Words*, 10.
34. Hannah Smyth, Julianne Nyhan, and Andrew Flinn, "Opening the 'Black Box' of Digital Cultural Heritage Processes: Feminist Digital Humanities and Critical Heritage Studies," in *Routledge International Handbook of Research Methods in Digital Humanities*, ed. Kirsten Schuster and Stuart Dunn (Abingdon: Routledge, 2020).
35. Sinclair and Rockwell, "Towards an Archaeology," 357.
36. Paul Tasman, "Literary Data Processing," *IBM Journal of Research and Development* 1, no. 3 (1957): 255.
37. Ibid.
38. Winter, "Roberto Busa," 16.
39. Though information processing has become synonymous with digital computing, a long history of the use of analogue and electromechanical devices for information processing precedes the use of digital machines and, to some extent, runs alongside them too. On the history of punched cards for information processing see, e.g., Lars Heide, *Punched-Card Systems and the Early Information Explosion, 1880–1945.* (Baltimore, MD: Johns Hopkins University Press, 2009); on paper-based computing see, e.g., Mark Lorenzo Jones, *The Paper Computer Unfolded: A Twenty-First Century Guide to the Bell Labs CARDIAC, the LMC, and the IPC* (Philadelphia, PA: SE Books, 2017).
40. Nyhan, *Hidden and Devalued Labour.*
41. Sinclair and Rockwell, "Towards an Archaeology."
42. This text has been reproduced, with permission, from Nyhan and Flinn, *Computation and the Humanities*, 63–4.
43. M. Halmann, "A Simple Multi-Sorter for Separating Edge-Punched Cards," *Journal of Chemical Documentation* 1, no. 2 (1961): 78.
44. Kevin Kelly, "One Dead Media," *The Techniu* (2008), online at http://kk.org/thetechnium/one-dead-media/ (accessed March 9, 2022).
45. A. Kreusler and Graf K. Ch. Rothkirtch-Trach, *Randlochkarten als Sprachwörterkartei* (Brussels: European Atomic Energy Community, 1963), 3, online at http://aei.pitt.edu/60342/ (accessed March 9, 2022).

46. Manfred Alexander, "Zur Verwendung von Lochkarten, elektronischer Datenverarbeitung und statistischen Methoden in der sowjetischen Historiographie," *Jahrbücher für Geschichte Osteuropas* 22, no. 1 (1974): 92 (translation ours).
47. Ibid. (translation ours).
48. For a wider discussion of how old technologies do not necessarily disappear but can go on to bolster and enable newer technologies in consequential yet often overlooked ways see David Edgerton, *The Shock of the Old: Technology and Global History since 1900* (London: Profile Books, 2006).
49. Sinclair and Rockwell, "Towards an Archaeology," 357.
50. On the longer history of text technologies and information management tools see, e.g., Ann M. Blair, *Too Much to Know: Managing Scholarly Information before the Modern Age* (New Haven, CT: Yale University Press, 2011) and Markus Krajewski, *Paper Machines: About Cards and Catalogs, 1548–1929*, trans. Peter Krapp (Cambridge, MA: MIT Press, 2011).
51. See Julianne Nyhan, Andrew Flinn, and Anne Welsh, "Oral History and the Hidden Histories Project: Towards Histories of Computing in the Humanities," *Digital Scholarship in the Humanities* 30, no. 1 (2015): 71–85.
52. Tom McArthur, *Living Words: Language, Lexicography, and the Knowledge Revolution* (Exeter: University of Exeter Press, 1998), 41–3.
53. Thank you to Herman Paul and Geoffrey Rockwell for their helpful comments on this chapter.

Part III

Values and Virtues

8

Practical Learning: The Transnational Career of an Epistemic Value in Japan

Michael Facius

Introduction

This chapter introduces a transnational approach to the history of the humanities by tracing how the epistemic values of practicality, utility, and applicability moved across national, cultural, and intellectual borders and, in doing so, changed in meaning and relevance. Practicality and usefulness are nowadays ranked among the most essential attributes of knowledge. Applied sciences, especially in the STEM fields, are seen as inherently useful because of their contributions to technological development and the economy. Scholars in the humanities also feel pressured to demonstrate the practical value and impact of their research in an increasingly competitive and underfunded academic marketplace. On the teaching side, practical learning in schools and universities, where students are engaging with so-called real-life problems, is supposed to enrich mere 'book learning' and aid professional development.

However, what practicality, usefulness, and applicability exactly mean is ambiguous and contested. In a narrow sense, practicality today is often about the conformance of knowledge production to academic capitalism and the needs of the work- and marketplace.[1] In a wider sense, it can refer to any type of knowledge that does some work in the world beyond the minds of scholars and the ivory tower. Practicality thus sets a norm that, by implying its opposite of useless, theoretical, or bookish knowledge, delineates the contours of desirable and negative forms of knowledge production. It is in this sense that this chapter will call practicality an epistemic value—less a "value that promotes the attainment of knowledge" than a perceived attribute of a certain body of knowledge.[2]

The contemporary debate about utility is a crucial one for the humanities, because economists and policymakers have much greater power to define public hierarchies of practical knowledge than humanities scholars or departments themselves, even while these definitions directly affect the public status, funding and research directions of these fields.[3] Researchers in the humanities are using different strategies to deal with this imbalance: they submit to the discourse of economic utility by focusing on research that produces quantifiable output and appeal to the labor-market value of their degrees;[4] they try to assert use values of the humanities beyond the economic realm, in the aid of self-realization or democratic discourse;[5] or they reject the centrality of practicality altogether and foreground other epistemic values.[6]

Given their power in structuring knowledge production, tracing the history of epistemic values is a fruitful task for the history of the humanities, both as a reflexive endeavor to interrogate contemporary value systems and as a historical research program in its own right.[7] By tracing genealogies of the value of practical learning and its changing relationship to humanistic scholarship in nineteenth-century Japan, this chapter will contribute to such a history of epistemic values from a global or transnational perspective.

One of the gains of such a global perspective is that it shows us the instability of the terms, institutions, and practices of humanistic scholarship across different localities. In the contemporary setting, despite the global interconnectedness of academic research and the pervasive influence of academic capitalism, value discourses follow local circumstances and trajectories. In China, for example, the humanities are receiving strong state support as a form of soft power and are thus following a different logic of utility.[8] Going back in time, these differences become even more pronounced as we enter the early modern period when the world was still divided prominently into different "republics of letters" and other spheres of knowledge exchange.[9]

This is where a transnational perspective can offer a complementary reading: it can show how the notion of practical learning accrued new meanings while moving across national, cultural, and intellectual borders, and how its prominence in the hierarchy of epistemic values changed while doing so. As the following discussion will show in detail, Japan is an informative case study for this kind of program because here, the idea of practical learning arose independently from Western discourses during the influx of Chinese Confucian thought. Japan's conceptualization of practical learning then evolved in response to domestic epistemic and political pressures, and it became central to Japanese knowledge production in reaction to Western imperialism and the state-building programs of the later nineteenth century. As sinologist Theodore de Bary pointed out in his influential work on practical learning in China and Japan, the Japanese understanding eventually converged with Western ones—from "an earlier focus on moral substantiality to the pursuit of objective, empirical investigation serving utilitarian ends"[10]—but had its own unique starting point and route, and thus presents a case of conceptual universalization that productively enriches the global history of the humanities.[11]

Practical Learning and Confucian Virtue in Early Modern East Asia

In East Asia, the epistemic value of "practical learning" originally surfaced in the context of Confucian thought. Practical learning is one possible translation of the Chinese word *shixue*: the first character, *shi*, means "fruit," so it could be literally translated as learning that bears fruit. The semantic connotation is that the learning so denoted has some relationship with reality and is of practical use, hence "real" or "practical" learning or scholarship. Given the strong normative implications, it is not surprising that Chinese rhetoric, not unlike the Western context, also makes ample use of its antonym *xuxue*—empty, false, and useless learning—succinctly juxtaposing two poles of virtuous and problematic scholarship. It is also equally true for the Chinese case that how intellectuals filled this value with life and what counted as practical learning was ambiguous, contested, and changed over time.

In the later Confucian tradition after Zhu Xi (1130–1200), the Song period scholar who founded what is often called Neo-Confucianism in the English literature, the purpose of learning was a deep understanding of the cosmic principle (*li*) and how it governed and unfolded in human society.

The ultimate goal was the realization of the moral order of society; in the *Great Learning*, a foundational text of this tradition, moral order is connected to knowledge and individual conduct through a causal chain:

> Those of antiquity who wished that all people throughout the empire would let their inborn luminous virtue shine forth put governing their states well first; wishing to govern their states well, they first established harmony in their households; wishing to establish harmony in their households, they first cultivated themselves; wishing to cultivate themselves, they first set their minds in the right; wishing to set their minds in the right, they first made their intentions true; wishing to make their intentions true, they first extended knowledge to the utmost; the extension of knowledge lies in the investigation of things.[12]

Through the study of the Confucian classics and moral reflection, the scholar would incrementally align and harmonize their own being with the cosmos. This is the "fruit" that the Chinese term originally referred to, and learning that went against or distracted from this goal was "empty." Despite Zhu Xi's dislike and disavowal of Zen Buddhism, the original notion of practical learning thus did not just link knowledge with morality, but was also deeply spiritual, similar to the Buddhist perfection of transcendent wisdom (*prajna paramita*) and connected with related introspective and meditative practices.[13]

Japanese scholars studied these teachings and adopted a similar view of practical learning. Confucian scholarship in Japan was read and written in Classical Chinese, so the term *shixue*, written with the same Sinitic characters, entered Japanese vocabulary with the Japanese pronunciation *jitsugaku*. The renowned seventeenth-century scholars Nakae Tōju (1608–48) and Kumazawa Banzan (1619–91) expressed a morally grounded understanding of the term close to its Chinese roots. Kumazawa, for example, exclaimed that "if there is no fondness of virtue, it is hard to speak of practical learning." However, this did not mean that Kumazawa was exclusively mandating the study of metaphysics and morality. He also found *jitsugaku* embodied in the study of poetry: "Good and evil, right and wrong, are all facts (*jitsuji*) of human nature. Thus, the study of [poetry] is practical learning."[14]

This quote from Kumazawa expresses a striking similarity to Western defenses of the humanities that emphasize their potential for providing students with skills and attitudes that allow them to participate actively in society and hone their capacities for an ethical and fully "human" life.[15] Theodore de Bary took note of this similarity:

By *tao wen hsüeh* Chu [i.e., Zhu Xi] described that aspect of the "Study of the Way" which was particularly concerned with scholarly and literary pursuits, in contrast to moral cultivation and social action. It was learning relevant to the humane concerns of the Confucian Way, and took many of the same forms as the *studia humanitatis* [in the Western Renaissance].[16]

This similarity of notions of humanistic scholarship between early modern East Asia and Europe is an interesting fact in its own right; more importantly for the history of epistemic values, it reveals a close alignment of humanistic scholarship with practicality—an association that slowly began to shift in the late eighteenth century.

Practical Learning and Japanese Statecraft

Over the course of the eighteenth century, Zhu Xi-Confucian learning in its earlier formulations lost some of its attraction as new generations of scholars moved away from the exegesis of the Confucian classics based on commentaries and personal reflection towards new, more empirically minded methodologies to study them. Scholar of Chinese thought Benjamin Elman called this trend a move from "philosophy to philology," as practical scholarship came to be reinterpreted less as rooted in a specific philosophical stance than in a methodology of what their proponents called evidential learning (*kaozhengxue*, J. *kōshōgaku*).[17]

Early modern Japan participated heavily in the East Asian circulation of Confucian thought. Every year countless Confucian texts and other learned treatises written in Classical Sinitic entered the country through the port of Nagasaki at the hands of Chinese traders, which were then circulated, copied, discussed, and built upon by Japanese scholars.[18] Both the original versions of Zhu Xi Confucianism and their critiques found echoes and equivalents in Japanese debates. Japanese intellectual history often identifies in the lexical studies of the eminent scholar Ogyū Sorai (1666–1728) a similar turn from "philosophy to philology."[19] While later scholars who directly engaged with Qing-period (1644–1912) evidential learning such as Ōta Kinjō acknowledged Ogyū as a forerunner in this type of scholarship, they also criticized him for having been too utilitarian to the point of heterodoxy, and for forgetting that true practical learning needs to be rooted in the practice of Confucian virtues.[20]

In other words, the eighteenth century saw the emergence of new scholarly trends in conversation with contemporary Chinese literature that introduced empirical methods as one new key ingredient of practical learning, but without going so far as to fully replace the older precedence of moral training in Japanese Confucian discourse.

On top of these purely scholarly discussions, a more pressing and worldly concern began to shift the notion of practical learning in a different direction. Both the central shogunal government and many of the approximately 250 feudal domains that made up the early modern Japanese polity had navigated themselves into an impasse: they were institutionally and intellectually ill-prepared to deal with the increasing complexity of the economy in the archipelago with its growing reliance on money, inter- and intra-domanial trade and private enterprise. As a result, they were faced with severe fiscal shortages, unstable price levels, and other economic problems. Practical learning now became connected to issues of good statecraft.[21] Political philosophy had always been at the core of Confucian learning and most scholars belonged to the hereditary ruling class of samurai and were learning the basics of virtuous rulership from the classics. Yet, tackling these political problems more systematically required the accumulation and analysis of financial data and political strategy, as well as domain officials that were adequately educated thus. Therefore, many feudal lords began to set up, revive, or reform domain-run schools.

In the Kansei era (1789–1801), the central government of the Tokugawa shogunate also initiated a wide-ranging reform program.[22] One element of this program was to strengthen the relationship between government and education. Reform-minded scholars were ordered to modernize accordingly the Shōhei Academy, the Confucian school of the Tokugawa government, by formally making it a state institution, reforming the curriculum, and setting up an examination system that would facilitate the recruitment of capable leaders into the Tokugawa bureaucracy.[23]

There was also a wider geopolitical background behind the Kansei reforms: the southward push of Russia in the North Pacific, including unwelcome visits of Russian ships to the northern island of Ezo (today Hokkaido) and later the defeat of China in 1842 at the hands of Britain in the first Opium War. Practical knowledge also came to mean knowledge about the world, and the need for better intelligence led to the creation of new institutions that gathered and translated information about current affairs.[24] Despite long periods of reform, the fundamental tensions built into the Tokugawa political economy could not be resolved, while recurring bad harvests and famines ensured recovery was always fragile, which meant that calls for reform continuously reemerged on the political agenda.

One particularly influential scholar in the lineage of the discourse on practical learning was Yokoi Shōnan (1809–69). He became a teacher and scholar at the domain-run school Jishūkan in Kumamoto on the southern island of Kyūshū. In 1844 he founded a "study group for practical learning" (*jitsugakutō*) at said school with four other scholars that met regularly to study subjects relevant to the reform of domanial politics and the replenishment of its coffers. The thrust of their brand of practical learning was also directed towards the poor state of the Jishūkan, which according to Yokoi and his group was attended by the sons of the hereditary samurai class with the purpose of securing posts and income in the domain government instead of actual study.[25]

The group's attempts eventually faltered, more due to personal conflicts and factional infighting in the domain government than its program per se. But Yokoi continued to push for the "unity of scholarship and government" to solve policy problems. In his *Dialogue on Schools* (1852), Yokoi attacked both scholars who kept away from politics and rulers who failed to seek out scholarly expertise. He argued that founding a school in and of itself is not a guarantee for the training of capable political leaders. If they are not managed properly, they devolve into a playground for "vulgar Confucians" with their "useless learning" (*muyō no gakumon*) of "words and phrases."

> Learned and common people equally tend to understand scholarship exclusively as self-cultivation. They call persons who read books and ponder their meanings, who are upright and modest, who renounce worldly matters and cultivate themselves, "true Confucians." Those that reflect on the classics, discuss historical works and are skillful in poetry, they call a "learned person." ... And so scholars become unfit for government (*keizai*), and those who govern lose their moral grounding.[26]

Here finally, we can observe a clear formulation of the sentiment that had been growing among intellectuals in the previous decades: that the value of scholarship lies not in a particular methodology or moral stance, but in its use value for the state; accordingly, scholars should not look for self-cultivation, but active participation in governmental affairs. Semantically, this change manifested in the character *yō* for "use," which, alone or in conjunction with *jitsu*, stresses the "practical use" (*jitsuyō*) of scholarship more explicitly.

Yet, Yokoi's plea was not a complete utilitarian break with previous notions, but more of a shift in focus, as self-cultivation and the good order of the realm and cosmos were still linked through the framework of Confucian philosophy as presented in the *Great Learning*. Neither did this shift imply that a complete overhaul of the curriculum was called for: Literature and speculative philosophy were harder to reconcile with this new ideal, but most knowledge that Yokoi and his peers would have understood as politically useful was fundamentally philological in form and method: from law codes and economic theory to translations of Dutch intelligence reports and even ancient Chinese political history, which provided models for virtuous decision-making and sharpened the faculties of future leaders.

Western Imperialism and Military Technology

It was in the midst of this growing political instability that the United States and European powers advanced into East Asia. Western ships had already been appearing on and off in Japanese ports since the early years of the nineteenth century, despite the strict official limits on trade and diplomatic intercourse imposed by the Tokugawa government. In 1853, the American Commodore Matthew Perry used gunboat diplomacy to push Japan to join a Western-centered global trade and diplomatic order.

The escalating foreign threat made it obvious to the Tokugawa government that they needed to step up organizational and technological efforts to strengthen coastal defense.[27] It encouraged domains such as Saga on the southern island of Kyūshū to experiment with Western military technology. Saga succeeded in building a Western-style reverberatory iron furnace based on a Dutch description in 1850 and started producing cannon for their own and for shogunal use. Production sites for shipbuilding and armaments soon followed.[28]

The external crisis precipitated further political turmoil: The perceived weakness of the Tokugawa shogunate in handling the foreign threat delegitimized their rule, and in the course of the 1860s, some of the stronger feudal domains who were staunchly opposed to the opening of Japanese ports and hoped to "expel the barbarians" aligned with the imperial court, which had never ceased to exist but had lost any political power centuries earlier, in order to overthrow Tokugawa rule and reinstall an imperial government.[29]

Under these circumstances, practical learning became a rallying cry for both factions to pursue European applied sciences to secure the survival of the Japanese polity under the slogan "rich country, strong army." As was the case with the iron furnace, most of the necessary knowledge in this period entered Japan in the form of written materials in Dutch via the trade and intellectual connections of the Dutch factory in Nagasaki, and after the opening of treaty ports these materials were increasingly also in English. Since its beginnings in the mid-eighteenth century, Dutch learning had become widespread and covered a variety of different fields from medicine to biology, but after the opening of treaty ports its focus shifted more and more to military sciences.[30]

Japanese scholars translated and disseminated technical handbooks and intelligence reports as fast as they were capable, but the government realized that it needed to increase its efforts. In a response to an inquiry on educational reform by the shogunal council of elders, the official for coastal defense Kawaji Toshiakira lamented that the shogunal Shōheizaka Academy "failed to carry out scholarship," as

> there is little practical use (*jitsuyō*) in reading books. They devote themselves to poetry and literature ... We need to tell the professors ... to attend to coastal defense as well, because if we are not able to discern conditions regarding the West, we will go against the principle of "knowing your enemy and knowing yourself." ... We need to give the military science and gunnery of Dutch studies (*rangaku*) the highest priority.[31]

The government reacted quickly to Kawaji's memorandum and expanded its translation bureau in 1855 into an "Institute of Barbarian Books," which was renamed Kaiseijo and further enlarged in 1863.[32] We can see here how practical value became tied to technological and military knowledge and de-emphasized book learning, a value judgment that simultaneously spilled over to the bodies of knowledge associated with these types of learning. In other words, philological expertise in Dutch and English gained in value relative to the corpus of Classical Chinese erudition that formed the mainstream of education and scholarship.

The Critique of Sinitic Humanities

After a decade of civil unrest and political chaos, the Meiji Restoration in 1868 brought to power a government centered on the imperial throne which was committed to opening the country and proactively adopting Western knowledge and institutions. The Charter Oath, a founding document of the new government, proclaimed: "Knowledge shall be sought throughout the world so as to strengthen the foundations of imperial rule."[33]

Right after the Meiji Restoration, the new government set up a short-lived deliberative body (*kōgisho*) in which political leaders and intellectuals from all parts of the country discussed some of the pressing issues of the time. Still high on the agenda was the problem of securing and educating talented people for positions in the government and bureaucracy. Following a proposal by Kanda Kōhei, director of the Kaiseijo, the assembled samurai discussed the merits of importing the Chinese model of imperial examinations and the shape of the curriculum.

Kanda asserted that the subjects to be prioritized should be those which can be "applied in real life" (*jitchi tekiyō*), and another discussant warned that scholars were prone to pursuing "idle erudition" and should focus on "practical use" (*jitsuyō*).[34] Which subjects should fall under this label, however, was hotly debated. For Kanda, it was Japanese studies, Sinitic studies, politics and economy, composition, astronomy, geography, military sciences, law, medicine, and natural history. Many objected to the inclusion of Japanese and Sinitic studies, i.e., the philology, literature, history, and philosophy of Japan and China, while others wanted to include moral education in the list.

Ironically, the new evaluative standard of *jitsugaku* turned against the type of scholarship from which it had emerged: During the 1870s, textual scholarship based on the Sinitic canon (not exclusively, but also of the Confucian variety) came to be seen by a majority of policymakers and intellectuals as useless across the board; an evaluation that was compounded by the immense time and effort it took to learn the thousands of characters of the Sinitic writing system.[35] *Kangaku* or Sinitic learning became the target of rash criticism, and scholars, intellectuals and politicians called in unison for the revision of curricula that gave pre-eminence to Confucian morality and Chinese history, literature, and poetry.[36]

The most extreme criticism leveled against Sinitic learning came from, of all people, a junior scholar at the Shōhei Academy, who also submitted a proposal to the *kōgisho* with the inflammatory title "Burning excessive books":

> In ancient times, Chinese books spread across the realm in accordance with the imperial will and there was a great benefit to studying them. Recently,

however, the number of imported publications has risen starkly, useless characters making up the majority, with vulgar scholars . . . spilling ink for irrelevant frivolities. . . . They do not only completely lack a sense of what is important in our times but also . . . inflict great harm on the education of our people. Those books full of superfluous glosses and frivolous banter and others without any benefit for the realm should without exception be turned to ashes and dust. That would sweep away all evil customs, people would rub their eyes, and devote themselves to learning useful to government affairs.[37]

As soon as the abolishment of feudal domains enabled a central education policy, the government set about to create a national school system and implemented drastic curricular reforms, starting with the First National Plan for Education in 1872, which prioritized the newly identified practical subjects at the expense of traditional curricula and even employed Western textbooks and translated editions in favor of the Confucian primers that had been in use throughout the Tokugawa period.[38] The turn towards technical and scientific Western disciplines was even more striking in the realm of higher education. The basis for the first academic institution of higher learning was not the old Shōhei Academy run by the shogunate, which was shut down, but the Kaiseijo school for Western learning and the school for Western medicine, which were merged and restructured in the style of Western universities in 1877 to form the Imperial University (now the University of Tokyo).

Some historians made the polemics against Kangaku in the 1870s out to be somehow anti-Chinese in nature. As foreshadowed in the debates on practical learning of the previous decades, however, the crucial point is rather that Kangaku became the discursive stand-in for text-based and thus useless humanistic scholarship. Consequently, some intellectuals also denounced Western scholarship if it did not contribute to technological progress, such as Yoda Hyakusen (1834–1909; also Yoda Gakkai), himself a Kangaku scholar, in a short polemic titled "Doubts about Western Learning":

> Nowadays, even small children talk about the uselessness of Kangaku, and there is no one who would not praise the utility of Western science for our time. There is no arguing with the fact that Kangaku is useless. However, I also have my doubts about Western science . . . If it departs from practical things and principles (*jitsubutsu jitsuri*), then people can shout "civilization and enlightenment" as loud as they want, but then it is no better than the useless and rotten Kangaku.[39]

Overall, however, the association of practical learning with the subjects of Western science and technology became so entrenched as to be almost automatic. It was further strengthened by new conceptual underpinnings that came as a result of Japanese thinkers beginning to engage with Western views of knowledge and civilization. The most well-known of these thinkers is Fukuzawa Yukichi (1835–1901), who had been a scholar of Dutch and English before the Meiji Restoration. Through a number of well-placed publications such as his *English-Japanese Dictionary* (1860), *Conditions in the West* (1866–70), *Encouragement of Learning* (1872) and *An Outline of a Theory of Civilization* (1875), he became one of the leading intellectuals of the day.[40]

In *An Outline of a Theory of Civilization*, Fukuzawa engaged with the thought of John Hill Burton, Samuel Mitchell, Henry Thomas Buckle and François Guizot to work out how Japan could attain the level of civilization of advanced European countries and the United States. The Western notion of civilization was the missing conceptual piece needed in order to distance the purpose of knowledge from Confucian morality and instead redefine it as an intrinsic good that drives human civilization towards progress. At the same time, for Fukuzawa just as much as for Yoda, knowledge seen as contributing to civilization was skewed toward the material and technical side, and he dismissed Western art, literature, music, and religion.[41]

In the 1880s, this view had become so mainstream that textbooks such as Fujita Mokichi's *History of the Eastward Expansion of Civilization* (1884) could present the beginning of Dutch studies in the Tokugawa period as the origin of civilization in Japan and as virtually homonymous with practical learning.[42]

Useful Sinitic Humanities? Reassertions of Value After 1880

As the epistemic value of practicality reconverged around the advancement of civilization and utility for the state and became associated with the natural sciences and the West, proponents and practitioners of humanistic scholarship were put in a difficult position. Especially the Sinitic humanities found themselves on the other side of the fence by default, which is why this section will concentrate on these fields.[43] The only way forward was to accept the rules of the dominant discourse and reclaim practicality on these terms. How could the Sinitic humanities become useful to the state again and aid civilization?

In the 1870s, "enlightenment and civilization" (*bunmei kaika*) was the buzzword of the day. From Western-style buildings to military uniforms, institutions like postal services and museums, to technology such as trains and telegraphs, Japan fervently engaged with the trappings of what they saw as useful elements of Western material civilization. The heavy focus on "rich country, strong army"-style state building and the immense pace of intellectual and material change became disorienting, however, and many people began to notice the lack of a spiritual foundation in this newly "civilized" Japan. Where else to look than to what had been there all along: Confucian morality. In the course of the 1880s, Confucian morality was reintroduced into public discourse and education, culminating in the *Imperial Rescript on Education* promulgated by the Meiji emperor in 1890, which extolled the Confucian virtues of loyalty and filial piety and admonished the emperor's subjects to "perfect [their] moral powers."[44] Far from a simple conservative backlash to Westernization, this was a new development that heralded the end of Confucian thought as a living philosophical tradition and its transformation into a narrow state ideology used to mold Japanese, and later colonial Korean and Taiwanese subjects.[45]

Not just Confucian morality, but Kangaku, too, had to transform into something else, and scholars and intellectuals took different paths to get there. An early attempt at swimming against the tide was the private Kangaku school Nishōgakusha founded by Mishima Chūshū (1831–1919) in 1879. In the school's manifesto, Mishima tried to recuperate practical value for Kangaku by asserting:

> The aim of *kangaku* is to cultivate oneself, to govern other people and to become a person who will be useful (*yūyō*) in their lifetime; it is not to become merely a Confucian scholar whose learning and literary skills are without practical application. . . . It is our purpose to produce people who are useful to the world, who read books, but do not fall into investigating texts to the smallest detail and pick out individual phrases.[46]

Mishima's attempt was successful and attracted capable students, many of whom went on to enroll in the law school of the ministry of justice or the military academy, and his school, now a university, still exists today. It was the exception, however, to the general trend of private Kangaku schools going out of business due to narrowing career options for their graduates and being actively shut down by the government to enforce the nationalization of the school system and its curriculum.⁴⁷

At the Imperial University, the search for a useful Kangaku took another route. The term had gained currency in the course of the nineteenth century not as a self-description but as a polemic term, and it was only in 1889 that a department and degree with this name were set up. The professors were at a loss to describe what held the field together, given that it was just named after the language of the written materials it studied. Temporarily, lectures and research followed the precedents of the late Tokugawa years. However, as the university came to be organized around departments and disciplines according to Western classification schemes, it became obvious that Kangaku had to adapt.

Shigeno Yasutsugu (1827–1910), eminent nineteenth-century scholar of Sinitic learning and history professor at the Imperial University since 1888, was one of the first to propose that Kangaku had to become more scientific. In a lecture on the topic of "Kangaku and practical learning," he explained how the "principle of science" could be applied to Kangaku. The massive archive of textualized knowledge in Classical Chinese contained not just Confucian philosophy after all, but many other subjects from botany and geography to astronomy. Kangaku scholars could contribute to the scientific endeavor by studying these, but also by interacting with the Chinese for scientific purposes, such as importing seeds and learning about their cultivation.⁴⁸

Becoming more scientific, in the wider nineteenth-century sense, could mean something else: regrouping Kangaku around humanistic disciplines and adopting the scientific methods associated with them. Since the production of scientific knowledge had become an intrinsic good, this would guarantee its practical value in a different manner. This is precisely what happened, and in 1904, the former Kangaku department at the Imperial University was split into Chinese history, Chinese literature, and Chinese philosophy.⁴⁹

Shigeno envisioned a second avenue for Kangaku: refashioning it into a type of area studies. A step ahead of his time, he proposed already in 1879 to make Kangaku a "regular discipline" and send students to China:

> People who hear the title [of this lecture] might say that . . . the use (*yō*) of Kangaku has already been exhausted and there is no further value in studying it. That is most certainly not the case. . . . The practical value of Kangaku is not yet running out. It is unavoidable that it will become the most useful of tools in the future.⁵⁰

While Kangaku, literally Sinitic learning, vaguely referred to China, it had been perceived as a universal form of learning much like Latin knowledge in Europe, which had a genetic, but no intrinsic, association with Italy. Being, as it was, founded on philological expertise in Classical Chinese—still the prevalent form of written communication in China at the time—Kangaku could easily turn to the study of contemporary China. Shigeno was on the right track: the demand for China-related expertise did gradually increase in the 1880s, as Japan revealed its economic and geopolitical ambitions in East Asia. Tensions with China grew and led to the First Sino-Japanese war of 1894–95, which ended with a victory for Japan and the acquisition of Taiwan as its first official colony. In its wake, China studies became institutionalized in colonial and area studies institutes and could demonstrate their practical use for commerce, diplomacy and colonial governance.[51]

Conclusion

The epistemic value of practical learning is one of the central concepts in the history of knowledge of nineteenth-century Japan. The debates surrounding practical learning and its shifting definitions were a catalyst for great conceptual and institutional changes at the interface of the Japanese epistemic and political order. As this chapter has shown, understandings of practical learning and humanistic scholarship were deeply intertwined and evolved together. Both became and ceased to be matters of epistemic and political concern around the same time. After 1900, the reconfigured humanities were an accepted part of academic knowledge production and the term Kangaku lost its deprecating nuance and more or less fell out of usage, alongside the departments and disciplines it had denoted in previous decades.[52] Similarly, while practicality and utility continued to be important values, they were no longer an existential problem or matter of survival to Japanese intellectuals.

The Japanese history of practical learning can only be understood in a transnational perspective. The concept was transformed through its movement across borders, intellectual interactions, and the changing relations with China, European countries, and the United States. These movements triggered reappraisals and redefinitions, starting with the importation of Zhu Xi-Confucian thought and shifts internal to Confucian discourse, and ending with a reaction to Western imperialism and the creation of a system of higher education centered on technological progress in the service of the nation state.

For a global history of the humanities, studying the Japanese case is intrinsically worthwhile, as it enriches our understanding of epistemic values in different parts of the world. It also offers a fascinating example of intellectual universalization in the nineteenth century, showing how the convergence of values that took shape during the globalization of the epistemic order had distinct starting points in different local settings.

Finally, the history of practical learning in Japan contributes to a genealogy of contemporary epistemic values and offers a critical point for comparison. It is striking how the debates in nineteenth-century Japan seem to foreshadow the contemporary predicament of the globalized humanities. Herman Paul writes in the introduction to this volume that the origin of the label humanities in Europe was already inseparable from a discourse of crisis. If we take the tradition and label of Kangaku as a rough equivalent to humanistic scholarship, the same can be said for the case of Japan, wherein the crisis hinged precisely on the question of its practical value.

Notes

1. See, e.g., *Retooling the Humanities: The Culture of Research in Canadian Universities*, ed. Daniel Coleman and Smaro Kamboureli (Edmonton: University of Alberta Press, 2011).
2. See Kevin C. Elliot and Daniel Steel, "Introduction: Values and Science. Current Controversies," in *Current Controversies in Values and Science,* ed. Kevin C. Elliot and Daniel Steel (New York: Routledge, 2017), 1–11, at 3. Due to the focus of this paper on transnational history, I omit an in-depth discussion of the relationship between epistemic and non-epistemic (i.e., social and religious) values in knowledge production; understandings of practical and useful knowledge, especially at the time and place in question, oscillated between these.
3. Rosário Couto Costa, "The Place of the Humanities in Today's Knowledge Society," in *Palgrave Communications* 5, no. 38 (2019), online at https://doi.org/10.1057/s41599-019-0245-6
4. E.g., Deloitte Access Economics, *The Value of the Humanities* (October 2018), online at https://www2.deloitte.com/au/en/pages/economics/articles/value-humanities.html
5. Poul Holm, Arne Jarrick, and Dominic Scott, *Humanities World Report 2015* (Basingstoke: Palgrave Macmillan, 2015), 12–41.

6. *Humanities in the Twenty-First Century: Beyond Utility and Markets*, ed. Eleonora Belfiore and Anna Upchurch (Basingstoke: Palgrave Macmillan, 2013).
7. See, e.g., Rik Peels, "Epistemic Values in the Humanities and in the Sciences," *History of Humanities* 3, no. 1 (2018): 89–111; see also Elliot and Steel, *Current Controversies*. For a closely related, well-defined research program on epistemic virtues, see Herman Paul, "What is a Scholarly Persona? Ten Theses on Virtues, Skills, and Desires," *History and Theory* 53, no. 3 (2014): 348–71 and *Epistemic Virtues in the Sciences and the Humanities*, ed. Jeroen van Dongen and Herman Paul (Cham: Springer, 2017).
8. Stuart Christie, "International Glow: The Contemporary Reinvention of a Chinese *Humanitas*," in *The Humanities in Contemporary Chinese Contexts*, ed. Evelyn T. Y. Chan and Michael O'Sullivan (Singapore: Springer Nature, 2016), 143–59.
9. E.g., Muhsin J. Al-Musawi, *The Medieval Islamic Republic of Letters: Arabic Knowledge Construction* (Notre Dame, IN: University of Notre Dame Press, 2015); David Mervart, "The Republic of Letters Comes to Nagasaki: Record of a Translator's Struggle," *Transcultural Studies* 6, no. 2 (2015): 8–37.
10. Wm. Theodore de Bary, "Introduction," in *Principle and Practicality: Essays in Neo-Confucianism and Practical Learning*, ed. Wm. Theodore de Bary and Irene Bloom (New York: Columbia University Press, 1979), 1–36, at 25.
11. Christopher L. Hill, "Conceptual Universalization in the Transnational Nineteenth Century," in *Global Intellectual History*, ed. Samuel Moyn and Andrew Sartori (New York: Columbia University Press, 2013), 134–58.
12. The Great Learning, section 4. Quoted in Daniel Gardner, *The Four Books: The Basic Teachings of the Later Confucian Tradition* (Indianapolis, ID: Hackett, 2007), 4f.
13. De Bary, "Introduction," xx.
14. Quoted in Minamoto Ryōen, "Jitsugaku no keifu: Tōju, Banzan, Shōnan," in *Yokoi Shōnan, 1809–1869. "Kōkyō" no senkusha*, ed. Minamoto Ryōen (Tokyo: Fujiwara Shoten, 2009), 72–8, at 75.
15. See Herman Paul's introduction to this volume.
16. De Bary, "Introduction," 7.
17. Benjamin Elman, *From Philosophy to Philology: Intellectual and Social Aspects of Change in Late Imperial China* (Los Angeles, CA: University of California Press, 2001).
18. Ōba Osamu, *Kanseki yu'nyū no bunkashi: Shōtoku taishi kara Yoshimune e* (Tokyo: Kenbun shuppan, 1997), esp. 117–66; see also Ōba Osamu, "Sino-Japanese Relations in the Edo Period (Part One: Forgotten Sino-Japanese Contacts)," trans. Joshua A. Fogel, *Sino-Japanese Studies* 8, no. 1 (1995): 40–52.

19. *Ogyū Sorai's Philosophical Masterworks: The Bendō and Benmei*, trans. John A. Tucker (Honolulu, HI: University of Hawai'i Press, 2006), 15.
20. Benjamin Elman, "The Search for Evidence from China: Qing Learning and Kōshōgaku in Tokugawa Japan," in *Sagacious Monks and Bloodthirsty Warriors: Chinese Views of Japan in the Ming-Qing Period*, ed. Joshua A. Fogel (Norwalk: East Bridge, 2002), 158–84.
21. Ōishi Manabu, "Kinsei kokka, shakai to han, hankō," in *Kinsei hansei hankō daijiten*, ed. Ōishi Manabu (Tokyo: Yoshikawa kōbunkan, 2006), 3–35.
22. Takeuchi Makoto, *Kansei kaikaku no kenkyū* (Tokyo: Yoshikawa kobunkan, 2009).
23. Kiri Paramore, "The Nationalization of Confucianism: Academism, Examinations, and Bureaucratic Governance in the Late Tokugawa State," *Journal of Japanese Studies* 38, no. 1 (2021): 25–53, at 39–42.
24. Iwashita Tetsunori, *Edo no kaigai jōhō nettowaaku* (Tokyo: Yoshikawa kōbunkan, 2006).
25. Kamata Hiroshi, "Jitsugakutō no tanjō, Jishūkan o meguru kyōiku to seiji," in *Yokoi Shōnan, 1809–1869. "Kōkyō" no senkusha*, ed. Minamoto Ryōen (Tokyo: Fujiwara Shoten, 2009), 79–86.
26. Yokoi Shōnan, "Gakkō mondōsho," in *Watanabe Kazan, Takano Chōei, Sakuma Shōzan, Yokoi Shōnan, Hashimoto Sanai*, ed. Satō Shōsuke, Uete Michiari, Yamaguchi Muneyuki (Tokyo: Iwanami Shoten, 1971), 428–33, at 429f.
27. Noell Wilson, *Defensive Positions: The Politics of Maritime Security in Tokugawa Japan* (Cambridge, MA: Harvard University Press, 2015), 135–70.
28. Tessa Morris-Suzuki, *The Technological Transformation of Japan: From the Seventeenth to the Twenty-First Century* (Cambridge: Cambridge University Press, 1994), 57–8.
29. For a general political history of the late Tokugawa years, see Andrew Gordon, *A Modern History of Japan: From Tokugawa Times to the Present* (Oxford: Oxford University Press, 2014), 47–59.
30. Satō Shōsuke, *Yōgakushi ronkō* (Kyoto: Shibunkaku, 1993), 287–323; on the history of Dutch/Western learning, see Numata Jirō, *Western Learning: A Short History of the Study of Western Science in Early Modern Japan* (Tokyo: The Japan-Netherlands Institute, 1992).
31. Quoted in Kurasawa Takashi, *Bakumatsu kyōikushi no kenkyū 1: Chokkatsu gakkō seisaku* (Tokyo: Yoshikawa Kōbunkan, 1983), 2.
32. Miyazaki Fumiko, "Kaiseijo ni okeru keiō kaikaku: Kaiseijo gakusei kaikaku o chūshin to shite," *Shigaku zasshi* 89, no. 3 (1980): 343–64.
33. Quoted in Marius B. Jansen, *The Making of Modern Japan* (Cambridge, MA: Harvard University Press, 2000), 338.
34. "Kōgisho nisshi," in *Meiji bunka zenshū: Dai ikkan: kensei hen*, 3rd edn, ed. Meiji bunka zenshū kai (Tokyo: Nihon hyōronsha, 1967), 44–8.

35. For the arguments against the use of Sinitic characters, see Nanette Twine, "Toward Simplicity: Script Reform Movements in the Meiji Period," *Monumenta Nipponica* 38, no. 2 (1983): 115–32.
36. On the history of Kangaku in early Meiji period Japan, see Margaret Mehl, "Chinese Learning (*kangaku*) in Meiji Japan (1868–1912)," *History* 85, no. 277 (2000): 48–66 and Michael Facius, *China übersetzen: Globalisierung und chinesisches Wissen in Japan im 19. Jahrhundert* (Frankfurt am Main: Campus, 2017), 139–93.
37. "Kōgisho nisshi," 156.
38. Richard Rubinger, "Education: From One Room to One System," in *Japan in Transition. From Tokugawa to Meiji*, ed. Marius B. Jansen and Gilbert Rozman (Princeton, NJ: Princeton University Press, 1986), 195–230; Benjamin Duke, *The History of Modern Japanese Education: Constructing the National School System, 1872–1890* (New Brunswick, NJ: Rutgers University Press, 2009), 61–76; E. Patricia Tsurumi, "Meiji Primary School Language and Ethics Textbooks: Old Values for a New Society?" *Modern Asian Studies* 8, no. 2 (1974): 247–61.
39. Yōda Hyakusen, "Yōgaku no gi," *Yōyōsha dan* no. 3 (1875): 6r–7v, at 6v, reprinted in *Yōyōsha dan* vol. 1, ed. Haga Shōji (Tokyo: Yumani Shōbo, 2007), 57–60, at 58.
40. Albert M. Craig, *Civilization and Enlightenment: The Early Thought of Fukuzawa Yukichi* (Cambridge, MA: Harvard University Press, 2009), 100–43.
41. Ibid., 103.
42. Fujita Mokichi, *Bunmei tōzen shi* (Tokyo: Hōchisha, 1884), 107–19, online at https://dl.ndl.go.jp/info:ndljp/pid/1918298
43. For a detailed look at the debates surrounding Kangaku in the 1880s and 1890s, see William Hedberg, "Paradise Lost and Regained: The Passion of Chinese Studies (*Kangaku*) in Meiji-Period Japan," *Sino-Japanese Studies* 26 (2019–20), article 1.
44. Translated in Richard Rubinger, "Education in Meiji Japan," in *Sources of Japanese Tradition*, 2nd edn, vol. 2, ed. Wm. Theodore de Bary, Carol Gluck and Arthur E. Tiedemann (New York: Columbia University Press, 2005), 750–88, at 780.
45. Kiri Paramore, *Japanese Confucianism: A Cultural History* (Cambridge: Cambridge University Press, 2016), 141–66.
46. Nishō gakusha, *Nishō gakusha shasoku* (1879), quoted in Margaret Mehl, *Private Academies of Chinese Learning in Meiji Japan: The Decline and Transformation of the Kangaku Juku* (Copenhagen: NIAS Press, 2003), 74.
47. Mehl, *Kangaku Juku*, 173–206.
48. Shigeno Yasutsugu, "Kangaku to jitsugaku," in *Zōtei Shigeno hakase shigaku ronbunshū. Jōkan*, ed. Ōkubo Toshiaki (Tokyo: Meicho fukyū kai, 1989), 412–20, at 415.

49. Tōkyō daigaku hyakunenshi henshū iinkai, *Tōkyō daigaku hyakunenshi. Bukyokushi 1* (Tokyo: Tōkyō daigaku shuppankai, 1986), 511.
50. Shigeno Yasutsugu, "Kangaku yoroshiku seisoku ikka o mōke shōnen shūsai o erami shinkoku ni ryūgaku seshimu beki ronsetsu," in *Zōtei Shigeno hakase shigaku ronbunshū. Gekan,* ed. Ōkubo Toshiaki (Tokyo: Meicho fukyū kai, 1989), 345–52, at 345. See also Michael Facius, "Transcultural Sinology in 19th-Century Japan: The Case of Shigeno Yasutsugu (1827–1910)," *Philological Encounters* 3, no. 1–2 (2018): 3–33.
51. See, e.g., Douglas R. Reynolds, "Training Young China Hands: Tōa Dōbun Shoin and Its Predecessors, 1886–1945," in *The Japanese Informal Empire in China, 1895–1937,* ed. Peter Duus, Ramon H. Myers, and Mark R. Peattie (Princeton, NJ: Princeton University Press, 1989), 210–71.
52. Facius, *China übersetzen,* 285–98.

9

An Ethos of Criticism: Virtues and Vices in Nineteenth-Century Strasbourg

Herman Paul

Introduction

One of the prisms through which historians have come to study scholars' activities in centuries past is that of virtues and vices: character traits that were perceived as beneficial and detrimental, respectively, to the pursuit of scholarly work. Historians study these virtues and vices partly because it allows them to add historical depth and nuance to contemporary academic performance criteria. While we think we know what "objectivity" entails, historical research forces us to rethink what we mean by the term, given that objectivity, from the mid-nineteenth century onwards, has taken on a range of forms, each with its own demands on scholars' intellectual habits. In their history of objectivity, historians Lorraine Daston and Peter Galison therefore present historical contextualization as a much-needed remedy against ahistorical thinking about scholarly norms and values: "It is not always the same kind of ethos, or the same kind of self, that is involved: both have histories."[1]

If historicizing contemporary virtues is one impetus behind the recent surge of interest in scholarly virtues and vices, a second one is that virtues and vices lend themselves well to transdisciplinary comparisons of the kind that especially historians of the humanities like to make.[2] No single field of study had a monopoly on objectivity, impartiality, or accuracy: both these virtues and their negative counterparts, the vices, traveled across disciplinary divides, either because scholars appropriated them from neighboring fields or because people drew on shared moral repertoires to which categories of virtue were central.[3] So by tracing how, for instance, "thoroughness" appealed to philologists, historians, chemists, and medical scholars alike, we can identify parallels and sometimes even transfers between fields of research that are conventionally studied in isolation from each other.[4]

Both of the approaches just mentioned, however, have the disadvantage of isolating single virtues or vices from broader clusters of qualities that scholars regarded as needed for research or teaching. A study that zooms in too closely on thoroughness, for instance, runs the risk of ignoring that the meanings and connotations of this virtue depended on other, contrastive, complementary, or overlapping virtues. Likewise, a study of objectivity may easily forget that the relative weight attached to this virtue can only be assessed by examining what I have elsewhere called the "constellations of virtues" to which scholars were committed.[5] Scholars never put all their cards on a single virtue: they cared about objectivity and patriotism alike or valued intellectual courage only as long as it was restrained by accuracy and love of truth. So, despite the rich layers of meaning that studies of individual virtues and vices may unearth, the challenge for historians of the humanities is not to lose sight of the fact that scholarly virtues always existed in the plural.

How can this be done? Analysing evaluative genres, such as book reviews, is one possible way of foregrounding interaction between scholarly virtues, given that reviewers until well into the twentieth century often judged scholarly publications on the virtues or vices that they displayed.[6] Along these lines, studies of book reviews and scholarly controversies have argued that a "balancing" of virtues was central to the moral economies of German and British scholars in the nineteenth century.[7] The relative importance assigned to different virtues can, however, also be examined in other ways. This chapter will do so by analysing the ethos of a particular community of humanities scholars, at the Kaiser-Wilhelms-Universität in Strasbourg. What were the constellations of virtues cherished by these late nineteenth-century German academics? What catalogs of virtues did they instill in their students and display in their research or writing?

By selecting the Kaiser-Wilhelms-Universität as its case study, this chapter discusses an example from the heyday of the German *Geisteswissenschaften* as well as from the height of nineteenth-century nationalism. That is to say, in the first place, that this chapter deals with a university that proudly presented itself as a stronghold of what the philosopher Wilhelm Dilthey called the "human sciences": fields of inquiry that tried to grasp human culture in all its complexity, not merely by explaining regularities in the human experience, as natural scientists allegedly did, but by "understanding" (*verstehen*) products of the human mind both in their historical settings and in their normative appeal to present-day audiences.[8] When asked for advice by Strasbourg university authorities, just a year before the German university in the newly conquered province of Alsace officially opened its doors (1872), Dilthey grasped the opportunity to recommend no less than eighteen chairs in the human sciences.[9] Although this plan turned out a little too ambitious, the importance that Germany's youngest university attached to the human sciences is apparent from the resources it invested in them. Not only could the Kaiser-Wilhelms-Universität boast to be the first continental university with a chair in English,[10] it also managed to attract both staff and students by offering modern seminar teaching in nearly all fields of study.[11]

These investments were made possible, financially and otherwise, by a wave of nationalist enthusiasm over the German occupation of the Alsace. Almost immediately after the region had been ceded to Germany, the idea of establishing a university in the Alsatian capital captured the imagination of German scholars and politicians alike. They believed that such an institution would be able, not only to showcase the supremacy of German *Wissenschaft*, but also to contribute to a "Germanification" of Alsace's French-speaking population.[12] This vision helps explain why the human sciences were granted such a privileged status. In Dilthey's words: "In the historical-philosophical sciences lies the power to stimulate national feeling and moral severity."[13] Importantly, this did not imply that Strasbourg faculty members eagerly posed as "political professors" or used the lectern as their pulpit.[14] On the contrary, especially in politically sensitive fields like history, university administrators carefully avoided appointing candidates known for patriotic styles of teaching.[15] Instead of loudly preaching love of country, Strasbourg professors were expected to teach by example, showing the superiority of German culture by demonstrating excellence in research and teaching alike.[16] Otto von Bismarck's suggestion to change the university motto *Litteris et patriae* into *Patriae et litteris* was therefore rejected: faculty believed they served their country best by strengthening Germany's reputation as a stronghold of *Wissenschaft*.[17]

What did this imply for the virtues in which Strasbourg students were being socialized? Focusing on the humanities—fields like philology, Biblical scholarship, history, philosophy, art history, and musicology—I will give an answer in two parts. In the first half of the chapter, I will argue that the dominance of philological and historical critique was such that virtues of criticism (accuracy, precision, attention to detail) were central to Strasbourg's academic ethos in the period under discussion, from 1872 to the turn of the century. In this context, I take the term "ethos" to refer to habits, expectations, norms, and values that scholars at the time believed to define good scholarship.[18] Yet while virtues of criticism were held in high regard, to the point of being seen as indispensable for each and every serious attempt at scholarly inquiry, the ethos at Strasbourg allowed for more than philological precision or historical accuracy. In writing books for general readers, for instance, humanities scholars also engaged in activities that required other qualities than carefulness and sharp-mindedness. So, in the second half of the chapter, I will offer three qualifications to the importance of virtues of criticism: (1) not all genres to which Strasbourg scholars contributed made an equally strong demand on virtues of criticism; (2) these virtues of criticism were compatible with different scholarly personae, or models of being of scholar; and (3) more often than not, they were colored by evaluative stances vis-à-vis the German past, the Christian tradition, or the non-European "other."

Scholarly Self-Images

Friedrich Max Müller's inaugural address, *Über die Resultate der Sprachwissenschaft* (On the Results of the Science of Language, 1872), is a good place to start. What makes this text stand out is that it abounds with language of virtue and vice. For instance, in explaining why the study of Indo-European languages was rapidly advancing, Müller pointed to the "unflagging industry," "mathematical exactness," "conscientiousness," and "great cautiousness" exercised by recent generations of linguistics. To some extent, these virtues had helped the field get rid of "prejudice," "speculations," and deference to authority.[19] To remedy some still prevalent vices, such as the arrogant thought of knowing better than others and the sloppy practice of quoting things at second hand, Müller went on recommending *Gewissenhaftigkeit* and *Bescheidenheit*: "Whoever devotes himself to the study of so comprehensive a science must try never to lose sight of two virtues: conscientiousness and modesty." To emphasize the critical importance of these character traits, Müller let his lecture culminate in a long quotation from Barthold Georg Niebuhr:

> Above all things, we must in all scientific pursuits preserve our truthfulness [*Wahrhaftigkeit*] so pure that we thoroughly eschew every false appearance; that we represent not even the smallest thing as certain of which we are not completely convinced; that if we have to propose a conjecture, we spare no effort in representing the exact degree of its probability. If we do not ourselves, when it is possible, indicate our errors, even such as no one else is likely to discover; if, in laying down our pen, we cannot say in the sight of God, "Upon strict examination, I have knowingly written nothing that is not true;" and if, without deceiving either ourselves or others, we have not presented even our most odious opponents in such a light only that we could justify it upon our deathbeds—if we cannot do this, study and literature serve only to make us unrighteous and sinful.[20]

One may wonder what to make of this exalted prose. What, if anything, does it reveal about the virtues in which Müller and his colleagues tried to socialize their students? Precisely to the extent that the passage depicts scholars at their Sunday best, as aspiring to what Daston and Galison call "the self-discipline of saints," it does not tell us much about everyday teaching or research habits.[21] This is partly because high-minded words about the scholar's vocation belonged to the standard features of the genre.[22] Also, because an *Antrittsvorlesung* offered professors a chance to stylize themselves as virtuous scholars, their appeal to modesty and conscientiousness is likely to tell us more about virtues that they *preferred* to have than about dispositions that they *actually* possessed. At least in Müller's case, the virtues hailed in his inaugural overlapped only partly with qualities that colleagues ascribed to him.[23] (Just months after the occasion, the secretary of the London Philological Society described the Strasbourg professor as a scientific lightweight, "not much thought of" by serious students of language.)[24]

Nonetheless, virtues of the kind emphasized in Müller's addresses were invoked by, or attributed to, many a Strasbourg professor. Especially obituary writers were eager to stress conscientiousness and carefulness as characteristic qualities of deceased Strasbourg scholars. Whereas the historian Julius Weizsäcker was remembered for his "most painful exactitude," "sharp-minded criticism," and "conscientious work," the classical philologist

Wilhelm Studemund was praised for his "erudition" and "scrupulous accuracy."[25] Yet another classical scholar, Rudolf Schöll, was hailed as a "sharp-minded researcher," who "in exemplary fashion [had] combined meticulousness with sharpness of judgment."[26] Just how persistent this discourse of precision, carefulness, and conscientiousness was, is apparent from the case of Theodor Nöldeke, the Strasbourg Orientalist who as late as the early 1930s was held up as a model of "conscientious research," "considerate judgment," "stringent matter-of-factness," and "exactitude in the smallest things."[27]

Obviously, such words of praise should not be taken at face value. Like inaugural addresses, obituaries tended to distribute light and shadow in such a way as to make scholars appear at their best.[28] Yet what matters for our purposes is not the degree of stylizing in a genre known for saying nothing but good of the dead (*de mortuis nil nisi bonum*). More relevant is that obituary writers, like Müller in his inaugural, chose to emphasize virtues like carefulness, accuracy, and conscientiousness. In their preferred mode of self-fashioning, at least, Strasbourg humanities scholars put a premium on what I will call "virtues of criticism": qualities like precision, exactitude, cautiousness, and sharp-mindedness that were seen as indispensable for philological and historical *Kritik*. Strasbourg professors, in other words, liked to see themselves, not as great orators or as influential teachers, but as dedicated researchers who privileged thoroughness and precision over bold hypotheses or grand visions.

Seminar Teaching

If virtues of criticism played a major role in the *discursive legitimation* of scholarship, then to what extent did these virtues also capture how Strasbourg scholars *actually* did their work as teachers and researchers? How important were virtues of criticism, not on Sunday, but on Monday, when scholars found themselves sitting at a desk cluttered with notes or in front of a student audience? One "weekday" practice that has recently been studied in some detail is the seminar: a small-scale teaching format that, unlike the traditional *Vorlesung*, allowed for group discussions and student presentations. Developed by classical philologists in the late eighteenth century, seminars or "exercises" found their way throughout the humanities, mainly because professors embraced them as means for socializing future colleagues into field-specific research habits. Seminar teaching therefore quickly acquired an aura of *Wissenschaftlichkeit*, which helps explain why the Kaiser-Wilhelms-Universität saw it as a matter of prestige to offer seminars in nearly all fields of study.[29]

Among the sources informing us about virtues and skills cherished in such seminars are eye witness accounts such as penned by François Collard, a classical philologist from Louvain who visited Wilhelm Studemund's Greek philology seminar in 1878.[30] What struck him most was the professor's habit of inviting seminar participants over for dinner. Like the many hours that Studemund spent daily on student supervision, these *soupers philologiques* appeared to him as evidence of great devotion to the students.[31] As soon as Greek texts appeared on the table, however, Studemund also turned out to be demanding. Collard observed that the philologist "attached great importance to dates," while pressing his students to resolve issues of authorship and authenticity to the best of their abilities. "Woe to the student who erred in haste or hesitated in a moment of doubt: a disquieting glance, an ironic smile, a nervous gesture, or a somewhat brusque remark made him feel that he would have done better to remain carefully silent."[32] If this depicts Studemund as a man with little tolerance for mistakes, Collard went on to emphasize that "rigorous method" in source critical matters was what the professor wanted his students to develop. Accordingly, the virtues highlighted in his report resemble those of Müller: accuracy, precision, and "extreme carefulness."[33]

Clearly, this account was written for a purpose: propagating a German teaching model at Belgian universities. This explain why Collard's text, like Müller's inaugural, is not free from idealizing tendencies. It is worth noting, therefore, that virtues of accuracy, exactitude, and carefulness were also emphasized in sources that were not intend on telling success stories. A memoir of Hermann Baumgarten, for instance, emphasized that the Strasbourg historian had felt reserved about *historische Übungen*. Instead of familiarizing his students with the do's and don'ts of source criticism, he wanted to teach them the importance of imagination, vision, and a good style of writing. Baumgarten realized, however, that these were things that could hardly be taught, while his students expected him to offer "critical" exercises. So he did what he could, drawing on his own philological training, but with less than convincing results: "The energetic life of a real seminar meeting was mostly absent with him."[34] If this indirectly confirms Collard's point of seminars focusing on philological training, so do the grievances of more outspoken critics like Alfred Dove, who abhorred "the narrowly philological school" of historical exercises.³⁵ Friends and foes, in other words, agreed that seminar teaching placed a premium on virtues of criticism.

Source Editions

Virtues of accuracy, precision, and patience were indispensable, too, in the realm of research, especially in a type of analysis known as *Kritik*. Echoing Immanuel Kant, who had proclaimed the eighteenth century "the real age of critique," Gustav Gröber, the Romanist philologist, and Georg Dehio, the art historian, proudly referred to "our century of critique" or "the century... that chose critique as its guide."³⁶ These were not empty phrases: many humanities scholars, in Strasbourg and elsewhere, saw *Kritik* as a defining mark of *Wissenschaftlichkeit*. Arguably, critique could achieve this prominence thanks to a semantic flexibility that allowed both neo-Kantian philosophers and classical philologists to present themselves as critical.³⁷ Clearly, though, for Gröber, Dehio, and their colleagues in Strasbourg, philological connotations of the term outweighed philosophical ones. When they engaged in "criticism of the Old Testament," subjected the Pastoral Epistles to "critical treatment," or offered "contributions to a critique of German and Italian source texts," they were critical in the sense of not accepting at face value the authorship, the dating, or the message of a text.³⁸

How much such "critical" research depended on the same sort of virtues that we encountered in the seminar is apparent from source editions, a genre to which many Strasburg scholars contributed at some point in their careers. Classical philologists led the way, with Rudolf Schöll editing Asconius Pedianus, Proclus, and Justinian, while Georg Kaibel published editions of Dionysius of Halicarnassus, Galen, Longinus, and Aristotle.³⁹ Chair holders in non-classical languages followed suit with editions of Geoffrey Chaucer and Francesco Petrarch, among others.⁴⁰ Medieval historians launched projects like the *Urkundenbuch der Stadt Straßburg* (Book of Records of the City of Strasbourg, 7 vols, 1879–1900), while the Sanskrit scholar Siegfried Goldschmidt made the ancient Indian Rāmāyana epic available to modern readers.⁴¹ Even the musicologist Gustav Jacobsthal contributed his share with a diplomatic edition of a thirteenth-century collection of medieval polyphonic music.⁴²

What kind of virtues such editorial work required, can be seen, first of all, from the pile of correspondence that Julius Weizsäcker and his assistants generated in the process of editing the German Reichstag Records. While some of these letters and postcards address travel plans or reimbursement of expenses, the lengthiest ones are almost invariably devoted to minutiae of spelling and punctuation. Should one read *expectat* or *expectatur*, *Galis* or *Gallis*, *volebat* or *volebant*, *quo* or *quod*?[43] Getting these details straight was not beyond the call of duty. Book reviewers wondering how *pendre* could have possibly be transcribed as *prendre* showed that they, too, valued textual accuracy over anything else.[44] Even more instructive is the example of Studemund preparing a Plautus edition based on a palimpsest in the Biblioteca Ambrosiana in Milan. The ancient script concealed beneath an early medieval manuscript was notoriously hard to decipher. Despite Studemund making unscrupulous use of chemical reagents to make the text more legible,[45] his notes are peppered with phrases like "difficult to read" and "it may be that someone who obtains permission to use new chemicals will be able to read a bit more."[46] Although a provisional edition of the text was finished within a couple of years, Studemund kept returning to Milan for further inspections of the manuscript, especially after two colleagues had proposed readings that differed from his.[47] Oskar Seyffert, who eventually helped Studemund finish his *opus magnum*, was not alone in expressing astonishment at the degree of "conscientiousness" that went into the project.[48] Colleagues near and far agreed that Studemund's work was characterized by "most conscientious care" and "truly admirable persistence, cautiousness, and discernment."[49]

So, time and again, we encounter similar kinds of virtues: carefulness, precision, and patience, sometimes also sharp-mindedness or perseverance, with a characteristic lack of emphasis on originality, creativity, or intellectual courage. It would be possible to call these qualities "philological virtues," thereby emphasizing their origin in what Franz Schultz called a "philological ethos."[50] I however prefer to call them "virtues of criticism," so as to highlight not their origin, but their goal. On the one hand, this allows us to say that qualities like attentiveness and meticulousness were supposed to contribute to historical and philological *Kritik* as practiced by Strasbourg historians, linguists, and philologists alike. On the other hand, this phrasing also leaves room for different virtues taking center stage in activities other than source editing and seminar teaching. For although *Kritik* and its accompanying virtues were central to how Strasbourg scholars conceived of their work, criticism was not the only thing that mattered to them. There were other genres to which they contributed—survey courses, narrative histories, occasional speeches—and other expectations that they had to meet.

Accordingly, if this chapter so far has illustrated the prevalence of an "ethos of criticism," I will use the rest of the chapter to add three points of nuance: (1) there were other virtues, too, that mattered; (2) typical for the ethos at Strasbourg were not only virtues, but also evaluative attitudes; and (3) a shared commitment to virtues of criticism did not prevent humanities faculty from developing different "personae" or ways of being a scholar.

Other Virtues

First of all, Strasbourg scholars did more than editing old sources: they also wrote monographs, research articles, and narrative histories, while some even edited textbooks or encyclopedic handbooks. Clearly, these genres made different demands on authors than an edition or medieval sources. Take Wilhelm Scherer, the historian of German literature, who shortly after his appointment at Strasbourg wrote a *Geschichte der deutschen Dichtung im elften und zwölften Jahrhundert* (History of German Poetry in the Eleventh and Twelfth Centuries, 1875). The book tried to offer a "comprehensive image" of early Middle High German poetry by tracing influences, pointing out analogies, and identifying developments over time.[51] According to a critical reviewer, this exercise was more "journalistic" than scientific, partly because preliminary studies were still missing, partly also because Scherer's habit of indicating uncertainties only in his footnotes showed a painful lack of "scientific love of truth."[52] Other colleagues, however, while granting that Scherer could "lose himself in clouds of conjectures, in the nimbus of parallels, in the realm of lightheartedness [and] of poetic euphoria," appreciated his interpretative courage and welcomed the book for the stimulus it provided.[53] Although most of its conjectures were impossible to prove, the author at least presented a possible picture of how things hang together.[54]

Scherer was not alone in trying his hands at narrative synthesis. In *Die geistigen und socialen Strömungen des neunzehnten Jahrhunderts* (The Spiritual and Social Currents of the Nineteenth Century, 1899), his philosophy colleague Theobald Ziegler also cast his net widely. Emerging out of a lecture series given in 1896–7,[55] the book offered a panoramic view of German intellectual life since the Enlightenment. Judging by reviews in the popular press, most attractive about the book was its perceived combination of "thoroughness of research" with an accessible style of writing.⁵⁶ Ziegler was hailed as an author who "thinks clearly and writes well."⁵⁷ Indeed, according to his Austrian colleague Friedrich Jodl, Ziegler was the right person for such a synoptic work because he possessed all the qualities needed for the job: an "unambiguous national attitude," an "unprejudiced and independent position" in religious matters, and a talent for writing both "lively" and "understandably to all."⁵⁸ Unmistakably, these were other qualities than those fostered in seminar rooms or needed for preparing source editions.

Similarly, in the realm of teaching, lecture courses (*Vorlesungen*) required different didactic qualities than research-intensive seminars. Given the frequency with which Strasbourg professors were being excused for not lecturing with the rhetorical power and emotional intensity of a Heinrich von Treitschke, it looks like mediocre performance in the lecture hall could be framed as a virtue rather than a vice.⁵⁹ Careful, conscientious scholars, after all, would betray their ethos by abstracting too much from what they could analyse in painstaking detail. Still, when Studemund, the meticulous source editor, taught a survey course on Roman literature, he did not hesitate to sacrifice on accuracy when necessary for the sake of clarity.⁶⁰ Others even acquired a reputation for inspirational lecturing. Otto Liebmann's philosophy lectures were described as "little pieces of art," delivered with contagious enthusiasm.⁶¹

Consequently, a first qualifying observation is that the ethos of criticism at Strasbourg was most manifest in *certain* genres of research and teaching, but not in *all* of them. Despite their great commitment to philological and historical critique, Strasbourg humanities scholars also contributed to genres that required other qualities than accuracy and attention to detail. Interestingly, the desire to engage in more than philological *Kleinarbeit* manifested itself not only among scholars skeptical about source editing projects. When Weizsäcker's assistants tried to discriminate between *habitationes* and *habitationibus*, they could also deeply long for more challenging or satisfying work. "Lost in the abysses of editions," Ernst Bernheim, for instance, envied his colleague Karl Lamprecht for book projects that allowed him to follow his own inclinations.⁶² Likewise, Theodor Nöldeke, while agreeing to contribute to Michael Jan de Goeje's large-scale edition of the *Tarikh al-Tabari*, warned his Dutch colleague in advance: "In particular, I have a horror of the work of transcribing; I prefer correcting ten proof sheets over transcribing half a sheet."⁶³ Or as Nöldeke sighed on another occasion: he would have greatly preferred to write a monograph on the Sasanian Empire instead of editing Tabari's account of it.⁶⁴ So, despite the fact that virtues of criticism were seen as indispensable for serious scholarship, Strasbourg scholars also engaged, or dreamt of engaging, in types of teaching and research that made demands on other, less philological virtues.

Evaluative Attitudes

If virtues of criticism existed alongside other virtues, a second point that needs to be made is that these virtues were often colored by *evaluative attitudes*. Criticism, after all, not only served the *wissenschaftliche* goal of acquiring knowledge; it was also charged with normative meaning, informed by religious assumptions, or loaded with political overtones, all of which left their mark on the ethos lived out by Strasbourg humanities scholars. Although these evaluative stances often remained implicit, they manifested themselves, among other things, in how scholars positioned themselves vis-à-vis their subject matter—how they identified with their topics of research or, by contrast, distanced themselves from it.

A vivid example of distanced criticism is offered by Theodor Nöldeke's history of the Qur'an. Reviewing a broad range of sources, from ancient Arabic biographies of Mohammed to manuscript commentaries on the Qur'an, Nöldeke tried to sort out what was historically reliable and what was not. In many cases, "lies," "pious frauds," and unbridled "phantasy" on the part of the authors yielded negative results: neither "dogmatic" nor "uncritical" sources could pass Nöldeke's reliability test.[65] So, while Nöldeke presented himself as open-minded, free from prejudice, cautious, and skeptical of tradition and authority alike,[66] these were exactly the virtues he found lacking in his source material. And this was not the only way in which Nöldeke contrasted between "us," modern European scholars, and them, "superstitious Muslims" haunted by religious phantasies "that no one seriously investigating the matter will believe sincerely."[67] In later years, he even stated, in private correspondence, that it were not "the worst features of our modern being" that make "dreamers and seers" like Mohammed appear to us as "incomprehensible."[68] In other words, the distance between Nöldeke, the self-declared rationalist, and the world of ancient Islam was almost complete.

Things were less clear cut for Heinrich Julius Holtzmann, a New Testament critic who argued that the gospel of Mark offered a more reliable image of Jesus than the gospel of Matthew.[69] In his scholarly publications, Holtzmann proceeded from the assumption that the Bible had to be treated like Homer or the pre-Socratic fragments, without any preconceived idea about their religious, philosophical, or literary value.[70] This, however, did not prevent him from climbing the pulpit of Strasbourg Cathedral on Sunday to deliver sermons that treated even Matthew's words as nourishment for the soul.[71] There are indications that even Holtzmann's "Marcan priority" hypothesis was informed by a liberal Protestant agenda. In the context of Bismarck's *Kulturkampf*, at least, the thesis that Matthew was of disputable reliability was welcomed by anticlerical Protestants, as it allowed them to dismiss Matthew 16,18 ("upon this rock I will build my church") as a proof text for apostolic succession.[72]

While Holtzmann negotiated distance and proximity, unambiguous identification with the past under study could be found in the fields of history and art history. At a time when even a specialist reference work like the *Urkundenbuch der Stadt Straßburg* could be presented as a monument of "national conviction,"[73] explicit glorification of the German past seemed hardly necessary: studying the national past as such already counted as an act of patriotism. Nonetheless, not a few scholars chose to write in the first person plural, thereby conveying how much they identified with the past under scrutiny. The art historian Georg Dehio, for instance, almost routinely referred to "our people," "our history," "our national life," and "the fortunes of our nation," even when writing in a professional journal.[74] Indeed, for Dehio, Holy Roman Emperor Frederick II was "one of ours, even when we gradually come to realize that he himself hardly felt German and was not [German] insofar as his upbringing, language, and way of thinking are concerned."[75] Arguably, this identification with a past claimed as "German" was one of the motives behind Dehio's dedication to heritage conservation. As he argued in 1905, at a university ceremony attended by Emperor Wilhelm II: "We do not conserve a monument because we think it is beautiful, but rather because it is a part of our national existence."[76] Clearly, Dehio's age of critique also was an age of nationalism. Historical criticism could serve nationalist history writing just as easily as it could support an Orientalist "othering" of the East.

One implication of this is that German nationalism at the Kaiser-Wilhelms-Universität was more than a matter of displaying patriotic virtues (as distinguished from scholarly virtues). Typical of the nationalist fervor cultivated at Strasbourg was that critical study *as such* was supposed to add to the glory of the fatherland. Historical or philological inquiry therefore not only demanded scholarly virtues (accuracy, precision, patience), but also an evaluative stance (identification with the German nation state) which lent a particular flavor to the virtues in which Strasbourg students were socialized. More generally, this implies that virtues, despite their prominence in nineteenth-century scholarly thinking, cannot capture each and every aspect of the ethos prevalent at Strasbourg. The academic ethos was characterized by virtues of criticism, but also, no less importantly, by identifications and dissociations—modes of "positioning" that revealed how Strasbourg scholars related normatively to the German past, the Christian tradition, and the Orientalist "other."

Different Personae

Finally, even if Strasbourg professors shared an ethos of criticism and found each other in love for the German Empire, these similarities did not prevent them from developing different "scholarly personae" or ways of being a scholar.[77] Patience and accuracy could be lived out in the seclusion of a scholar's own study, in careful manuscript study, but could be practiced also in Egyptian kings' tombs, by scholars who tried to decipher ancient hieroglyphs while being surrounded by hordes of startled bats.[78]

A Strasbourg professor who came close to personifying the first persona was Paul Scheffer-Boichorst, a historian whose virtuosity in historical criticism was known near and far.[79] Unlike Bernheim and Nöldeke, Scheffer did not dream of writing monographs or survey texts: he willingly restricted himself, more exclusively as time went on, to issues in medieval history of which he thought that truth and falsehood had not yet been sufficiently sorted out.[80] This type of research required ingenuity and sharp-mindedness, but also great familiarity with printed and archival sources. Consequently, if Scheffer was not teaching, he could be found in archives, bent over medieval manuscripts, or in his study, surrounded by notes and books.[81] Reportedly, even during dinner, Scheffer (a lifelong bachelor) sometimes had a transcript laid next to his plate.[82] Although it was a commonplace in obituaries to exonerate a deceased scholar from the charge of having been a *Stubengelehrte*, Scheffer seemed to live the cliché: "The young Strasbourg professor expected nothing from life except comfortable silence for his work."[83]

The Egyptologist Johannes Dümichen, by contrast, was an "outdoor" type of scholar: a fieldworker who was most in his element when traveling in the Nile valley. At a time when fieldwork abroad was anything but common, Dümichen's research trips were a rich source of stories about suffering and sacrifice, complete with anecdotes about the indefatigable scholar spending long hours copying inscriptions under the burning Egyptian sun.[84] If these travels already brought him a reputation beyond academic circles,[85] richly illustrated books like the *Geschichte des alten Aegyptens* (History of Ancient Egypt, 1879) added to this fame. As a result, Baedeker, the German travel guide, contracted Dümichen to co-author a volume on Upper Egypt, thereby following the example of the Prussian crown prince, who had chosen Dümichen as his personal guide when touring the pyramids in 1869.[86] All this explains why, in his Strasbourg inaugural, Dümichen could literally call his chair "the office of a guide through ancient Egypt," while comparing his course syllabus to a "travel itinerary."[87]

As apparent as the differences between Scheffer's and Dümichen's personae are, these differences do not imply, however, that Scheffer's virtues of criticism were of only marginal importance to Dümichen. The *Geschichte des alten Aegyptens* was largely based on inscriptions that the author himself had transcribed. Moreover, apart from this narrative history book, Dümichen's scholarly output largely consisted of source publications full of carefully copied hieroglyphs.[88] The exactitude and sharp-mindedness required for this transcription work were not entirely unlike the precision and sagacity that Scheffer needed at his desk. Indeed, at times, Dümichen's work in Egypt resembled Studemund's research in Milan: both men tried to decode ancient scripts, with help of modern technologies, to produce transcripts that were as reliable as possible.[89] So, despite the fact that Dümichen was less of a scholarly recluse than Scheffer, he did engage in work to which virtues of criticism were crucial. Judging by obituaries appearing after Dümichen's death in 1894, this collecting and publishing of valuable inscriptions was what his fellow Egyptologists eventually judged his greatest contribution.[90]

What these examples show is that a broadly shared commitment to virtues of criticism among humanities scholars in Strasbourg was, to some extent, compatible with a variety of personae and scholarly ways of life. Not all professors were *Stubengelehrten*; not all of them were hesitant to reach out to educated middle-class readers.

Conclusion

Where does all this leave us? When in 1897 the historical economist Gustav Schmoller looked back on the years of his professoriate in Strasbourg, he noticed that many of his colleagues at the time shared a commitment to what he called "realism." For Schmoller, this term referred to a conception of scholarship in which empirical research, driven by what had become known as the "scientific method," mattered more than bold attempts at determining how all human knowledge fits together. Realism thus indicated dissociation from the idealist legacy that had shaped so much of German university life in earlier parts of the century. Also, it implied a focus on scientific work, with professors engaging in research instead of occupying parliamentary seats and writing for *bildungsbürgerliche* audiences, as had been customary in earlier decades. For Schmoller, it was "sharper criticism," "stricter methods," and "new results" that captured the *corps d'esprit* in the Alsatian capital.[91]

Although the picture sketched in this chapter is broadly compatible with Schmoller's, I have emphasized the *ethos* displayed by Strasbourg humanities scholars rather than their methodologies, partly to understand why they spoke so highly about virtues like precision, accuracy, and sharp-mindedness, but partly also to examine how such virtues of criticism related to the nationalist ambitions of the Kaiser-Wilhelms-Universität. One of the things this chapter has made clear is that the ethos prevalent at Strasbourg consisted of more than virtues of criticism. Even though *Kritik* was seen as a defining mark of *Wissenschaftlichkeit*, scholars also engaged in activities for which imagination, creativity, and synthetic abilities were just as indispensable qualities as sharp-mindedness and meticulousness. Also, this chapter has shown that *Kritik* was not a matter of virtues alone: virtues of criticism were often colored by evaluative attitudes, which made visible how scholars normatively positioned themselves vis-à-vis their subject matter. Finally, a shared commitment to *Kritik* did not prevent Strasbourg humanities scholars from embracing different scholarly personae. Far from being homogeneous, their ethos of criticism could be lived out in different ways, by fieldworkers in far-away countries as well as by scholars absorbed in ancient manuscripts.

All this implies that a research focus on communities of scholars, at a single university or otherwise, may bring to light certain aspects of scholarly habits, norms, and values that tend to remain invisible in studies of single virtues or vices. Apart from that this research focus can show how virtues overlapped and interacted with each other, it can highlight the extent to which such constellations of virtues were genre specific. Lecture courses, after all, made other demands on professors than private exercises, just as wide-ranging handbooks required other abilities than critical editions of medieval texts. Also, the perspective adopted in this chapter allows us to see that scholars' self-representations (self-congratulatory accounts like Müller's inaugural address) not always matched with their actual working practices (Studemund pouring chemical reagents on old manuscripts in Milan). Even if Schmoller was right in emphasizing "sharper criticism" and "stricter methods" as distinctive of the ethos cultivated at Strasbourg, historians of the humanities not only want to know what standards scholars propagated, but also how these standards worked out in practice.[92]

Notes

1. Lorraine Daston and Peter Galison, *Objectivity* (New York: Zone Books, 2007), 40.
2. Rens Bod et al., "A New Field: History of Humanities," *History of Humanities* 1, no. 1 (2016): 1–8.
3. Rens Bod et al., "The Flow of Cognitive Goods: A Historiographical Framework for the Study of Epistemic Transfer," *Isis* 110, no. 3 (2019): 483–96; *Epistemic Virtues in the Sciences and the Humanities*, ed. Jeroen van Dongen and Herman Paul (Cham: Springer, 2017).
4. Herman Paul, "German Thoroughness in Baltimore: Epistemic Virtues and National Stereotypes," *History of Humanities* 3, no. 2 (2018): 327–50.
5. Herman Paul, "Virtue Language in Nineteenth-Century Orientalism: A Case Study in Historical Epistemology," *Modern Intellectual History* 14, no. 3 (2017): 689–715.
6. See, e.g., Aleksei Pleshkov and Jan Surman, "Book Reviews in the History of Knowledge," *Studia Historiae Scientiarum* 20 (2021): 629–50; Christiaan Engberts, "Scholarship, Community Formation and Book Reviews: The *Literarisches Centralblatt* as Arena and Meeting Place," ibid., 651–79; Richard L. Kremer and Ad Maas, "A Tale of Reviews in Two History of Science Journals," ibid., 755–85.
7. Christiaan Engberts, *Scholarly Virtues in Nineteenth-Century Sciences and Humanities: Loyalty and Independence Entangled* (Cham: Palgrave Macmillan, 2022); Léjon Saarloos, "The Scholarly Self under Threat: Language of Vice in British Scholarship (1870–1910)" (PhD thesis Leiden University, 2021).
8. Rudolf Makkreel, *Dilthey: Philosopher of the Human Studies* (Princeton, NJ: Princeton University Press, 1975), 35–44.
9. Wilhelm Dilthey, "Entwurf zu einem Gutachten über die Gründung der Universität Straßburg" (1871), *Die Erziehung* 16 (1941): 81–5.

10. Renate Haas and Albert Hamm, *The University of Strasbourg and the Foundation of Continental English Studies: A Contribution to a European History of English Studies* (Frankfurt am Main: Peter Lang, 2009).
11. Stephan Roscher, *Die Kaiser-Wilhelms-Universität Straßburg 1872–1902* (Frankfurt am Main: Peter Lang, 2006), 147–8.
12. John E. Craig, *Scholarship and Nation Building: The Universities of Strasbourg and Alsatian Society, 1870–1939* (Chicago, IL: University of Chicago Press, 1984).
13. Dilthey, "Entwurf," 82. Unless otherwise noted, all translations are mine.
14. On the "political professor," see Ulrich Muhlack, "Der 'politische Professor' im Deutschland des 19. Jahrhunderts," in *Materialität des Geistes: Zur Sache Kultur: Im Diskurs mit Ulrich Oevermann*, ed. Ronald Burkholz, Christel Gärtner, and Ferdinand Zehentreiter (Weilerswist: Velbrück, 2001), 185–204.
15. Craig, *Scholarship and Nation Building*, 57.
16. As the youngest daughter of economics professor Georg Friedrich Knapp recalled in her memoirs: "We almost never used the word 'Germanifying'. My father . . . did not talk about Germanness, but lived it." Elly Heuß-Knapp, *Ausblick vom Münsterturm: Erlebtes aus dem Elzaß und dem Reich* (Berlin: Hans Bott, 1934), 16.
17. Craig, *Scholarship and Nation Building*, 84–5.
18. This draws on Robert K. Merton's classic definition in "Science and the Social Order," *Philosophy of Science* 5 (1938): 321–37, at 326 n. 16 and "A Note on Science and Democracy," *Journal of Legal and Political Sociology* 1 (1942): 115–26, at 116.
19. F. Max Müller, *Über die Resultate der Sprachwissenschaft: Vorlesung gehalten in der Kaiserlichen Universitæt zu Strassburg am XXIII. Mai MDCCCLXXII* (Strasbourg: Karl J. Trübner, 1872), 9, 10, 15, 17, 12, 13, 14, here cited in the English translation (modified in one case) published as "On the Results of the Science of Language: Inaugural Lecture, Delivered in the Imperial University of Strassburg, May 23, 1872," in F. Max Müller, *Chips from a German Workshop*, vol. 4 (New York: Charles Scribner's Sons, 1881), 199–226, at 205, 209, 211, 207, 208, 209.
20. Müller, *Über die Resultate*, 29, 32; "On the Results," 223, 225–6. The Niebuhr quote was taken from *Lebensnachrichten über Barthold Georg Niebuhr aus Briefen desselben und aus Erinnerungen einiger seiner nächsten Freunde*, vol. 2 (Hamburg: Friedrich Perthes, 1838), 208.
21. Lorraine Daston and Peter Galison, "The Image of Objectivity," *Representations* 40 (1992): 81–128, at 83.
22. Mark-Georg Dehrmann, "Prüfung, Forschung, Gruß: Antrittsprogramme und Antrittsvorlesungen als akademische Praktiken im 19. Jahrhundert," *Zeitschrift für Germanistik* 23, no. 2 (2013): 226–41.

23. Arie L. Molendijk, "Multiple Personae: Friedrich Max Müller and the Persona of the Oriental Scholar," in *Scholarly Personae in the History of Orientalism, 1870–1930*, ed. Christiaan Engberts and Herman Paul (Leiden: Brill, 2019), 45–63, esp. 48–51.
24. Frederick J. Furnivall to William Dwight Whitney, December 27, 1872, as quoted in Stephen G. Alter, *William Dwight Whitney and the Science of Language* (Baltimore, MD: Johns Hopkins University Press, 2005), 177.
25. [Ludwig Quidde], "Julius Weizsäcker †," *Deutsche Zeitschrift für Geschichtswissenschaft* 2 (1889): 327–40, at 328, 329, 330; P. Thomas, "Nécrologie," *Revue d'instruction publique en Belgique* 32 (1889): 362–4, at 362.
26. [Wilhelm von Christ], "Rudolf Schöll," *Sitzungsberichte der philosophisch-philologischen und historischen Classe der k. b. Akademie der Wissenschaften zu München* (1894): 149–52, at 150–1.
27. Enno Littmann, "Theodor Nöldeke: Gedächtnisrede gehalten am 9. Mai 1931," in *Nachrichten von der Gesellschaft der Wissenschaften zu Göttingen: Geschäftliche Mitteilungen aus dem Berichtsjahr 1930/31* (Berlin: Weidmann, 1931): 48–57, at 50; C. H. Becker, "Theodor Nöldeke," *Der Islam* 20 (1932): 43–8, at 43, 45.
28. Anna Echterhölter, *Schattengefechte: Genealogische Praktiken in Nachrufen auf Naturwissenschaftler (1710–1860)* (Göttingen: Wallstein, 2012).
29. Carlos Spoerhase, "Seminar Libraries as Laboratories of Philology: The Modern Seminar Model in Nineteenth-Century German Philology," *History of Humanities* 4, no. 1 (2019): 103–23; Kasper Risbjerg Eskildsen, "Virtues of History: Exercises, Seminars, and the Emergence of the German Historical Discipline, 1830–1900," *History of Universities* 34, no. 1 (2021): 27–40. See also Eskildsen's chapter in this volume.
30. Other relevant sources include annual seminar reports, such as those written by Wilhelm Scherer: "Bericht des Prof. W. Scherer über das Seminar für deutsche Philologie während der drei ersten Semester seines Bestehens (Winter 1872/3—Winter 1873/4)," May 25 1874, in Scherer, *Briefe und Dokumente aus den Jahren 1853 bis 1886*, ed. Mirko Nottscheid and Hans-Harald Müller (Göttingen: Wallstein, 2005), 377–81 and Scherer, "Seminarbericht 1874/75," June 4, 1875, in Scherer and Elias von Steinmeyer, *Briefwechsel 1872–1886*, ed. Horst Brunner and Joachim Helbig (Göppingen: Kümmerle, 1982), 320–1. See also, more generally, Uwe Meves, "Die Jahresberichte der Seminardirektoren als Quellen für die Seminarpraxis," *Zeitschrift für Germanistik* 23, no. 2 (2013): 242–58.
31. F. Collard, *Trois universités allemandes considérées au point de vue de l'enseignement de la philologie classique (Strasbourg, Bonn et Leipzig)* (Louvain: Ch. Peeters, 1879–82), 54–5.
32. Ibid., 36.

33. Ibid., 37, 39, 45.
34. Erich Marcks, "Hermann Baumgarten (III)," *Beilage zur Allgemeinen Zeitung* (October 4, 1893): 2–5, at 3.
35. Alfred Dove to Heinrich von Treitschke, May 13, 1873, in Dove, *Ausgewählte Briefe*, ed. Oswald Dammann (Munich: F. Bruckmann, 1925), 32–5, at 34. I discuss some other disapproving responses in Herman Paul, "The Heroic Study of Records: The Contested Persona of the Archival Historian," *History of the Human Sciences* 26, no. 4 (2013): 67–83.
36. Immanuel Kant, *Critik der reinen Vernunft* (Riga: Johann Friedrich Hartknoch, 1781), xi*; Gustav Gröber, "Geschichte der romanischen Philologie," in *Grundriss der romanischen Philologie*, ed. Gustav Gröber, vol. 1 (Strasbourg: Karl J. Trübner, 1888), 3–139, at 34; Georg Dehio, *Geschichte des Erzbistums Hamburg-Bremen bis zum Ausgang der Mission*, vol. 1 (Berlin: Wilhelm Hertz, 1877), 43.
37. See Benedetto Bravo, "*Critice* in the Sixteenth and Seventeenth Centuries and the Rise of the Notion of Historical Criticism," in *History of Scholarship: A Selection of Papers from the Seminar on the History of Scholarship Held Annually at the Warburg Institute*, ed. Christopher Ligota and Jean-Louis Quantin (Oxford: Oxford University Press, 2006), 135–95; Claus von Bormon, Helmut Holzhey, and Giorgio Tonelli, "Kritik," in *Historisches Wörterbuch der Philosophie*, dl. 4, ed. Joachim Ritter, Karlfried Gründer, and Gottfried Gabriel (Basel: Schwabe & Co., 1976), 1250–82; Giorgio Tonelli, "'Critique' and Related Terms Prior to Kant: A Historical Survey," *Kant-Studien* 69 (1978): 119–48; J. Colin McQuillan, *Immanuel Kant: The Very Idea of a Critique of Pure Reason* (Evanston, IL: Northwestern University Press, 2016), 3–20.
38. Theodor Nöldeke, *Untersuchungen zur Kritik des Alten Testaments* (Kiel: Schwers, 1869); Heinrich Julius Holtzmann, *Die Pastoralbriefe, kritisch und exegetisch behandelt* (Leipzig: Wilhelm Engelmann, 1880); P. Scheffer-Boichorst, "Beiträge zur Kritik deutscher und italienischer Quellenschriften," *Forschungen zur deutschen Geschichte* 11 (1871): 483–527.
39. See the titles listed in Fr. Schöll, "Rudolf Schöll, geb. 1. Sept. 1844, gest. 10. Juni 1893," *Biographisches Jahrbuch für Altertumskunde* 20 (1897): 9–40 and W. Radtke, "Georg Kaibel, geb. 30. Oktober 1849, gest. 12. Oktober 1901," *Biographisches Jahrbuch für Altertumskunde* 27 (1904): 15–71, at 66–71.
40. *Der Prolog zu den Canterbury Tales: Versuch einer kritischen Ausgabe*, ed. Bernhard ten Brink (Marburg: N. G. Elwert, 1871); Francesco Petrarca, *Rerum vulgarium fragmenta*, ed. [Gustav Gröber] (Strasbourg: J. H. Ed. Heitz, [1906]).
41. *Râvaṇavaha oder Setubandha*, ed. Siegfried Goldschmidt (Strasbourg: Karl J. Trübner, 1880).
42. Gustav Jacobsthal, "Die Texte der Liederhandschrift von Montpellier H. 196: Diplomatischer Abdruck," *Zeitschrift für romanische Philologie* 3 (1879): 526–56 and 4 (1880): 35–64, 278–317.

43. Julius Weizsäcker to Ernst Bernheim, May 1, 1884, Greifswald University Library, Ms 1588.
44. H. Ulmann, review of *Deutsche Reichtstagsakten*, vol. 1, *Deutsche Litteraturzeitung* 15 (1894): 495-8, at 498.
45. Mario Varvaro, "Wilhelm Studemund e il 'martire illustre della paleografia,'" *Seminarios Complutenses de Derecho Romano* 25 (2012): 281-318.
46. *T. Macci Plauti fabularum reliquiae Ambrosianae Codicis rescripti Ambrosiani Apographum*, ed. Guilelmus Studemund (Berlin: Weidmann, 1889), fol. 235r, 235v. The English translations are taken from Walter Stockert, "The Rebirth of a Codex: Virtual Work on the Ambrosian Palimpsest of Plautus," in *The Oxford Handbook of Greek and Roman Comedy*, ed. Michael Fontaine and Adele C. Scafuro (Oxford: Oxford University Press, 2014), 680-98, at 682, 683.
47. O. Seyffert, review of *T. Macci Plauti Fabularum Reliquiae Ambrosianae*, *Zeitschrift für das Gymnasial-Wesen* 44 (1890): 557-61, at 557.
48. Ibid., 559.
49. E. A. Sonnenschein, "A Plautine Palimpsest of the Ambrosian Library," *The Classical Review* 4, no. 7 (1890): 308-10, at 308; F[ritz] S[chöll], review of *T. Macci Plauti Fabularum Reliquiae Ambrosianae*, *Literarisches Centralblatt für Deutschland* (1890): 1375-8, at 1375.
50. Rainer Kolk, "Liebhaber, Gelehrte, Experten: Das Sozialsystem der Germanistik bis zum Beginn des 20. Jahrhunderts," in *Wissenschaftsgeschichte der Germanistik im 19. Jahrhundert*, ed. Jürgen Fohrmann and Wilhelm Voßkamp (Stuttgart: J. B. Metzler, 1994), 48-114, at 76, quoting Franz Schultz, "Die Entwicklung der Literaturwissenschaft von Herder bis Wilhelm Scherer," in *Philosophie der Literaturwissenschaft*, ed. Emil Ermatinger (Berlin: Juncker und Dünnhaupt, 1930), 1-42, at 37.
51. Wilhelm Scherer, *Geschichte der deutschen Dichtung im elften und zwölften Jahrhundert* (Strasbourg: Karl J. Trübner, 1875), vii.
52. [Friedrich Zarncke?], review in *Literarisches Centralblatt für Deutschland* (1876): 151-3, at 153.
53. [Franz] Sachse, review in *Archiv für das Studium der neueren Sprachen und Literaturen* 31 (1877): 93-9, at 97; Erich Schmidt, review in *Deutsche Rundschau* 7 (1876): 294-9, at 295.
54. [Elias] Steinmeyer, review in *Anzeiger für deutsches Alterthum und deutsche Litteratur* 1 (1876): 234-40, at 235; W. Wilmanns, review in *Historische Zeitschrift* 36 (1876): 518-23, at 519.
55. Roscher, *Kaiser-Wilhelms-Universität*, 372, n. 1030.
56. F. D. in "Litterarische Rundschau," *Westermanns Illustrierte Deutsche Monatshefte* 90 (1901): 530-40, at 536.
57. Adolf Hausrath, "An der Neige des Jahrhunderts," *Deutsche Rundschau* 98 (1899): 313-15, at 315.

58. Fr. Jodl, review in *Euphorion* 6 (1899): 772–9, at 775. More critical was the Austrian Catholic *Allgemeines Litteraturblatt* 11 (1902): 39–42.
59. Marcks, "Hermann Baumgarten (III)," 3; Hermann Bloch, "Paul Scheffer-Boichorst (25. Mai 1843—17. Januar 1902)," *Historische Zeitschrift* 89 (1902): 54–71, at 66; C. Snouck Hurgronje, "Theodor Nöldeke: 2. März 1836—25. Dezember 1930," *Zeitschrift der Deutschen Morgenländischen Gesellschaft* 85 (1931): 239–281, at 279.
60. Collard, *Trois universités allemandes*, 21.
61. R. Eucken, "Ansprache bei der Bestattung," *Kant-Studien* 17 (1912): 1–5, at 3.
62. Ernst Bernheim to Karl Lamprecht, February 9, 1883, in *"Über das eigentliche Arbeitsgebiet der Geschichte": Der Briefwechsel zwischen Karl Lamprecht und Ernst Bernheim sowie zwischen Karl Lamprecht und Henri Pirenne 1878–1915*, ed. Luise Schorn-Schütte and Mircea Ogrin (Cologne: Böhlau, 2017), 49–51, at 50.
63. Theodor Nöldeke to Michael Jan de Goeje, April 7, 1874, as quoted in Snouck Hurgronje, "Theodor Nöldeke," 262.
64. Theodor Nöldeke to Georg Hoffmann, October 24, 1877, as quoted in Bernhard Maier, *Gründerzeit der Orientalistik: Theodor Nöldekes Leben und Werk im Spiegel seiner Briefe* (Würzburg: Ergon, 2013), 69.
65. Theodor Nöldeke, *Geschichte des Quorâns* (Göttingen: Dieterich 1860), xxix, 5, 20, xxi.
66. Ibid., xxxi, 214, v, xvi, 51. Reviewers also hailed Nöldeke's "thorough" and "critical" habits of mind: [Moritz Steinschneider], review in *Hebräische Bibliographie* 4 (1861): 67–9; H[einrich] E[wald], review in *Göttingische Gelehrte Anzeigen* (1860): 1441–57, at 1444.
67. Nöldeke, *Geschichte des Quorâns*, 38, 223 (cf. ibid., 50, 214).
68. Nöldeke to Hoffmann, February 22, 1886, as quoted in Maier, *Gründerzeit der Orientalistik*, 66.
69. John S. Kloppenborg, "Holtzmann's Life of Jesus according to the 'A' Source," *Journal for the Study of the Historical Jesus* 4 (2006): 75–108, 203–23.
70. Heinrich Holtzmann, *Recht und Pflicht der biblischen Kritik: Ein Vortrag* (Karlsruhe: G. Braun, 1874).
71. H. J. Holtzmann, *Gesammelte Predigten*, [vol. 1] (Berlin: Hans Friedrich, 1901), chapters 2, 3, 8, 9, 11, and 13.
72. William R. Farmer, "State Interesse and Markan Primacy: 1870–1914," in *Biblical Studies and the Shifting of Paradigms, 1850–1914*, ed. Henning Reventlow and William R. Farmer (Sheffield: Sheffield Academic Press, 1995), 15–49, at 32–33.
73. "Vorwort," in *Urkundenbuch der Stadt Strassburg*, vol. 1, ed. Wilhelm Wiegand (Strasbourg: Karl J. Trübner, 1879), v–vii, at vi.
74. G. Dehio, "Deutsche Kunstgeschichte und deutsche Geschichte," *Historische Zeitschrift* 100 (1908): 473–85, at 480, 482, 484, 479.

75. Georg Dehio, "Die Kunst Unteritaliens in der Zeit Kaiser Friedrichs II.," *Historische Zeitschrift* 95 (1905): 193–205, at 194.
76. Georg Gottfried Dehio, *Denkmalschutz und Denkmalpflege im neunzehnten Jahrhundert: Rede zur Feier des Geburtstages Sr. Majestät des Kaisers, gehalten in der Aula der Kaiser-Wilhelms-Universität Strassburg am 27. Januar 1905* (Strasbourg: J. H. Ed. Heitz, 1905), 9.
77. I elaborate on the concept of personae in Herman Paul, "Introduction: Scholarly Personae: What They Are and Why They Matter," in *How To Be a Historian: Scholarly Personae in Historical Studies, 1800–2000*, ed. Herman Paul (Manchester: Manchester University Press, 2019), 1–14 and "Introduction: Scholarly Personae in the History of Orientalism," in Engberts and Paul, *Scholarly Personae in the History of Orientalism*, 1–16.
78. Georg Ebers, *Richard Lepsius: Ein Lebensbild* (Leipzig: Wilhelm Engelmann, 1885), vii.
79. Bloch, "Scheffer-Boichorst," 62.
80. Ibid., 58–9; E. Dümmler, "Gedächtnissrede auf Paul Scheffer-Boichorst," in *Abhandlungen der Königlich Preussischen Akademie der Wissenschaften aus dem Jahre 1902* (Berlin: Verlag der Königlichen Akademie der Wissenschaften, 1902), 1–16, at 14.
81. Ibid., 13; Bloch, "Scheffer-Boichorst," 66.
82. K. Hampe, "Paul Scheffer-Boichorst," *Historische Vierteljahrschrift* 5 (1902): 280–90, at 286.
83. Bloch, "Scheffer-Boichorst," 57.
84. Georg Ebers, "Johannes Dümichen," *Beilage zur Allgemeinen Zeitung* (February 26, 1894): 1–6, at 2.
85. See "Dümichen," in *Brockhaus' Conversations-Lexikon*, 13th edn, vol. 5 (Leipzig: F. A. Brockhaus, 1883), 634.
86. K. Baedeker, *Ägypten: Handbuch für Reisenden*, vol. 2 (Leipzig: Karl Baedeker, 1891), v; Ebers, "Johannes Dümichen," 4.
87. Johannes Dümichen, *Über die Tempel und Gräber im alten Ägypten und ihre Bildwerke und Inschriften: Vorlesung gehalten in der Kaiserlichen Universität zu Strassburg am XIX. November MDCCCLXXII* (Strasbourg: Karl J. Trübner, 1872), 4, 22.
88. See, among other titles, Johannes Dümichen, *Altägyptische Kalenderinschriften in den Jahren 1863–1865 an Ort und Stelle gesammelt* (Leipzig: J. C. Hinrichs, 1866); *Altägyptische Tempelinschriften in den Jahren 1863–1865 an Ort und Stelle gesammelt* (Leipzig: J. C. Hinrichs, 1867); *Historische Inschriften altägyptischer Denkmäler in den Jahren 1863–1865 an Ort und Stelle gesammelt* (Leipzig: J. C. Hinrichs, 1867).
89. In Dümichen's case, photography was the technology that facilitated his transcription work. See Johannes Dümichen, *Resultate der auf Befehl Sr.*

Majestät des Königs Wilhelm I. von Preußen im Sommer 1868 nach Aegypten entsendeten archäologisch-photographischen Expedition, vol. 1 (Berlin: Alexander Duncker, 1869).
90. H[einrich] B[rugsch] and A[dolf] E[rman], "Johannes Dümichen, geb. 15. October 1833, gest. 7. Februar 1894," *Zeitschrift für Ägyptische Sprache und Alterthumskunde* 32 (1894): 63; Wilhelm Spiegelberg, "Johannes Dümichen: Geb. 15. October 1833, gest. 7. Februar 1894," *Recueil de travaux relatifs à la philologie et à l'archéologie égyptiennes et assyriennes* 16 (1894): 74–7, at 75.
91. Gustav Schmoller, "Von der Straßburger Jubelfeier: Worte in Namen der früheren Lehrer der Kaiser Wilhelm-Universität gesprochen zu Straßburg am 1. Mai 1897," *Beilage zur Allgemeinen Zeitung* (May 7, 1897): 6–7, at 7. On the *Methodenstreit* that caused Schmoller to emphasize this empiricist leaning, see Jens Herold, *Der junge Gustav Schmoller: Sozialwissenschaft und Liberalkonservatismus im 19. Jahrhundert* (Göttingen: Vandenhoeck & Ruprecht, 2019), 189–93.
92. Funding was generously provided by the Dutch Research Council (NWO).

10

Producing the Masculine Scholar: Europe in the Nineteenth and Twentieth Centuries

Falko Schnicke

Introduction

The history of gender in the humanities is no simple add-on, no supplement to the "real story" of the disciplines, which could otherwise stand alone. On the contrary, gender is part of the very essence of humanistic scholarship and studying it reveals structures, hierarchies, habitus, and perceptions fundamental to it. Since their establishment as modern university disciplines, all humanities are deeply intertwined with gendered norms—be it the establishment of research seminars as "masculine marketplace[s] of knowledge"[1] and the marginalization of early attempts to study women and gender in nineteenth-century historical research,[2] be it late nineteenth-century male classics scholars imagining themselves as hard-working miners and brave warriors,[3] be it the understanding of reading as masculine practice in English studies in the 1920s and 1930s,[4] the notion of teaching as affectionate and thus female and research as cognitive and masculine in American Studies during the 1930s to 1960s,[5] or be it the canon centered on male authors and artists in literature studies and art history to the present.[6]

Academic merits, too, are defined masculine as reflected in academic awards. The Faculty of Humanities of the University of Hamburg, for example, bestowed only five out of fifty-two honorary doctorates to women until 1989; most of them since the late 1970s.[7] The praise of "womanly qualities" as methodological advantage for sociological studies in the late nineteenth-century circles of economist Gustav Schmoller was a rare exception.[8] On the contrary, for a long time for women universities turned out to be nothing like a kind mother (*alma mater*), as the Berlin women's education activist Helene Lange at the same time derisively noted, but rather like a "cantankerous stepmother."[9] While there were a few supporters of female students, the vast majority of humanity scholars during the nineteenth century approved German historian Heinrich von Sybel's view that "if our universities were suited for ladies, they were inappropriate for students, and vice versa."[10] How persistent these ideas of academically unfit femininity were is demonstrated by a survey among male university personnel during the 1950s in West-Germany. Participants found women's voices too weak to become professors and believed they would not be able to assert themselves in the classroom.[11] Only a critical history of gender in the humanities therefore can decipher elementary disciplinary logics, social practices of scholarship, and its symbolic orders, hierarchies of power, and structures of knowledge.[12]

To offer an overview, in the first of the five parts of this chapter I will begin by making the point that it would be falling short to reduce the history of gender in the humanities to counting how many men and women occupied which positions and when. Vital as this information is, more complex histories are necessary. Second, I will briefly outline the research arena of a gendered history of the humanities. The deliberately abstract catalogue of topics it might encompass is supported by two examples to underscore that the masculine nature of the humanities can only be investigated by including masculinity and femininity at the same time. Third, I will explore how late eighteenth- and early nineteenth-century male scholars in art history and archaeology were (re-)produced in portraits. Academic portraits and their gendered coding are still an understudied subject but offer extensive insights into both the self-fashioning of masculine scholars and academic values. Fourth, I will investigate how the masculine scholar was narrated: in the late nineteenth-century, Theodor Wiedemann, long-term assistant to German historian Leopold von Ranke, portrayed him in writing. Memoirs are a highly instructive genre because, again, they present prevailing academic criteria aimed at setting and solidifying disciplinary standards. This was true for Wiedemann's account for which he used gendered concepts to describe Ranke, as well as himself. The conclusion, finally, compiles desiderata for future research.

More Than Numbers: Complex Histories

The gendered history of the humanities should not be confused with simply collecting statistical data about how many women were formally registered students or employed researchers. These facts are crucial but the gender history of the humanities is not exhausting itself in the mere collection of biographical information. Instead, it should use them as starting point for further research and a broader argument. Turned into histories of exclusion and inclusion, biographical studies are highly informative, especially for periods of transformation and/or as group biographies (prosopography).[13] They contribute to the vital question of inclusion and exclusion that reveals the underlying masculine coding of the humanities and how it worked in practice.

Already the issues mentioned indicate that the gender history of the humanities is not primarily about women or men. Instead, as historian of science Ludmilla Jordanova concluded, gender "is a concept that expresses a widespread and highly complex phenomenon: the representation of the multiple relationships between masculine and feminine."[14] In addition to that, Joan Scott made the point that "[g]ender is, after all, a primary way of signifying power."[15] This is true for societies in general and for the academic world in particular. Combining individuals, institutions, and topics, biographical studies are instead, as the following examples show, an effective way to explore the gendered nature of the humanities and the politics around it. By embedding statistical data into complex analyses they can explain their significance for the individuals mentioned and the disciplinary contexts at the same time.

For Austria, Elizabeth Grabenweger in her study of the first three female *Privatdozentinnen* (adjunct professors) in German philology at the University of Vienna has shown that the occurrence of female scholars in the first third of the twentieth century depended on historical coincidences such as the appointment of the open-minded head of institute. Another promotive factor was the increasing numbers of students after the Great War. They made it necessary to hire more adjunct professors for teaching purposes making it more and more unlikely for them to gain a full professorship in the end. This loss of prestige of the position of adjunct professors during the 1920s opened up this position for women.[16] On the one hand, the female scholars' intellectual work brought new topics to the canon, as Christine Touaillon wrote in her postdoctoral thesis on the hitherto-neglected eighteenth-century novels by women writers, and Marianne Thalmann who focused on Romantic cheap literature.[17] The framing of these topics as niche topics by the male academic establishment, on the other hand, made it easy to marginalize them, reaffirming the proper scholar and his topics as masculine. Touaillon obviously knew about this risk and stressed that her work was academic and not politically associated with the women's movement.[18] The reviews, however, were mostly negative, and Touaillon remained an outsider.[19]

For Weimar, Nazi, and post-war Germany, Heike Berger's study of the first generations of female historians holding a *Habilitation* shows that their entrance to the universities was only a partial one. Within the first fifty years after the permission to earn the formal postdoctoral qualification in 1920 (and the initial National Socialist prohibition of it) only eighteen female historians obtained their *Habilitation*. Male networks managed to keep them away from the center of the discipline and assigned less prestigious, new subdisciplines and peripheral branches such as prehistory or Eastern European history to them. What is more, many female historians served as editorial staff for academic journals, a time-consuming activity which reduced their research output and, again, resulted in the situation that research was primarily associated with male scholars.[20] During the Third Reich, a research career for female historians was possible only at non-university research institutions for National Socialist Eastern Studies (*Ostforschung*), which for male colleagues was a springboard back to a university post, for female historians the final destination.[21] After the Second World War, some women kept working academically. Their National Socialist biography could be of value because in some cases it helped that they were recognized as a prevented *Habilitand* under the Nazi regime. In other cases, different to most male historians, a gap-free curriculum vitae was interpreted as a disadvantage and a moral burden and led to exclusion from further employment after 1945. For women academics, therefore, the Nazi period marked a considerable caesura.[22]

Both examples (out of many) demonstrate that studying male and female actors applying a gender perspective leads to information about their individual careers in context and thus evidence about structural elements, academic practices, and cultures of scholarship. Such an approach offers insights into the multi-layered historical processes of gendering academic disciplines that point beyond the mere counting of actors.

Masculinity and Femininity: Five Trajectories

Following Jordanova and Scott and considering the gendering of the humanities a complex phenomenon, different histories of it are possible: "Gender is indeed everywhere."[23] Summarizing to some extent, five trajectories of historical research can be distinguished: first, actors; second, institutions; third, bodies of knowledge; fourth, academic practices; and finally symbolic orders.[24] While these trajectories can be separated retrospectively, they were interconnected, intertwined, and overlapping in the times under investigation. The outlined trajectories go far beyond the statistical distribution of men and women and combine biographical research with history of knowledge, institutional and cultural history approaches towards a gender-sensitive history of the humanities. The presented set might seem broadly defined. It is, however, specific for humanistic scholarship and intended as call for a multi-layered and complex study of gender in the humanities that will suffice for its multi-layered and complex nature. Notwithstanding the differences between disciplines, they are meant to be applicable to all humanities.

(1) *Actors*: The level of actors is fundamental because it explores who the important players at universities and research institutions were and what agency they had. Insiders are able to form and influence disciplinary policies as well as fill official functions. Different to outsiders and people denied access, it is for them to shape academic discourses, decide on quality criteria or to define regulations for access to name just a few capabilities. Following intersectional approaches, next to gender further social categories are important for access such as class, religion, sexuality, or race.[25] It is also necessary to deconstruct the insider's success. The question of how scholars are supported by whom is vital. Exploring what kind of support they could draw on in their household, family, or offices and who financed them reveals networks and social structures such as marriage or aristocratic sponsors as basic conditions for successful academic careers.

However, to stop the research on the gendered nature of the humanities here would mean to reproduce former academic power structures and memory practices, while a critical gender history of the humanities should do exactly the opposite.[26] Scholars are constantly involved in the boundary work of distinguishing themselves from people they consider outsiders or so-called amateurs. It is necessary to study how this often-gendered boundary work[27] operates and who is excluded by which arguments, and there are two ways of doing this. First, a focus on the scientific persona helps to explain how insiders and their "cultural identity" are produced and reaffirmed and which features are considered elementary.[28] Second, outsiders themselves must be part of the gender history of the humanities because excluding them from the disciplines again and again went hand-in-hand with the marginalization of topics, approaches, and sources. How productive and innovative their consideration can be is shown by Johanna Gehmacher in her study on alternative persona concepts of excluded learned women around the turn of the century, with which she additionally enriches the history of scholarship with the dimension of the perception of the humanities from the outside.[29]

(2) *Institutions*: As framework and structure for individual action, academic institutions are fundamental to the gender history of the humanities. Individuals are not subjected to institutions because they are capable of shaping them but to some extent, as the new intuitionalism has highlighted, institutions are capable of structuring the actions of individuals.[30] Institutions are not identical to actors because they follow their own logics, as the mentioned example of unintentionally increasing number of students and its partly unwanted consequences in early 1920s Vienna proves. Universities and non-university research institutes that exclude or discriminate certain groups are biased, or gendered institutions. One level below, faculties and departments are crucial as they decide how to implement policies and to allow exceptions for whom. Academic institutions are dependent on political institutions which is why legal regulations allowing or working against discrimination are part of this as is the latitude they offered actors. The same is true for political bodies overseeing academic institutions such as ministries of education or parliamentary commissions. They set the fundamental rules for academic institutions, provide funding and are therefore in the position to force gender equality or not.

Further, informal institutions are of interest because research is driven from working groups, private seminars, and networks which form powerful decision-making bodies often predetermining decisions by official bodies.

Informal networks running publication series or journals are prime examples, these informal institutions define focus areas, set priorities about content and sources, and possess gate-keeping functions that can hinder or promote individuals and groups.

(3) *Bodies of knowledge*: To include the content humanistic disciplines produce or are based on is vital because these bodies of knowledge are by no means gender-neutral. As the example of Touaillon quoted above shows, certain topics are considered to be more important than others, more scientific than others. These hierarchies of topics are often gendered, and in turn gender the humanistic persona. Exploring both accepted and neglected or marginalized topics is therefore exploring implicit disciplinary values and its unwritten rules vital for academic success. This must include research and teaching because novel topics are likely to enter teaching syllabuses first.[31] The story of Touaillon also indicates that traditional hierarchies of topics often go together with the exclusion of sources, which is why new actors typically point to new sources. They form part of the humanistic bodies of knowledge because research and therefore knowledge production depends on them. What is more, subdisciplines and academic innovation often trace back to the exploration or acceptance of new source material or novel readings of it. Moreover, next to content and sources also analysis systems such as periodization should be included. They are informative for a gender history of the humanities as they reveal how priorities are set, what is considered important and formative and who's perspectives, views, and experiences are included or left out.

(4) *Practices*: The humanities, as all academic subjects, are more than simply intellectual production but also consist of practices understood as collective actions and recurring routines. The practice history of the humanities is not only a history of what happened but also of how it happened. Such a perspective contributes to its gender history because, first, gender itself is produced and reaffirmed through practices.[32] Second, as political scientists Emanuel Adler and Vincent Pouliot highlight, gendered "knowledge is not only located 'behind' practices, in the form of intentions, beliefs, reasons, goals, etc. It is also 'bound up' in the very execution of the practice."[33] Third, practices are dependent on approval by peers: "Social recognition is thus a fundamental aspect of practice; its (in)competence is never inherent but attributed in and through social relations," as they point out.[34] Teaching, for example, is one of the most neglected issues in the history of the humanities, but can reveal gendered styles of academic training and discussions as well as hierarchies of topics. Also, analysing academic

congresses can elucidate who is presenting research findings in what way, and what cultures of criticism are existing. Furthermore, academic rituals and ceremonies themselves are of interest as they are crucial for group formation processes. Anniversaries, graduation ceremonies, academic days, or opening ceremonies commemorate academic values and traditions. They are performances of institutional self-perceptions and therefore inform about their gendered structures.

(5) *Symbolic orders*: The final trajectory are symbolic orders, that is conceptions of what is scientific and its relations to gendered ideas of scholarship, a set of tacit rules of the academic sphere and its representations, habitus, tacit systems, and regulating self-images. It is a coincidence that the bourgeois gender order and the humanities emerged at the same time. However, historically they influenced and reinforced one another which resulted in gendered understandings of the nature of research, universities, and (higher) education in general. The language of the humanities used to describe individual research steps or the humanist scholar exposes this connection: metaphors proved a gendered and sexualized concept of research, and in turn contributed to the establishment of modern gender norms. Such concepts had social consequences as they shaped the university as action space for some and excluded others. The same is true for spatial and body orders inscribed to the modern research institutions creating them as masculine institutions, often spatially separated from women. Against this historical development, a critical history of the humanities has to reflect on their gendered nature and how it formed past versions of historiography. Historiography, as memory politics in general, is a powerful instrument of producing gendered concepts of the humanities, as it is in deconstructing them.

All these five trajectories make it clear that gendering the humanities was a complex process. It involves femininity as well as masculinity because both are interrelated and produced interdependently.[35] Two examples illustrate this. For England, a study of early women's colleges, that touches on trajectories 1, 2, 4, and 5, is instructive. Sophie Forgan explains that their history is in fact a history of the spatial separation of the sexes. While the traditional colleges in the city center of Oxford or Cambridge remained male spaces not to be entered by women,[36] around 1870 a number of additional women's colleges were founded in both cities. To meet the intentions of medical protection and to ward off lustful male glances or to counter them preventively by physical displacement, they were deliberately located at the outskirts.[37] (Re-)producing higher education as a masculine sphere thus was not primarily a question of existing institutions, but of social practice.³⁸ For other universities that admitted women, such as the King's College in London, there is evidence of male guards escorting female students. They did not primarily serve their defense, but above all their protection: "At the end of the lecture, it could happen . . . that the professor escorted the ladies out of the lecture hall and out of the building, as if he were leading them through enemy territory."³⁹ What is more, the foundation of women's colleges was not necessarily accompanied by the questioning of existing gender stereotypes, for where they existed in England, they could even reinforce the thesis of physical female weakness: for example, infirmaries were set up in Somerville, Girton, and Newnham to respond to any overexertion due to academic work. These institutions contributed to women's identification with weakness.⁴⁰

For France, Denis Provencher and Luke Eilderts, in an article that connects to trajectory 3, have argued that Ernest Lavisse, after the defeat in the Franco-Prussian War of 1870–1, used motifs of masculinity and femininity to achieve his program of French resurrection. In the textbook *Histoire de France: cours élémentaire* (1884), Lavisse, professor at and director of the l'École normale, claimed that for France to regain its strength, it had to rely on the reinforcement of masculine honor and militaristic nationalism. To support this claim, he provided examples from French national history and presented pointed interpretations of historical figures. While he praised masculine political and military leaders, he criticized exuberant masculinities such as Napoleon: failing to subject himself to an economy of moderation, he "explains Napoleon's ultimate defeat at Waterloo by way of his uncontrollable love for war."⁴¹ On the other hand, Lavisse ascribed phases of weakness in French history to feminine qualities.⁴² Female protagonists are important for his account but he draws their strength "from a mix of male support and divine powers."⁴³ The authors therefore conclude that Lavisse's manual on citizenship and future glory of France was a "gender manual" in the first place.⁴⁴

Seeing the Masculine Scholar: Academic Portraiture

To offer some empirical insights after this programmatic overview, this section focuses on how portraiture functioned as a tool of gendering the humanities. Visual culture, and portraiture among them, has been a major factor in establishing modern gender norms.⁴⁵ This is true for general history and the history of the humanities. In her study *Defining Features*, Ludmilla Jordanova has argued that the social establishment of doctors and men working in medical professions in the eighteenth and nineteenth centuries was supported by public portraiture. Portraits were "an integral part" of cultivating esteem for their professions.[46] "Medical identities were being built around a middle-class ideology, of merit, education, first-hand observation, of progress and reform."[47] Conveying this meaning was possible because of the special features of visual culture. "Portraits can do this social and cultural work," Jordanova explains, "because there is an extensive and widely recognized range of visual devices for endowing an individual with heroic qualities."[48] Humanistic scholars, too, were featured in portraits and often introduced by a number of objects. Such enriched or interior portraits showed more than just the sitter but surrounded him by his work environment and used additional attributes to characterize him. This practice was not limited to scholars,[49] but also applied to them. Humanistic scholars were thus typically presented next to books, in front of libraries, and with desks to point towards their academic activities. Highlighting their social background in the educated middle classes, these attributes situated the scholar in a setting which introduced him individually and his profession.

How exactly did these visual arrangements (re-)produce the masculine scholar? The self-portrait of German art historian Johann Dominik Fiorillo (1748–1821) and Carl Oesterley's portrait of German archaeologist Karl Otfried Müller (1797–1840) (see Figure 10.1) provide answers. Fiorillo, who worked as an art historian at the University of Göttingen, depicted himself in 1798 in a medallion-shaped portrait in which he was surrounded by a color palette and a canvas stand to identify him as the artist he also was. In addition to that, he added a volume next to him, inscribed "Giorgio Vasari."[50] This arrangement alerted viewers to the fact that Fiorillo was also an art historian and author of one of the first academic histories of art; the first volume of his *History of Draughtsmanship* appeared in the same year as his portrait.[51] At the end of the eighteenth century, books—and academic books in particular—still represented a masculine world for publishing and authorship were becoming increasingly accessible to women, but only slowly. Writing women were mostly associated with genres considered private and emotional such as letters, diaries or autobiographies and understood as "amateurs," as Bonnie Smith described them, or they appeared as editors of their husbands' works and *salonnières*.[52] However, the volume placed in Fiorillo's portrait did more. Referring to the authoritative collection of biographies of artists by Vasari, the proximity of this well-known volume put

Fiorillo himself into this line of tradition. Vasari devoted only one of the over three hundred *vitae* in his collection to a woman and had thus created a strongly male-coded canon of art,[53] a "hagiography of masculine genius."[54] By the notion of this book, Fiorello placed himself not only in that tradition but suggested also that he was about to follow in Vasari's footsteps which meant to continue the masculine tradition of writing the history of art.

Oesterley's portrait of Müller operated similarly. Originally trained as classical philologist, Müller became a star of the emerging subject of archaeology. In 1830, he published his *Handbook of the Archaeology of Art*, which soon became a standard reference at home and abroad.[55] He also took huge interest in archaeological discoveries at his time. As many others in Europe, he was particularly fascinated by the Parthenon Marbles which, brokered by Lord Elgin, were taken to the British Museum in London in 1816.[56] Müller convinced the minister for the affairs of Hanover at the German Chancery in London to commission plaster impressions of them for his home university at Göttingen. Previously impressions were given to selected monarchs and a few museums only, and so bringing copies of the famous and highly coveted Parthenon Frieze of Athens to Göttingen was a major success for Müller. Their arrival upgraded the university's collection of plaster casts, and Osterley's portrait celebrates what was seen as stroke of a genius.[57] It shows Müller sitting at a desk and writing in front of the Frieze which dominates the entire picture. The archaeologist is thus presented next to naked ancient cavalrymen. Their muscular bodies and those of their strong, energetic, and even aggressive horses surrounded Müller. Again, proximity is crucial because it reminded viewers not only of his political success of securing the impressions, but also situated Müller within a context of militaristic masculinity. Thus, he himself appeared as a proper man in this picture dealing with important objects of study. Raewyn Connell coined this relationship "complicit masculinity" and explained that it means without incorporating the high-ranking hegemonic masculinity of military men "accepting the privilege of their gender."[58] Since Müller's head is positioned among the cavalrymen the portrait suggests that his academic mind was even capable of taming and ordering, thus mastering the ancient military masculinity. The fact that he, unlike Fioillo, used this notion for a private representation—the portrait was commissioned as a gift to his parents[59]—illustrates how natural and acceptable the (re-)production of his masculinity was for him. It also proves how deeply rooted in bourgeois culture the production of nineteenth-century academic masculinities was.

Establishing propinquity to prestigious masculinities was no rare phenomenon and occurred in other disciplines as well. Historians later also

Figure 10.1 Carl Oesterley, Karl Otfried Müller (1830), oil on canvas, 74 × 63 cm, private collection. © Photo Stephan Eckardt, Archäologisches Institut der Universität Göttingen.

were presented next to military masculinities. In a portrait made by Eduard Bendemann for the German national gallery in 1885, Johann Gustav Droysen was shown encircled by the Prussian military leaders he had written about: he was thus presented as one of them. In a portrait (1881) by Ludwig

Knaus, Droysen's Berlin colleague Theodor Mommsen was placed in front of a bust of Caesar, writing his *History of the Roman Empire*.[60]

Further features of the portraits help to shape the masculine scholar. Müller's posture is telling. He is positioned at his desk, and while his right hand holds a quill his left arm rests on the table and supports his head. Evoking the impression of thoughtfulness, it presents Müller as a man of reason, as an intellectual, and a thinker. His view bolsters this characteristic as it is turned sideways and diagonally upwards, as well as directed to the light. Daniel Graepler convincingly reads this as an expression of inspiration and productive restlessness without any semblance of reverie or cloying sentimentality.[61] It should be added that, notwithstanding the ostentatiously white shirt (pointing to the high prestige of cleanliness and tidiness among the middle classes), Osterley situated Müller's head in the light making it the portrait's brightest spot. Highlighting the masculine scholars' heads by, for example, focusing the image section on them was a common technique in characterizing humanistic scholars as brain workers.[62] Another technique was emphasizing the head by bright color, as in the case of Müller.

What is more, academic portraits provide information on how masculine scholars worked scientifically. Addressing methods was a powerful tool of coding academic disciplines masculine because of the long forced absence of women from methodical discussions. For the most part the nineteenth and first half of the twentieth centuries, scientific methods were applied to men only and considered the most manly part of the disciplines because women could play no role since they were denied access to academic professions in the first place. This is why talking methods was considered a purely masculine affair.[63] So, while it was possible to depict women as educated, it was not possible to include hints of their scientific methods into those portraits because of their formal disqualification from the academy. Quite different for men: in Osterley's portrait of Müller the specificity of his method is made unambiguously clear by painting the Parthenon Frieze in the background as fragment with parts missing and beveled edges. Some of the heads of the horses and cavalrymen therefore are given broken off. The plaster impressions in his picture are therefore shown as true to original which in turn suggests that Müller's work is not that of an effusive amateur looking for superficial beauty or perfection but that of a precise, scientific scholar, an academic studying the true transmission of antique material.[64]

A further case in which a particular approach to sources is part of the portrait is a photograph of Austrian art historian Julius Schlosser (1866–1938). Produced to be published in a biographical volume on art historians that appeared in 1924,[65] it presented him sitting in a chair in front of a bookcase looking at a small bronze Renaissance statuette of Hercules held in his hands. Avoiding the eye of the viewers, he is concentrated on, even immersed in the object. Schlosser was reluctant to take part in the publication project at first because he feared it too shallow.[66] After he had convinced himself, he decided to present himself by highlighting his original-oriented approach to art. Schlosser, professor at the University of Vienna and director of the Vienna Art Museum, believed in studying and teaching art history by consulting the originals. His portrait expressed this (in his view threatened) conviction visually by showing him with a concentrated look focusing on nothing than the bronze. To underscore his orientation to the original once again, the table in front of him was deliberately left empty.[67]

Finally, to cite an additional example, in Bendemann's aforementioned oil painting Droysen is presented not only as historian, and not only as historian of Prussian history, but more precisely as a biographer. Droysen is shown in his study surrounded by his completed works; the portrait is an intellectual retrospection of his career. While all his major publication projects are present in some way or another, his biographies are represented as crucial. They are completely assembled and specially arranged: in the painting, Droysen stands next to a bookstand and rests his arm on a volume laid on top of it. Carefully chosen, this book is his famous and very popular history of a Prussian war hero from the battles against Napoleon, Ludwig Yorck von Wartenburg. It is given in red. Biographical research was a contested method of scientific historiography at that time, and the artist Bendemann knew that Droysen approved it and was its leading representative because both were long-term personal friends and discussed their work in letters. The whole scene in the portrait therefore is arranged to give a portrait of Droysen's methodological standpoint and to show the masculine scholar as historical biographer whose contemporary fame was based on his biographies.[68]

Narrating the Masculine Scholar: Remembering Historian Leopold von Ranke

The masculine scholar is not only produced and reaffirmed visually but also—and, in fact, more regularly—in writing. Biographical accounts are a major genre for what has been called the study of scholarly personae.[69] To provide an example from the "intermediate level" combining models of scholarship with individual biographies,[70] the following considers Theodor Wiedemann's (1823–1901) biographical essay on Leopold von Ranke (1795–1886), who himself had come a model for historical scholarship by this time within the German discourse and beyond.[71] Both German historians stood in close contact as Ranke, one of the most important historians of the nineteenth century who became famous for his formative all-male seminars,[72] employed Wiedemann as a personal assistant. He supported Ranke in his research activities in his later years after he had ended his career as a lecturer at Berlin university. Wiedemann, himself a historian holding a doctorate and one of his pupils, spent sixteen years with Ranke working in his house in the center of Berlin on several publication projects, among them revisions of his works and a monumental world history in nine volumes (six of which appeared during Ranke's life time, the rest posthumously).[73] Ranke had weak eyes[74] and was becoming increasingly deaf. In addition to the household staff, he was therefore dependent on the help of scientific assistants. Wiedemann's account on that time providing information on Ranke's style of working and research routines appeared in several pieces in the *Deutsche Revue über das gesamte nationale Leben der Gegenwart*, an open-minded monthly that was quite influential in the early 1890s.

Like the visual portraits, the genre of memoirs as such was a marker of masculine success. Human interest stories of the kind that Wiedemann's text undoubtedly, if not primarily, were published only about the most eminent and most productive German historians, such as Ranke, Mommsen, and (to a lesser extent) Sybel. Therefore the genre itself testified to Ranke being elevated to the status of a heroic genius, a category which was only populated by figures of masculine strength. At the turn of the nineteenth and twentieth centuries, this was true for literature in general[75] and for historiography in particular.[76] Martina Kessel has shown that memoirs and biographical texts were a privileged locus for such narratives because they allowed the male professional persona to be distinguished from female domestic work. Based on the (at least ideal) separation of private and public spheres of the sexes, domestic work was devalued as repetitive and professional work was valorized as part of the nineteenth-century discourse of progress. Kessel therefore refers to titles of memoirs and biographies in which terms such as "becoming," "willing," "creating," or "working" occurred as the doing gender of this distinction. They underlined the male potential for development and creativity, and accentuate individual achievements.[77] Against this background, it is not surprising but downright obvious that Wiedemann is on this line with the title of his text: he entitled it "Sixteen Years in Leopold von Ranke's Workshop," evoking associations of male-coded long-lasting and permanent productivity, efficiency, and creative power. In the age of industrial high modernity—the German Empire was among the world's leading industrial nations in the 1890s—Wiedemann used the term "workshop" (*Werkstatt*) to distance himself from the uninspired piecework of the unskilled proletarian lower classes in the factories and to suggest associations with the perfection of trained craftsmen working on individual pieces on the one hand and the ingenious power of visual artists on the other. In this way, Wiedemann undertook to idealize Ranke and further consolidate his academic masculinity, implicitly meaning himself as well—in the sense of the complicit masculinity already mentioned—because, after all, Wiedemann was part of Ranke's success and achievement.

Also in terms of content, Wiedemann's text is a prime example of how genius masculinity was (re-)produced in the biography of science in the nineteenth century. The somewhat lengthy treatise cannot be treated exhaustively here, but already a few selected topics give an insight into its tone and argumentation. It was not necessary to make a special elaborate claim for Ranke that he had been of genius, for Ranke, although not without criticism, enjoyed high esteem in Imperial Germany.[78] Wiedemann therefore wove it in casually again and again, and placed him on a high pedestal. It took him to the third part of his essay until he called him a "genius."[79] Already before, he had named him a "great man" and put him on a par with Pierre Bayle, Gottfried Wilhelm Leibniz, Alexander von Humboldt, Theodor Mommsen, and Immanuel Kant.[80] Wiedemann saw Ranke moving in a "higher sphere of thought and imagination"[81] and did not regard his works as productions, but as "creations" (*Schöpfung*), again evoking the association with genial male artists.[82] He pointed to "the strength of Ranke's receptivity" and alluded to his superior intellectual capacity.[83]

Despite this status, Ranke needed assistants, or at least he made use of them. While Wiedemann used his text to show how devotedly and effectively he worked for him, proving he was able to do the genius' groundwork, he also shared with his readers how Ranke saw the relationship with his assistants: he described, according to Wiedemann, his working with him as "some sort of intellectual marriage" (*geistige Vermählung*).[84] This metaphor represents a gendering of the working relationship. It can be assumed that Ranke imagined himself as the man in this marriage and thus framed his assistants' scholarly work as a feminized activity.

It fits with the genius claim that Ranke did not want to call his assistants that. In his perception, this label invoked a false connotation:

> The term assistant or scientific assistant, which is probably also used, appeared to Ranke to be quite inappropriate and was downright repugnant to him: for one thinks of the completely different position of a medical assistant. He saw in this designation an intolerable presumption, very likely to give rise to the false opinion that he did not create his works completely independently.[85]

Ranke made clear with this stance an awareness of his prestigious position, and the perception that it was potentially at risk. His preferred designation of "secretary" for his assistants testifies to the fact that hierarchy was important to him in his professional relationships. On the one hand, it is unusual that such a rather unfavorable message is mentioned in a rather hagiographic essay. On the other hand, Wiedemann was thus able to prove authenticity for his report. At the same time, however, he called Ranke's thesis into question, for he repeatedly reported that he had indeed contributed significant portions to Ranke's publication. Already in the more or less immediate surroundings of the quotation, he points out that he compiled important research literature for Ranke,[86] prepared correction proposals for manuscripts,[87] or even carried them out independently.[88] All these examples show that for Wiedemann, the characterization of Ranke was also an opportunity for self-representation, for the presentation of his share in the genius's work.

Notwithstanding, Wiedemann was unambiguous in making it clear that Ranke was the hardest worker. He described him as a restless scholar who had to achieve his scientific successes manfully and bravely against the manifold infirmities of his body—and was able to do so. The first context in which Wiedemann addressed this was the question of Ranke's daily routine. After a morning's work, which began between 9:00 and 10:00 a.m. and lasted until about 1:30 or 2:00 p.m., Ranke used to take an extended walk through Berlin, accompanied by a servant since 1871. On his return at about 5:00 p.m., he would have lunch and rest afterwards: "The start [of work] in the afternoon, however, shifted as the years went on, as Ranke became in need of a longer rest." Ranke first started work again around 6:30 p.m., later only around 10:00 p.m. He kept other breaks short in order to work more effectively. His breakfast and dinner lasted fifteen minutes only.[89] Wiedemann emphasized that Ranke, despite his age, worked "until the end with a fresh mind and restless activity" and that he possessed an "extraordinary capacity for work." He had always pursued his scientific work "untiringly and without fatigue."[90] Wiedemann's narration suggested that Ranke may have been physically limited, but that this was not accompanied by mental exhaustion. Rather, Wiedemann presented Ranke in his late seventies and eighties as someone who arranged his life in such a way that he could work in any situation. In one of his study rooms, for example, Wiedemann mentions, Ranke had set up a sofa on which he lay down so that he could continue working even when he got tired.[91]

This description points to the fact, that, as I have argued elsewhere, nineteenth-century German historians had a profound understanding of how deeply the body influenced their very definition of the scholar and academic research.[92] In letters and obituaries, historians—Ranke among them—connected intellectual work with corporeality and physical ability in order to prove their middle-class work ethic and to highlight their productivity. It was also connected with masculinity as proven in overcoming physical conditions. In their perception of masculine scholarly identity, physical dysfunctions meant dysfunctions in historical study. The gender history of the humanities should therefore take a broader view of academic research, which takes into consideration the body's role.[93] Wiedemann's account on Ranke's late years is another example for that as it argues that Ranke managed to stay productive against the obstacles his body provided him. He was a masculine scholar because he did not let his body put him down, but actively resisted such a situation and virtually fought for his productivity against the physical infirmities of his age.

The same was true for his handling of illnesses. Wiedemann describes that Ranke was hard of hearing and yet listened intently for hours to the reading aloud of manuscripts or research literature by his assistants in order to be able to complete his works. While his hearing weakened, Ranke's mind remained of "the same intense attention" and he of "never flagging mental tension."[94] When Ranke fell asleep, when his assistants read to him what had also become necessary due to his deteriorating eyesight, he would wake up after finishing and be able to discuss the content with a sharp mind.[95] To make the aspect of heroic overcoming of the body even clearer, Wiedemann also emphasized that Ranke found longer breaks from work "unbearable."[96] Not his physique, but Ranke's mind determined his scientific activity, was the message. Wiedemann also mentions Ranke's outbursts towards his assistants, in which he became hot-tempered towards them. He excused them with the pain Ranke is said to have had almost continuously for the last decade and a half of his life.[97] He had suffered from a hemorrhoidal and bladder condition, as Wiedemann frankly tells his readers for the purpose of aggrandizement, that had led to life-threatening seizures and had frequently interrupted his sleep: "Nights in which he did not wake up at least five to seven times for shorter or longer periods and needed the assistance of [his staff] . . . almost did not occur at all; at times, however, the interruptions increased twice as much."[98]

Even this, however, did not prevent Ranke from keeping up his work rhythm and continuing to dictate his voluminous world history in his old age, so that a volume could appear every year. Wiedemann's narration presents Ranke not only as a brilliant historian of superior intellect, but also as a manly and heroic character of discipline and stamina. The latter, he suggests with a multitude of examples and just intimate details, was the condition of the former. With his essay, Wiedemann claimed between the lines to have a share in his success indicating the multi-faced functions of scientific biography.

Conclusion: Old Questions Still Pressing for Answers

Studying the masculine scholar is no new research agenda. Facing the hostile or reluctant higher education system of their time, already the first women's movement at the end of the nineteenth century understood this need. When Arthur Kirchhoff's famous collection *The Academic Woman*—a fascinating and still understudied collection of so called "opinions" (*Gutachten*) on the question if women are able to study by a male-only group of professors and women's teachers—came out in 1897,[99] feminist activists published amused and ironic reviews. Käthe Schirmacher, for example, was pleased to note that the resistance to the admission of women was no longer the majority opinion and recommended the volume as a study guide for women to choose a university based on what the professors there said.[100] Schirmacher, herself one of the first female students holding a doctoral degree obtained in Zurich in 1895,[101] used it to reflect upon the "men's universities," male professors and their defense mechanism against female students.[102] Helene Lange, in her review, believed that the book would say nothing about women, but rather about male universities: it would, she said in 1897, provide information "about the gentlemen's own minds"[103]—and rightly so, as later research proved.[104]

Against this background—which must be supplemented by the fact that the second women's movement in the 1970s also criticized the masculine constitution of universities as a social problem and named it as a research topic[105]—it is astonishing that so comparatively little research has been done on this topic of historiography. Moreover, in view of the cognitive potentials and possibilities explained above to enlighten fundamentally about logics and modes of functioning of scholarship in general, this reticence is not comprehensible and must be surmounted in the future in order to contribute to a critical history of the humanities.

Future research should focus on more humanities, because there is a whole range of disciplines that have not yet been studied in their specific way of establishing themselves as masculine realms. Although the masculinization of the humanities is not limited to individual disciplines, discipline-specific research makes sense because, as the works available so far show, it follows the logics of the respective disciplines with their specific forms of research, institutions, networks, and sources. In addition, we need further detailed studies on the disciplines already examined in order to continue the differentiation of concepts of academic masculinities in the humanities.[106]

Next to that, six other fields of work stand out.[107] First, thematically, there is a need for further research, especially in the area of academic teaching, which is still little researched in general, and even less in terms of its gendering effects. Secondly, the everyday history of the humanities (committee meetings, examinations, daily work routines, schedules, etc.) should receive more attention, because they allow insights into (male) work contexts and routines, outsourced auxiliary work, but also constraints and decision-making cultures. Thirdly, in an epochal perspective, there is still a lack of work on the conditions and developments of the universities and humanities after 1945, with closure periods of (personal) files proving to be a central problem. Fourthly, from a methodological point of view, (inter-)national comparisons are still pending. Their difficulty lies above all in the fact that there is often not only a lack of the necessary preliminary studies (which is why discipline-specific research was emphasized as a basis), but also already a lack of comparable structures across national borders. Fifthly, transfer analyses are still lacking that can clarify in a diachronic perspective how gender was appropriated in different—national as well as regional—academic cultures and which exchange processes and interactions existed, for example, between academic cultures with early admission for female students such as Switzerland and latecomers such as Germany. Finally, on a theoretical level, gender as an intersectional category of analysis must be more strongly inscribed in the existing approaches of disciplinary history, discourse analysis, historical epistemology, sociology of science, philosophy of science, science studies, history of knowledge and more. Even if many of these approaches have not been developed as gender-critical approaches, as research has already pointed out, they can be developed into such. As a result, gender should not be seen as an arbitrary or incidental category, but should always be critically considered in the theoretical conception of research projects due to the fundamental importance for the university and scholarship that has hopefully become clear in this chapter.

Notes

1. Bonnie G. Smith, *The Gender of History: Men, Women, and Historical Practice* (Cambridge, MA: Harvard University Press, 2001), 111.
2. Barbara Stollberg-Rilinger, "Väter der Frauengeschichte? Das Geschlecht als historische Kategorie im 18. und 19. Jahrhundert," *Historische Zeitschrift* 262 (1996): 39–71.
3. Falko Schnicke, "Wissenschaftsmetaphern: Zur männlichen Kodierung der Germanistik und Klassischen Philologie in der zweiten Hälfte des 19. Jahrhunderts," *Jahrbuch für Universitätsgeschichte* 20 (2017) [2019]: 67–96, at 87–90.
4. Ben Knights, "Reading as a Man: Women and the Rise of English Studies in England," in *Gendered Academia: Wissenschaft und Geschlechterdifferenz 1890–1945*, ed. Miriam Kauko, Sylvia Mieszkowski, and Alexandra Tischel (Göttingen: Wallstein, 2005), 65–81.
5. Levke Harders, *American Studies: Disziplingenese und Geschlecht* (Stuttgart: Franz Steiner, 2013), 113–94.
6. Linda Nochlin, *Women, Art, and Power and Other Essays* (Boulder, CO: Westview Press, 1988); Renate von Heydebrand and Simone Winko, "Arbeit am Kanon: Geschlechterdifferenz in Rezeption und Wertung von Literatur," in *Genus: Zur Geschlechterdifferenz in den Kulturwissenschaften*, ed. Hadumod Bußmann and Renate Hof (Stuttgart: Kröner, 1995), 206–61; Griselda Pollock, *Differencing the Canon: Feminist Desire and the Writing of Art's Histories* (London: Routledge, 1999); Claudia Benthien and Inge Stephan, "Einleitung," in *Meisterwerke: Deutschsprachige Autorinnen im 20. Jahrhundert*, ed. Claudia Benthien and Inge Stephan (Cologne: Böhlau, 2005), 9–19.
7. Angelika Schaser, "Gabentausch: Eine Geschlechtergeschichte der Ehrenpromotionen von 1919 bis 1989 am Beispiel der Universität Hamburg," *Jahrbuch für Universitätsgeschichte* 20 (2017) [2019]: 145–76.

8. Marynel Ryan Van Zee, "'Womanly Qualities' and Contested Methodology: Gender and the Discipline of Economics in Late Imperial Germany," *Gender and History* 22, no. 2 (2010): 341–60.
9. Helene Lange, "Die akademische Frau" (1897), in Lange, *Kampfzeiten: Aufsätze und Reden aus vier Jahrzehnten* (Berlin: Herbig, 1928), 217–26, at 226.
10. The German original makes the identification of students as exclusively male even clearer: "Wenn unsere Universitätscollegien für Damen taugten, so wären sie unzweckmäßig für die Studenten, und umgekehrt." Heinrich von Sybel, "Ueber die Emanzipation der Frauen," in Sybel, *Vorträge und Aufsätze* (Berlin: Hofmann, 1874), 59–79, at 79.
11. Hans Anger, *Probleme der deutschen Universität: Bericht über eine Erhebung unter Professoren und Dozenten* (Tübingen: J. C. B. Mohr, 1960), 451–502.
12. A critical gender history is defined by challenges to historically established inequality as well as categories of historical research. Joan Scott in her seminal article explains: "If we treat the opposition between male and female as problematic rather than known, as something contextually defined, repeatedly constructed, then we must constantly ask not only what is at stake in proclamations or debates that invoke gender to explains or justify their positions but also how implicit understandings of gender are being invoked and reinscribed. . . . Investigation of these issues will yield a history that will provide new perspectives on old questions . . ., redefine the old questions in new terms . . ., make women visible as active participants, and create analytic distance between the seemingly fixed language of the past and our own terminology." Joan W. Scott, "Gender: A Useful Category of Historical Analysis," *The American Historical Review* 91 (1986): 1053–75, at 1074–5.
13. Levke Harders and Hannes Schweiger, "Kollektivbiographische Ansätze," in *Handbuch Biographie: Methoden, Traditionen, Theorien*, ed. Christian Klein (Stuttgart: J. B. Metzler, 2009), 194–8; Krista Cowman, "Collective Biography," in *Research Methods for History*, ed. Simon Gunn and Lucy Faire (Edinburgh: Edinburgh University Press, 2012), 83–100.
14. Ludmilla Jordanova, "Gender and the Historiography of Science," *British Journal for the History of Science* 26 (1993): 469–83, at 474.
15. Joan W. Scott, "Unanswered Questions," *The American Historical Review* 113, no. 5 (2008): 1422–9, at 1423.
16. Elisabeth Grabenweger, *Germanistik in Wien: Das Seminar für deutsche Philologie und seine Privatdozentinnen (1897–1933)* (Berlin: Walter de Gruyter, 2016), 40–88.
17. Ibid., 102–29 and 144–64.
18. Ibid., 102.
19. Ibid., 129–38.

20. Heike Anke Berger, *Deutsche Historikerinnen 1920–1970: Geschichte zwischen Wissenschaft und Politik* (Frankfurt am Main: Campus, 2007), 48–112.
21. Ibid., 113–201.
22. Ibid., 263–310.
23. Jordanova, "Gender and the Historiography of Science," 474.
24. For an extended account of the following catalogue including examples, see Falko Schnicke, "Fünf Analyseachsen für eine kritische Geschlechtergeschichte der Geisteswissenschaften: Aufriß eines Forschungsfeldes," *Jahrbuch für Universitätsgeschichte* 20 (2017) [2019]: 43–68.
25. *Intersectionality*, ed. Patricia Hill Collins and Sirma Bilge (Cambridge: Polity, 2016); Brittney Cooper, "Intersectionality," in *Oxford Handbook of Feminist Theory*, ed. Lisa Disch and Mary Hawkesworth (Oxford: Oxford University Press, 2015), 385–406.
26. Pierre Bourdieu, *Masculine Domination*. transl. Richard Nice (Stanford, CA: Stanford University Press, 2001); Martina Kessel, "Gendering Historiography? Problems and Suggestions," in *Gendering Historiography: Beyond National Canons*, ed. Angelika Epple and Angelika Schaser (Frankfurt am Main: Campus, 2009), 225–33.
27. Thomas F. Gieryn, "Boundary-Work and the Demarcation of Science from Non-Science: Strains and Interests in Professional Ideologies of Scientists," *American Sociological Review* 48 (1983): 781–95; Tanja Paulitz, *Mann und Maschine: Eine genealogische Wissenssoziologie des Ingenieurs und der modernen Technikwissenschaften, 1850–1930* (Bielefeld: Transcript, 2012).
28. Lorraine Daston and H. Otto Sibum, "Introduction: Scientific Personae and Their Histories," *Science in Context* 16 (2003): 1–8, at 2. See also Herman Paul, "Introduction: Scholarly Personae: What They Are and Why They Matter," in *How to Be a Historian: Scholarly Personae in Historical Studies*, ed. Herman Paul (Manchester: Manchester University Press, 2019), 1–14.
29. Johanna Gehmacher, "Im/possible Careers: Gendered Perspectives on Scholarly Personae around 1900," *European Journal of Life Writing* (forthcoming).
30. *New Institutionalism: Theory and Analysis*, ed. André Lecours (Toronto: University of Toronto Press, 2005); B. Guy Peters, *Institutional Theory in Political Science: The New Institutionalism*, 4th edn (Cheltenham: Edward Elgar, 2019).
31. Angelika Schaser and Falko Schnicke, "Der lange Weg in die Institution: Zur Etablierung der Frauen- und Geschlechtergeschichte an westdeutschen Universitäten (1970–1990)," *Jahrbuch für Universitätsgeschichte* 16 (2013) [2015]: 79–110, at 93–6.
32. Bourdieu, *Masculine Domination*; *Männlichkeit und Reproduktion: Zum gesellschaftlichen Ort historischer und aktueller Männlichkeitsproduktionen*, ed. Andreas Heilmann et al. (Wiesbaden: Springer, 2015).

33. Emanuel Adler and Vincent Pouliot, "International Practices," *International Theory* 3 (2011): 1–36, at 17.
34. Ibid., 6.
35. See for an overview regarding the first 120 years of the historical discipline Falko Schnicke, *Die männliche Disziplin: Zur Vergeschlechtlichung der deutschen Geschichtswissenschaft 1780–1900* (Göttingen: Wallstein, 2015).
36. Sophie Forgan, "Eine angemessene Häuslichkeit? Frauen und die Architektur der Wissenschaft im 19. Jahrhundert," in *Zwischen Vorderbühne und Hinterbühne: Beiträge zum Wandel der Geschlechterbeziehungen in der Wissenschaft vom 17. Jahrhundert bis zur Gegenwart*, ed. Theresa Wobbe (Bielefeld: Transcript, 2003), 137–57, at 139.
37. Ibid., 142–3.
38. Ibid., 140.
39. Ibid., 147.
40. Ibid., 142.
41. Denis M. Provencher and Luke L. Eilderts, "The National According to Lavisse: Teaching Masculinity and Male Citizenship in Third-Republic France," *French Cultural Studies* 18 (2007): 31–57, at 44.
42. Ibid., 42.
43. Ibid., 48.
44. Ibid., 52.
45. George L. Mosse, *The Image of Man: The Creation of Modern Masculinity* (Oxford: Oxford University Press, 1996); Mary D. Sheriff, "How Images Got Their Gender: Masculinity and Femininity in the Visual Arts," in *A Companion to Gender History*, ed. Teresa A. Meade and Merry E. Wiesner-Hanks (Malden, MA: Blackwell, 2006), 146–69.
46. Ludmilla Jordanova, *Defining Features: Scientific and Medical Portraits 1660–2000* (London: Reaktion Books, 2000), 102.
47. Ludmilla Jordanova, "Medical Men 1780–1820," in *Portraiture: Facing the Subject*, ed. Joanna Woodall (Manchester: Manchester University Press, 1997), 101–15, at 104.
48. Jordanova, *Defining Features*, 127.
49. *Interior Portraiture and Masculine Identity in France, 1789–1914*, ed. Temma Balducci et al. (Farnham: Taylor & Francis, 2011).
50. Anja Zimmermann, "Schaustellung im Kollegenkreise: Repräsentationen von Kunsthistorikern und Kunsthistorikerinnen in der Moderne," in *Gesichter der Wissenschaft: Repräsentanz und Performanz von Gelehrten in Porträts*, ed. Christian Vogel and Sonja E. Nökel (Göttingen: Wallstein, 2019), 99–113, at 99.
51. Johann Dominik Fiorillo, *Geschichte der zeichnenden Künste von ihrer Wiederaufblebung bis auf die neuesten Zeiten* (Göttingen: Rosenbusch, 1798).

52. Smith, *Gender of History*, 37–69; Angelika Epple, *Empfindsame Geschichtsschreibung: Eine Geschlechtergeschichte der Historiographie zwischen Aufklärung und Historismus* (Cologne: Böhlau, 2003).
53. Maike Christadler, *Kreativität und Geschlecht: Giorgios Vasaris "Vite" and Sofonisba Anguissaolas Selbst-Bilder* (Berlin: Reimer, 2000).
54. Deborah Cherry and Griselda Pollock, "Patriarchal Power and the Pre-Raphaelites," *Art History* 7 (1984): 480–95, at 493.
55. Karl Otfried Müller, *Handbuch der Archäologie der Kunst* (Breslau: Max, 1830).
56. William St Clair, *Lord Elgin and the Marbles* (Oxford: Oxford University Press, 1998); Rochelle Gurstein, "The Elgin Marbles, Romanticism and the Waning of 'Ideal Beauty,'" *Daedalus* 131 (2002): 88–100.
57. Daniel Graepler, "Sehnsuchtsziel Akropolis: Der Archäologe Karl Otfried Müller im Porträt," in Vogel and Nökel, *Gesichter der Wissenschaft*, 233–7, at 233–4.
58. R. W. Connell, *Masculinities* (Berkeley, CA: University of California Press, 2005), 114.
59. Graepler, "Sehnsuchtsziel Akropolis," 236.
60. Schnicke, *Männliche Disziplin*, 138–99.
61. Graepler, "Sehnsuchtsziel Akropolis," 234–5.
62. Zimmermann, "Schaustellung im Kollegenkreise," 103.
63. Schnicke, *Männliche Disziplin*, 349–61.
64. Graepler, "Sehnsuchtsziel Akropolis," 236.
65. *Die Kunstwissenschaft der Gegenwart in Selbstdarstellungen*, ed. Johannes Jahn (Leipzig: Meiner, 1924).
66. Zimmermann, "Schaustellung im Kollegenkreise," 104.
67. Ibid., 105.
68. Falko Schnicke, *Prinzipien der Entindivualisierung: Theorie und Praxis biographischer Studien bei Johann Gustav Droysen* (Cologne: Böhlau, 2010), 21–53.
69. Paul, "Scholarly Personae."
70. Ibid., 6–8.
71. Herman Paul, "Ranke vs Schlosser: Pairs of Personae in Nineteenth-Century German Historiography," in Paul, *How to Be a Historian*, 36–52, at 41.
72. Smith, *Gender of History*, 111; Schnicke, *Männliche Disziplin*, 501–40.
73. Leopold von Ranke, *Weltgeschichte*, vols 1–6 (Berlin: Duncker & Humblot, 1881–5); Ranke, *Weltgeschichte*, vols 7–9, ed. Alfred Dove, Georg Winter and Theodor Wiedemann (Berlin: Duncker & Humblot, 1886–8).
74. On that topic now: Heinz Duchhardt, *Blinde Historiker: Erfahrung und Bewältigung von Augenleiden im frühen 20. Jahrhundert* (Stuttgart: Kohlhammer, 2021).

75. Falko Schnicke, "19. Jahrhundert," in Klein, *Handbuch Biographie*, 243–50, at 248–9; Julia Barbara Köhne, *Geniekult in den Geisteswissenschaften und Literaturen um 1900 und seine filmischen Adaptionen* (Vienna: Böhlau, 2014), 58–400.
76. Schnicke, *Prinzipien der Entindivualisierung*, 72–95; Herman Paul, *De deugden van een wetenschapper: karakter en toewijding in de geesteswetenschappen, 1850–1940* (Amsterdam: Amsterdam University Press, 2018), 101–15.
77. Martina Kessel, "Heterogene Männlichkeit: Skizzen zur gegenwärtigen Geschlechterforschung," in *Handbuch Kulturwissenschaften: Themen und Tendenzen*, ed. Friedrich Jaeger et al. (Stuttgart: J. B. Metzler, 2004), 372–84, at 374–5.
78. Hans-Heinz Krill, *Die Rankerenaissance: Max Lenz und Erich Marcks: Ein Beitrag zum historisch-politischen Denken in Deutschland 1880–1935* (Berlin: Walter de Gruyter, 1962); Elisabeth Fehrenbach, "Rankerenaissance und Imperialismus in der wilhelminischen Zeit," in *Geschichtswissenschaft in Deutschland: Traditionelle Positionen und gegenwärtige Probleme*, ed. Bernd Faulenbach (Munich: C. H. Beck, 1974), 54–65.
79. Theodor Wiedemann, "Sechzehn Jahre in der Werkstatt Leopold von Ranke's: Ein Beitrag zur Geschichte seiner letzten Lebensjahre," *Deutsche Revue über das gesamte nationale Leben der Gegenwart* 17 (1892): 95–102, 208–20 and 342–53, at 100.
80. Theodor Wiedemann, "Sechzehn Jahre in der Werkstatt Leopold von Ranke's. Ein Beitrag zur Geschichte seiner letzten Lebensjahre," *Deutsche Revue über das gesamte nationale Leben der Gegenwart* 16 (1891): 164–79 and 322–39, at 330.
81. Wiedemann, "Sechzehn Jahre" (1892): 95.
82. Ibid., 97.
83. Wiedemann, "Sechzehn Jahre" (1891): 334.
84. Ibid., 167.
85. Ibid., 325.
86. Ibid., 333.
87. Ibid., 336.
88. Wiedemann, "Sechzehn Jahre" (1892): 97.
89. Wiedemann, "Sechzehn Jahre" (1891): 328.
90. Ibid., 330.
91. Ibid., 331.
92. Falko Schnicke, "Rituale der Verkörperung: Seminarfeste und Jubiläen der Geschichtswissenschaft des 19. Jahrhunderts," *Zeitschrift für Geschichtswissenschaft* 63 (2015): 337–58.
93. Falko Schnicke, "Kranke Historiker: Körperwahrnehmungen und Wissenschaft im 19. Jahrhundert," *Historische Anthropologie* 25 (2017): 11–31.
94. Wiedemann, "Sechzehn Jahre" (1891): 333.

95. Ibid., 334.
96. Ibid., 335.
97. Wiedemann, "Sechzehn Jahre" (1892): 101.
98. Ibid., 102.
99. *Die Akademische Frau: Gutachten hervorragender Universitätsprofessoren, Frauenlehrer und Schriftsteller über die Befähigung der Frau zum wissenschaftlichen Studium und Berufe*, ed. Arthur Kirchhoff (Berlin: Steinitz, 1897).
100. Käthe Schirmacher, "Die akademische Frau," *Die Frauenbewegung* (January 1, 1897): 2–4, at 3. I thank Johanna Gehmacher (Vienna) for pointing out this source to me.
101. Johanna Gehmacher, Elisa Heinrich and Corinna Oesch, *Käthe Schirmacher: Agitation und autobiographische Praxis zwischen radikaler Frauenbewegung und völkischer Politik* (Vienna: Böhlau, 2018), 84–158.
102. Käthe Schirmacher, "Die akademische Frau," *Die Frauenbewegung* (January 15, 1897): 15–7, at 16.
103. Lange, "Akademische Frau," 219.
104. Peter Gay, *The Bourgeois Experience: Victoria to Freud*, vol. 1 (Oxford: Oxford University Press, 1984), 221–5; Karin Hausen, "Warum Männer Frauen zur Wissenschaft nicht zulassen wollten," in *Wie männlich ist die Wissenschaft?* ed. Karin Hausen and Helga Nowotny (Frankfurt am Main: Suhrkamp, 1986), 31–40; Schnicke, *Männliche Disziplin*, 93–113.
105. Ibid., 13–6.
106. See, e.g., Herman Paul, "The Whole Man: A Masculine Persona in German Historical Studies," in *Gender, Embodiment and the History of the Scholarly Persona: Incarnations and Contestations*, ed. Kirsti Niskanen and Michael J. Barany (Cham: Palgrave Macmillan, 2021), 261–86.
107. The following list draws on Angelika Schaser and Falko Schnicke, "Wege zu einer Geschlechtergeschichte der Universitäten und Geisteswissenschaften: Forschungsstand und Desiderata," *Jahrbuch für Universitätsgeschichte* 20 (2017) [2019]: 27–42, at 40–2.

11

Scholarly Activism in Africa: The *General History of Africa* (1964–98)

Larissa Schulte Nordholt

Introduction

In what way do scholars within the humanities try to change the societies they live in? This chapter discusses the persona of the activist scholar. Arguably, activism within the humanities has played an important role post-Second World War, specifically from the 1960s onwards.[1] Both in the global North and South, scholars started to ask themselves how the humanities, in their potential for shaping the "meaning making practices" of human society, could be made useful for what they saw as political progress through advocacy.[2] Movements for change, such as the Women's movement, advocacy for LGBTQ rights as well as movements for religious freedom and against racial and ethnic discrimination have often looked at public intellectuals, and specifically historians, for some kind of intellectual guidance.[3]

However, as Stefan Berger notes in the introduction to a 2019 edited volume on the "engaged historian," the study of the interrelationship between activism and history writing is still in its infancy. This is the case despite the fact that historical studies and social and political engagement are intimately intertwined.[4] Politics, history, and adjacent moral imperatives have always been entangled endeavors. At the same time, conceptions of impartiality and ideals of detached historical scholarship have been key parts of the professionalization of that discipline.⁵ This entanglement stems from the fact that the humanities tend to study culture and society while at the same time being part of that society. The chapter aims to shed light on the entanglement between academia and activism through an exploration of the persona of the activist scholar. Scholars, after all, are people too and engaged in the society around them in all manners of ways.

I argue that the "scholarly activist" can be studied specifically as a scholarly persona, that is to say, as an archetype or model of scholarship, that emerged alongside social changes within academia. It is within the persona of the activist scholar that particular traditional nineteenth- and twentieth-century ideas on a desired distance between politics and academia tended to clash. The study of personae may help illuminate how scholars nevertheless tried to harmonize two seemingly conflicting loyalties in their performance of scholarship. As Lorraine Daston and Otto Sibum have noted in a seminal article, personae primarily tell us something about a collective cultural rather than individual identity.⁶ Scholarly personae, moreover, can be studied as models of selfhood and identity, that encompass dispositions, attitudes, and skills deemed necessary for the execution of scholarly work—or any other professional activity, as Herman Paul has argued. He also notes that the study of personae permeates different levels, the literary and individual or the collective, otherwise known as the "micro" and the "macro." The former may be studied through individual life writing. The latter may delineate what scholars are and how they are recognizable as a group through templates that are broadly shared amongst groups.⁷ On the crossroads of the individual and collective level, scholarly personae may be studied as performances of collective social positions through individual lives, often as part of an attempt to gain credibility. Paul advocates for such an intermediate, or "meso," perspective to show how collective types are subject to negotiation in different contexts in order for scholars to be seen as trustworthy producers of knowledge.⁸

In the context of activist scholarship especially this negotiation surrounding the creation of reliable knowledge is important.⁹ The scholar as activist may rely on skills, habits, virtues, or competencies that delineate scholarly templates in different contexts to justify their position as academic. At the same time they may in this way strive towards the creation of an "activist ethos."¹⁰ Mineke Bosch as well as Julia Dahlberg have noted that categories such as gender, class, and race may influence in what way a scholar will need to seek credibility.¹¹ They thereby highlight the relationship between the creation of knowledge and the bearer of knowledge.¹² This is of particular interest in a postcolonial context, where exclusionary racism played a role in deciding who could be seen as a good scholar. We can therefore use personae to study the emergence of collective change within the history of the humanities through the lens of individual scholars and their position within a given historical context and as part of disciplinary change.

For the purpose of this chapter, it is important to delineate the difference between scholarly activism and political or social activism that scholars engaged in. By scholarly activists I mean those academics who advocate for change within academia itself, for instance, by arguing for the inclusion of a new discipline (e.g., LGBTQ studies, women's history, black studies). Such advocacy, however, is always connected to larger society as well. The wish to incorporate new fields of study within existing academic frameworks almost always stems from some kind of social movement and the rising social mobility of a specific group—for instance (black) women. This activism within the academy is somewhat different, although not distinct, from activists who also operate as scholars, or scholars who spent time as political activists next to and often informed by their scholarship. For instance, by intellectualizing their efforts to change the world, at least partly, through scholarship. This is subject to critique from those activists who argue that intellectualization of the cause may create too great a distance between theory and practice.[13] Institutionalization itself, moreover, has also been criticized as having a de-radicalizing influence on the field of study to be incorporated. As Judith Bennett has noted: "The greatest challenge to women's history may come, indeed, from the debilitating effects of institutionalization itself, which has nurtured the field's slow and ongoing severance from feminism."[14] To become incorporated into academia is possibly to be neutralized. There is considerable overlap and mutual influence between these two conceptualizations of what it means to be an activist and a scholar at once.

My specific case study is the Africanization of history during the period of political decolonization in Africa, a time of great global political change when history seemed capable of shaping futures. In this chapter I will take the UNESCO-funded eight-volume *General History of Africa* (*GHA*, 1964–98) as a starting point to explore how the historians working on it came to combine activism and scholarship in their wish to decolonize or Africanize African history. They aimed to prove that researching the history of Africa was a viable academic endeavor and, secondly, that it could contribute to the political emancipation of Africans worldwide. By the adage "knowledge is power," the group of mostly historians, but including archaeologists and anthropologists among others, set out to write the *GHA* in 1964 under the auspices of UNESCO in both French and English. Most, but not all, of these scholars were Africans who started the project with the epistemic, political, and moral goals of setting the record of Africa's history straight. The *GHA* contained both the wish to change academia as a result of changing societal contexts as well as the wish to change society itself through scholarship, particularly African societies. To some of the historians working on the *GHA*, activism and scholarship could not be separated due to the Euro-American academies' involvement in imperialism and the creation of racialized thinking.[15] If one was to engage in scholarship, it was with the aim to improve it and by extension the society in which it was embedded. This chapter therefore analyses why and how African historians, and their Euro-American partners, came to envision the persona of the scholarly activist and explains why scholarship and activism were so deeply intertwined in the writing of African history.

The chapter will first explore and analyse why the *GHA* framed its historical research goals along activist lines and sketch its wider context in society in order to explain why scholarly activism is a useful frame with which to regard the work. I will offer a conceptualization of the persona of the activist scholar as it emerged from the *GHA*. Retrospectively, the activist scholar was presented as an ideal: scholars had successfully enlarged the realm of historical knowledge so as to include the history of forgotten pasts, in this case the African past. Secondly, I will look into the contributions to the work made by Adu Boahen (1929–2006) and Ali Mazrui (1933–2014). Both were exemplary in how they operationalized activism within (historical) scholarship, while also acting as political activists proper. The ensuing tensions illustrate in how far academia and activism could actually be merged harmoniously when faced with the reality of conflicting ideas on scholarship during the drafting of two *GHA* volumes.

Activist Scholarship in the *General History of Africa*

The history of African studies is filled with scholarly activism. African or African descended intellectuals engaged with Africa have nearly always called for liberation from European points of view. From the early nineteenth century mostly Caribbean pan-African nationalists who aimed to revalue African history for reasons of cultural pride, to the twenty-first-century Fallist movement in South Africa, where activists are continuing this tradition by calling for a decolonization of the academy—yet again.[16] Activism has flowed through African historical studies as a red thread because of the still unfinished business, many would argue, of epistemological and racial colonization by Europeans, often dated back to the trans-Atlantic slave trade. The *GHA* has often been identified as part of that African nationalist historiography of the post-independence period.[17] The historians working on the *GHA* challenged the existing historiography of Africa, as it conceived of the continent as an unhistorical part of the world. The *GHA* was part of the process of political decolonization in that it wanted to help establish an autonomous African historical discipline. That was also what UNESCO set out to do by sponsoring the project. UNESCO had come to believe that the postcolonial world had a right to history.[18] The eight-volume series, which included over three hundred authors, was a project that aimed to encompass many different points of view. It included historians from all over Africa and beyond with different historical creeds, making use of a variety of methods and ideas on the history of Africa. At its very core, the work aimed to change the way the Euro-American academy regarded the African past by Africanizing the production of knowledge about that past. The *GHA* therefore argued that African history should primarily be written from a point of view internal to the continent. Its *raison d'être* was inherently activist and this activism was borne out of political necessity. Simultaneously, the *GHA* strove to be taken seriously by the scholarly community. How far could it take its political activism before it lost its credibility as a scholarly work of authority? And how did the scholars working on the project and African nationalist history more broadly, present themselves towards the outside world?

One genre that shaped the perception of what it meant to be an impartial historian and also at the forefront of decolonization were obituaries written to commemorate prominent *GHA* historians. Obituaries could be made to mold scholars into a narrative of disciplinary progress and, moreover, idealize them to present an image of what the discipline should look like or what was important when the obituary was written, rather than what it looked like in reality.[19] The obituaries for the African pathfinders within the academic study of African history usually emphasized their activist focus on an African perspective to include them in the disciplinary history and to press a continued need for advocacy, but without turning away from academic scholarship and associated scholarly virtues. In doing so, they created an ideal image of the activist historian that was perhaps more harmonious than reality allowed.

Many obituaries written for *GHA* members emphasized activist scholarship, while simultaneously emphasizing high scholarly quality and, specifically, a critical attitude. The activist scholarship in these obituaries therefore connected the scholar being commemorated to an epistemic and moral imperative to do the right thing, to further both knowledge that has been hidden by obscurantists and to further the emancipation that was made possible by that knowledge. Activism here then, is meaningful in that it is upheld by a simultaneous focus on objectivity and critical scholarship. In that way, having a critical attitude towards colonial knowledge produced about Africa rather than taking it at face value, became a scholarly virtue that functioned within a constellation of virtues.[20] It is important to note that "critical scholarship" here differs from the "ethos of criticism" described by Herman Paul in Chapter 9. One the one hand, a critical attitude in the sense of being meticulous with source material in the context of African history could add to the strengthening of the political goals of decolonization, by emphasizing the seriousness of African historical studies in similar fashion to what Paul describes in the context of the strengthening of patriotism in the nineteenth-century German humanities. However, somewhat paradoxically, but more important for our purpose here, "critical" also had political undertones as it meant to overtly critique received colonial knowledge about Africa as biased and racist, rather than only referring to specific philological virtues used to dissect texts.[21]

A positive emphasis on the value of political engagement played a big role in the obituaries for Adu Boahen. In 1959 Boahen became the first Ghanaian to obtain a PhD in African history at SOAS in London. When he subsequently returned to Legon in Accra, he had come to believe that African history needed to be Africanized and decolonized—but without completely getting rid of Euro-American influences.[22] When Boahen passed away in 2006, the *Journal of African History* published an editorial obituary for "Ghana's foremost historian and a distinguished statesman." It stated that Boahen had been a political activist all his life: "A scholar-activist, he demonstrated a consistent opposition to dictatorial rule and military regimes that earned him stints in prison."[23] The importance of Boahen's politics for his historical work becomes evident too in the obituaries written for him in the *New African*, a pan-African publication. Its two obituaries mention the *GHA* and connect the UNESCO project to Boahen's role as a trailblazer in African history: "Recognising him as Africa's voice to its postcolonial past, UNESCO made him the president and consultant (1983–99) of its International Scientific Committee for the eight-volume *General History of Africa*."[24] Both obituaries, moreover, place their pan-African hero, Boahen, opposite the British scholar Hugh Trevor-Roper, who functions as a personified example of what to avoid as a historian of Africa. They thereby evoke a different time of perhaps simpler dichotomies of good and bad.[25] Referring to Trevor-Roper's infamous phrase about Africa as a "dark" place without history, one of the obituaries states: "When the British don, Hugh Trevor-Roper, wrote this, little did he know that an African colossus, Albert Adu Boahen, would one day rise and make him look quite foolish."[26] The obituary placed Boahen opposite the whole establishment of British history, including such historians as Roland Oliver and John Fage, calling the latter "probably racist."[27] This opposition towards European historiography possibly served to cement the idea that scholarly activism was meant as a correction to existing bias and scholarly inaccuracy.

Within the *GHA*, Eurocentrism itself was constructed as a vice to avoid, for it had previously caused the production of unsound historical scholarship on Africa as a result of bias.[28] Within African studies throughout the twentieth century more generally, a negative stereotype of what it meant to be a historian of Africa became personified through the trope of "Hugh Trevor-Roper," as becomes clear in the obituaries written for Boahen. His presence as an anti-historian of Africa had been etched into the collective consciousness of early Africanists by a rather infamous comment already referred to above, that equated African history with darkness. For years African historians, such as Boahen's obituary writers and including Boahen himself, would place the Trevor-Roper remark within a long and insidious tradition of Euro-American denial of African historicity.[29] As a result of the cultural position of Trevor-Roper as a negative stereotype, his name was used as a rhetorical device to contrast bad historical scholarship against good historical scholarship. The obituary writers therefore relished in narrating how Boahen had once corrected "the high and mighty of African Studies in Great Britain" on their own turf.[30] Both obituaries, moreover, celebrated Boahen's political activities, describing him as an Ashanti warrior who challenged not just the racist historiography from Britain, but also the authoritarian politicians from Ghana.[31] Boahen, then, was a scholarly activist as well as a political activist. His obituary writers thought the two could not be separated. Importantly they also appealed to scholarly precision and a critical attitude to show how Boahen had put the arrogant Britons in their place. Activist scholarship, as well as political activism, is here portrayed as a reaction against the hubris of others and, crucially, incorrect assumptions regarding the African past.

The connection between scholarly activism and good historical scholarship on Africa is even more pronounced in the obituaries written for Joseph Ki-Zerbo (1922–2006), the editor of the first *GHA* volume. When Ki-Zerbo passed away in 2006 the pan-African literary magazine *Présence Africaine* published a special issue in his honor. The editorial introduction focuses almost exclusively on Ki-Zerbo's contribution to the *GHA* and the problem of a continuing European denial of African historicity that Ki-Zerbo and the *GHA* had reacted to. It connected Ki-Zerbo's political and public engagement to his editing of the first *GHA* volume, illustrating how for Ki-Zerbo politics, knowledge creation and history were not separate endeavors. *Présence Africaine* described how the *GHA* under Ki-Zerbo's direction had as its task to further knowledge on the African continent: "The challenge of this undertaking was also epistemological."[32] Epistemology, however, could not be separated from the struggle that had become part and parcel of the African past as *Présence Africaine* saw it. African history then was a public and therefore political enterprise.

In the obituaries for Ki-Zerbo an image develops of the Burkinabé historian as an anti-colonial political activist who fought valiantly against colonial stereotypes and was equally a critical scholar. The characteristic that is reiterated most in the obituaries, was that Ki-Zerbo was a man who did not identify a difference between being an intellectual and a politician.[33] As one of the obituaries stated: "Joseph Ki-Zerbo never accepted the fictional divide between intellectuals and politicians."[34] We should read that comment to understand how Ki-Zerbo and arguably other African historians of his generation, understood the historical discipline. History to them was and always had been at the service of a political or social cause, be it nationalism or Marxism or something else again. The construction of history for the reinstatement of a specific identity was therefore as much an academic as it was an anti-colonial political project during the era of independence.[35] Like the other historians discussed in this chapter, Ki-Zerbo after all grew up and was educated under a colonial yoke. Ki-Zerbo felt a responsibility to develop a new way of thinking and writing history that would capture the specificity of the African past accurately in order to contribute to the development of his country and even his continent.[36] In the obituary written by Adame Ba Konaré there is decisive defense of activist historiography as academic:

And this is precisely where we find the merit of the historical science, as it is the only way to curb falsifications, conveniently reassuring interpretations, knowing that they are nimble and inevitable, hence the need to make room in historiographic thinking for a mechanism of observance and vigilance. But is this not an admission of activism, even if it is scientific?[37]

As Ba Konaré saw it, African historians seemed to have had no choice but to be "activist," given the role of history in society and the falsifications that surrounded African history. This, however, did not mean it was unscientific. And this identification of Ki-Zerbo with activism focused on scholarly accuracy may be the reason that the obituaries written for him so explicitly link him to the *GHA*, which was a civic project that aimed to rehabilitate African history as an academic endeavor.

As Catherine Coquery-Vidrovitch and Bogumil Jewsiewicki have both emphasized, however, African historians were well aware of the predicament in which they found themselves vis-à-vis the historians' imperative to be objective. As Coquery-Vidrovitch aptly writes: "While making their history, the African historians were perfectly aware of the affective mode from which they could not escape because of both the recent wounds inflicted by Europe and the urgency to construct a new political and cultural identity."[38] For the African historians working on the *GHA* political imperatives and historical knowledge could not always be neatly separated. The *GHA* aimed to change the status quo and could therefore never escape some semblance of political engagement. A historian, as follows, had to be both critical towards existing knowledge about Africa and militant enough to challenge this knowledge in order to rehabilitate African history.[39] Scholarly activism engendered political activism in equal amounts and vice versa. The development of new scholarly standards could be seen as political, but as the obituaries argued, that did not necessarily disqualify historians from striving towards truth. They made the claim that excluding African perspectives was inaccurate and unscholarly more than they argued that it was morally wrong. Ki-Zerbo's life, moreover, was easily adapted to such a blending together of scholarship and activism, given his anti-colonial political view on African history and activities as a public intellectual.

Whereas the obituaries for Ki-Zerbo function to smoothen the inherent tension between political activism and scholarly distance, the availability of an anti-persona in the obituaries for Boahen served to heighten the contrast between the historian commemorated and the history he sought to disprove. Obituaries generally serve a function as a reflective practice, not just towards the individual that is being commemorated, but towards their field of scholarship as part of a system of justification as well.[40] The need to emphasize certain parts of disciplinary history over others may be especially pertinent in a context of boundary work as a result of disciplinary innovation or change, as was the context of the *GHA*.[41] The obituaries discussed here all use a combination of praise for scholarly and/or political activism or nation-building, with an emphasis on their subject's scholarly qualities, in order to place them in opposition to biased European historiography. The obituary writers aimed to reconcile two previously different public personae: that of the political activist and the detached scholar. They presented this combination as much more compatible than it might have felt when the agitation against colonial visions of African history actually took place. The obituaries therefore served to smoothen the tension between historical scholarship and political activism. The point was that activism engendered more accurate and sounder historical scholarship on Africa.

What this material has also shown, moreover, is that the virtues in the obituaries discussed above were perhaps most meaningful as part of a "constellation" that transcended the merely epistemic.[42] Virtues such as a critical disposition towards colonial knowledge were seen as necessary for conducting good historical research on Africa because they showed the historian had moral as well as epistemic norms. Having a critical attitude was both an epistemic as well as a moral virtue. It was the combination of those goals that made "activism" a virtue to be celebrated. Activism, in the context of decolonization, was a positive descriptor because it emphasized that the historian was willing to go against the grain of colonial historiography and, moreover, use their learning for a broad public good, rather than just the academic advancement of knowledge.

Disputing the Fluidity Between Politics and Academia

The necrologies analysed above suggested a considerable overlap or harmony between political engagement and scholarship. The archival documents pertaining to the *GHA* volumes, however, show there was also tension between politics and scholarship. This section will detail how scholarly activism worked in scholarly practice during the editing process of the *GHA*. For that purpose, I look into the archival documents pertaining to the editing of volume 7 of the *GHA*, which dealt with Africa's history under colonial occupation, as well as volume 8, which dealt with the history of decolonization. Because the volumes pertained to the history of European invasion in Africa—relatively recent events—they were particularly prone to attract debate surrounding the balance between political imperatives and research standards. It was fundamental for the *GHA* to write the history of European colonization from an African perspective if the project wanted to honor its foundational ideals of African-centered African history. European colonization of Africa had been justified and made possible by a denial of African history and agency, and now it was up to the *GHA* to justify the creation of national African states through a reappraisal of African historicity. This assignment was nowhere more pronounced than in the writing of the history of (de)colonization.

In the introduction to volume 7, its editor, Boahen, therefore espoused an idea of African society as united through a common resistance to colonialism. Simultaneously, he emphasized that the colonial period had only been a short interlude between two periods of state-formation. "African nations" were forced to reconcile with "sudden change" and needed to "adapt or perish."[43] What mattered, however, and what the volume would be about, was how Africans responded to that challenge.[44] Volume 7 of the *GHA* had as its task, Boahen continued, to bring to light African resisters, such as Prempeh I of Asante, Wobogo, King of the Mossi, or Menelik of Ethiopia, because their actions had been "grossly misrepresented or entirely ignored" by colonial historians, such as Lewis Henry Gann, Peter Duignan, and Margery Perham. He balked specifically at the latter's use of the term "pacification", calling it "Eurocentric."[45]

Boahen, as is reflected in the obituaries that would later be written for him, specifically argued that historical scholarship should have some connection to political realities in order to be meaningful. To ignore that history was political, was to be disingenuous. Boahen's focus on African initiatives and perspectives marked him as a near-perfect representative of the *GHA* as a whole. He, moreover, was one of the towering figures of what Toyin Falola and others later labeled the nationalist school of historiography.[46] Boahen believed history should explicitly contribute to nation-building and for that purpose colonial history needed to be reinterpreted to show how Africans had resisted their European colonial oppressors. Africans had been engaged in state-building and had been able to preserve their culture and heritage despite colonialism. Not all authors completely agreed on Boahen's view of history, however, as some of the correspondence between the editor and his authors shows.

An exchange between Boahen and the well-known historian of nationalism and African resistance, Terence Ranger, became especially heated, partly due to a different perspective on the history of colonialism in Africa. Ranger had been commissioned to write a historiographical overview on African resistance to colonialism. However, in 1978, after Ranger had handed in the chapter, Boahen wrote him to ask for a complete revision of the chapter, pointing to "the general psychological approach" which needed correction, taking offense at

> the notion that some states were new and therefore lacked legitimacy and consequently could not resist Europeans. . . . It appears to me now that many historians, including you, have considered African reaction to the imposition of colonial rule from the 1880s to the 1940s and 1950s as essentially a *simple phenomenon*.[47]

Ranger replied angrily to Boahen: "I seek to be co-operative man but I can do very little of the things you suggest in your letter." Ranger did not agree with the comments on the legitimacy of African states, writing:

> it is unclear to me why the Bureau [the *GHA* committee] took particular exception to the idea that some states lacked the legitimacy required for effective resistance. Do they merely dislike the thought? Or are they prepared to say on scholarly grounds that it is unfounded? To my mind the idea of an important aspect of making African historiography fully mature as well as true in fact. . . . Moreover, this emphasis is one which characterizes a great deal of recent, radical work on African resistance by both black and white scholars.[48]

Ranger's intention was for African history to be treated seriously, with the same rigor as European history and he took injury to Boahen's suggestion that his account of African resistance had been too simple. He intimated that perhaps it was Boahen and the rest of the *GHA* who oversimplified matters. Ranger had come to believe that it did not serve African realities to draw a direct line between precolonial sovereignty and postcolonial nation-states, connecting the endeavor to what he called bourgeois history and arguing that the role of African nationalist history had purely been to contribute to cultural nationalism.[49] For the bulk of the people European colonialism only meant a change of political overlord, rather than a loss of sovereignty. Resistance could therefore also be understood as resistance to local elites.[50] Ranger wanted to emphasize local agency—hence his comments on radicalism.[51] For Boahen it was important to focus on state-building and African resistance through nationalism, whereas Ranger wanted to create a history that would be both analytically sound as well as relatable to local realities. Both were invested in politics—Ranger had been an anti-colonial activist—but what those politics were differed. Ranger ended the letter by stating that it was "absurd" to ask him to change the chapter substantially.[52]

Boahen in turn responded equally angrily in a very short letter. He took offense at Ranger's use of the word "absurd": "I never expected that one could use such a word in a letter to a colleague, even if that colleague happens to be an African."[53] Boahen thus emphasized his identity as African in his letter to Ranger, more or less accusing the latter of racism in the process. The altercation between Boahen and Ranger rested on two very different interpretations of the function of African history and resistance within that history. Boahen was engaged in history for nation-building, while Ranger had come to criticize that endeavor as elitist. It seems that what was and was not the right kind of politics for African history in general and the *GHA* in specific was in the eye of the beholder.

Another example of a debate surrounding this question was the so-called "post-face," or epilogue, to the last volume. Because the *GHA* ran out of UNESCO-funds halfway through the process of drafting volume 8, the French translation of that volume took much longer than expected. Whereas the English version was published in 1993, the French version did not appear until 1998. Obviously, the years between 1993 and 1998 were not devoid of changes in Africa—ranging from the tragic in the form of the Rwandan genocide to the ecstatic regarding the formal end of apartheid in South Africa. The idea was therefore developed to add a "post-face" to the volume. When the editor of volume 8, Ali Mazrui (1933–2014), drafted this afterword, however, protest erupted.

Jan Vansina (1929–2017), a Belgian historian of oral traditions who came to play a crucial role within the *GHA*, rejected the text completely, stating that it undermined the very goal the *GHA* had set out to achieve:

> All of this is much too current and superficial to merit inclusion in this volume—one should not provide a lethal weapon to powerful critics of this history of Africa, who are inclined to accuse it of being partisan and a political tool, which is what the Committee and its Bureau generally avoided for twenty-five years![54]

Vansina's commentary on the afterword may tell us more about his general idea of what the *GHA* was to achieve than about the afterword itself. Vansina shied away from the idea that the work should be overtly political. Mazrui had evidently crossed the boundary guiding professional scholarly behavior in the direction of political partisan involvement. Although not quite the same as wanting to shy away from political partisanship, there is a tacit link between needing to be seen as a respectable scholar, with respectable source-material, and shying away from overt political involvement. Scholarly respectability, in this instance, seems to have been contingent on scholarly values associated with "the" imagined or perceived Euro-American academy. Vansina had famously and strategically applied the method of historical source criticism to oral traditions to argue that oral traditions were in fact legitimate historical sources and that the African continent, which lacked an abundance of written sources, could therefore be studied historically.[55] For him, scholarly respectability was important because of what it could achieve. Therefore, Mazrui's apparent failure of self-distanciation in his political partisanship and his supposedly incorrect application of method (because the afterword pertained to contemporary events that could not count as history) were linked. That Vansina did not think it should be published in the volume, therefore, was perhaps connected to his wish to be seen as a respectable scholar and to have African history being accepted as a respectable scholarly discipline by his peers. Fundamentally, Vansina seems not to have liked the afterword because it did not align with his idea of what historical scholarship ought to be.

That point may be underlined more clearly by looking at those *GHA* committee members who did like it, or disliked it for reasons different from Vansina's. Boahen thought it was "interesting and a typical Mazrui piece—informed, well-written, contrasting and analytical."[56] He did not at any point suggest that the piece was too political or that the history of the early 1990s was too contemporary to be included in the volume. His critique, rather, suggested that the piece was not sufficiently engaged with the continent's affairs. Boahen had radically different ideas on the purpose of academic history than Vansina. Whereas Boahen thought of African history as overtly political, for Vansina it was only covertly political. As a result, they judged the Mazrui piece very differently.

This difference in judgment on how to write (contemporary) history echoed throughout the drafting of volume 8 and was connected to the question how political a historian could be before they would no longer be taken seriously. Evidently, there were several different ideas at work within the *GHA* concerning the question of political engagement and in how far that engagement could cross into the realm of political partisanship. Vansina was committed to guarding the boundary between the historian as a professional and its traditional other—the politician. For Boahen and Mazrui, this boundary seems to have been not only less important, but also less obvious as they recognized an inherent overlap between these roles. Nevertheless, the exchange between Ranger and Boahen shows that there were still many different ways in which one could exercise one's scholarly activist commitments.

Conclusion

The *GHA* was an activist academic project. As a result of the juxtaposition in between academia and political decolonization, the project attracted a myriad of different personalities, who sometimes blended what it meant to a scholar with notions of political activism. The boundaries between scholarship and politics were therefore blurred within the *GHA*, causing debates among *GHA* historians. In remembering the project retrospectively, however, obituary writers for some of its most important African personalities argued that the *GHA*'s scholarly activism was made possible by a constellation of virtues that included both a critical attitude towards colonial knowledge as well as an emphasis on accuracy. They projected an image of scholarly activism back in time that seemed more harmonious than it had perhaps been in reality. The latter point can be illustrated through the archival documents pertaining to volumes seven and eight of the *GHA*. What it meant to be a politically active scholar and for what political purpose, was by no means agreed upon by all.

This chapter has shown, through a specific case study, how the humanities—in this case the discipline of history—were engaged with what I have called scholarly activism, the aim to change the wider world through scholarship. There were different repertoires of scholarly personae available for the scholars working on the *GHA*—from the scholarly activist to more traditional ideas of what it meant to be a historian. Through a study of these personae and their virtues and vices, as well as the way they were retrospectively projected back into time, it becomes possible to better understand the entanglement between historical work, in this case a decolonization of history, and political advocacy. Perhaps what has emerged from this exploration of the activist scholar most ardently is the perceived need to posit activism as a legitimate activity for scholars and it may be that this was the case especially within the *GHA* because the scholarly activists were black Africans advocating for a form of emancipation. The perspective of the persona has illustrated that the activist scholar was an ideal type that was deployed to break through traditional boundaries of clearly delineated, but equally ideal-typical, political and scholarly personae. This delineation, it should be made clear, was always an idealization of the way scholars operated in reality. The scholarly activist as a persona cut through this delineation while adapting previously existing scholarly templates to a specific context. It is therefore all the more telling that in the obituaries presenting this ideal type as well as in the denunciation of the anti-persona of Trevor-Roper, it was made important to emphasize the absence of bias and the truthfulness of what the scholarly activists were attempting. The African historians advocating for African history on its own terms emphasized the accuracy and rigor of their work, perhaps because African history had not yet been accepted as reputable when the *GHA* had come into being in 1964.

The persona lens, therefore, exposes existing tensions between politics and scholarship as they are often present in times of disciplinary change. The scholarly activist persona shows us an antithesis of the scholar as neutral, but not because the scholarly activist is necessarily more political than the scholar who portrays themselves as above political tensions. Rather, the scholarly activist accepts the entanglement between scholarship in the humanities and politics as inherent to the nature of the knowledge scholarship in the humanities produces. The African historians advocating for their perspective were not necessarily more political than the colonial historians before them, but they were perceived as such. The persona lens therefore shows the difference between collective ideals, as becomes visible in the obituaries for both Boahen and Ki-Zerbo, and the practice of scholarship. The latter is illustrated by both the discussion between Boahen and Ranger as well as the dispute over the *GHA*'s afterword. The question how history could be made useful for emancipation has since remained a key feature of African historical studies from an African perspective. It may be interesting to research how tensions between political advocacy and legitimation were resolved or, rather, exacerbated within other types of emancipatory historiography, such as women's history or black studies.

Notes

1. David Bromwich, "Scholarship as Social Action," in *What's Happened to the Humanities?* ed. Alvin B. Kernan (Princeton, NJ: Princeton University Press, 1997), 220.

2. Helen Small, *The Value of the Humanities* (Oxford: Oxford University Press, 2014), 56.
3. Stefan Berger, "Introduction: Historical Writing and Civic Engagement," in *The Engaged Historian: Perspectives on the Intersections of Politics, Activism and the Historical Profession*, ed. Stefan Berger (New York: Berghahn, 2019), 3.
4. Berger, "Introduction," 2–3.
5. Herman Paul, "Distance and Self-Distanciation: Intellectual Virtue and Historical Method Around 1900," *History and Theory* 50, no. 4 (2011): 104–16 and Herman Paul, "Performing History: How Historical Scholarship is Shaped by Epistemic Virtues," *History and Theory* 50, no. 1 (2011): 17.
6. Loraine Daston and H. Otto Sibum, "Introduction: Scientific Personae and Their Histories," *Science in Context* 16, no. 1–2 (2003): 7.
7. Herman Paul, "Introduction: Scholarly Personae: What They Are and Why They Matter," in *How to Be a Historian: Scholarly Personae in Historical Studies 1800–2000*, ed. Herman Paul (Manchester: Manchester University Press, 2019), 3–7.
8. Ibid., 3–7.
9. Kirsti Niskanen and Michael J. Barany, "Introduction: The Scholar Incarnate," in *Gender, Embodiment, and the History of the Scholarly Persona: Incarnations and Contestations*, ed. Kirsti Niskanen and Michael J. Barany (Cham: Palgrave Macmillan, 2021), 3.
10. Paul, "Introduction," 3, 7.
11. Mineke Bosch, "Scholarly Personae and Twentieth Century Historians: Explorations of a Concept," *Low Countries Historical Review* 131, no. 4 (2016): 33–54 and Julia Dahlberg, "Gifts of Nature? Inborn Personal Qualities and Their Relation to Personae," in Niskanen and Barany, *Gender, Embodiment*, 181–214.
12. Niskanen and Barany, "Introduction," 3.
13. Paulo Freire asserted that true liberation cannot be reduced completely to either practice or theory: Paulo Freire, *Pedagogy of the Oppressed*, trans. Myra Bergman Ramos (London: Penguin Random House, 2017 [1970]), 98.
14. Judith M. Bennett, "Feminism and History," *Gender and History* 1, no. 3 (1989): 253.
15. The term "Euro-American" here is used to refer to predominantly white European and American institutions or, more generally, white European or American scholars, in preference to "Western" to convey a more precise geographical and historically situated meaning. The term "Western" or "the West" has often functioned as a rhetorical device without clear-cut reflection in historical reality. Neil Lazarus, "The Fetish of the 'the West' in Postcolonial Theory," in *Marxism, Modernity, and Postcolonial Studies*, ed. Crystal Bartolovich (Cambridge University Press: Cambridge, 2002), 43–64.

16. Toyin Falola, *Decolonizing African Studies: Knowledge Production, Agency, and Voice* (Rochester, NY: Rochester University Press, 2022) and Susan Booysen, *Fees Must Fall: Student Revolt, Decolonisation and Governance in South Africa* (Johannesburg: Wits University Press, 2016).
17. Toyin Falola, "Nationalism and African Historiography," in *Turning Points in Historiography: A Cross-Cultural Perspective*, ed. Q. Edward Wang and Georg G. Iggers, (Rochester, NY: University of Rochester Press, 2002), 224.
18. Sunil Amrith and Glenda Sluga, "New Histories of the United Nations," *Journal of World History* 19, no. 3 (2008): 253, 269.
19. Léjon Saarloos, "Virtue and Vice in Academic Memory: Lord Acton and Charles Oman," *History of Humanities* 1, no. 2 (2016): 340.
20. The notion of "constellations of virtues" is described in more detail in Chapter 9 of this volume.
21. See Chapter 14 of this volume for a broader exploration of what "critique" can mean.
22. Toyin Falola, "Adu Boahen: An Introduction," in *Ghana in Africa and the World: Essays in Honor of Adu Boahen*, ed. Toyin Falola (Trenton, NJ: Africa World Press, 2003), 10–11.
23. "Editorial: Professor Emeritus Albert Adu Boahen (1932–2006)," *The Journal of African History* 47, no. 3 (2006): 359.
24. Ivor Agyeman-Duah, "The Historian Who Made History Himself," *New African* (July 2006): 58–60.
25. Ibid.; Cameron Duodu, "The Man Who Rescued African History," *New African* (July 2006): 60–3.
26. Ibid.
27. Ibid,; Agyeman-Duah, "Historian."
28. Larissa Schulte Nordholt, "What Is an African historian? Negotiating Scholarly Personae in UNESCO's *General History of Africa*," in Paul, *How to Be a Historian*, 182–201.
29. A. Adu Boahen, *Clio and Nation-Building in Africa: An Inaugural Lecture delivered at the University of Ghana Legon, on Thursday, 28th November, 1975* (Accra: Ghana Universities Press, 1975), 17.
30. Duodu, "Man Who Rescued."
31. Ibid,; Agyeman-Duah, "Historian."
32. "L'histoire africaine: l'après Ki-Zerbo," *Présence Africaine* 173, no. 1 (2006): 5. All translations are my own.
33. See: Salim Abdelmajid, "Joseph Ki-Zerbo: le savant, le politique et l'Afrique," *Esprit* (2007–8): 85 and Assane Seck, "Un nationaliste sans concession," *Présence Africaine* 173, no. 1 (2006): 40.
34. Mangoné Niang, "Le veilleur de jour," *Présence Africaine* 173, no. 1 (2006): 22.

35. Mamadou Diouf and Mohamad Mbodj, "The Shadow of Cheikh Anta Diop," in *The Surreptitious Speech: Présence Africaine and the Politics of Otherness, 1947–1987*, ed. V. Y. Mudimbe (Chicago, IL: University of Chicago Press, 1992), 122–3.
36. J. Ki-Zerbo, "Histoire et conscience nègre," *Présence Africaine* 16 (1957).
37. Adame Ba Konaré, "L'histoire africaine aujourd'hui," *Présence Africaine* 173, no. 1 (2006): 35.
38. Catherine Coquery-Vidrovitch, "Présence Africaine: History and Historians of Africa," in Mudimbe, *Surreptitious Speech*, 75.
39. Ibid., 77.
40. Anna Echterhölter, *Schattengefechte: Genealogische Praktiken in Nachrufen auf Naturwissenschaftler (1710–1860)* (Göttingen: Wallstein, 2012), 10, 20–1.
41. Ian Hesketh, "Diagnosing Froude's Disease: Boundary Work and the Discipline of History in Late-Victorian Britain," *History and Theory* 47, no. 3 (2008): 384.
42. Camille Creyghton et al., "Virtue Language in Historical Scholarship: The Cases of Georg Waitz, Gabriel Monod and Henri Pirenne," *History of European Ideas* 42, no. 7 (2016): 925–6 and Saarloos, "Virtue and Vice," 341–2.
43. Adu Boahen, "Africa and the Colonial Challenge," in *General History of Africa*, vol. 7, ed. A. Adu Boahen (Paris: UNESCO, 1985), 3.
44. Ibid.
45. Ibid.
46. Kwabena O. Akurang-Parry, "A. Adu Boahen," in *The Dark Webs: Perspectives on Colonialism in Africa*, ed. Toyin Falola (Durham, NC: Carolina Academic Press, 2005), 387 and Toyin Falola, *Nationalism and African Intellectuals* (Rochester, NY: Rochester University, 2001), 227.
47. UNESCO Archives Paris (hereafter UAP), CLT CS 7, A. Adu Boahen to Terence Ranger, December 19, 1978 (emphasis mine).
48. UAP, CLT CS 7, Terence Ranger to A. Adu Boahen, January 4, 1979.
49. Terence Ranger, "Towards a Usable African Past," in *African Studies since 1945: A Tribute to Basil Davidson*, ed. Christopher Fyfe (London: Longman, 1976), 17–29.
50. Michael Twaddle, "Historians and African History," in *The British Intellectual Engagement with Africa in the Twentieth Century*, ed. Douglas Rimmer and Anthony Kirk-Greene (London: MacMillan, 2000), 144–5.
51. Ranger had come to self-criticize for a failure to engage with the implication of colonialism and global interactions. See E. S. Atieno-Odhiambo, "From African Historiographies to an African Philosophy of History," *Afrika Zamani: revue annuelle d'histoire africaine* 7 (1999/2000): 17 and Megan Vaugh and Luise White, "Terence Ranger," *Past & Present* 228 (2015): 6.
52. UAP, CLT CS 7, Terence Ranger to A. Adu Boahen, January 4, 1979.
53. UAP, CLT CS 7, A. Adu Boahen to Terence Ranger, January 30, 1979.

54. UAP, CLT CID 103, Jan Vansina to Christophe Wondji, February 8, 1997.
55. David Newbury, "Contradictions at the Heart of the Canon: Jan Vansina and the Debate over Oral Historiography in Africa, 1960–1985," *History in Africa* 34 (2007): 215–6.
56. UAP, CLT CID 103, Adu Boahen to Christophe Wondji, February 13, 1997.

Part IV

Teaching Practices

12

The Humanities in the Vocational University: On the Unity of Teaching and Research

Kasper Risbjerg Eskildsen

The Humanities and Universities

The history of the modern humanities is closely connected to the history of higher education. Academics are not born academics, but become so at universities. Future scholars are here introduced to the working practices and dominant theories of their disciplines. Textbooks, readers, and syllabi cultivate their sense of what is important and what is not, which questions deserve attention and which do not. During their studies, students have the chance to mirror themselves in their teachers and fellow students and learn to behave and think as scholars. University professors write many of the books and articles, edit academic journals, control peer-review, and lead most professional societies. Museum curators and archivists may contribute to humanities research as well, but professors educate the new generations of researchers and generally decide what counts as valid and significant knowledge within their disciplines.[1]

The relationship between the humanities and universities has changed over time. During the early modern period, academics also became academics at universities, but universities did not control the production of knowledge in the humanities.[2] The Renaissance inventor of the *studia humanitatis*, Francesco Petrarca, never taught at a university. Many central figures of early modern humanities scholarship, including Ficino, Peiresc, Leibniz, and Winckelmann, were not university professors. Core parts of today's humanities scholarship, such as history and the study of material culture, were not considered as proper academic knowledge and not accepted as independent fields of study within the faculty of philosophy.[3] These matters were primarily cultivated elsewhere, among antiquarians, connoisseurs, salonnières, and courtiers.[4]

Only during the eighteenth and nineteenth centuries, initially in the German states, universities came to dominate humanities scholarship. Some large research projects, such as the *Thesaurus Linguae Latinae* (see Chapter 6), continued to be housed at academies and other research institutions rather than at universities. However, by the end of the nineteenth century, almost all central figures of German humanities scholarship were also university professors. When Eduard Wöfflin started on the *Thesaurus* in 1894, he did so as a professor of classical philology at the University of Munich and he remained in this position, despite embarking on the enormous task. Other countries followed the German example.[5] In 1891, the American historian John Franklin Jameson celebrated that "an increasing proportion of the annual product [of historical books] now comes from the teachers of history in universities and colleges, and the signs are that the immediate future belongs to the professorial class."[6] American history writing, he confirmed in 1901, had come under a new "professorial régime."[7] So, there was no longer any distinction between the humanities and universities. During the late nineteenth and early twentieth century, university administrators even adopted the word "humanities" to describe the remains of the faculty of philosophy, after the exodus of the natural and social sciences.[8]

The Vocational University

An important reason for the new connection between the humanities and universities was the emergence of, what I will call, the *vocational university*. Universities always have been in the business of educating for vocational purposes. However, this was not the primary function of the faculty of philosophy. The faculty instead prepared students for the so-called higher faculties of theology, medicine, and law. This ranking of faculties,

Immanuel Kant noted as late as 1798, proved "that not the scholarly community, but the government, was asked about this division and naming. For among the higher [faculties] are only counted those ... of interest to the government; that [faculty], on the contrary, which only has to serve the interest of scholarship is called the lower."[9] During the eighteenth and nineteenth centuries, however, German universities transformed dramatically. Many new fields were accepted as legitimate branches of academic knowledge making. The universities acquired a new role in a society, where knowledge became ever more important. This transformation especially impacted the faculty of philosophy and eventually resulted in its dissolution.

One characteristic of the vocational university was an emphasis on training *practices*. Students should not only acquaint themselves with accumulated knowledge, but also learn how to work, in a predictable way and according to standardized procedures. The primary purpose of this training was to prepare students for future work. For the humanities, this first of all meant as teachers in secondary schools. The training also prepared students for a kind of research that in itself became increasingly vocational. A second characteristic was the division of academic labor into *disciplines*, with different methods and fields of investigation. During the eighteenth and nineteenth centuries, new specialized trade schools threatened the dominance of the university in higher education. When the university anyhow succeeded, it was not least because the institution was remade in the image of these specialized schools.[10] The faculty of philosophy gradually lost its old role as a preparatory school for the higher faculties during the first half of the nineteenth century.[11] But the faculty also expanded with numerous new specialized disciplines.

The disciplines delivered the standards that made vocational training possible. This training, at the same time, ensured the coherence of the disciplines. The division of labor allowed professors to abandon considerations about the higher purpose of the university. The university was no longer the keeper of universal knowledge or the moral center of society, but just another part of the modern bureaucratic state. This new role of the university was especially evident in the transformation of faculty of philosophy.[12] As the Graz professor Anton Schönbach explained in 1897:

> Our universities ... as it is rather widely known, don't correspond to the name that they bear. If this [name] signified the unity of all scholarly studies, the university today scatters into a number of disciplinary schools, which

prepare for this or that vocation. Even the faculty of philosophy, where the ideal connection between all studies, as known in the Middle Ages, lasted the longest, is now alienated from its original purpose through its educational aims as well as through its specialized disciplines, which almost no longer can be overviewed.[13]

Practices

When late nineteenth-century scholars discussed the rise of the modern university, they often pointed to the introduction of seminars.[14] The first seminar for classical philology was established at the University of Göttingen in 1738. After 1770, this seminar became the model for a series of similar seminars at other German universities.[15] By the end of the nineteenth century, seminars had been introduced at all German universities and in all humanities disciplines.[16] The seminars were institutions, funded by the state, and not just a type of instruction. They had their own statutes, directors, and budgets for expenses, scholarships, prizes, and books. The teaching focused upon so-called "exercises" (*Übungen*). Professors seldom lectured, but instead gave the students tasks to solve. Friedrich August Wolf, who served as the first director of the philological seminar in Halle, established in 1787, offered two kinds of exercises, interpretation and disputation.[17] For the interpretation classes, the students themselves acted as teachers and presented classical texts. For the disputation classes, they wrote papers, which could be as long as forty pages. Wolf would write critical comments and afterwards the students defended their papers orally in class against an opponent. Other seminars adopted similar teaching methods, including the focus on writing. The statutes demanded that students regularly handed in papers and those who failed to do so could be excluded from the seminar and lose their scholarships.[18]

The aim of the first philological seminar in Göttingen was from the beginning to educate teachers.[19] In Halle, Carlos Spoerhase and Mark-Georg Dehrmann have argued, Wolf wanted to teach his students to do research and transformed the seminar for this purpose.[20] However, the official task of his seminar was to educate "future school teachers, equipped with state scholarships, aided by a modern library, excited by competition and prices,"[21] Apart from participating in Wolf's exercises, the students also taught classes in the pietist Waisenhaus school, just outside the city walls of Halle. Similar stipulations can be found in other seminar statutes. The philological seminar in Freiburg, established in 1828, demanded not only that students should participate in exercises and write papers, but also that they, during the last semester of their studies, should teach one hour each week in a local school.[22]

During the nineteenth century, the expansion of German secondary schools, and the gradual introduction of state exams to certify teaching qualifications, increased the significance of teacher training.[23] The school disciplines, classical philology, history, and modern languages, were the first to open seminars. Seminars for classical philology were established at most German universities during the first half of the century. The first historical seminars were introduced in Königsberg and Breslau in 1832 and 1843 and at many other German universities from the 1850s. The first seminar for German philology opened in Rostock in 1858. In 1867, the University of Tübingen established a seminar for modern languages, which five years later split into three seminars for German, English, and Romance studies.[24] A parallel development happened in the natural sciences with teaching laboratories, which, as Kathryn M. Olesko has shown in her study of Franz Neumann's physics seminar in Königsberg, also focused upon training technical practices and educating future secondary school teachers.[25]

Two-thirds of all seminars in the humanities and social sciences that existed at German universities in 1907 were established after 1870.[26] Lectures remained the most common form of teaching, but exercises became increasingly widespread. At the University of Tübingen, Sylvia Paletschek has calculated, exercises only constituted around 14 percent of classes in 1870. In 1930, the number had risen to almost 40 percent. In the Faculty of Philosophy, the proportion grew from around 21 to 45 percent.[27] During this period, the seminars also grew bigger. When the University of Strasbourg was re-established in 1872, after the German conquest of Alsace-Lorraine, seminars were introduced in all humanistic disciplines, each with its own rooms and a large seminar library (see Chapter 9). Other universities followed and constructed new buildings with libraries, teaching rooms, study facilities for students, and an office for the director.

The continuous need for qualified secondary school teachers partly justified this expansion, but the seminars increasingly also offered other kinds of vocational training. One example, recently discussed by Anne Kwaschik, is the emergence of "colonial sciences and scholarship," *Kolonialwissenschaften*.[28] In 1887, the University of Berlin opened a seminar for oriental languages to support German trade in Asia and Africa and educate translators. With German colonial expansion, the seminar changed its focus to colonial training. Among its graduates in 1912 were 101 civil servants, 64 postal officers, and 228 military officers bound for the colonies. Other institutions of higher education also contributed and, in 1908, the German government together with the city of Hamburg established a large *Kolonialinstitut* with numerous seminars, including Carl Heinrich Becker's groundbreaking seminar for the history and culture of the Orient.

Another reason for the numerous new and bigger seminars was increased enrollment. The number of students at German universities rose from around twelve thousand in 1860 to around sixty thousand in 1914. Many started in the faculty of philosophy, which expanded from a bit less than a third to more than half of all German students, between 1870 and 1910.[29] The students were far more diverse than previously and some had not attended classical gymnasium, but more practically-oriented secondary schools, *Realgymnasien* and later *Oberrealschulen*.[30] Professors had to adjust their teaching practices to these changed realities. They produced textbooks, which explained the methods and practices of their disciplines, and standardized their exercises.[31] The exercises were then made available to a larger portion of the student body.[32] Seminar regulations increasingly differentiated students in groups, according to their qualifications, with different requirements.[33] The German seminar at the University of Marburg, Uwe Merves has shown, accepted 233 students during the first five years after its establishment in 1876. Only three were considered as full members. The remaining students were extraordinary members, who did not hand in written papers. The director of the seminar, Karl Lucae, instead practiced the students' philological practices, through close readings of printed medieval texts as well as famous text-editions.[34] In the historical seminar in Leipzig, founded in 1877, students were also not supposed to write research papers, but instead worked on preplanned assignments, changing from week to week, that could be solved with books and source-editions in the seminar library.[35]

Disciplines

Nineteenth-century discipline formation, as Rudolf Stichweh pointed out, was closely connected to teaching.[36] University affiliation not only ensured institutional recognition, but also opened a career path, from student to full professor. The unity of teaching and research enabled reproduction and recruitment and the dissemination of disciplinary standards and working practices between generations. These shared standards and practices delivered continuity and allowed for disciplinary histories, which often were told as family histories.[37] They also enforced coherence within the discipline and distinguished insiders from outsiders. During the nineteenth century, however, scholars disagreed about the usefulness of seminars for this purpose. Many even considered the seminars, and the kind of vocational training they promoted, as an obstacle to the progress of research and contrary to the mission of the university.

In the history of the natural sciences, the Giessen professor Justus von Liebig's teaching laboratory, established in 1826 in a former army barracks, is often considered as an important turning point towards the unity of teaching and research.[38] However, his vision initially encountered opposition within the academic community. In 1840, Liebig published a harsh critique of the state of chemistry at Prussian universities. Most universities did not have teaching laboratories and professors with private laboratories did not receive enough compensation. Practical education was instead exiled to specialized trade schools that reduced chemistry to a craft and lacked the scientific knowledge to harvest its full potential. The Prussian government asked the universities to respond and, as R. Steven Turner has shown, opinions were split.[39] Liebig received enthusiastic support from Franz Neumann and his colleague Friedrich Dulk in Königsberg, but many professors did not share his concerns. The Berlin philosophical faculty answered that the trade schools already delivered this training, which was anyway "only indispensable for those who are going to dedicate themselves to industry and manufacturing."[40]

Professors, who advocated the use of exercises, often preferred to offer these in their private homes instead of in institutionalized seminars. The Berlin professor Leopold von Ranke, often celebrated as the founder of the historical discipline, never taught in a seminar and the University of Berlin was one of the last German universities to establish a historical seminar. Ranke instead gathered his most promising students for exercises at home, around a large desk in his study. The few students who were accepted here were expected to do original research, write publishable papers, and present them to one another.[41] Some of Ranke's students also rejected the new institution and continued with private exercises.[42] His most celebrated student, the Göttingen professor Georg Waitz detested the seminars and complained that students here learned "method, but not the spirit and art of history writing."[43]

During the second half of the nineteenth century, however, scholars started to consider the seminars as beneficial for research. As early as 1853, the German-born secretary of the French Société Asiatique, Julius von Mohl, reported that the causes of the great progress of German orientalist research over the past thirty years were the "number and organization of German universities and the scholarly education that the clergy receives there."[44] These advantages, he claimed, matched the benefits of French government support and British colonial possessions. In seminars as well as teaching laboratories, Lorraine Daston has argued, students came to embody a new ideal of *Wissenschaftlichkeit* that emphasized precision and the elimination of error over erudition and the cultivation of imagination. They learned, in Daston's words, "diligence, attention to minute detail, devotion to technique, an ethos of responsibility and exactitude, and the habits of collective discussion."[45]. The ideal of *Wissenschaftlichkeit* permitted collaboration between many scholars, large research projects, and the formation of schools of research. If scholars proceeded according to rigid rules and standardized producers, and avoided speculation, it was possible to compare results and build upon one another's work. The training enabled the emergence of, what late nineteenth-century German scholars started to call, "big science and scholarship," *Großwissenschaft*.[46]

The University of Berlin, where the philosophical faculty had protested against Liebig's teaching ideas in 1840 and Ranke had taught his private exercises, also established several seminars, laboratories, and institutes during the second half of the nineteenth century. When the Prussian government in the early 1860s hired A. W. Hofmann and August Kekulé as professors of chemistry in Berlin and Bonn, it also endowed them with generous funding for establishing large teaching laboratories. One of Ranke's former students, Julius Weizsäcker, introduced a historical seminar in 1883, with a considerable budget, a large working library, and its own rooms in a former birth-clinic behind the main university buildings.[47] By 1914, the university had seminars and institutes for different modern and ancient languages, psychology, philosophy, archaeology, art history, and several other fields.[48] German academics had come to consider the establishment of a seminar or a teaching laboratory as a precondition for the creation of a discipline.[49]

The disciplines did not become associated with seminars because the seminars had become less vocational. The dramatic transformation of the German universities during the last decades of the nineteenth century only emphasized the importance of vocational training. A more likely explanation is that research itself had become more vocational. Humanities professors increasingly compared their seminar exercises to laboratory work as well as to manual labor.⁵⁰ In Berlin, Weizsäcker described his historical seminar to a "work room," where the students, always and at all times of the day, could find "the necessary hand tools." The need for such a venue, he explained, had emerged because "one everyday becomes more practical."⁵¹ "Handcraft remains handcraft," the founder of the German seminar at the University of Graz, Anton Schönbach, noted, "no matter, if it done with the microscope or with the reading apparatus of an old authors."⁵² So, the requirements for research and vocational work were not that different. Researchers and secondary school teachers, the Greifswald history professor Ernst Bernheim argued in 1898, both needed "a similar overview of the entire field of knowledge of the discipline and an intimate familiarity with the engrained working methods."⁵³ The general principle applied that "the aim of all academic instruction is to teach [students] to think, to observe, and to work in a disciplinary way," *fachwissenschaftlich*.⁵⁴

The Myth of Humboldt

Since the beginning of the twentieth century, many scholars in the humanities have preferred to tell themselves another story about the beginning of the modern university. According to this story, the history of the modern university started in 1810 with the establishment of the University of Berlin. The university was inspired by German idealism and neo-humanism and promoted academic freedom, the equality of the disciplines, and the value of pure research. The unity of teaching and research was based upon these ideals and the rejection of utilitarian concerns. Professors and students were joined in a common pursuit of knowledge. The end of the role of the faculty of philosophy as a preparatory school for the higher faculties was not the beginning of specialization, but a liberation which allowed professors to offer the courses they wanted and students to choose freely among them, according to the principles of freedom of teaching and learning, *Lehr- und Lernfreiheit*. The establishment of the University of Berlin ushered in a dramatic change from mere "education" (*Ausbildung*) to "self-cultivation" (*Bildung*).

Some scholars are still retelling this story, but in recent decades German historians have pointed to, what they have called, the "myth of Humboldt" (*Mythos Humboldt*).⁵⁵ Central to the story of the University of Berlin as the birthplace of the modern university was the role of Wilhelm von Humboldt. Humboldt briefly served as head of the section for religion and education in the Prussian interior ministry. During his sixteen-months tenure, he helped establish the university and drafted a short essay, which contained many of the ideas which later became associated with the university. However, those debating university reform in the nineteenth century did not consider the University of Berlin as a model and did not refer to Humboldt. Humboldt's famous essay was discovered in an archive only at the end of the century and published in full in 1903.[56] The University of Berlin was not institutionally that different from other German universities, even if from the beginning it attracted brilliant professors and soon became one of the largest.

German scholars invented the myth during the first decades of twentieth century to defend the university against utilitarian demands. They were concerned about the loss of the prestige of the humanities, in the face of the progress of the natural and technical sciences, and about the division of the old institution into specialized disciplines and vocational schools.[57] The myth mirrored anxieties among German academics about what they and the university had become.[58] The university, the orientalist Carl Heinrich Becker argued in 1925, should be a "castle for the grail of pure science and scholarship." It was therefore evident that "the essence of the university fundamentally doesn't have much to do with utilitarian considerations, with disciplinary schooling and vocational education." Becker, who himself had taught at the Hamburg *Kolonialinstitut* and fathered the discipline of *Islamwissenschaft*, admitted that German universities had taken on these tasks. But he demanded understanding for "the profound tension between [the university's] fully rationalized methods and practical purposes and its ultimate entirely irrational, ideal, and unified final aim."[59]

Teaching and Research in the Modern University

The Humboldtian vision for a unified university did not prevail. After the catastrophe of the Nazi-regime, Humboldt's name became a fixture in German discussions about higher education and his ideas for the University of Berlin have been invoked in many different contexts.[60] However, German universities continued on a path of increasing specialization. The connection between teaching and research was also still justified with the utilitarian needs for vocational training. In 1962, in an influential report which laid the foundation for subsequent reforms of higher education, the German *Wissenschaftsrat* offered the following description of the contemporary situation:

> The connection between research and teaching today means the connection between a strongly specializing research task, only to be archived in collaboration with many people ... and the task of educating a quickly growing number of young people for their functions in a society, which only is able to solve its problems with the help of science and scholarship.[61]

Since the beginning of the twentieth century, many have challenged the idea that universities should only offer disciplinary and vocational training. One influential alternative has been North American liberal arts education. During the last decades of the nineteenth century, American universities started adopting the German model of higher education. New universities, most prominently Johns Hopkins University and the University of Chicago, emulated the example of German universities. This, James Turner recently has shown for the humanities at Johns Hopkins, meant establishing seminars that focused narrowly on disciplinary training.[62] Older universities, like Princeton, Yale, and Harvard, were reformed according to German ideals and abandoned their previous religious and moral missions.[63] The modern university, to many American scholars, was the German university.[64]

American universities, however, also differed in important ways from their German counterparts. The most important difference was the separation between college and graduate and professional schools. The college acquired a role similar to that of a German faculty of philosophy before the rise of the vocational university, as a preparatory school for later vocational studies. Many colleges introduced general education requirements, demanding a distribution of courses across the liberal arts or dictating a core curriculum (see Chapter 13).[65] University administrators considered these requirements as a bulwark against overspecialization. General education should ensure broadness of mind and that students were familiar with the major works and thoughts of "Western Civilization." The requirements guaranteed a central role for the humanities within American higher education, but also created a new division between teaching and research.

Another challenge was the establishment of reform universities from the 1960s and onwards, often informed by the American example. If German public universities were a model for emulation before the First World War, American elite universities became the beacon to follow after the Second

World War.⁶⁶ In response to increasing specialization, the 1962 rapport of the German *Wissenschaftsrat* recommended the establishment of interdisciplinary institutes as well as reorganization of universities, to encourage students to attend courses from different disciplines. In the following years, the reform universities of Konstanz and Bielefeld were founded, both with an interdisciplinary mission for education and research and a strong profile in the humanities and social sciences.⁶⁷ Similar institutions were established in other parts of Europe and the world.⁶⁸ Within many universities, a parallel development was the emergence of "studies," which drew upon insights from both the humanities and social sciences, such as women's studies, postcolonial studies, gay and lesbian studies, cultural studies, and science studies. Like the reform universities, these studies served as supplements, or correctives, but did not fundamentally change the disciplinary system. In the end, neither American liberal arts education nor the reform movement nor the emergence of studies halted the march towards specialization. The system also proved remarkably flexible and accommodating to new disciplines and subspecialities.⁶⁹

However, the system may no longer fulfill its educational function, at least for the humanities. Today, many more students graduate in the humanities than are needed as secondary school teachers or for other specific humanities vocations, such as archivist or museum curator. The vocational university, as it emerged during the nineteenth century, was based upon the premise that disciplinary training ensured that students acquired particular working habits which would be useful in their later vocational life. Teaching and research belonged together because the work that academics would do inside and outside the university was somewhat similar. With increasing student numbers, this may no longer be the case. The rarefication of research only exacerbates this problem. The specific qualifications needed to become a researcher in a specialized field are often not the generalist qualifications that a likely employer of a humanities graduate is looking for.⁷⁰ One imaginable outcome is that the humanities again separate from universities and only are maintained at a few elite institutions, the graduates of which will find employment anyway.⁷¹ But we may also question if training for particular vocations should be the only purpose of higher education. The humanities, as often claimed at liberal arts colleges and reform universities, may serve the students' personal development and convey some generalist qualifications.⁷² If this is the purpose of studying the humanities, it should have consequences for teaching as well as research. A system designed to certify secondary school teachers and facilitate *Großwissenschaft* may not be the best option. The unity of teaching and research should not become an excuse to ignore students' needs.

Notes

1. Michèle Lamont, *How Professors Think: Inside the Curious World of Academic Judgement* (Cambridge, MA: Harvard University Press, 2009).
2. For a parallel argument for the natural sciences, Daniel Garber, "Philosophia, Historia, Mathematica: Shifting Sands in the Disciplinary Geography of the Seventeenth Century," in *Scientia in Early Modern Philosophy: Seventeenth-Century Thinkers on Demonstrative Knowledge from First Principles,* ed. Tom Sorell, G. A. J. Rogers, and Jill Kraye (Dordrecht: Springer, 2010), 1–17.
3. On the status of historical and empirical knowledge as academic knowledge, see Arno Seifert, *Cognitio historica: die Geschichte als Namengeberin der frühneuzeitlichen Empirie* (Berlin: Duncker & Humblot, 1976), *Historia: Empiricism and Erudition in Early Modern Europe,* ed. Gianna Pomata and Nancy Siraisi (Cambridge: MIT Press, 2005), and Per Landgren, *Det aristoteliska historiebegreppet: historieteori i renässansens Europa och Sverige* (Gothenburg: Acta Universitatis Gothoburgensis, 2008).
4. On the Renaissance study of history and material culture, Peter N. Miller, *History and Its Objects: Antiquarianism and Material Culture since 1500* (Ithaca, NY: Cornell University Press, 2017), 55–75.
5. Also, on the global dissemination of the German university model, *Humboldt International: Der Export des deutschen Universitätsmodells im 19. und 20. Jahrhundert,* ed. Rainer Christoph Schwinges (Basel: Schwabe, 2001), 163–346, and the special issue "A Global History of Research Education: Disciplines, Institutions, and Nations, 1840–1950," ed. Ku-ming Chang and Alan Rocke, *History of Universities* 34, no. 1 (2021).
6. John Franklin Jameson, *The History of Historical Writing in America* (Boston, MA: Houghton, Mifflin and Company, 1891), 159.
7. John Franklin Jameson, "The Influence of Universities upon Historical Writing," in *John Franklin Jameson and the Development of Humanistic Scholarship in America,* ed. Morey Rothberg and Jacqueline Goggin, vol. 1 (Athens, GA: University of Georgia Press, 1993), 262–73, at 271. Also, for a more nuanced discussion, Peter Novick, *That Noble Dream: The "Objectivity Question" and the American Historical Profession* (Cambridge: Cambridge University Press, 1988).
8. Kasper Risbjerg Eskildsen and Rens Bod, "The Forgotten Curriculum of the Humanities," *History of Humanities* 4, no. 2 (2019): 219–227, esp. 223–5.

9. Immanuel Kant, *Der Streit der Fakultäten in drey Abschnitten* (Königsberg: Friedrich Nicolovius, 1798), 6–7. All translations, unless otherwise noted, are my own.
10. Gert Schubring, "Spezialschulmodell versus Universitätsmodell: die Institutionalisierung von Forschung," in *"Einsamkeit und Freiheit" neu besichtigt: Universitätreformen und Disziplinenbildung in Preussen als Modell für Wissenschaftspolitik in Europa des 19. Jahrhunderts*, ed. Gert Schubring (Stuttgart: Franz Steiner, 1991), 276–326.
11. Harm-Hinrich Brandt, "Studierende im Humboldt'schen Modell des 19. Jahrhunderts," in Schwinges, *Humboldt International*, 131–50, at 132–4.
12. On the moral import of the humanities, see also Kasper Risbjerg Eskildsen, "Commentary: Scholarship as a Way of Life: Character and Virtue in the Age of Big Humanities," *History of Humanities* 1, no. 2 (2016): 387–97.
13. Anton E. Schönbach, *Über Lesen und Bildung: Umschau und Ratschläge* (Granz: Leuschner & Lubensky, 1897), 12–3.
14. For example, Wilhelm Erben, "Die Entstehung der Universitäts-Seminare," *Internationale Monatschrift für Wissenschaft, Kunst und Technik* 7 (1913): 1247–64, 1335–48.
15. William Clark, "On the Dialectical Origins of the Research Seminar," *History of Science* 27 (1989): 111–54.
16. For an overview, Bernhard vom Brocke, "Wege aus der Krise: Universitätsseminar, Akademiekommission oder Forschungsinstitut: Formen der Institutionalisierung der Germanistik und Deutschen Literaturwissenschaft in Rahmen der Geistes- und Naturwissenschaften," in *Zur Geschichte und Problematik der Nationalphilologien in Europa*, ed. Frank Füberth, Pierre Krügel, Ernst E. Metzner, and Olaf Müller (Tübingen: Max Niemeyer, 1999), 359–78. Also, Gert Schubring, "Kabinett—Seminar—Institut: Raum und Rahmen des forschenden Lernens," *Berichte zur Wissenschaftsgeschichte* 23, no. 3 (2000): 269–85.
17. Carlos Spoerhase and Mark-Georg Dehrmann, "Die Idee der Universität: Friedrich August Wolf und die Praxis des Seminars," *Zeitschrift für Ideengeschichte* 5, no. 1 (2011): 105–17.
18. William Clark, *Academic Charisma and the Origins of the Research University* (Chicago, IL: University of Chicago Press, 2006), 176–9 and Otto Kruse, "The Origins of Writing in the Disciplines: Traditions of Seminar Writing and the Humboldtian Ideal of the Research University," *Written Communication* 23, no. 3 (2006): 331–52.
19. Johannes Tütken, "Die Anfänge der Pädagogik im 18. Jahrhundert," in *Pädagogik an der Georg-August-Universität Göttingen: Eine Vorlesungsreihe*, ed. Dietrich Hoffmann (Göttingen: Vandenhoeck & Ruprecht, 1987), 13–49, at 46–9.
20. Spoerhase and Dehrmann, "Idee der Universität."

21. Ibid., 106.
22. Sylvia Paletschek, "Geisteswissenschaften in Freiburg im 19. Jahrhundert: Expansion, Verwissenschaftlichung und Ausdifferenzierung der Disziplinen," *550 Jahre Albert-Ludwigs-Universität Freiburg*, vol. 3 (Freiburg: Alber, 2007), 44–71, at 51–2.
23. Heinz-Elmer Tenorth, "Lehrerberuf und Lehrerausbildung," in *Handbuch der deutschen Bildungsgeschichte*, vol. 3, ed. Karl-Ernst Jeismann and Peter Lundgreen (Munich: C. H. Beck, 1987), 250–70, at 250–6.
24. Also, vom Brocke, "Wege aus der Krise."
25. Kathryn M. Olesko, *Physics as a Calling: Discipline and Practice in the Königsberg Seminar for Physics* (Ithaca, NY: Cornell University Press, 1991). Also, "Commentary: On Institutes, Investigations, and Scientific Training," in *The Investigative Enterprise: Experimental Physiology in Nineteenth-Century Medicine*, ed. William Coleman and Frederic L. Holmes (Berkeley, CA: University of California Press, 1988), 295–332.
26. Brocke, "Wege aus der Krise," 365.
27. Sylvia Paletschek, *Die Permanente Erfindung einer Tradition: Die Universität Tübingen im Kaiserreich und in der Weimarer Republik* (Stuttgart: Franz Steiner, 2001), 392–402.
28. Anne Kwaschik, "Die Verwissenschaftlichung des Kolonialen als kultureller Code und internationale Praxis um 1900," *Historische Anthropologie* 28, no. 3 (2020): 399–423 and *Der Griff nach dem Weltwissen: Zur Genealogie von Area Studies im 19. und 20. Jahrhundert* (Göttingen: Vandenhoeck & Ruprecht, 2018), 64–75.
29. Konrad H. Jarausch, "Universität und Hochschule," in *Handbuch der deutschen Bildungsgeschichte*, vol. 4, ed. Christa Berg (Munich: C. H. Beck, 1991), 313–45, at 315.
30. Jarausch, "Universität und Hochschule," 324–5 and Brandt, "Studierende," 139–41.
31. On the natural sciences, Michael Gordin, "Beilstein Unbound: The Pedagogical Unraveling of the Man and His Handbuch," in *Pedagogy and the Practice of Science: Historical and Contemporary Perspectives*, ed. David Kaiser (Cambridge: MIT Press, 2005), 11–39 and Kathryn M. Olesko, "The Foundation of a Canon: Kohlrausch's Practical Physics,," ibid., 323–56. For the historical discipline, Rolf Torstendahl, "From All-Round to Professional Education: How Young Historians Became Members of an Academic Community in the Nineteenth Century," *Leidschrift* 25, no. 1 (2010): 17–31.
32. Jarausch, "Universität und Hochschule," 330.
33. Also, Thorsten Pohl, *Die studentische Hausarbeit: Rekonstruktion ihrer ideen- und institutionsgeschichtlichen Entstehung* (Heidelberg: Synchron, 2009), 99–107.

34. Uwe Merves, "Die Jahresberichte der Seminardirektoren as Quellen für die Seminarpraxis," *Zeitschrift für Germanistik* 23, no. 2 (2014): 242–58, at 250–2.
35. Kasper Risbjerg Eskildsen, "Private Übungen und verkörpertes Wissen: Zur Unterrichtspraxis der Geschichtswissenschaft im neunzehnten Jahrhundert," in *Akademische Wissenskulturen: Praktiken des Lehrens und Forschens vom Mittelalter bis zur Moderne*, ed. Martin Kintzinger and Sita Steckel (Bern: Schwabe, 2015), 143–61, at 155–6.
36. Rudolf Stichweh, *Zur Entsehung des modernen Systems wissenschaftlicher Disziplinen: Physik in Deutschland 1740-1890* (Frankfurt am Main: Suhrkamp, 1984). Also, for a recent discussion of early discipline formation in the anglophone world, James Turner, "Discipline Formation and Research Training: Chicken or Egg?," *History of Universities* 34, no. 1 (2021): 11–26 and, for a contemporary perspective, Stephen Turner, "What Are Disciplines? And How is Interdisciplinarity Different?," in *Practicing Interdisciplinarity*, ed. Nico Stehr and Peter Weingart (Toronto: University of Toronto Press, 2000), 46–65.
37. Also, Eskildsen, "Private Übungen."
38. J. B. Morrell, "The Chemist Breeders: The Research Schools of Liebig and Thomas Thomsen," *Ambix* 19 (1972): 1–46; Frederic L. Holmes, "The Complementarity of Teaching and Research in Liebig's Laboratory," *Osiris* 2, no. 5 (1989): 121–64, and Alan Rocke, "The Rise of Academic Laboratory Science: Chemistry and the 'German model' in the Nineteenth Century," *History of Universities* 34, no. 1 (2021): 41–64.
39. R. Steven Turner, "Justus Liebig versus Prussian Chemistry: Reflections on Early Institute-Building in Germany," *Historical Studies in the Physical Sciences* 13, no 1 (1982): 129–62.
40. Ibid., 137. Turner's translation.
41. Kasper Risbjerg Eskildsen, "Leopold von Ranke, la passion de la critique et le séminaire d'histoire," in *Lieux de savoir*, vol. 1, ed. Christian Jacob (Paris: Albin Michel, 2007), 462–82.
42. Jo Tollebeek, "A Domestic Culture: The mise-en-scène of Modern Historiography," in *The Making of the Humanities*, vol. 3: *The Modern Humanities*, eds. Rens Bod, Jaap Maat and Thijs Weststeijn (Amsterdam: Amsterdam University Press, 2014), 129–43 and Eskildsen, "Private Übungen." Also, for a recent comparison of private teaching in history and physics, see Sjang L. ten Hagen, "History and Physics Entangled: Disciplinary intersections in the Long Nineteenth Century" (PhD thesis University of Amsterdam, 2021), 115–97.
43. Georg Waitz, *Friedrich Christoph Dahlmann: Gedächtnisrede gehalten in der Aula der Universität Kiel am 13. Mai 1885* (Kiel: Universitäts-Buchhandlug, 1885), 5. Also, Kasper Risbjerg Eskildsen, "Virtues of History: Exercises,

Seminars, and the Emergence of the German Historical Discipline, 1830–1900," *History of Universities* 34, no. 1 (2021), 27–40.
44. Jules Mohl, *Vingt-sept ans d'histoire des études orientales: rapports faits à la Société Asiatique de Paris de 1840 à 1867* (Paris: Reinwald et cie., 1879), 478.
45. Lorraine Daston, "Objectivity and Impartiality: Epistemic Virtues in the Humanities," in *The Making of the Humanities*, vol. 3, ed. Rens Bod, Jaap Maat, and Thijs Weststeijn (Amsterdam: Amsterdam University Press, 2014), 27–41, at 37.
46. Eskildsen, "Commentary."
47. Max Lenz, *Geschichte der Königlichen Friedrich-Wilhelms-Universität zu Berlin*, vol. 3 (Halle: Buchhandlung des Waisenhauses, 1910), 247–60, and Wolfgang Eric Wagner, *Die Bibliothek der Historischen Gesellschaft von Johann Gustav Droysen* (Berlin: Akademie Verlag, 2008), 13–34.
48. On the transformation of the University of Berlin, Heinz-Elmar Tenorth, "Transformation der Wissensordnung: die Berliner Universität vom ausgehender 19. Jahrhundert bis 1945: zur Einleitung," *Geschichte der Universität Unter den Linden 1810–2010*, vol. 5 (Berlin: Walter de Guyter, 2010), 9–50. For lists of seminars, ibid., 19, 27.
49. The establishment of seminars, laboratories, and institutes, however, did not guarantee disciplinary recognition. For the troubled early history of German experimental psychology, see Mitchell G. Ash, "Academic Politics in the History of Science: Experimental Psychology in Germany, 1879–1941," *Central European History* 13, no. 3 (1980): 255–86.
50. For the comparison with laboratories, see Bonnie G. Smith, "Gender and the Practices of Scientific History. The Seminar and Archival Research in the Nineteenth Century," *The American Historical Review* 100, no. 4 (1995): 1150–76, and Carlos Spoerhase, "Seminar Libraries as Laboratories of Philology: The Modern Seminar Model in Nineteenth-Century German Philology," *History of Humanities* 4, no. 1 (2019): 103–23.
51. Lenz, *Geschichte*, 255.
52. Schönbach, *Über Lesen und Bildung*, 13.
53. Ernst Bernheim, *Der Universitätsunterricht und die Erfordernisse der Gegenwart* (Berlin: Calvary & Co, 1898), 16–7.
54. Ibid., 28.
55. Gert Schubring proposed an investigation into the twentieth-century origins of the myth in "Spezialschulmodell versus Universitätsmodell," 309. Also, *German Universities Past and Future: Crisis or Renewal*, ed. Mitchell G. Ash (Providence, RI: Berghahn, 1997).
56. Sylvia Paletschek, "Verbreitete sich ein 'Humboldtsches Modell' an den deutschen Universitäten im 19. Jahrhundert?," in Schwinges, *Humboldt International*, 75–104.

57. Sylvia Paletschek, "Die Erfindung der Humboldschen Universität: Die Konstruktion der deutschen Universitätsidee in der ersten Hälfte des 20. Jahrhunderts," *Historische Anthropologie* 10, no. 2 (2002): 183–205.
58. Also, Fritz K. Ringer, *The Decline of the German Mandarins: The German Academic Community, 1890–1933* (Cambridge, MA: Harvard University Press, 1969), esp. 102–13.
59. Carl Heinrich Becker, "Vom Wesen der deutschen Universität," in *Die Universitätsideale der Kulturvölker*, ed. Reinhold Schairer and Conrad Hoffmann, Jr. (Leipzig: Quelle & Mayer, 1925), 1–30, at 1–2.
60. For an overview, Peter Uwe Hohendahl, "Humboldt Revisited: Liberal Education, University Reform, and the Opposition to the Neoliberal University," *New German Critique* 113 (2011): 159–96. Also, Ash, *German Universities*.
61. *Anregungen des Wissenschaftsrates zur Gestalt neuer Hochschulen: verabschiedet von der Vollversammlung des Wissenschaftsrates am 10. Februar und 26. Mai 1962*, online at https://www.wissenschaftsrat.de/download/archiv/0398-62.html, 9.
62. Turner, "Discipline Formation."
63. Julie E. Reuben, *The Making of the Modern University: Intellectual Transformation and the Marginalization of Morality* (Chicago, IL: University of Chicago Press, 1996) and Jon H. Roberts and James Turner, *The Sacred and the Secular University* (Princeton, NJ: Princeton University Press, 2000).
64. Roy Steven Turner, "Humboldt in North America: Reflections on the Research University and its Historians," in Schwinges, *Humboldt International*, 289–312. Also, Herman Paul, "German Thoroughness in Baltimore: Epistemic Virtues and National Stereotypes," *History of Humanities* 3, no. 2 (2018): 327–50.
65. For an overview, Louis Menand, *The Marketplace of Ideas: Reform and Resistance in the American University* (New York: Norton, 2010), 23–57. Also, W. B. Carnochan, *The Battleground of the Curriculum: Liberal Education and American Experience* (Stanford, CA: Stanford University Press, 1993).
66. For the German case, Stefan Paulus, *Vorbild USA? Amerikanisierung von Universität und Wissenschaft in Westdeutschland 1945–1976* (Munich: Oldenbourg, 2010).
67. Susanne Schregel, "Interdisziplinarität im Entwurf: Zur Geschichte einer Denkform des Erkennens in der Bundesrepublik (1955–1975)," *NTM Zeitschrift für Geschichte der Wissenschaften, Technik und Medizin* 24 (2016): 1–37. Also, Moritz Mälzer, *Auf der Suche Nach der neuen Universität: Die Entstehung der "Reformuniversitäten" Konstanz und Bielefeld in den 1960er Jahren* (Göttingen: Vandenhoeck & Ruprecht, 2016).
68. For a recent discussion of, primarily, the anglophone world, see *Utopian Universities: A Global History of the New Campuses of the 1960s*, ed. Jim Pellew and Miles Taylor (London: Bloomsbury, 2021).

69. Jerry A. Jacobs, *In Defense of Disciplines: Interdisciplinarity and Specialization in the Research University* (Chicago, IL: University of Chicago Press, 2013).
70. Martin Humburg, Rolf van der Velden and Annelore Verhagen, *The Employability of Higher Education: The Employers' Perspective* (Maastricht: European Union, 2013), online at https://op.europa.eu/en/publication-detail/-/publication/ecbcc42d-349e-4903-a844-9820680baa1a, esp. 75–8.
71. Stefan Collini, himself a Cambridge professor, recently proposed such an outcome in "On Not 'Justifying' the Humanites," in *The Humanities in the World*, ed. Anders Engberg-Pedersen (Copenhagen: U Press, 2020), 24–53.
72. For different defenses of the humanities, see Helen Small, *The Value of the Humanities* (Oxford: Oxford University Press, 2013).

13

On the Purpose of Humanities Education: A Historical Perspective from the Mid-Twentieth-Century United States

Claire Rydell Arcenas

Three questions animate contemporary discourse on the humanities' role in public life.[1] First, how should we understand the humanities' purpose and value? Put another way, what are the humanities good for? Second, how should we communicate their payoff(s) and to whom? Third, should discussions of the humanities' contributions—whether to the flourishing of individuals or society—be framed as *defenses* of the humanities? Should we, in short, be defending the humanities?

The first two questions are relatively old ones dating back to nineteenth-century conversations and disagreements about the benefits of "liberal" *versus* "useful" education. The third question is new, although not because the humanities have only recently been put on the defensive. To the contrary. As one historian has observed, "liberal education [of the sort provided by humanistic study] is usually on the defensive."[2] Rather, what is new is that in an ever-growing discourse on the humanities' purpose and value, defending the humanities has gone out of vogue. When, for example, Helen Small advanced a "pluralistic account" as being the only plausible way to make a "persuasive account of the humanities' contribution to the public good," in

The Value of the Humanities (2013), she framed her discussion as intentionally not a defense of the humanities.[3] Simon During, a scholar of British literature, was blunt in his assessment of the situation at hand: "Stop defending the Humanities," he wrote in 2014.[4] "One of the key things that hasn't worked," concluded professor of English Kathleen Fitzpatrick in her 2019 book *Generous Thinking: A Radical Approach to Saving the University* "is the impassioned plea on behalf of humanities fields." In recent years, she explained, "a welter of defenses of the humanities from both inside and outside the academy" has appeared, "each of which has seemed slightly more defensive than the last, and none of which has had the desired impact."[5] From a survey of recent works such as these, it is clear that existing approaches to defending the humanities have fallen short and, consequently, that believers in the humanities' value need to think long and hard about how best to advocate on their behalf.[6]

In this chapter, I approach these vital questions from a historical perspective. I ask what we can learn from arguments on behalf of the humanities and, secondarily, how this history of defending and advocating for the humanities can inform contemporary conversations about their relevance. More specifically, I focus on a crucial, but underappreciated, moment in the history of the humanities in the mid-twentieth-century United States: the 1940s, when humanities teaching and learning at US colleges and universities came under siege for being "non-essential" in a nation at war.

The discussion that follows examines how, in response, the humanities—or rather their practitioners, teachers, and advocates—defended and thus advocated their study and pursuit. It shows that, beginning in early 1942, public-facing academic defenses of the humanities combined two crucial elements and features: first, they embraced (rather than disputed) the case for their practical utility—often framed in geopolitical terms; second, they pursued decidedly forward-looking lines of argumentation. Rather than frame their responses as *defensive* reactions to criticisms, advocates for the humanities framed their arguments in unequivocally positive, even optimistic, terms. These public-facing, future-oriented, utility-based arguments conjured and deployed during the Second World War became an essential component of the humanities' postwar flourishing. Taken as a whole, my argument in this chapter offers a necessary complement to standard narratives of the humanities in twentieth-century America, which overwhelmingly focus on the postwar, Cold War years, and initiatives such as the GI Bill. It shows that the history of the humanities in the postwar era cannot be properly understood without taking the wartime moment of crisis into account.

From here, this chapter proceeds in three parts. In part one, I sketch a brief history of arguments regarding the purpose of liberal education to situate the humanities' 1940s defense in a wider context of previous renderings of the value and purpose of the humanities and liberal education more broadly. Arguments in the 1940s for the usefulness of the humanities were not new, but they were made differently and to different ends than at other periods. In part two, I introduce the "crisis" facing the humanities in the early 1940s and the range of arguments deployed in defense of their teaching and study. Put on the defensive during the early years of the Second World War, teaching and studying the humanities was, in the immediate postwar years, perceived and portrayed as playing offense in new Cold War battles that pitted democracy and capitalism against authoritarianism and communism. Finally, this chapter concludes by briefly considering what lessons this story can offer both historians and teachers of the humanities today.

I

In the nineteenth century, "the humanities" arose as a new classification for secular subjects—such as classics, history, literature, and philosophy—to distinguish them from theological ones, the "divinities."[7] Their study, which comprised an essential feature of a liberal education was understood and talked about in terms of the cultivation and shaping of an individual's mind and character. As its proponents articulated, a liberal, humanities-based education entailed an education of the whole person. A liberal education stressed breadth over specialization and emphasized a student's fullness of life.

The famous Yale Report of 1828, for example, described a liberal education as being "broad, and deep, and solid" and its payoffs as providing both "the *discipline* and the *furniture* of the mind; expanding its powers, and storing it with knowledge." This liberal education, which ensured that "*all* the important mental faculties be brought into exercise" was, in short, about "form[ing] in the student a proper *balance* of character." Its purpose was understood essentially entirely in terms of an individual's self-improvement. When the Yale Report spoke about "usefulness," it did so in the context of imagining a liberally educated man's "commanding influence in [not on or for] society."[8]

Nearly half a century later, in his public writings and addresses on educational reforms in the 1860s, Harvard President Charles W. Eliot echoed this earlier emphasis on liberal education as the cultivation of individual intellect. But he pushed back on the uniformity of education prescribed by the Yale Reports. Instead, he made the case for more individualized, elective or choice-based education that would allow an individual to pursue his own, unique, interests—"his own peculiar taste and capacity." Eliot's well-articulated shift from uniformity to variety indicated, and was a product of, his new and different understanding of a liberal education's purpose. For Eliot, as he put it in his inaugural address at Harvard in 1869, when considering the purpose of an education, the needs of "the State" were paramount. In the context of the immediate past—i.e., the Civil War—and the urgent need to reconstruct the American nation, this was a vitally important insight. An individual's college education was not only so he could be as well-rounded and "balanced" a person as possible (and thus, through his life as much as his work, contribute somehow positively to society), now it was about what was "needful," as Eliot put it, for the operation of the state.[9]

In the early-twentieth-century Progressive Era, Eliot's understanding (and framing) of the relationship between the needs of the state and the purpose of an individual's liberal education found clear expression in the writings and addresses of a new generation of educational leaders. At Dartmouth College, in 1916, for example, President Ernest Martin Hopkins articulated a vision of liberal education's purpose that also underscored service to meet the "needs of the state." Addressing the student body, faculty, alumni, and wider community only months before the United States entered World War One, Hopkins argued that an individual's success was secondary to the success of the wider community. The college and its liberal education existed not for "the individual student" but "for the social group which is the state." Hopkins was clear about what this meant and what made his vision different from previous arguments along similar lines: "The college has always stood for fullness of life for the individual and has thus by indirection benefited the group," he explained. "It must from now on," he continued, "have as its first aim, fullness of life for the group, depending for this largely upon the advantage it can afford the individual."[10]

Hopkins' arguments that moved beyond "fullness of life" for the individual to "fullness of life" for the group—i.e., the state—mirrored those made by historian and former British Ambassador to the United States James Bryce. In his co-authored 1916 "Memorandum on the Limitations of Scientific Education," Bryce had argued that "the shock and stress of the war" opened the possibility that "we may ignore elements in education vital to the formation and maintenance of national character."[11] As indicated by the report's title, the payoffs of a purely scientific education, at least as far as the needs of society or the state were concerned, were limited. While earlier proponents of liberal education had emphasized the development of individual character, now it was clear that the "character" of a nation was also at stake in discussions of liberal education's purpose.

Broadly speaking, between the early nineteenth and early twentieth century, arguments about the purpose of a liberal education, particularly connected to the pursuit of humanistic study, shifted from emphasizing the payoffs or value for the individual receiving the education to emphasizing the importance of this education for a group's greater good—namely, the good of the state or character of the nation. As a result, university and college leaders confronted head-on the popular "contention," as Hopkins articulated, "that all education, to be worth while [sic], must be made utilitarian."[12] They did so by shifting conversations about utility away from a narrow conception of "individualism," professional or career readiness, or "too narrow a regard for practical efficiency," as Bryce had put it, to frame utility in terms of societal or state contributions.[13]

These points that framed the humanities' payoffs and significance beyond an individual's own life or career laid the foundation for arguments, two decades later, about the nature of the humanities' purpose and usefulness. But these arguments in the 1940s would take on a new tenor—that of a *defense* in response to a new and very immediate crisis.

II

In the early 1940s, the humanities, as a subset of the liberal arts, were in crisis.[14] From the outside, they faced opposition from government officials in Washington, D.C., who saw little reason or purpose for their pursuit in a nation now at war. Deeming the teaching and study of the humanities "non-essential," these government officials declared the importance of "technical" over "cultural" training.[15] As a result, at US institutions of higher education, demand for technical training, in the form of engineering and applied science courses that were deemed more relevant for building and operating wartime machinery, soared.

From the inside, the crisis was one of rhetoric, but also one of numbers. Even those elite, private institutions with long, respected traditions of liberal arts education announced a precipitous decline in liberal arts enrollments, as a direct result of the war. In 1941, even before US entry into World War Two, Princeton University, for example, reported a 10 percent decrease—from 27.6 percent of students in 1939 to 17.7 percent in 1941—in the percentage of their students concentrating in the liberal arts. Even the humanistic social sciences—subjects such as history and political science—noted dropping enrollments. Meanwhile, at Princeton, enrollment in the School of Engineering was accelerating.[16]

In 1942, the Office of University Admissions at Columbia University also identified a steep decline in the number of students pursuing liberal arts—especially humanities—degrees, which it attributed to the rise of specialized training programs for servicemen. The Office indicated that the vast majority—some 90 percent—of the 625 freshmen enrolling at Columbia "would pursue courses directly related to one or more of the deferred service plans offered by the Army and Navy." A July 1943 report painted an even more dire picture noting "an even greater decrease," as the *Columbia Spectator* reported, "not only in the number of non-scientific pre-professional students, but also in the registration for straight liberal arts courses." "Of the two hundred and twenty-seven entering Freshman," the student paper explained, citing numbers reflective of a precipitous decline in wartime enrollment overall, "only five have been classified as straight liberal arts students."[17] At the same time that it recorded a figure of less than 2 percent for the number of Columbia's incoming freshman who were liberal arts students, the Office of Admissions identified a full two-thirds of the incoming class as "pre-scientific" students pursuing training and "careers in medicine and engineering."[18]

As war raged overseas, American university officials and faculty themselves knew full well that their institutions would be called upon to deliver more obviously useful and "practical" training than the liberal arts provided. In anticipation of such demands, Princeton President Harold W. Dodds traveled to Nashville, Tennessee in October 1941 to address 1,200 alumni on the topic of the continuing necessity of liberal education. "There is a need as never before," Dodds declared, "for the product of the liberal arts college, the whole man."[19]

But what, exactly, was this need, as Dodds put it, for whole-person education? Why was an education in the humanities important? Was the purpose of "whole-person" learning primarily for the individual, as had been the case in the nineteenth century? Or was it for society, the nation, or even the world, as had been the case earlier in the twentieth century? Or was it for something else entirely? In the face of external opposition and internal skepticism as evidenced by plummeting enrollment numbers, answers to these questions became central for defenders of the humanities in the early 1940s.

Broadly speaking, beginning in 1942, two interconnected sets of arguments emerged—from administrators, faculty, and students—in defense of continuing education in the humanities during the war. Both yoked liberal arts education to the war effort. But they did so in strikingly different ways.

The first set of arguments that emerged made the case that the liberal arts were practical, erasing an old distinction between what did and did not constitute useful education. As Columbia English professor Mark Van Doren argued pointedly in a 1943 book on the subject, liberal education *was* useful education. No education is more useful, Mark Van Doren explained, "than the kind that makes men free to possess their nature." "It is both useful and liberal to be human," he wrote, "just as it takes both skill and knowledge to be wise. If education is not practical when it teaches men to do the things which become men, then no education is practical."[20] At Brown University, President Henry M. Wriston echoed the emphasis on the particular individual, moral preparation liberal education provided, when he argued that humanities training provided its students with "moral preparedness," which was of the utmost importance.[21]

As a teacher of undergraduates, Van Doren himself had no patience for arguments about the inutility of humanities training for the young men of a nation now embroiled in the century's second global war. A veteran of the First World War, the Pulitzer-Prize-winning poet and popular instructor was adamant that a "well rounded education" of the sort the humanities provided was essential, not just for those on the home front, but for soldiers facing action in the heat of battle. In fact, countering opinions of those government officials who stressed technical over humanistic skills as more valuable—and important—for the wartime needs of the nation, Van Doren made a compelling case to the community beyond his classroom that an education in the humanities produced the best soldiers. As reported by the college's student paper the *Columbia Spectator*, he portrayed the humanities as essential because they trained students, through studies of different cultures and different times, to understand "how the mind reacts in situations of danger." The humanities, in short, helped a young man think beyond the particularities of his moment—his own self-interest and limited perspective—to understand his place in history and his role in solving, as the Columbia Humanities Department put it, "the great permanent problems of human life." The result of the cultural and historical perspective this humanities training provided was, as the paper was sure to quote for their readers, "tougher and braver soldiers."[22]

If the liberal-arts-as-useful-arts arguments responded to criticisms of the liberal arts' inutility, the second set of arguments moved the conversation in a new, forward-looking direction—to that of postwar planning. In a variety of ways, these arguments were not so much a defensive reaction to attacks against the liberal arts as they were about shifting the terms of the debate by refocusing the time frame (chronological perspective) for questions to do with utility or usefulness. Advocates of technical training alone, or those who suggested deferring or suspending humanities teaching and learning until after the war, were, according to this argument, decidedly short-sighted. They were unable to see beyond the immediate context of the present moment. Defenders of the humanities, by contrast, portrayed themselves as those with an eye to the future.

Even as Army and Navy training programs at colleges expanded across 1942 and 1943, university leaders doggedly addressed audiences on the importance of planning for a "post-war world."[23] An education in the liberal arts "should help men make democracy work"—not just today, but for tomorrow and the future, Princeton's President Dodds explained. Indeed, the job—that of "making democracy work"—as Dodds framed it, was not the job of a single moment; it was a "ceaseless task," or to repeat Van Doren's words quoted above, one of "the great permanent problems of human life."[24] The humanities' twentieth-century defenders promoted their study in universalizing, forward-looking language that would have been familiar to previous generations of Americans who saw, as the eighteenth-century pamphleteer Thomas Paine put it, their cause being that of "posterity . . . even to the end of time."[25] Qualities that were important in 1943—"trained intelligence, wide range of vision, discipline of mind and spirit, and the other related objectives of education in the liberal arts"—would, Dodds argued, "continue to be of vital importance . . . in all the years to follow."[26]

From the student's perspective—perhaps one tinged by youthful optimism—these diachronic arguments were especially popular. Consider, for example, the well-covered debate that unfolded on the pages of a student newspaper of Dodd's own institution, Princeton, in winter and summer 1942 on the necessity of education in the humanities. Engineering students, students studying in the field of the humanities, and an alumnus headed for officers' training school weighed in on the purpose of the humanities during the war for after the war. While one "would-be humanist," a graduating senior, argued that just as "we must temporarily sacrifice much of our individual freedom to make possible enduring freedom for all, so the humanist must for the moment give up his humanistic pursuits . . . so that it will in the future be possible to make them available to a wider circle," most others who offered up opinions firmly disagreed.[27] A junior engineering student put the situation this way:

> It may take engineers to put planes in the air or tanks in the field, but it's going to take men who have studied in the realms of the humanities and the social sciences to establish a just and a lasting peace when this war is over. Winning the war may be the primary objective right now, but only a fool will advocate that studying in the humanities should be discontinued 'for the duration' thereby eliminating the store of men we will need in the future to establish a permanent peace.[28]

These defenses—embraced and articulated by humanists and non-humanists alike—juxtaposed the narrowness of "essential" wartime contributor classifications with the expansiveness of the humanities' present *and* future necessity. Students "studying the liberal arts are making as definite and important a contribution to the broad strategy of national manpower planning as the technically trained engineer or scientist whose immediate contribution to the war effort brands him as 'essential,'" another Princeton student explained. "The continuance of the liberal arts training looks to immediate and active participation in the war," he acknowledged. But "as a preparation for *after* the war, its importance grows enormously."[29] As one freshman explained, "to win this war is not enough," because "when [the war's] end does come, peace must be established, and the only peace which is lasting is the one which is based on an understanding of men."[30] And, as this young man was learning from his coursework, an understanding of men was what the humanities provided.

How then did these two arguments—for the humanities' present utility and future necessity—translate into practice? On one—immediate—level, the optimistic rhetoric embraced by students and administrators alike did little to prevent the reality that, during the war, true liberal arts education was, in fact, "almost completely suspended" as Van Doren observed in 1943.[31] One another level, however, these defenses accomplished precisely what their proponents wanted: the long-term flourishing of the humanities and social sciences at American universities after the war. Their optimistic, public-facing defenses positioned the humanities to thrive as both an engine and an example of liberal-democratic values during the Cold War.

Despite earlier fears to the contrary, the humanities and humanistic social sciences were not victims of wartime emphases on technical training as the only "essential" training. Instead, they became—or rather were made—central to American foreign and domestic policy in the immediate aftermath of the Second World War. Their teaching and study became essential components of a postwar political-educational project that sought to demonstrate the vitality of American institutions—political, intellectual, social, religious, economic—against perceived threats of totalitarianism and communism at home and abroad.

The humanities early 1940s crisis and response had impacts real and rhetorical, both institutional and intellectual. For example, several specific projects and developments that encapsulated early-Cold War educational policy in the United States had roots in the humanities crisis moment of the early 1940s. President Harry Truman's 1946 Commission on Higher Education produced a multi-volume report on *Higher Education for American Democracy* that echoed earlier emphases on articulating the objectives of liberal education in specifically democratically useful terms.[32] And Harvard's famous postwar program on General Education in a Free Society emerged from its president James Bryant Conant's committee on "The Objectives of a General Education in a Free Society," which he convened in early 1943 both predicting and desiring "strong growth of liberal arts studies in post-war period."[33] The 1945 report "consider[ed] ways and means by which a great instrument of American democracy [its educational system] can both shape the future and secure the foundations of our free society."[34]

Having conceived of liberal education in the humanities as an engine to secure society's *foundations* and shape its *future*, its defenders also construed and portrayed teaching and studying the humanities an essential example of their liberal-democratic values. In these ways, the legacy and impact of the humanities' early 1940s crisis and response was also about the intellectual content—not just the structures—of education. When practitioners and advocates of humanistic education in the late 1940s argued that "today's world must develop a renewed respect for the humanities," their case was essentially this: the challenges and complexities that defined both the present moment and the foreseeable future made the humanities essential and indispensable for both individuals and society.[35] When Columbia President Frank D. Fackenthal addressed his students on the occasion of their graduation in June 1947, for example, he underscored the challenges wrought by the fragility of democracy and the particular *need* for students' humanistic training as a result. Democracy and democratic life were not, nor would they ever be, easy, he declared. To the contrary. It required active, nimble minds to navigate the great "variation and transition" that defined the "challenging, stimulating system" of democracy. "[H]ere," Fackenthal explained, "in the liberal, progressive, democratic life—is the educated man's greatest field of usefulness."[36]

Once a watchword of vocationalism or technical training, "usefulness" was embraced as a celebrated outcome of what was portrayed as necessary training in the humanities. One component of the humanities' new status as essential training was framed in terms of the complexity facing individuals and society in the immediate aftermath of the Second World War. When Fackenthal, for example, made public in 1947 Columbia's case for prioritizing the humanities and social sciences, rather than just focusing on the physical sciences, he explained that "the problems of man in society is [sic] far more complex, and infinitely more important" than those problems that were purely scientific. "Political and humanistic research," the student newspaper summarized for readers, "is the only way to lead the world out of its present chaotic state of affairs."[37]

But at Columbia and elsewhere, it wasn't just research, but also teaching in the humanities and humanistic social sciences that offered paths out of "chaos" to (what those making the arguments saw as) a better, more equitable, prosperous, and secure future. One striking example of the impact these arguments had on the taught curriculum in the late 1940s can be found in the content of courses that focused on the modern history of political thought. As it would turn out, instructing students in the writings of thinkers understood as articulating ideas or values at the heart of "the American way" proved central to the construction, i.e., the postwar invention, of what historian Richard Hofstadter termed in 1948 the American Political Tradition.[38] The American Political Tradition, as it emerged from the writing and teaching of humanists and social scientists, was a made-to-seem-timeless set of commitments to liberalism, democracy, and capitalism that were perceived and presented as standing in opposition to tenets of, for example, socialism associated with, for example, Karl Marx. Its invention entailed and coincided with the creation of a canon of texts—books—intended to provide Americans with "the power to generalize their position and their aims" and thus effectively combat Communists, who had "their book," that is, Marx's *Das Kapital*.[39]

Beginning in the 1940s, university programs in the humanities and humanistic social sciences enthusiastically participated in a postwar, early-

Cold War project of canon formation to create a set of texts that could encapsulate and undergird this American Political Tradition. They reinvented and repurposed old works such as John Locke's *Second Treatise of Government*, Alexis de Tocqueville's *Democracy in America*, and the *Federalist* as essential reading for understanding the origins of American—and what they called Western—political thought. In so doing, they demonstrated both inside and outside their classrooms how a liberal education in the humanities could serve as both an engine and an example of liberal-democratic values.

In accounts of the humanities' and humanistic social sciences' postwar flourishing, it is easy to focus solely on geopolitical, demographic, or financial factors that enabled what Fackenthal observed as "a greater interest than ever in the humanities" in 1949—factors like the GI Bill and the Cold War.[40] It is easy to miss how different things might have looked, and how differently things might have gone, had the moment of crisis for the humanities in the early 1940s prompted teachers, students, or supporters of the humanities to relinquish classifications of "useful" or "essential" or confine their responses—their defense—to pure rebuttal and only to the most immediate threats. In standard narratives of higher education and the history of the humanities in the twentieth-century United States, this wartime moment of crisis for the humanities is easily forgotten, overshadowed by the flourishing and heyday of the humanities in the postwar—Cold War—United States, when young men on the GI Bill flocked to college campuses to study subjects like history, English, and philosophy in record numbers and young women, discouraged from remaining in the workforce, joined a baby-boom generation of humanities degree seekers. But the moment in the early 1940s when academic study and teaching of the humanities faced hostility is worth remembering. And it is worth remembering precisely for what it reveals about the long history of defending the humanities and the need to keep reminding Americans of their value to society.

III

What can we learn from examining past defenses of the humanities? And what can we learn from examining the defenses of the humanities offered up and deployed in the 1940s United States in particular? Answers to these questions are not, despite this chapter's US-focus, restricted to an American setting.[41] They are, moreover, polyvalent. On the one hand, as practitioners of the humanities, we might draw particular inspiration or useful models (positive or negative) from past defenses that framed arguments for the humanities' value in terms of usefulness or that shifted the timeframe of a debate beyond the present—that is, only the most immediate—"needs" of individuals or society to imagining the future. We might think not just in terms of the questions *who* or *what* are the humanities for, but also the question of *when* are the humanities needed? On the other hand, we might quarry past defenses not for inspiration or models for our work but for material to inform our own teaching and writing on the role responding to an opposition or to criticism—be it intellectual, institutional, financial, or demographic—has played in the history of the humanities.

What might this second approach look like? From an instructional standpoint, it could entail sharing with our students and the public how the humanities, in the past, have countered perceptions of their perceived irrelevance. In doing so, it could illuminate that discussing and debating the value of the humanities is not an aberration or the result of a crisis unique to contemporary society anywhere in the world today. Rather, in whatever ways we conceive of and wish to articulate the humanities' relevance and worth today, we are part of a long, dynamic history of the humanities enmeshed in a complex web of questions and concerns that stretch beyond the walls of the academy. In this way, teaching about these past public-facing portrayals of the humanities' value would be less a project of defending the humanities, per se, and more one of understanding and illuminating our place in what is an unfinished and ongoing story of what makes the humanities essential.

Notes

1. One excellent recent discussion of the purpose of the humanities and other liberal arts is Johann N. Neem, *What's the Point of College? Seeking Purpose in an Age of Reform* (Baltimore, MD: Johns Hopkins University Press, 2019).
2. Sheldon Rothblatt, "Old Wine in New Bottles, or New Wine in Old Bottles? The Humanities and Liberal Education in Today's Universities," in *A New Deal for the Humanities*, ed. Gordon Hutner and Feisal G. Mohamed (New Brunswick, NJ: Rutgers University Press, 2016), 34.
3. Helen H. Small, *The Value of the Humanities* (Oxford: Oxford University Press, 2013), 3. For further discussion of Small's decision to avoid framing her account as a defense, see Serena Golden, "The Value of the Humanities," *Inside Higher Ed* (April 28, 2014), online at https://www.insidehighered.com/

news/2014/04/28/new-book-explores-various-arguments-value-humanities (accessed March 9, 2022).
4. Simon During, "Stop Defending the Humanities," *Public Books* (March 1, 2014), online at https://www.publicbooks.org/stop-defending-the-humanities/ (accessed March 9, 2022).
5. Kathleen Fitzpatrick, *Generous Thinking: A Radical Approach to Saving the University* (Baltimore, MD: Johns Hopkins University Press, 2019), 19.
6. For one compelling defense—framed as such—of the humanities, see Martha C. Nussbaum, *Not for Profit: Why Democracy Needs the Humanities* (Princeton, NJ: Princeton University Press, 2010).
7. James Turner, *The Liberal Education of Charles Eliot Norton* (Baltimore, MD: Johns Hopkins University Press, 1999), 257, 380–8, and 449 n. 8 and, especially, Caroline Winterer, *The Culture of Classicism: Ancient Greece and Rome in American Intellectual Life 1780–1910* (Baltimore, MD: Johns Hopkins University Press, 2002).
8. *Reports on the Course of Instruction in Yale College; By a Committee of the Corporation, and the Academical Faculty* (New Haven, CT: printed by Hezekiah Howe, 1828), 6–8, 15. For an account of the Yale Report (1828) as a "forward-looking manifesto for educational reform," see Peter Dobkin Hall, *The Organization of American Culture, 1700–1900: Private Institutions, Elites, and the Origins of American Nationality* (New York: New York University Press, 1982) and Peter Dobkin Hall, "Noah Porter Writ Large? Reflections on the Modernization of American Education and Its Critics, 1866–1916," in *The American College in the Nineteenth Century*, ed. Roger L. Geiger (Nashville, TN: Vanderbilt University Press, 2000), 196–220, at 197.
9. Charles W. Eliot, "Inaugural Address," in *Addresses at the Inauguration of Charles William Eliot President of Harvard College, Tuesday, October 19, 1869* (Cambridge, MA: Sever and Francis, 1869), 40. See also "The New Education: Its Organization," *The Atlantic Monthly* 23 (1869): 203–20. My use of the male pronoun when referring to students is purposeful; it reflects the reality that the students I write about here were all young men.
10. Ernest Martin Hopkins, "The College of the Future" (October 6, 1916), in *Builders of American Universities: Inaugural Addresses*, ed. David Andrew Weaver, vol. 1 (Alton, IL: Shurtleff College Press, 1950), 126, 129, 135.
11. James Bryce et al., "Memorandum on the Limits of Scientific Education," *School and Society* 4, no. 79 (1916): 31.
12. Hopkins "College of the Future," 123.
13. Bryce et al., "Memorandum," 31.
14. The liberal arts also included mathematics and the basic (not applied) sciences.
15. For a summary of this position, see Walter D. Scott, "Van Doren Declares Liberal Arts Vital in War Education," *Columbia Spectator* (19 November 1942).

16. For a summary of these numbers, see "Choice of Courses is Affected by War," *Princeton Herald* (April 18, 1941).
17. "Educators Witnessed Decline in Enrollment in Liberal Arts Last Year; Opinions Reviewed," *Columbia Spectator* (July 23, 1943).
18. "Report Shows Decrease in Liberal Arts Enrollment," *Columbia Spectator* (July 23, 1943).
19. The speech was reported in "Dodds Lauds Students in Report to Trustees; Addresses 1200 Princeton Alumni at Nashville," *Daily Princetonian* (October 28, 1941).
20. Mark Van Doren, *Liberal Education* (New York: Henry Holt, 1943), 166.
21. Quoted in "H. M. Wriston Defends Liberal Arts Training: President of Brown Says College Men Must Prepare for Emergencies During and After War," *Daily Princetonian* (October 13, 1942).
22. Scott, "Van Doren Declares Liberal Arts Vital."
23. At Brown, for example, Wriston emphasized the "great readjustment" after the war and spoke in terms of a liberal arts education preparing students "for emergencies during and after war." Quoted in "H. M. Wriston Defends Liberal Arts Training."
24. Quoted in "E. V. Case '22 Made Colgate President; Dodds is Main Speaker at Ceremonies," *Daily Princetonian* (September 25, 1942).
25. Thomas Paine, *Common Sense; Addressed to the Inhabitants of America . . .* (Philadelphia, PA: printed and sold by R. Bell, 1776), 30.
26. Quoted in "Liberal Arts Program Will Be Kept Intact During Coming Months, Dr. Dodds Promises," *Princeton Herald* (January 8, 1943).
27. Donald Mackenzie, letter to the editor, *Daily Princetonian* (February 11, 1942).
28. "Engineer, '43," letter to the editor, *Daily Princetonian* (February 11, 1942).
29. "The Liberal Arts Again," *Daily Princetonian* (July 6, 1942). Emphasis mine.
30. Paul W. Taylor, letter to the editor, *Daily Princetonian* (February 11, 1942).
31. Van Doren, *Liberal Education*, vii.
32. Not all observers were pleased with or satisfied by the report's definition of the concept of democracy and its emphasis on giving "students every possible experience in democratic processes within the college community." See, e.g., Richmond C. Beatty, "The Truman Report on Higher Education," *Georgia Review* 2, no. 3 (1948): 362–72, at 362. On the Commission's report, see Ethan Schrum, "Establishing a Democratic Religion: Metaphysics and Democracy in the Debates Over the President's Commission on Higher Education," *History of Education Quarterly* 47, no. 3 (2007): 277–301.
33. This was the title the *Daily Princetonian* gave an article covering Conant's committee: "Harvard President Predicts Strong Growth of Liberal Arts Studies in Post-War Period," *Daily Princetonian* (January 18, 1943).

34. James Bryant Conant, introduction to *General Education in a Free Society: Report of the Harvard Committee* (Cambridge, MA: Harvard University Press, 1950), x.
35. "President's Report to Trustees Lauds University's War Contributions," *Columbia Spectator* (March 17, 1947).
36. Frank Diehl Fackenthal, "Equal Opportunity: Address delivered June 3, 1947, at the 193d Commencement of Columbia University," in Fackenthal, *The Greater Power and Other Addresses* (New York: Columbia University Press, 1949), 14.
37. "President's Report to Trustees Lauds University's War Contributions;" "The University's Place," *Columbia Spectator* (March 17, 1947).
38. On the invention of "the American way," see Wendy L. Wall, *Inventing the "American Way": The Politics of Consensus from the New Deal to the Civil Rights Movement* (Oxford: Oxford University Press, 2008); Richard Hofstadter, *The American Political Tradition and the Men Who Made It* (New York: Knopf, 1948).
39. Editorial, "Western Faith: At Last a Good Basic Book to Fling at the Communists," *LIFE Magazine* (March 21, 1949): 36. The pretext of the editorial is its review of Paul McGuire, *There's Freedom for the Brave: An Approach to World Order* (New York: W. Morrow, 1949), which the editors suggest Americans might "fling in the faces of the Communists."
40. Quoted in "President's Report Out," *Columbia Spectator* (February 1, 1949).
41. Indeed, scholars have demonstrated the extent to which recent crises in the humanities are global phenomena. See, e.g., Kristofer Schipper, *The Gene Bank of Culture: Reflections on the Function of the Humanities* (Wassenaar: NIAS, 1994); Henk Wesseling, *The Idea of an Institute for Advanced Study: Some Reflections on Education, Science and Art* (Wassenaar: NIAS, 2002); and Nussbaum, *Not for Profit*, Ch. 7.

Part V

Visions of the Future

14

The Postcritical Turn: Unraveling the Meaning of "Post" and "Turn"

Herman Paul

Introduction

What Napoleon Bonaparte and postmodernism have in common, a Marxist film critic once quipped, is that they ruled their empires through a throng of loyal relatives. Like the French emperor, who appointed siblings to thrones across Europe, postmodernism conquered the humanities with help of various "discursive uncles, brothers-in-law, and cousins," such as post-capitalism, post-Marxism, post-feminism, and post-theory.[1] Clearly, this Napoleonic analogy, with its depiction of postmodernism as a foreign invader, conveyed a sense of unease about the rise to popularity of "post-concepts" (post-ideology, poststructuralism, postcolonialism) in the late twentieth-century humanities. In addition, however, the analogy hints at something of historical interest: intellectual affinities or even kinship relations between post-terms that entered academic parlance with so much force that already by the late 1980s, several commentators had the impression that they were living in an "era of posts."[2] This raises some intriguing questions: Where did post-concepts like postmodernism come from? What made them so irresistible that scholars could not stop inventing new ones, from post-political and post-traditional to post-racist and post-sexual? What kind of aspirations did the prefix express? And if it is true, as this chapter will argue, that "post" was malleable enough to denote a range of different things—intellectual debt and independency, individual self-fashioning and broad societal change, progress and regression—what was the point of bringing all this together under a single heading?

This chapter explores these questions through a recent case study: the rise of "post-criticism" as a rallying cry in, most notably, the field of literary studies. Although the term goes back to the 1950s, post-criticism or "postcritique," as some prefer to say, became a household term only by the second decade of the twenty-first century. To no small degree, this was due to Rita Felski, an American literary scholar whose provocative musings on the limitations of the "critical" paradigm in literary studies were enthusiastically welcomed by colleagues who dreamt of new directions in the study of literature. At the same time, Felski met with bitter opposition from scholars who feared that postcritique would amount to a sell-out of critical thinking in a neoliberal age. This caused large numbers of especially American literary scholars to engage in spirited debate. Was Felski right to argue that literary studies had become too much embroiled in critique, too much intent on exposing ideological complicity, and therefore too negative? Was it true that critical theory as practiced by Theodor Adorno, Fredric Jameson, or Judith Butler had been insufficiently responsive to the affective appeals of literary texts? And how fair was it to argue that critique, sometimes even caricatured as *crrritique*,[3] did not allow for attitudes other than the suspicious, interrogative stance of a critic interested only in unearthing hidden assumptions?

What is notable about these questions is that they touch not only on the ethos of humanities scholars—on dispositions, attitudes, and virtues characteristic of the persona of the scholar—but also on how academics do or do not wish to carry on approaches inherited from the past. This is perhaps the most important reason why post-concepts are so much *en vogue* these days. Like the equally popular trope of a "turn"—the linguistic turn, the cultural turn, the practice turn, and so on—post-concepts allow scholars to articulate in highly condensed form how they want to relate to their discipline's past. Both "post" and "turn," therefore, show what scholars identify with, what they seek to get rid of, to what or whom they feel indebted, and what they regard as obstacles to progress. To illustrate how historians of the humanities might approach such "posts" and "turns," this chapter analyses the "postcritical turn" through three different lenses. It starts with a brief exercise in *conceptual history* (where did the adjective "postcritical" come from?), continues with a *rhetorical analysis* (what gave the term its rhetorical power?), and concludes with an attempt to unravel the *temporalities* implied in "post" and "turn."

A Concise History of the Term

Tracing a concept's origins, spread, and changing meanings over time is what historians call "conceptual history" (*Begriffsgeschichte*). In the case of "postcritical," conceptual historical analysis shows that, in English at least, the term established itself shortly after the Second World War, perhaps not coincidentally at a time that also saw the rise to prominence of other post-concepts, such as post-Christian, post-secular, and post-industrial.[4] Philosophers were among the earliest adopters of the term. Although, prior to the 1950s, the adjective post-critical had already been applied to thinkers who tried to break the spell of Immanuel Kant's critical heritage,[5] it was Michael Polanyi who, in 1958, firmly put the term on the agenda. Dissociating himself from critical rationalism as practiced by Karl Popper, among others, Polanyi argued that all knowledge rests on idioms, attitudes, and impulses that "shape our vision of the nature of things."[6] The subtitle of his book, *Towards a Post-Critical Philosophy*, pointed out what a recovery of this "non-rational" element would entail: a philosophy freed from the illusion that the world could be rationally mastered.

Meanwhile, in the 1950s and 1960s, post-criticism got currency among theologians, too. Almost without exception, the term was applied to Karl Barth and other "neo-orthodox" theologians who tried to get beyond the legacy of nineteenth-century Biblical criticism by emphasizing that, in spite of its historical materiality, Scripture was chiefly a locus of divine revelation.[7] Although Barth himself did not like the label,[8] the term post-critical stuck, especially in the United States, where Barth-inspired theologians like Hans Frei and George Lindbeck would develop a "postliberal" school at Yale Divinity School that was explicitly committed to post-critical Biblical hermeneutics.[9] Interestingly, this project also drew on the French philosopher Paul Ricoeur, whose 1960s explorations into the possibilities of "post-critical faith" tried to develop an alternative to what the author called a "hermeneutics of suspicion."[10]

For two or three decades, philosophers and theologians had a near-monopoly on post-critical theorizing.[11] Only by the late 1980s, this began to change, partly through the influence of a widely discussed essay by literary theorist Gregory Ulmer. This piece was not about Biblical interpretation, but about artistic techniques of collage and montage as advocated by a host of twentieth-century avant-gardists, from Walter Benjamin and Bertolt Brecht to Jacques Derrida. Taking his cue from Roland Barthes, Ulmer argued that the rise to prominence of these techniques revealed the collapse of an age-old distinction between literature and criticism. Instead of seeing criticism as a realm of second-order reflection on the first-order discourse of literature, Ulmer followed Barthes in thinking that the reflective stances that literature allows for can be as "meta" as those associated with criticism. Consequently, for Ulmer, post-criticism denoted a situation in which critics could no longer claim a privileged position vis-à-vis literature: they had all become "writers."[12] This implied that, for Ulmer, post-criticism was not an emerging possibility, as it had been for Polanyi, but a fait accompli: most twentieth-century avant-gardists had already become post-critical.

Although Ulmer occupies a relatively minor place in the history of the humanities, citation patterns reveal that his article helped introduce post-criticism to fields other than philosophy and theology. (In that respect, Ulmer resembles Ihab Hassan, the American literary critic who contributed much to postmodernism and posthumanism entering academic parlance.)[13] In the late 1980s and 1990s, the idea of a postcritical move began to circulate, initially in fields were "critical" was understood to denote a specific school or approach. Critical pedagogy is a case in point: the adjective referred to a type of pedagogy inspired by Paulo Freire and the Frankfurt School. Consequently, the term postcritical appealed to feminists like Patti Lather, who took her lead from Ulmer in arguing that "postmodern" attentiveness to difference and otherness could help feminist pedagogues move beyond the "largely male inscribed liberation models of critical pedagogy."[14] Similarly, post-criticism could be envisioned as challenging the reign of critical theory, as literary scholar R. Lane Kauffmann did in response to Derrida-inspired deconstructionism as practiced at Yale by Paul de Man and J. Hillis Miller.[15]

Whereas in these cases the word "critical" had a rather clearly identifiable referent, post-criticism increasingly also found its way into debates where such tangible referents did not exist. For instance, in the early 1990s, Elizabeth Lester used post-criticism ("a concept developed by Gregory Ulmer") to challenge the hegemony of a scientifically oriented research culture in media and communication studies.[16] A few years later, cultural theorist Sari Thomas used the label for a type of study that "both follows from and disengages with traditional critical perspectives." Notably, Thomas did not specify what she regarded as traditional, while the contours of her post-critical alternative also remained shrouded: "Included as postcritical theory is much of what is called poststructuralism, postmodernism and... cultural studies"—to which Thomas added names as varied as those of Jean Baudrillard, Pierre Bourdieu, Michel Foucault, and Jean-François Lyotard.[17] Apparently, post-criticism did not always serve a well-defined purpose. The term could also be invoked as a sign of the times or be mentioned in one breath with other post-concepts (postmodernism, postconstructivism, postcolonialism) that hinted at some fundamental changes being in the air. This explains why English professor Rob Latham could equate "what Ulmer calls 'postcriticism'" with "postmodern theory" in general and why, by the turn of the century, "postcritical theories" could be lumped together with deconstructionism, poststructuralism, and postcolonialism as "major new theories" to which cultural studies had to relate.[18]

The early years of the twenty-first century witnessed a further spread of the term, increasingly in its adjective form, "postcritical." In addition to ongoing discussions on postcritical pedagogy and Biblical hermeneutics, ethnographers and political economists began to search for avenues beyond a type of critique that they perceived as indebted to colonial thinking ("ethnography is the ultimate colonialist project and critical theory the ultimate modernist project").[19] Janet Wolff proposed a "postcritical aesthetics," intent on rescuing the concept of beauty from decades of feminist critique, while art curators found themselves discussing post-critical museology, characterized by a greater diversity of agents than customary in academic museum criticism.[20] In the early 2010s, even "postcritical social science" entered the conversation, premised on the idea that research is not only a methodologically controlled investigation, but also a human activity fraught with tensions and imbued with relational meaning.[21] Clearly, these ventures into postcritical territory did not have a common agenda. If they shared anything at all, it was an interest in exploring hitherto neglected elements of interpretation—personal, emotional, affective dimensions in particular—or, negatively, a sense of fatigue with academics who always seem to "hide" behind theories and methods.

Although the late 1990s and early 2000s also saw the publication of texts that have been identified retrospectively as foundational for Felski's postcritical movement—Eve Sedgwick's "Paranoid Reading and Reparative Reading," Bruno Latour's "Why Has Critique Run Out of Steam?" and Stephen Best's and Sharon Marcus's plea for "surface reading"—none of these celebrated essays actually spent a single word on post-criticism.[22] They became known as postcritical only after 2013, when Felski proposed "postcritical reading" as an umbrella term for a broad assortment of attempts at fostering non-suspicious readerly attitudes.[23]

> Like others, I find the vagueness of the term to be also its singular strength, allowing it to serve as a placeholder for emerging ideas and barely glimpsed possibilities. It is a term that is gaining traction in various fields to denote pragmatic and experimental modes of engagement that are not prefortified by general theories. The role of the term "postcritical," then, is neither to prescribe the forms that reading should take nor to dictate the attitudes that critics must adopt; it is to steer us away from the kinds of arguments we know how to conduct in our sleep.[24]

Notably, in these lines, Felski not only continued her long-time advocacy for modes of reading that merge "analysis and attachment, criticism and love."[25] She also strategically aligned this project to a range of other intellectual pursuits, in and outside of the field of literary studies, all of which she called postcritical. Accordingly, like Ulmer twenty years before, Felksi used the term for bringing a variety of trends together under one rubric. What lent additional force to this "act of seeing things together" was that Felski depicted the postcritical brigade as a scholarly vanguard, bored by a type of criticism that most scholars still experienced as "normal science." By moving beyond the critical paradigm, this academic avant-garde would pave the way for "a new era of 'postcritique.'"[26]

Four Features of the Term

What does this little exercise in conceptual history reveal? Clearly, it does not offer a Whiggish genealogy of the postcritical movement around Felski—one that identifies "forerunners," "contributors," or "sources of inspiration."[27] Instead, I have sketched how the term post-criticism entered the humanities as a tool that allowed scholars in and outside of the field of literary studies to negotiate their relations with existing paradigms in their disciplines, while opening up spaces for conceptual, methodological, or attitudinal reorientation. To understand how post-criticism made this possible, it is worth highlighting four features of the term.

First, the story of how post-criticism found its way into the humanities clearly shows that the term had different meanings in different fields. Postcritical philosophy as envisioned by Polanyi showed only little overlap with post-critical pedagogy as promoted by Lather. Even within fields, the "multivalent character of the 'post-critical' trend" was frequently noted.[28] As a Biblical scholar observed in 1995: "Postcritical exegesis can be poststructuralist exegesis, for example, and can amount to a critique of traditional historical criticism for being insufficiently critical. Such exegesis, in the New Testament context, also tends to be post-Christian. Then again, postcritical exegesis can be confessional ... , unabashedly taking its inspiration from precritical exegesis."[29] According to sociologist-ethnographer George Noblit, this heterogeneity implied that the quest for an unequivocal definition of post-criticism was doomed to fail from the outset: "Postcritical ethnography is not one thing, rather it is a critical *space* where many things can go on simultaneously."[30]

Secondly, in this realm of academic reflexivity, post-criticism did not roam alone: it almost always shared this space with other post-concepts. Polanyi's post-critical philosophy, for instance, was also dubbed post-rationalist,[31] whereas the Yale theologians who advocated post-critical hermeneutics became known as post-liberals. When in the 1980s postmodernism came to dominate the intellectual agenda, post-criticism was habitually associated with the buzzwords of postmodernism, poststructuralism, and postcolonialism (not to mention post-Marxism and post-feminism). From this it follows that the appeal of post-criticism as a tool for negotiating intellectual debts and aspirations can only be explained in the context of an entire "world of 'posts'"—a world that a somewhat skeptical historian in 1994 described as one "that knows where it has been and needs to assert that it is no longer there."[32]

Clearly, however, not everyone used post-criticism as a call to arms. The case of Ulmer shows that the term could also be used descriptively, as label for a gradual dissolving of the literature-criticism divide that had already started with Benjamin and Brecht. Likewise, the American art critic Hal Foster—perhaps not coincidentally the editor of the volume in which Ulmer's piece appeared—used post-criticism as designator for an era in which neither curators nor art critics still seemed to give a dime for criticism: "Bullied by conservative commentators, most academics no longer stress the importance of critical thinking for an engaged citizenry, and, dependent on corporate sponsors, most curators no longer promote the critical debate once deemed essential to the public reception of advanced art."[33] As his tone betrayed, Foster did not exactly applaud this silencing of critical thinking. In a time when, politically speaking, states of emergency seem to become the rule instead of the exception, "it is a bad time to go post-critical."[34] What this shows is that *first-order* uses of the term, by authors dreaming of a postcritical future, and *second-order* uses, by academics analysing postcritical trends in the present, could have different evaluative connotations. Whereas first-order uses were almost always affirmative, second-order discourse could also be outspokenly dismissive.[35]

Finally, in terms of its ability to provoke debate and stimulate fresh thinking, post-criticism was most successful when authors used it to bring a broad range of existing trends, developments, or perspectives together under a single heading. Just as Ulmer's text resonated widely because it depicted figures as diverse as Derrida, Marshall McLuhan (the media theorist) and John Cage (the composer) as engaged in one postcritical project, so Felski's post-criticism stuck because it identified a single "mood" among intellectuals as diverse as Franco Moretti, Eve Sedgwick, and Amanda Anderson.[36] Sari Thomas therefore hit the nail on its head when she interpreted the term "as a rubric-of-convenience in which to collapse a number of extant movements."[37] The strength of post-criticism, or any other post-concept for that matter, lay in its ability to serve as a "colligatory concept"—a concept that identifies a common denominator in what seems a heterogeneous variety of trends.[38]

Past-Present Relations

Still, this "lumping together" did not prevent authors from using post-criticism for a variety of purposes, to the point of challenging the very unity in diversity that the concept was supposed to identify. Take the volume *Critique and Postcritique* (2017) that Felski co-edited with Elizabeth Anker. It contains eleven chapters by authors who are all broadly sympathetic to postcritical reading. What they find appealing, however, differs considerably. Some authors feel attracted to the *aesthetic* possibilities that postcritique seems to offer. They envision a rehabilitation of "pleasurable engagement with artistic works for their own sake" or "for the sake of feelings" that works of art can evoke.[39] Others are intrigued by the *political* aspirations of post-critical criticism an in age when faith in a better future—a premise on which the classic aims of liberation and emancipation were based—has become difficult to sustain.[40] Christopher Castiglia, in his turn, speaks in an *ethical* register about hopefulness, idealism, and imagination as values central to postcritical reading, as do the editors in highlighting interpretative virtues like "respect, care, and attention."[41]

How different the angles are from which scholars approach postcritical criticism is even more apparent from reviews of *Critique and Postcritique* and Felski's earlier book, *The Limits of Critique* (2015). Unsurprisingly, *aesthetic* considerations loomed large in responses to an author who asked provocatively: "Why are we ... so excruciatingly tongue-tied about our loves?"[42] Although most reviewers agreed that love of literature and identification with literary characters have a legitimate place in literary criticism, some feared that Felski's almost unreserved endorsement of readers' affections runs the risk of "fetishization."[43] *Ethical* questions were raised by reviewers who did not see Anker and Felski practice the virtues they preached. Andrew Lyndon Knighton, for instance, lamented their "reckless oppositional swashbuckling," while Bruce Robbins took issue with the editors' style of reasoning, which he described as "aggressive" and "arrogant" despite its rhetoric of humility.[44] At another occasion, Robbins even went so far as to say that Felski personified the very "holier-than-thou self-righteousness" that she said to find objectionable in suspicious reading.[45] Thirdly, in a country where the outcome of the 2016 presidential election caused a shock throughout the humanities, *political* considerations were not far away either. One reviewer argued that privileging "affects" over "arguments" might bring postcritique in dangerously close proximity to post-truth, while another said that its fashionable bashing of critical theory reminded him of "political correctness-baiting" on the right end of the political spectrum.[46]

Crucially, however, regardless whether commentators privileged aesthetic, ethical, or political considerations (not to mention religious ones),[47] the key issue for all of them was how twenty-first-century academics could or should relate to an established tradition of critical reading. Even though both authors and reviewers adopted different perspectives and spoke in different idioms, what they had in common was that they explored, each from their own point of view, to what extent "critique" or "criticism" was a project worthy of being continued in the twenty-first century. Sympathizers and critics alike thus positioned themselves in a "now" that they distinguished from a "then" when critique, however defined, was still in its heyday. This move, in its turn, allowed them to assess the continuity or discontinuity between what literary scholars did back then and what their successors here and now should do. Even though this continuity, or lack thereof, was obviously not a matter of black and white—which explains why authors felt a need to distinguish between aesthetic, ethical, and political aspects— the red thread running through their exchanges was a negotiating of "past-present relations": modes of relating one's activities in the present to those of predecessors in the past.[48]

In this negotiating of past-present relations, four major moments can be distinguished. First, the past at stake had to be defined: What was "criticism" or "critique"? Did it denote something as broad as aesthetic criticism since the eighteenth century or, more specifically, the legacy of Frankfurt School-style critical theory?[49] Secondly, how accurate was Felski's portrayal of this tradition? To what extent did someone like Jürgen Habermas, with his strong commitment to communicative action, fit Felski's picture of critique as adversarial?[50] Thirdly, in what sense, if any, could critique be classified as "past"? Was its ethos of suspicion indebted to Cold War rationality or did ideology critique depend on narratives of modernization that were no longer seen as plausible?[51] Finally, taking a stance vis-à-vis the past as defined in step three required a normative assessment. How fruitful, compelling, important, or inspiring was this past according to present-day readers? If scholars seek to move beyond the critical past (however defined), what should they leave behind and what should they take forward?

Interestingly, while commentators seldom tried to solve definitional issues, they spent a lot of energy on the second issue: the fairness of Felski's accusations. Wasn't it ungenerous to argue that "critique sounds unmistakably foreign, in a sexy, mysterious, pan-European kind of way, conjuring up tableaus of intellectuals gesturing wildly in some-wreathed Parisian cafes"?[52] Did such images do any justice to critique in its various historical incarnations? "Is againstness really an accurate description of Marx? Freud? Derrida? Foucault? Judith Butler?"[53] And how convincing was it to depict Jameson as a suspicious reader, given that he had also welcomed Ricoeur's "positive hermeneutics" as a corrective to the "negative dialectic" of Marxist ideology critique?[54] The fourth moment elicited much commentary, too. Even scholars firmly committed to defending critique had to admit that feminist or anticolonial criticism as practiced in the postwar decades no longer fitted the present moment, if only because, for many people across the globe, its promise to bring justice and equality had not been fulfilled. Although not all of them shared Daniel Scott's diagnosis of critique having developed from "romance" (a project based on utopian hope) into "tragedy" (a mode of diagnosis that leaves the critic in the position of a spectator, without much transformative capacity),[55] several authors recommended a toning down of expectations, a "trimming" of grand gestures, or a rearticulation of critique "in a minor key."[56] Even Felski's opponents agreed that "a change of tactic" was needed.[57] As the editors of a broadly anti-postcritical volume voiced the challenge: "What sort of critical thinking is needed in a time when its very existence seems threatened? . . . To be faithful to its core principle, critique must involve its self-critique. That is the only way, in these critical times, to move forward."[58]

One may wonder: Doesn't all this heterogeneity—the aesthetic, ethical, and political aspects of the debate, the different definitions of critique, the multiple positions from which scholars contributed to the conversation, and their lack of agreement on how critique should adapt to the times—warrant the conclusion that the colligation achieved by "postcritical" is merely illusionary? As long as we expect the phrase to operate *descriptively*, as representing a reality "out there," some dose of skepticism is justified indeed. As a descriptive term, postcritique has something potentially misleading. There is no cohort of postcritical readers united by a common sense of where they come from and where they want to go. Arguably, however, the strength of the term does not lie in its descriptive potential. Instead of *representing* reality, it does the performative work of *creating* its own reality. Postcritique is "real" to the extent that literary scholars engage in lively debate on "where they come from" and "where they want to go." Postcritique consists of book reviews, journal articles, special issues, forum sections, and blog posts that all, in one way or another, reflect on what criticism entails and whether or how scholars should move beyond its supposed limitations. Seen in this light—"If men define situations as real, they are real in their consequences"[59]—postcritique is best understood as a realm of reflection in which scholars try to relate to the past, assess the current state of their field, and dream about routes to the future.

Post-Prefixes and Turn Talk

This eventually enables us to address the question with which this chapter started: What is the meaning of "post" and "turn" in "postcritical turn"? Clearly, the post-prefix not only conveys that change is in the air, but also that this change should be welcomed as a step towards a more self-reflective, socially relevant type of critical activity. Even if the temporality implied in the "post" is not straightforwardly progressive, it does depict postcritique as inaugurating a new era in literary criticism. This, in its turn, draws on an understanding of time that can be described as "a unidirectional chronology, where things and phenomena succeed each other along a metaphorical line of time."[60] Arguably, this notion of time accounts for much of the concept's rhetorical power. The strength of the "post" lies in its ability to make the postcritical vanguard appear as more up to date, more attuned to the present, more responsive to the demands of the time than its predecessor, the critical paradigm that is no longer at the cutting edge of things.

To see more clearly what this does and does not mean, it is helpful to distinguish the kind of transition implied here from two related, but different understandings of change. First, the "post" in postcritical does not imply an epochal transformation of the kind that "post-industrial" and "post-Christian" once denoted. In the decades following the Second World War, these two post-terms were used to convey that mechanical industry would not have much of a future in the United States and that Europe was no longer a Christian continent. Both post-terms thus hinted at broad societal changes.[61] What distinguishes postcritique from these older concepts is not only its more limited scope—the term refers exclusively to academic work done in the humanities and social sciences—but also its focus on individuals intentionally changing their minds. Even if authors invoke the concept of an era ("This is where we are: in what can be viewed as a post-critical era"),[62] this doesn't refer to scholars involuntarily entering a new stage of history. It rather denotes a moment when a conversation about the limits of critique is perceived as more "advanced" than simple continuation of the critical enterprise.

Second, the "post" in postcritical does by no means imply a rupture with the past. It should rather be interpreted as denoting a realm of reflection where scholars can "clear their throat" to indicate disagreement, doubt, or a desire to do things differently. As such, it resembles the "post" in postmodern and postcolonial, of which Kwame Anthony Appiah has argued that it served as a "space-clearing gesture," aimed at broadening a conversation rather than abandoning it.[63] Nonetheless, this space-clearing gesture is always imbued with temporal meaning. It points to something *beyond* the current state of affairs, *beyond* the way we do things now. The post-prefix thus invokes a notion of temporality that, despite its resistance to supersessionary schemes of periodization, does assume that raising new questions and exploring new avenues is better than continuing with existing ones.

If this already implies a state of "restless movement,"[64] the metaphor of a postcritical "turn" even stronger suggests that *mobilitas loci* rather than *stabilitas loci* is the norm of our time.[65] Turns are, of course, related to posts (not to mention "waves" in feminist studies and "new" or "neo" prefixes as in New Historicism and Neo-Victorianism).[66] Turns, however, carry more explicit connotations of either-or, judging by the fact that they are typically visualized by road junctions or described in terms of vehicles turning right or left. As Judith Surkis observes in a study of American historians debating the linguistic turn: "The 'turn' was increasingly described as something that historians should or should not take, as if it were a road or a means of transport."[67] Just how little room the image left for continued negotiation of past-present relations, is apparent from Joyce Appleby's not exactly flattering description of the linguistic turn:

> After historians made that last turn marked "linguistic," they ran into some dangerous curves. Scholarly vehicles were totaled; avenues of inquiry left in disrepair. The timid got out their maps to look for alternative routes to the past; die-hards demanded that the dividers be repainted. Some who managed to drive beyond the curves recommended ditching the cars for buses. Fueled by renewable verbal meanings, these buses, they said, add *jouissance* to the trip, even if they never take you where you want to go.[68]

Even if others were more excited about the journey and its destination, the image of a turn, whether used positively or negatively, always seems to imply movement through space: travel from one location to another. This makes "turn talk" potentially more radical in its implications than post-prefixes. While "post" still allows for continuity amid change, the image of a turn implies a more rigid either-or: "It logically prohibits further co-habitation between what you turn to and thereby turn away from."[69] Against this background, one may wonder whether David Sessions was right in characterizing the postcritical turn "as the latest instance of a scholarly phenomenon in which expansive constellations of philosophical ideas and methodological approaches are reduced and consolidated into a single object for the purposes of establishing a supersession narrative."[70] Even if Anker and Felski explicitly denied the charge of abandoning the critical tradition,[71] didn't their invocation of the "turn" metaphor imply, unintentionally perhaps, that colleagues less receptive to the idea of exploring affective dimensions of literary reading were stuck in the past? Would it at all be possible to propose a "turn" without suggesting, however subtly, the arrival of a new era that will turn existing paradigms into anachronisms?[72]

Conclusion

This chapter has explored three ways of approaching "posts" and "turns" in the history of the humanities. First, it has shown the importance of *conceptual history* for tracing how concepts travel across time, space, and disciplines. In the case of post-criticism, this exercise managed to challenge Whiggish narratives of the kind that depict Polanyi and Ricoeur as "forerunners" of Felski, while leaving Biblical scholars out of the picture. Secondly, a *rhetorical analysis* of post-terms as "colligatory concepts," intent on creating unity in diversity, revealed that the strength of these concepts typically lies in their ability to connect a heterogeneous set of ideas and trends. This explains why post-terms have the habit of generating ever new meanings instead of acquiring stable definitions. Thirdly, an analysis of *temporalities* and *past-present relations* brought to light a deep ambiguity in how postcritique relates to critique. Even if the post-prefix is not intended to imply a rupture with the past, the suggestion of supersession is hard to avoid, especially when spatial images of a "turn" are paired with temporal notions of an era "beyond" critique. Finally, throughout the chapter, it became evident that each of these three modes of analysis can benefit from comparison with other "posts" and "turns" in the humanities, if only because the terms are often entangled in various ways.

Clearly, the analysis provided in this chapter is not exhaustive. In addition, one might engage in *reception history*, for instance by tracing how Felksi's proposal has been received in other disciplines, such as history and art history. More importantly, perhaps, one might probe deeper into an *academic market economy* that puts a premium on restless innovation.[73] What does the proliferation of post-prefixes—think of post-feminism being superseded by post-postfeminism and even post-post-postfeminism[74]—tell us about the forces that shape contemporary academic life? An examination of what Jameson calls the "cultural logic of late capitalism" might well reveal that post-terms, instead of being loyal siblings of a Napoleonic emperor, are signs of the power of a regime that forces even humanities scholars to innovate at ever-accelerating speed.[75]

Notes

1. Andrew Britton, "The Myth of Postmodernism: The Bourgeois Intelligentsia in the Age of Reagan," *CineAction* 13/14 (1988): 3–17, at 3.
2. Richard J. Bernstein, *Philosophical Profiles: Essays in a Pragmatic Mode* (Philadelphia, PA: University of Pennsylvania Press, 1986), 9; Allan Megill, "The Identity of American Neo-Pragmatism; or, Why Vico Now?" *New Vico Studies* 5 (1987): 99–116, at 110.

3. Rita Felski, *The Limits of Critique* (Chicago, IL: University of Chicago Press, 2015), 120.
4. Herman Paul, "Introduction: Post-Concepts in Historical Perspective," in *Post-Everything: An Intellectual History of Post-Concepts*, ed. Herman Paul and Adriaan van Veldhuizen (Manchester: Manchester University Press, 2021), 1–14.
5. E.g., Arthur E. Murphy, review of *Symbolism, Its Meaning and Effect* by Alfred North Whitehead, *The Journal of Philosophy* 26, no. 18 (1929): 489–98, at 493; John Leard, review of *Intuition* by K. W. Wild, *Philosophy* 13, no. 51 (1938): 371–2, at 371.
6. Michael Polanyi, *Personal Knowledge: Towards a Post-Critical Philosophy* (London: Routledge & Kegan Paul, 1958), 266.
7. E.g., Charles T. Harrison, "A Post-Critical Guide to the Bible," *The Sewanee Review* 58, no. 4 (1950): 738–40; David Wesley Soper, *Major Voices in American Theology: Six Contemporary Leaders* (Philadelphia, PA: Westminster Press, 1953), 71–105. See also, in German, Rudolf Smend, "Nachkritische Schriftauslegung," in *ΠΑΡΡΗΣΙΑ: Karl Barth zum achtzigsten Geburtstag am 10. Mai 1966*, ed. Eberhard Busch, Jürgen Fangmeier, and Max Geiger (Zurich: EVZ, 1966), 215–37, at 218–9.
8. Eberhard Jüngel, "Theologie als Metakritik: Zur Hermeneutik theologischer Exegese," in Jüngel, *Barth-Studien* (Zürich: Benziger; Gütersloh: Gütersloher Verlagshaus, 1982), 83–98, at 88.
9. Mark I. Wallace, *The Second Naïveté: Barth, Ricoeur, and the New Yale Theology* (Macon, GA: Mercer University Press, 1990); Paul J. DeHardt, *The Trial of the Witnesses: The Rise and Decline of Postliberal Theology* (Malden, MA: Blackwell, 2006).
10. Paul Ricoeur, *De l'interprétation: essai sur Freud* (Paris: Du Seuil, 1965), 37, 40.
11. See, e.g., Jeffrey Kay, "Hans Urs von Balthasar: A Post-Critical Theologian?" *Concilium* 141 (1981): 84–9; Edward Joseph Echeverria, *Criticism and Commitment: Major Themes in Contemporary "Post-Critical" Philosophy* (Amsterdam: Rodopi, 1981); William H. Poteat, *Polanyian Meditations: In Search of a Post-Critical Logic* (Durham, NC: Duke University Press, 1985).
12. Gregory L. Ulmer, "The Object of Post-Criticism," in *The Anti-Aesthetic: Essays on Postmodern Culture*, ed. Hal Foster (Port Townsend, WA: Bay Press, 1983), 83–110, at 86. See also Gregory L. Ulmer, "The Post-Age," *Diacritics*, 11 (1981): 39–56.
13. Hans Bertens, "The 'Post' in Literary Postmodernism: A History," in Paul and Van Veldhuizen, *Post-Everything*, 135–54; Yolande Jansen, Jasmijn Leeuwenkamp, and Leire Urricelqui, "Posthumanism and the 'Posterizing Impulse,'" ibid., 215–33.
14. Patti Lather, "Post-Critical Pedagogies: A Feminist Reading," *Education and Society* 9, no. 1–2 (1991): 100–11, at 106. See also, in the same field, Ellen

Schwartz, "Emancipating Pedagogy: A Postcritical Response to 'Standard' School Knowledge," *Journal of Curriculum Studies* 28, no. 4 (1996): 397–418 and Bill Green, "Teaching for Difference: Learning Theory and Post-Critical Pedagogy," in *Teaching Popular Culture: Beyond Radical Pedagogy*, ed. David Buckingham (London: UCL Press, 1998), 177–97.

15. R. Lane Kauffmann, "Post-Criticism, or the Limits of Avant-Garde Theory," *Telos* 67 (1986): 186–95.
16. Elli Lester-Massman, "The Dark Side of Comparative Research," *Journal of Communication Inquiry* 15, no. 2 (1991): 92–106, at 100, 103.
17. Sari Thomas, "Dominance and Ideology in Culture and Cultural Studies," in *Cultural Studies in Question*, ed. Marjorie Ferguson and Peter Golding (London: SAGE, 1997), 74–85, at 79, 78.
18. Rob Latham, "Coda: Criticism in the Age of Borges," *Journal of the Fantastic in the Arts* 1, no. 4 (1988): 87–94, at 92; Kathleen S. Berry, *The Dramatic Arts and Cultural Studies: Acting Against the Grain* (New York: Falmer, 2000), 35.
19. *Postcritical Ethnography: Reinscribing Critique*, ed. George W. Noblit, Susanna Y. Flores, and Enrique G. Murillo (Creskill, NJ: Hampton, 2004) (quote from the back cover); Gary Browning and Andrew Kilmister, *Critical and Post-Critical Political Economy* (Basingstoke: Palgrave Macmillan, 2006).
20. Janet Wolff, *The Aesthetics of Uncertainty* (New York: Columbia University Press, 2008); Andrew Dewdney, David Dibosa, and Victoria Walsh, *Post-Critical Museology: Theory and Practice in the Art Museum* (London: Routledge, 2013).
21. Casper Bruun Jensen, "Experiments in Good Faith and Hopefulness: Toward a Postcritical Social Science," *Common Knowledge* 20, no. 2 (2014): 337–62.
22. Eve Kosofsky Sedgwick, "Paranoid Reading and Reparative Reading; or, You're So Paranoid, You Probably Think This Essay Is About You," in *Novel Gazing: Queer Readings in Fiction*, ed. Eve Kosofsky Sedgwick (Durham NC: Duke University Press, 1997), 1–37; Bruno Latour, "Why Has Critique Run Out of Steam? From Matters of Fact to Matters of Concern," *Critical Inquiry* 30, no. 2 (2004): 225–48; Stephen Best and Sharon Marcus, "Surface Reading: An Introduction," *Representations* 108, no. 1 (2009): 1–21.
23. Rita Felski, "Digging Down and Standing Back," *English Language Notes* 51, no. 2 (2013): 7–23, at 22. Four years earlier, she had still preferred "reflective reading" over "postcritical reading": Rita Felski, "After Suspicion," *Profession* (2009): 28–35, at 34. Felski's analysis of "suspicious reading" as a preeminent mood in literary studies shows some affinity with Peter Baehr's diagnosis of "unmasking" as a dominant style of thought in the social sciences: Peter Baehr, *The Unmasking Style in Social Theory* (London: Routledge, 2019).
24. Felski, *Limits of Critique*, 173.
25. Rita Felski, *Uses of Literature* (Malden, MA: Blackwell, 2008), 22.

26. Gila Ashtor, "The Misdiagnosis of Critique," *Criticism* 61, no. 2 (2019): 191–217, at 192.
27. The standard arguments against such Whiggish history writing are laid out in Stefan Collini, "'Discipline History' and 'Intellectual History': Reflections on the Historiography of the Social Sciences in Britain and France," *Revue de Synthèse* 109 (1988): 387–99.
28. Echeverria, *Criticism and Commitment*, 11.
29. Stephen D. Moore, review of *The Good Wine: Reading John from the Center* by Bruno Barnhart, *Interpretation* 49, no. 4 (1995): 426.
30. George W. Noblit, "The Possibilities of Postcritical Ethnographies: An Introduction to This Issue," *Educational Foundations* 13, no. 1 (1999): 3–6, at 5.
31. Karl R. Popper, *The Logic of Scientific Discovery* (London: Hutchinson, 1959), 23.
32. Joyce Appleby, "Introduction: Jefferson and His Complex Legacy," in *Jeffersonian Legacies*, ed. Peter S. Onuf (Charlottesville, VA: University Press of Virginia, 1993), 1–16, at 14.
33. Hal Foster, "Post-Critical," *October* 139 (2012): 3–8, at 3.
34. Ibid., 8.
35. As illustrated also by the case of Bruce M. Knauft, "Pushing Anthropology Past the Posts: Critical Notes on Cultural Anthropology and Cultural Studies as Influenced by Postmodernism and Existentialism," *Critique of Anthropology* 14, no. 2 (1994): 117–52, at 132–3.
36. On "mood," see Felksi, *Limits of Critique*, 20–2.
37. Thomas, "Dominance and Ideology," 78.
38. W. H. Walsh, "Colligatory Concepts in History," in *Studies in the Nature and Teaching of History*, ed. W. H. Burston and D. Thompson (London: Routledge & Kegan Paul, 1967), 65–84. On post-concepts as colligatory concepts, see also Adriaan van Veldhuizen, "Epilogue: Lessons for Future Posts," in Paul and Van Veldhuizen, *Post-Everything*, 235–49.
39. Jennifer L. Fleissner, "Romancing the Real: Bruno Latour, Ian McEwan, and Postcritical Monism," in *Critique and Postcritique*, ed. Elizabeth S. Anker and Rita Felski (Durham NC: Duke University Press, 2017), 99–126, at 101.
40. John Michael, "Tragedy and Translation: A Future for Critique in a Secular Age," ibid., 252–78.
41. Christopher Castiglia, "Hope for Critique?" ibid., 211–29; Elizabeth S. Anker and Rita Felski, "Introduction," ibid., 1–28, at 16. Castiglia elaborates his argument in his *The Practices of Hope: Literary Criticism in Disenchanted Times* (New York: New York University Press, 2017).
42. Felski, *Limits of Critique*, 13.
43. Foster, "Post-Critical," 7.

44. Andrew Lyndon Knighton, review of *Critique and Postcritique* by Elizabeth S. Anker and Rita Felski, *American Literary History Online Review* 12 (2017): 1–4, at 2; Bruce Robbins, "Fashion Conscious Phenomenon," *American Book Review* 38, no. 5 (2017): 5–6, at 6.
45. Bruce Robbins, "Not So Well Attached," *PMLA* 132, no. 2 (2017): 371–6, at 371.
46. Robert Cashin Ryan, review of *The Limits of Critique* by Rita Felski, *Victoriographies* 7, no. 3 (2017): 271–4, at 273; Robbins, "Fashion Conscious Phenomenon," 5. See also Esther Peeren, "Suspicious Minds: Critique as Symptomatic Reading," in *The Ends of Critique: Methods, Institutions, Politics*, ed. Kathrin Thiele, Birgit M. Kaiser, and Timothy O'Leary (Lanham, MD: Rowman & Littlefield, 2021), 97–116, at 104 ("an uncannily accurate description of the hermeneutical stance taken by hardcore Trump supporters").
47. Religious motifs abounded in a forum section that *Religion and Literature* 48, no. 2 (2016) devoted to *The Limits of Critique*.
48. Herman Paul, "Relations to the Past: A Research Agenda for Historical Theorists," *Rethinking History* 19, no. 3 (2015): 450–8; Mark Day, "Our Relations with the Past," *Philosophia* 36, no. 4 (2008): 417–7.
49. Nathan Lee, "Postcritique and the Form of the Question: Whose Critique Has Run Out of Steam?" *Cultural Critique* 108 (2020): 150–76.
50. Amanda Anderson, *Psyche and Ethos: Moral Life after Psychology* (Oxford: Oxford University Press, 2018), 101.
51. Castiglia, "Hope for Critique," 215–7; Michael, "Tragedy and Translation," 255–6.
52. Felski, *Limits of Critique*, 120; Ryan, review in *Victoriographies*, 273.
53. Robbins, "Fashion Conscious Phenomenon," 5. See also Diana Fuss, "But What about Love?" *PMLA* 132, no. 2 (2017): 352–5, at 354: "Might not many of the modes and moods of postcritique – 'joy, hope, love, optimism' – already be found inside critique, if we only cared to look?"
54. Knighton, review in *American Literary History Online Review*, 3; Fredric Jameson, *The Political Unconscious: Narrative as a Socially Symbolic Act* (Ithaca, NY: Cornell University Press, 1981), 285.
55. David Scott, *Conscripts of Modernity: The Tragedy of Colonial Enlightenment* (Durham, NC: Duke University Press, 2004), 10–11, 20–21. Transformative capacity ("the capability to intervene in a given set of events so as in some way to alter them") is a term borrowed from Anthony Giddens, *The Nation-State and Violence* (Berkeley, CA: University of California Press, 1985), 7.
56. Ayşe Parla, "Critique Without a Politics of Hope?" in *A Time for Critique*, ed. Didier Fassin and Bernard E. Harcourt (New York: Columbia University Press, 2019), 52–70, at 52, 62; Fadi A. Bardawil, "Critical Theory in a Minor Key to Take Stock of the Syrian Revolution," ibid., 174–92, at 176.

57. Felski, *Limits of Critique*, 107.
58. Didier Fassin and Bernard E. Harcourt, "Introduction," in Fassin and Harcourt, *Time for Critique*, 1–10, at 2, 3. Similarly: Birgit M. Kaiser, Kathrin Thiele, and Timothy O'Leary, "Introduction," in Thiele, Kaiser, and O'Leary, *Ends of Critique*, 1–16.
59. This is the so-called "Thomas theorem," formulated by William I. Thomas and Dorothy Swaine Thomas in *The Child in America: Behavior Problems and Programs* (New York: Alfred A. Knopf, 1928), 572.
60. Dan Karlholm, "Postcritical or Acritical? Twelve Steps for Art History Writing in the Anthropocene," *Journal of Art History* 89, no. 2 (2020): 150–64, at 152.
61. Howard Brick, "Optimism of the Mind: Imagining Postindustrial Society in the 1960s and 1970s," *American Quarterly* 44, no. 3 (1992): 348–80; Herman Paul, "'Our Post-Christian Age': Historicist-Inspired Diagnoses of Modernity, 1935–70," in Paul and Van Veldhuizen, *Post-Everything*, 17–39.
62. Antoine Hennion and Line Grenier, "Sociology of Art: New Stakes in a Post-Critical Time," in *The International Handbook of Sociology*, ed. Stella R. Quah and Arnaud Sales (London: SAGE, 2000), 341–55, at 345.
63. Kwame Anthony Appiah, "Is the Post- in Postmodernism the Post- in Postcolonial?," *Critical Inquiry* 17, no. 2 (1991): 336–57, at 348.
64. Homi K. Bhaba, *The Location of Culture* (London: Routledge, 1994), 1.
65. The phrase "postcritical turn" already enjoyed some popularity among architects before it founds its way into literary studies. See, e.g., George Baird, "Criticality and Its Discontents," *Harvard Design Magazine* 21 (2004): 16–21 and Rachel Sagner Buurma and Laura Heffernan, "Interpretation, 1980 and 1880," *Victorian Studies* 55, no. 4 (2013): 615–28, at 615.
66. Jeffrey C. Alexander, "Modern, Anti, Post, and Neo: How Social Theories Have Tried to Understand the 'New World' of 'Our Time,'" *Zeitschrift für Soziologie* 23 (1994): 165–97.
67. Judith Surkis, "When Was the Linguistic Turn? A Genealogy," *The American Historical Review* 117, no. 3 (2012): 700–22, at 710.
68. Joyce Appleby, "One Good Turn Deserves Another: Moving Beyond the Linguistic; A Response to David Harlan," *The American Historical Review* 94, no. 5 (1989): 1326–32, at 1326.
69. Karlholm, "Postcritical or Acritical," 152.
70. David Sessions, "Intellectual History and the Postcritical Turn," at https://sites.bc.edu/davidsessions/2016/11/29/ (accessed March 9, 2022).
71. Anker and Felski, "Introduction," 1.
72. Gary Wilder, "From Optic to Topic: The Foreclosure Effect of Historiographic Turns," *The American Historical Review* 117, no. 3 (2012): 723–45.
73. As illustrated by the introduction to a recent special issue on post-criticism: "While discussing the topic for this special issue . . . we were told to *hurry*.

Suggesting alternatives to critique, we were further told, is already yesterday's news." Sara Callahan, Anna-Maria Hällgren, and Charlotte Krispinsson, "A Farewell to Critique? Reconsidering Critique as Art Historical Method," *Journal of Art History* 89, no. 2 (2020): 61–5, at 61.
74. Stéphanie Genz, "Busting the 'Post'? Postfeminist Genealogies in Millennial Culture," in Paul and van Veldhuizen, *Post-Everything*, 195–214.
75. Fredric Jameson, *Postmodernism, or, the Cultural Logic of Late Capitalism* (Durham, NC: Duke University Press, 1991); Hartmut Rosa, *Social Acceleration: A New Theory of Modernity*, trans. Jonathan Trejo-Mathys (New York: Columbia University Press, 2013). Funding for this chapter was generously provided by the Dutch Research Council (NWO).

# 15

Environmental Humanities: Entangled Interdisciplinarity

Kristine Steenbergh

Introduction

When the editor of this volume invited me to write a chapter on the historiography of the environmental humanities as an interdisciplinary field, I sensed a slight trepidation.[1] How to write the history of such a young field? My mind turned initially to the histories of the individual disciplines that contribute to the environmental humanities. The discipline of environmental history, for example, has roots reaching back to the 1970s and beyond. I thought of Lynn White's now canonical article on "The Historical Roots of our Ecologic Crisis," published in *Science* in 1967, which argued persuasively that "what people do about their ecology depends on what they think about themselves in relation to things around them."[2] As a literary scholar working on the cusp of the history of emotions, ecocriticism, and early modern literature, I experienced a desire to also write my own disciplinary roots into this overview. Surely, ecocriticism's roots reached back as far as those of environmental history? I could juxtapose Lynn White, Donald Worster, and William Cronon with the names of Raymond Williams and William Rueckert to trace another disciplinary root engrained in canonical (male) literary scholars. An art historian might wish to include the early ecocritical work of Jack Burnham or György Kepes into this family tree. The history of the environmental humanities began to take shape in my mind's eye as a tree trunk with several distinct roots in canonical works, reaching back into the academic past. These disciplinary roots in environmental history, ecocriticism, environmental philosophy, and environmental art history stabilize and feed the young interdisciplinary sapling, which has now grown into a young tree of twenty years. But would such tracing of separate disciplinary pasts do justice to the history of the field? Where among these roots would I place the interdisciplinary work of Carolyn Merchant, Val Plumwood, and Donna Haraway? Even as I was shaping distinct roots for the tree, then, I found that my attempts at a historiography of the field were difficult to contain within disciplinary boundaries.

In this chapter, I explore the notion of interdisciplinarity in the environmental humanities from a historiographic perspective. Surveying how the history of the field has been written in handbooks and introductions, I signal that records of its young history do indeed trace a progress from disciplinary roots to a shared, interdisciplinary present, but at the same time note that these models do not quite fit with the actual history of the field. Historiographic metaphors of roots—or its recurrent alternative of waves—suggest that distinct disciplinary knowledges blend together to merge into a unified whole, whether that be a great bole or an ocean. These metaphors' conjuring of ideals of integration and blending jostle against the kinds of interdisciplinarity envisaged and practiced in the environmental humanities, which seek to foster and maintain plurality in an experimental approach to entangled, complex problems. I look for ways to describe the environmental humanities as an interdisciplinary project using the messier metaphor of entanglement. Indeed, I argue that the metaphor of entanglement resonates not only with the historiography of the field, but also with the field's sensitivity to the entangled nature of ecological questions. I close with the argument that the qualitative methodologies of the humanities are especially attuned to analysing problems in their entanglement with other problems, and that such study of entanglements may require science to slow down a little, even in the midst of this pressing ecological crisis.

The Environmental Humanities

Central to the environmental humanities is the idea that the ecological crisis cannot be tackled by the exact sciences alone: environmental challenges are bound up with social, cultural, and human factors, and therefore need to be addressed as complex problems.[3] As a key introduction to the field also notes, the idea of interconnectedness grounds the work of scholars in the field, based as it is in "the urgent need for critical reflection on the state of our environment, on human subjectivity and actions, but most importantly, on their inextricable entanglement and how to then research this."[4] The environmental humanities seek to problematize and bridge the traditional (Western) binary divide between nature and culture, exploring the entanglement of environmental issues with questions of the imagination, storytelling, ideologies, culture, ethics, politics, and justice. Humanities scholars approach ecological crises "as questions of socioeconomic inequality, cultural difference, and divergent histories, values, and ethical frameworks."[5] The field therefore seeks to bring to bear the fundamental concerns within the humanities on questions of the environment.[6] Climate scientists, for example, demonstrate that human influence is changing our climate, but have found that it is not enough to communicate these results to the general public in order to solve the problem.[7] As the authors of a recent volume on climate change and interdisciplinarity argue, this lack of response to the urgency of the climate crisis may be "a result of a science-dominated debate that has underplayed the role[s] of industrialization; consumption, governance; local, regional and international political and historical intersections in creating the crisis."[8]

In response to the complexity of the problem, the environmental humanities ask questions such as: How is climate change entangled with questions of inequality, environmental justice and multispecies ethics; and which cultural and historical practices, systems, ideologies, customs, stories, and imaginaries have shaped human impact on the climate; how did past societies and ecologies respond to changing climates; which alternative narratives, images, and artworks could help shape a different relation to human and non-human others? The field goes beyond disciplinary borders in many ways: it not only brings together various disciplines within the humanities, but also collaborates with disciplines in the social and natural sciences, as well as with citizens, artists, and activists outside academia.

How, then, to write the history of this interdisciplinary field? In one sense, the story could be relatively brief: the environmental humanities took shape in the early years of the twenty-first century and now blossom in journals, conferences, research initiatives, centers, and academic teaching programs across the globe. It is possible to trace the start of the field to the first use of the name in an institutional context, which was in 1995, when a Center for Environmental Arts and Humanities was erected at the University of Nevada.

Around 2010, the field became more institutionalized in Europe, the US, and Australia, and the journal *Environmental Humanities* was founded.[9] If we take into account the different disciplines that fed into the field, however, the history of the environmental humanities can be followed further back. Textbook introductions to the environmental humanities—another sign that the field is consolidating—commonly trace the contours of merging disciplinary traditions. In *The Routledge Companion to the Environmental Humanities* (2017), for example, Ursula K. Heise traces the origins of the fields of environmental philosophy, environmental history, and ecocriticism from the 1970s to the 1990s, and indicates that as these fields grew more confident, they began to collaborate with disciplines such as environmental anthropology, cultural geography, political science, and urban studies.[10] In *The Environmental Humanities: A Critical Introduction* (also from 2017), Robert S. Emmett and David E. Nye argue that "one can trace the origins of the environmental humanities back more than a century, but the field originated most immediately through the confluence of simultaneous developments during the 1970s and the 1980s in departments of literature, philosophy, history, geography, gender studies, and anthropology."[11] Each introduction inflects its history slightly differently. Whereas Heise focuses on environmental philosophy, environmental history, and ecocriticism as the three disciplines that form the roots of the field, Emmett and Nye cast a broader net and include geography, gender studies, and anthropology among the foundational disciplines. Astrida Neimanis, Cecilia Åsberg and Johan Hedrén argue that areas of the (qualitative) social sciences concerned with values, behaviors, meaning, and ideologies are an integral part of the field as well.[12] Moreover, they urge their readers not to overlook less canonical roots of the field: "anti-racist, feminist and anti-colonial theories and ethical frameworks have long encouraged a view of nature as a human and social issue, but have rarely enjoyed a privileged place . . . within the mainstream of environmental humanities."[13] Alternatively, the history of the field is shaped through references to key scholars in the field who wrote classics that have become shared points of reference across the environmental humanities. Names often mentioned in this context include Donald Worster and William Cronon in environmental history, Lawrence Buell and Ursula Heise in ecocriticism, Sherry Ortner, Val Plumwood, and Carolyn Merchant in ecofeminism, Bruno Latour and Donna Haraway in philosophy and science and technology studies. Some texts also incorporate older authors, such as the nineteenth-century writer Henry Thoreau, into their canon; and Emmett and Nye trace "a direct line" from Alexander von Humboldt and Aimé Bonpland's advocacy for an integrated planetary study of nature to the environmental humanities today.[14]

Such a discipline-based historiography, however, suggests that the field was shaped by a meeting between distinct and coherent wholes. Starting from disciplinary traditions, this type of historiography privileges the kinds of knowledge produced in academic contexts, while erasing other knowledges. In an article that shaped my thinking on this topic, Hannes Bergthaller et al. write that the traditional metaphor of "waves" used to trace progressive developments in the discipline of ecocriticism obscures "the untidy, uneven character of ecocriticism's development"—although this untidiness is "perhaps a better indicator of its health than the rapid growth and linear progression . . . posited by the 'wave' model."[15] This argument also applies to the environmental humanities as a whole: the model of roots merging into a whole hides the untidy character of interdisciplinarity. The history of the field could be told differently: "It could anachronistically collect many of the different (and predominantly peripheral or non-Western) cosmologies, philosophies, and histories that extend across millennia to tell the stories of human implication with non-human worlds," for example.[16] While at the same time highlighting the "artificiality and contingency" of historiographic metaphors, ecocritic Scott Slovic suggests that rather than thinking of "waves" or "roots" to imagine the development of a field, we could envisage "a vast intellectual drainage system or watershed." This would involve tracing "small creeks of intellectual, artistic, and activist thought that later merged with each other to form broader, swifter currents, eventually converging with other systems of thought and then finally emptying into the vast sea of 'environmental studies,' which encompasses all human efforts to understand our place on this planet."[17]

Historiographies of the field, then, tend to use natural metaphors to trace a development from smaller origins to a broader, more unified whole. In this greater whole, disciplinary knowledges blend and merge in a sea of transdisciplinarity. And yet, many texts that seek to define the field also signal that the environmental humanities resist this movement towards overarching synthesis, especially if it threatens to reduce existing pluralism of concepts, methodologies and theories, or if the ideal of transdisciplinarity is coupled with a desire to find directly applicable solutions to isolated problems that have been taken out of their deep contexts. Can interdisciplinarity be practised in a way that safeguards plurality?

Interdisciplinarity in the Environmental Humanities

Although interdisciplinarity is often understood as a merging of wholes, the term is in essence quite slippery: it can refer to connections and collaborations between disciplines, to the conceptual space in between established disciplines, or to new kinds of knowledge shaped by transcending disciplines and creating new conceptual or theoretical frameworks or methodological toolkits.[18] Characterizations of interdisciplinarity vary widely, and new prefixes are continually suggested to indicate new forms of collaboration and consilience between disciplines. For working definitions, I turn here to the work of Julia Thompson Klein, who distinguishes between multidisciplinarity, interdisciplinarity, and transdisciplinarity. In her view, what is called interdisciplinarity is often *multi*disciplinarity. In the latter case, separate disciplines are juxtaposed within a framework of a course, a conference, a research project, or publication. These disciplines may present themselves as an interdisciplinary group, but their "inputs are not integrated around core questions, topics, themes, or problems."[19] Individual researchers remain tethered to their own expertise, their knowledge is not transformed by the collaboration with other disciplines. In contrast, interdisciplinarity is characterized by "integration of information, data, methods, tools, concepts, and/or theories from two or more disciplines or bodies of specialized knowledge." By connecting and blending disciplinary outputs, interdisciplinary projects "foster a more holistic understanding of a question, topic, theme, or problem by individuals or teams."[20] Transdisciplinarity, as the most integrative concept of the three, brings the disciplines to an overarching synthesis, in which new conceptual frameworks or paradigms are shaped.

Whereas the notion of integration and blending is central to these definitions of interdisciplinarity, however, the growth of interdisciplinary alliances often does not progress as smoothly as these descriptions suggest. These processes are not linear in shape, but grow organically around specific questions and collaborations. Indeed, disciplines have been compared to biological cultures: like cells, they "subdivide and recombine, changing shape and disposition."[21] In the Routledge New Critical Idiom's book on interdisciplinarity, Joe Moran urges his readers not to "discipline" these interdisciplinary initiatives: "The value of the term, 'interdisciplinary,' lies in its flexibility and indeterminacy, and there are potentially as many forms of interdisciplinarity as there are disciplines." Rather than envisaging a linear progress towards synthesis, the move towards interdisciplinarity can also be characterized as a more "radical questioning of the nature of knowledge itself and our attempts to organize and communicate it."[22] An example of such radical questioning is Des Fitzgerald and Felicity Callard's argument that the ideals of transdisciplinarity are perhaps a defense mechanism employed by new fields to define their position in the academic landscape. Paradoxically, even if these fields are theoretically invested in plurality, they circumscribe their sites of analysis in order to define themselves as a discipline.[23] The desire for integration "mobilises a very particular account ... of what kind of things disciplines are; about what forms of spatial arrangement position them against one another; about what relations of exchange are appropriate across them; and about what must thereby constitute the, variously, human, cultural, biological and embodied agencies to which they attend."[24] Questioning whether the medical humanities should strive for integration of the humanities with the medical sciences, they propose to think these relations in terms of entanglement. I propose that the concept of entanglement is also useful in thinking about the history of interdisciplinarity in the environmental humanities.

The concept of entanglement invokes a way of thinking about relationality not as a process in which two bounded, whole subjects (such as academic disciplines) interact with each other, but as a process of intra-action in which there is no prior wholeness. Karen Barad, who introduced the term to the environmental humanities, writes that "what often appears as separate entities, does not actually entail a relation of absolute exteriority at all."[25] Rather than a movement from two cleanly separated cultures, interdisciplinary approaches "enter a long history of binding, tangling and cutting" in which differences matter and in which relations are shaped in the intra-action.[26] In this model of entanglement, then, disciplines such as ecocriticism and environmental history did not exist as separate entities, but as dynamic projects that were always already tangling and commingling before the arrival of the interdisciplinary field of the environmental humanities. Concepts and ideas traveled between disciplines, scholars read each other's work and drew on similar developments within the humanities in their research. The environmental historian Richard Grove, for example, included analyses of literary representations of green paradises in his canonical study *Green Imperialism* (1995).[27] And Rachel Carson opened her book *Silent Spring*, which incited an environmental movement in the US in the 1960s, with a fictional dystopia.[28] Indeed, Bergthaller et al. argue that Lynn White's influential article (1967) on the history of ecological crisis can be seen as an early meeting place between ecocriticism and environmental history, as it connects a change in the reception of the text of the Bible to the development of new relations and technologies of production in response to a specific environment. Similarly, they mention the field of early modern ecocriticism as an example of such common ground between environmental history and ecocriticism.[29]

This view of the environmental humanities as always already entangled has consequences for its historiography. As Frank Uekötter has argued in relation to the environmental history of the COVID-19 pandemic, the consequences of the entanglements of a Chinese wet market with home offices across the globe go straight to the heart of historical storytelling. Linear narratives of cause and event prove inadequate for entangled phenomena such as a global pandemic. Nevertheless, he writes, "words will remain the primary tool of historical storytelling for lack of something better."[30] I propose that we look for words that invite us to let go of the model of individual agency and help shape this entanglement in our imaginations. What if we revisit the metaphor of tree roots from this perspective?

Recent research into the entanglement of tree roots with the mycelium of fungi challenges the idea of the tree as an individual, bounded organism and invites us to revisit the metaphor of the environmental humanities as a young tree with disciplinary roots. As Merlin Sheldrake writes, fungi challenge the very idea of an individual and invite thinking in terms of porous bodies and entanglement: "a mycelial network is … a helpful reminder that all life forms are in fact processes, not things."[31] Similarly, scholars in the environmental humanities have developed concepts such as entanglement, transcorporeality, and intra-activity, which challenge anthropocentrism as well as the notion that individuals are bounded wholes. As a historiographic metaphor for interdisciplinarity in the environmental humanities, then, I would suggest an image of a living network of tangled roots and mycelium. This metaphor resonates with the plurality of concepts, methodologies and theories in the field, and also with the intention to view questions in their entangled contexts, rather than in isolation. It also enables us to think of the reciprocity between academic disciplines, writers, artists, citizens, and activists that took and still takes place under the name of environmental humanities. Finally, the metaphor of entanglement aligns with the field's practice of a mode of thought that is specifically attuned to analysing entanglements.

Ecological Thought: Practising Entanglement

When the first SARS-CoV-2 virus particles arrived in the Netherlands in March 2020, the Dutch government's initial response was to deal with the virus as a medical problem requiring the expertise of virologists. In the course of the year, however, it became more and more clear that the pandemic was not a purely virological problem: its causes were entangled with globalization, market economies, deforestation, and urbanization, as well as with inequality, political frictions.[32] As Frank Uekötter recently put it, "there is no Archimedean point from which we can understand the COVID-19 pandemic."[33] Rather, it is necessary not only to understand the particularities of the coronavirus particle, but also to harness the knowledge of other disciplines, and to connect these different knowledges in a web of entangled knowledges. Disciplinary specializations tend to shape a focus on specific factors, but the complex kind of problem that is a pandemic requires attentiveness to the multiplicity and interconnectedness of hugely diverse factors.[34] On a political level, however, this realization may need more time to take root: during the pandemic, the Dutch prime minister has repeatedly declared that he is not a sociologist, nor wishes to become one.[35]

Likewise, diversity is a key aspect of the environmental humanities. It is the diversity of methods within the environmental humanities, as well as its experimental ethos and preparedness to enter into conversations and relations with others, that enable the field to deal with the entangled problems of ecological crisis. The field's pluralism and its desire to understand complex problems in their layered contexts means that it uses methodologies different from those of the natural sciences. As Libby Robin notes, "attitudes and values are not easily measured, nor do they readily yield data that can be incorporated into modeling of future scenarios."[36] For this reason, the moral, political and ethical dimensions of the ecological crisis were long considered "outside the expertise" of environmental sciences. As the ecologist Frank B. Golley notes in his *Primer for Environmental Literacy*, "in science we face a poverty of tools for exploring the nature of whole systems." Philosophy and religion offer alternative approaches, and the "arts and humanities . . . are a crucial part of environmental studies." He warns that while analysis and synthesis are both necessary elements of an ecological analysis, the emphasis in (US) science tends to lie on analytical problem solving. The context is either ignored or is "considered outside the area of responsibility of the problem solver."[37] To counter global warming, for example, the late Dutch atmospheric chemist (and coiner of the name "Anthropocene" for our current geological epoch) suggested technologies for solar radiation management, such as spraying minute particles into the stratosphere, which would reflect sunlight and thereby lower the temperature on Earth.[38]

Focusing on one aspect of a complex problem, however, risks having unforeseen consequences: assessing only the temperature-related benefits and harms of such interventions is too narrow a basis for climate justice.[39] The danger of a scientific approach that focuses on specific questions in isolation, is that it proposes a solution for that narrow aspect of the problem, without taking into account its entanglement with more complex issues. As philosopher Isabel Stengers argues, a scientific approach of rationality and objectivity invites questions that can be answered in a "purified or constrained environment." On the basis of "what is well-controlled and clean," this approach then formulates a "truth that transcends the mess."[40] In other words, such an approach produces measurable and reproducible outcomes which suggest an objective truth. They are based, however, on the exclusion of other problems and questions that the selected aspect is intricately interconnected with. Lorraine Code similarly writes that the legacy of the Enlightenment emphasizes "the calculability of the world" and thereby excludes everything that does not conform to the "rule of computation and utility" from its definitions of knowledge.[41] In her words, the current ecological crisis shows "the messiness of the world" returning with a vengeance.[42]

What is this messiness that both Code and Stengers refer to, and what kind of approach is needed to understand it? It is important to note that the complexity excluded by a reductionist approach consists of relations and interdependencies. In the words of Stengers, it is an "irreducible and always embedded interplay of processes, practices, experiences, and ways of knowing that makes up our common world."[43] In the case of climate engineering, for example, environmental philosophers impress the need for a care ethics that would be attentive to "neglected considerations such as relationships, context, power, vulnerability, narrative, and affect (amongst others)."[44] To work towards social and climate justice, they argue, quantitative research into biophysical and economic impacts will not suffice: what is needed is a qualitative approach that involves listening to those who are affected to appreciate their perspectives on social, political, cultural, and ecological impacts. This includes the perspectives of vulnerable humans as well as more-than-human species affected by the problem.[45] Both Code and Stengers have argued that in order to be attentive and responsive to such entanglements, a different epistemology and alternative scientific practices are needed.

This "messiness" of problems calls for a new epistemology that Code calls "ecological thinking." The name does not seek to imply that this type of thinking concerns itself only with the environmental crisis, although it can certainly be applied to it. Rather, ecological thinking refers to a sensitivity to the entanglement of different aspects of a problem. As Code writes, it is grounded in an ecology of partial connections, which involves "ways of engaging with the implications of patterns, places, and interconnections of lives and events in and across the human and other-than-human world."[46] Rather than studying problems in isolation, it brings situated enquiries together and maps their interrelations and frictions. As an example of such ecological thought, she discusses Rachel Carson's book *Silent Spring* (1962) on the destructive effects of the use of pesticides. The book, written to include scientists as well as the general public in its readership, had a major impact on the United States' pesticide policies, and inspired a world-wide environmental movement. Carson's modes of research and writing are an example of ecological thinking: *Silent Spring* weaves together laboratory research with fieldwork, the situated experiences of those affected by the pesticides with the histories of the sites and species studied. Carson thus shapes a "more participatory, democratic epistemology" which is "bound neither by regulative contrasts between intellectual and emotional activity, nor between mental and manual labour; it evinces no separation between abstract thought and concrete, sensuous activity, nor between the ideas and practices of 'everyday life' and those that derive from formal institutions of knowledge production."[47]

Many scholars in the environmental humanities consider this kind of ecological thought, which is sensitive to the entanglements of complex problems, at the heart of their practice. When the working group on the Environmental Humanities of the Swiss Academy of Humanities and Social Sciences conducted a survey among scholars, they found that many of their respondents "suggested that the environmental humanities perspective is one that attempts to gain a holistic and context-sensitive view of problems instead of dividing it up by disciplines into sub-problems."[48] Their report concludes that a move towards transdisciplinarity might threaten to reduce this kind of pluralism, especially if this move is aimed at creating an overarching synthesis, or at finding quick fixes for isolated sub-problems.[49] Similarly, Neimanis, Åsberg, and Hedrén encourage "a version of this field that self-reflexively acknowledges and even nurtures its own contradictions, variances, and necessary open-endedness."[50]

The Humanities: Tools for Studying Interconnectedness

The methodologies of the humanities provide a valuable addition to those of the natural sciences in approaching such complex problems. As Jonathan Bate puts it in *The Public Value of the Humanities*, "the very nature of the humanities is to address the messy, debatable and unquantifiable but essentially human dimensions of life."[51] Humanities research in such disciplines as literary studies, history, art history, or cultural anthropology is qualitative rather than quantitative, and is attentive to situated knowledges: to the roles of specific stories and their narrators, to cultural specificity, and to historical context. And indeed, the very notion of entanglement is central to the environmental humanities. Scholars in this field are interested in the environment not as a landscape surrounding human life, but precisely in the interconnectedness and entanglements of nature with culture, or, in Bruno Latour's concept, in "natureculture"; in conceptions of all living, embodied organisms as intermeshed with the dynamic material world. In exploring these entanglements, the environmental humanities employ modes of thought traditionally associated with humanities disciplines. Bergthaller and his co-authors sketch this mode of thought by contrasting it to empirical research methods, where a problem is broken down into separate, smaller questions addressed from the perspective of a general theory. "By contrast," they write, "the enterprise of the humanities is hermeneutic and much less straightforward methodologically—it involves shuttling back and forth between the whole and its parts, between the past, the present, and the future, and in the case of the environmental humanities, between the environment and culture."[52] In this sense, environmental humanities scholars resemble ecologists, who also weave back and forth between local, situated ecologies and specific organisms, focusing on the interconnectedness of complex systems.

Moreover, humanities researchers have the critical tools to analyse diverse aspects of a topic in relation to each other, connecting poetics to politics and ethics. The traditional assumption that humanities research aims to understand (*verstehen*) rather than explain (*erklären*), originally applied by Wilhelm Dilthey and resonating also in C. P. Snow's idea of two cultures, has been characterized as one of the root problems of the current image problem of the humanities. Rens Bod, Jaap Maat, and Thijs Weststeijn regret that

Dilthey's interpretative approach ultimately led to a perception of the humanities not as "the pinnacle of intellectual development but as a luxury pastime with little relevance for society and even less for economy."[53] In his book-length history of the field, Bod therefore seeks to demonstrate that practices in the sciences and the humanities are not on opposite ends of this spectrum, but on a continuum between interpretative and analytical, subjective and objective.[54] Seeking to counter the notion that the humanities are irrelevant to society and economy, he stresses that the field uses empirical as well as hermeneutic methodologies.

I suggest that alongside this argument about the use of empirical methods, we should re-emphasize the hermeneutical methods of the humanities. For these hermeneutic, slow techniques of interpretation that connect text to context are highly useful to explore complex problems. If Code defines the methodologies of ecological thinking as working "by analogy from example to example, case to case, reaffirming a wariness of reductionism and premature closure, opening new deliberative spaces for epistemic negotiation," such methods can be grounded in the techniques of humanities research.[55] Indeed, the imaginative nature of many of the object of study in the environmental humanities (from literature to art works) adds to the complexity of such ecological thinking. This kind of hermeneutic practice is traditional in a variety of humanities disciplines, ingrained into the spacious monographs that characterize their publication culture. Such research does not render swift and definite knowledge claims, as it is characterized precisely by a resistance to reducing a problem to isolated aspects. It does, however, render a situated and layered understanding of interconnections that could enrich and deepen quantitative findings, and help prevent quick solutions that turn out to have unforeseen consequences. In other words, to address the pressing entangled problems of our world, a slower interdisciplinary science rooted in qualitative as well as quantitative humanities methodologies is an urgent requirement, and not a luxury pastime.

Slow Scholarship

To allow such methodological diversity to take root and flourish, science needs to slow down a little. The speed and competitiveness ingrained into contemporary scientific practice fosters an approach focused on isolated problems and quick solutions, without attention to these solutions' broader ramifications. As Stengers notes, "speed demands and creates an insensitivity to everything that might slow things down: the frictions, the rubbing, the hesitations that make us feel we are not alone in the world."[56] Interdisciplinary research is all too often modeled on this fast and competitive model: researchers from different backgrounds all contribute their parcel of knowledge to a project, without learning from other contributors, or being transformed by that experience. In such an approach, the scale of the project is expanded, without changing the framework of knowledge or action.[57] This kind of upscaling is based in a scientific practice that values the fast output of disciplinary knowledge, and which refuses to be slowed down by messy questions that fall outside of the demarcated research questions. Bergthaller et al. note that many areas of science also resist this pattern: they "cannot always generate results so quickly and are not necessarily geared towards technological solutions—most relevant here are the ecological sciences, where research may take decades to complete, and development of new products is rarely if ever the goal."[58]

To address complex problems like the ecological crisis, Stengers writes, we need to "gain something like the slow knowledge of the gardener as opposed to the fast knowledge of 'rationalised' industrial agriculture."[59] Slow science may seem to return to the virtues of conscientiousness and precision espoused by nineteenth-century criticism discussed by Herman Paul in this volume (Chapter 9), but in the context of the environmental humanities, this attention to detail is combined with an understanding of interdependence across different scales. Stengers' metaphor refers not to the lawn-mowing type of suburban gardener, but rather to the mindful gardener who carefully notices plants and the relations between them, the soil, its critters, human and non-human inhabitants of the garden. In the spirit of permaculture, I envisage Stengers' gardener as having a reciprocal relation with life in the garden.[60] In the environmental humanities, such "slow" methods include careful reading, with attention to texts and contexts, to ambiguities and contradictions. Moreover, the objects studied afford the development of what Anna Tsing has called "arts of noticing."[61]

Literary and art works, for example, stimulate a mindful attention to non-human others, and invite readers, viewers, and listeners to pay mindful attention on different scales than that of everyday human cognition, imagining interconnectedness through new words and images. Such techniques of careful observation and witnessing the lives of non-human others are central to ecological thought. As an example, Stengers refers to the work of female primatologists who invented a "slow primatology" in which they "allowed themselves to be affected by the beings with whom they were dealing, looking for suitable relationships with them, putting the adventure of shared relevance above the authority of judgement."[62] Deborah Bird Rose and Thom van Dooren consider multispecies ethics as an attentiveness to the non-human other:

> [It is] ethics as an openness to others in the material reality of their own lives: noisy, fleshy, exuberant creatures with their multitude of interdependencies and precarities, their great range of calls, their care and their abundance along with their suffering and grief. Within entangled worlds of mutual becoming, attentiveness is necessarily a complex mode of participation.[63]

A science capable of addressing complex problems, then, is not an objective view from the outside, but a situated knowledge shaped by a process which affects both the subject of research and the researcher.

This kind of slow science roots itself in relations of interdependency, reciprocity, and transformation, rather than competition and linear growth. It values practices that are less suitable for upscaling, such as "the moment when someone feels transformed by having understood someone else's perspective; or the gathering that discovers the transformative power of its participants thinking together; or the experience that something which until now seemed insignificant may indeed matter."[64] Such processes are not easily reproduced or scaled up and require time, effort, and the shaping of relations of interdependency. The practices needed to work with complex problems may seem messy and feel like a waste of time when considered from the perspective of fast science, but like the slow knowledge of the gardener, they are based in an ethics of care equipped to stay with complex problems and trace their interconnections from the inside out.

Conclusion

I began this article by suggesting that entangled underground life is an apt metaphor for the interdisciplinary history of the environmental humanities, in which strands of thought, writing, art, activism from within the humanities, other academic disciplines, artistic practice, and the world at large come together to shape an academic practice that is actively attuned to the entanglement of ecological problems with cultural, social, ethical, and economical, and political problems. While histories of the young field outline a progress from disciplinarity to interdisciplinarity, they at the same time resist the drive to blend the plurality of knowledges and practices in the field into a unified whole. I argued that this resistance resonates with key epistemologies and practices in the field, in which the concept of entanglement invites a sensitivity to the complexity of problems. A dynamic and entangled interdisciplinarity that roots itself in relations of interdependency, reciprocity, and transformation rather than competition and linear growth, is what is needed to stay with the complex troubles of our times.

Notes

1. I would like to thank Herman Paul and my colleagues Petra van Dam and Katja Kwastek for their stimulating feedback on earlier versions of this chapter.
2. Lynn White, Jr., "The Historical Roots of Our Ecologic Crisis," *Science* 155, no. 3767 (1967): 1205.
3. For introductions to the field, see Deborah Bird Rose et al., "Thinking Through the Environment, Unsettling the Humanities," *Environmental Humanities* 1, no. 1 (2012): 1–5; Astrida Neimanis, Cecilia Åsberg and Johan Hedrén, "Four Problems, Four Directions for Environmental Humanities: Toward Critical Posthumanities for the Anthropocene," *Ethics and the Environment* 20, no. 1 (2015): 67–97; *The Routledge Companion to the Environmental Humanities*, ed. Ursula K. Heise, Jon Christensen, and Michelle Niemann (London: Routledge, 2017); Robert S. Emmett and David E. Nye, *The Environmental Humanities: A Critical Introduction* (Cambridge, MA: MIT Press, 2017); *Environmental Humanities: Voices from the Anthropocene*, ed. Serpil Oppermann and Serenella Iovino (Lanham, MD: Rowman & Littlefield, 2017); *Humanities for the Environment: Integrating Knowledge, Forging New Constellations of Practice*, ed. Joni Adamson and Michael Davis (London: Routledge, 2017); Eva Horn and Hannes Bergthaller, *The Anthropocene: Key Issues for the Humanities* (London: Routledge, 2020).
4. Neimanis, Åsberg, and Hedrén, "Four Problems," 68.
5. Bruno Latour, *We Have Never Been Modern*, trans. Catherine Porter (Cambridge, MA: Harvard University Press, 2012), 7; Stacy Alaimo, *Bodily Natures: Science, Environment, and the Material Self* (Bloomington, IN: Indiana University Press, 2010); Ursula K. Heise, "Introduction: Planet, Species, Justice—and the Stories We Tell about Them," in Heise, Christensen, and Niemann, *Routledge Companion to the Environmental Humanities*, 2.
6. Neimanis, Åsberg, and Hedrén, "Four Problems," 69.

7. See also Heise, "Introduction," 3.
8. Alexander Elliott, Vinita Damodaran, and James Cullis, "Introduction," in *Climate Change and the Humanities: Historical, Philosophical and Interdisciplinary Approaches to the Contemporary Environmental Crisis*, ed. Alexander Elliott, James Cullis, and Vinita Damodaran (London: Palgrave Macmillan, 2017), 5.
9. Scott Slovic, "Seasick among the Waves of Ecocriticism: An Inquiry into Alternative Historiography Metaphors," in Oppermann and Iovino, *Environmental Humanities*, 106.
10. Heise, "Introduction," 1.
11. Emmett and Nye, *Environmental Humanities*, 3.
12. Neimanis, Åsberg, and Hedrén, "Four Problems," 71.
13. Ibid., 72. See also Emmett and Nye, *Environmental Humanities*, 4.
14. Emmett and Nye, *Environmental Humanities*, 4.
15. Hannes Bergthaller et al., "Mapping Common Ground: Ecocriticism, Environmental History, and the Environmental Humanities," *Environmental Humanities* 5, no. 1 (2014): 269.
16. Neimanis, Åsberg, and Hedrén, "Four Problems," 72.
17. Slovic, "Seasick," 109.
18. Joe Moran, *Interdisciplinarity* (London: Routledge, 2010), 15.
19. Julie Thompson Klein, *Interdisciplining Digital Humanities: Boundary Work in an Emerging Field* (Ann Arbor: University of Michigan Press, 2015), 15.
20. Ibid.
21. Tony Becher as quoted in Julie Thompson Klein, *Humanities, Culture, and Interdisciplinarity: The Changing American Academy* (Albany, NY: State University of New York Press, 2005), 83.
22. Moran, *Interdisciplinarity*, 15–6; See also *Valences of Interdisciplinarity: Theory, Practice, Pedagogy*, ed. Raphael Foshay (Edmonton, AB: Athabasca University Press, 2011), 8–9.
23. Des Fitzgerald and Felicity Callard, "Entangling the Medical Humanities," in *The Edinburgh Companion to the Critical Medical Humanities*, ed. Anne Whitehead and Angela Woods (Edinburgh: Edinburgh University Press, 2016), 45.
24. Ibid., 38.
25. Karen M. Barad, *Meeting the Universe Halfway: Quantum Physics and the Entanglement of Matter and Meaning* (Durham, NC: Duke University Press, 2007), 93.
26. Fitzgerald and Callard, "Entangling," 39.
27. Richard Grove, *Green Imperialism: Colonial Expansion, Tropical Island Edens, and the Origins of Environmentalism, 1600-1860* (Cambridge: Cambridge University Press, 1995). See, for example, his use of Shakespeare and Dante (33).
28. Rachel Carson, *Silent Spring* (Boston, MA: Houghton Mifflin, 1962), 1–4.

29. Bergthaller et al., "Mapping Common Ground," 270.
30. Frank Uekötter, "It's the Entanglements, Stupid," *Journal for the History of Environment and Society* 5 (2020): 105–9.
31. Merlin Sheldrake, *Entangled Life: How Fungi Make Our Worlds, Change Our Minds and Shape Our Futures* (London: Bodley Head, 2021), 60.
32. See also Andreas Malm, *Corona, Climate, Chronic Emergency: War Communism in the Twenty-First Century* (London: Verso, 2020).
33. Uekötter, "It's the Entanglements," 107.
34. Elza Bontempi, Sergio Vergalli, and Flaminio Squazzoni, "Understanding COVID-19 Diffusion Requires an Interdisciplinary, Multi-Dimensional Approach," *Environmental Research* 188 (2020).
35. Jan Willem Duyvendak et al., "Rutte heeft de sociologie juist nodig," *Trouw* (February 6, 2021), online at https://www.trouw.nl/gs-b034a9b4 (accessed March 7, 2022).
36. Libby Robin as quoted in David E. Nye et al., *The Emergence of the Environmental Humanities* (Stockholm: MISTRA, 2015), 6.
37. Frank B. Golley, *A Primer for Environmental Literacy* (New Haven, CT: Yale University Press, 1998), 16–7.
38. Paul J. Crutzen, "Albedo Enhancement by Stratospheric Sulfur Injections: A Contribution to Resolve a Policy Dilemma?," *Climatic Change* 77, no. 3 (2006): 211.
39. Christopher Preston and Wylie Carr, "Recognitional Justice, Climate Engineering, and the Care Approach," *Ethics, Policy and Environment* 21, no. 3 (2018): 308–23; Augustine Pamplany, Bert Gordijn, and Patrick Brereton, "The Ethics of Geoengineering: A Literature Review," *Science and Engineering Ethics* 26 (2020), 3069–119.
40. Isabelle Stengers, *Another Science Is Possible: A Manifesto for Slow Science*, trans. Stephen Muecke (Cambridge, MA: Polity Press, 2018), 120.
41. Lorraine Code, *Ecological Thinking: The Politics of Epistemic Location* (Oxford: Oxford University Press, 2006), 8–9.
42. Ibid., 100.
43. Stengers, *Another Science*, 120.
44. Preston and Carr, "Recognitional Justice," 313. On the role of the humanities with regard to "easy solutions," see also Jonathan Bate, *The Public Value of the Humanities* (London: Bloomsbury Academic, 2011), 2.
45. Thom van Dooren and Deborah Bird Rose, "Encountering a More-than-Human World: Ethos and the Arts of Witness," in Heise, Christensen, and Niemann, *Routledge Companion to the Environmental Humanities*, 120–8.
46. Lorraine Code, "Ecological Thinking as Interdisciplinary Practice Situation, Silence, and Skepticism," in *Valences of Interdisciplinarity: Theory, Practice, Pedagogy*, ed. Raphael Foshay (Edmonton: University of Alberta Press, 2011), 192.

47. Ibid., 195–6.
48. Christoph Kueffer, Katharina Thelen Lässer, and Marcus Hall, *Applying the Environmental Humanities: Ten Steps for Action and Implementation* (Bern: Swiss Academic Society for Environmental Research and Ecology, Swiss Academy of Humanities and Social Sciences, 2017), 16.
49. Ibid., 17.
50. Neimanis, Åsberg, and Hedrén, "Four Problems," 69.
51. Bate, *Public Value*, 6.
52. Bergthaller et al., "Mapping Common Ground," 265.
53. Rens Bod, Jaap Maat, and Thijs Weststeijn, "Introduction: The Making of the Modern Humanities," in *The Making of the Humanities*, vol. 3, ed. Rens Bod, Jaap Maat, and Thijs Weststeijn (Amsterdam: Amsterdam University Press, 2014), 13.
54. Rens Bod, *A New History of the Humanities: The Search for Principles and Patterns from Antiquity to the Present*, trans. Lynn Richards (Oxford: Oxford University Press, 2013).
55. Code, "Ecological Thinking," 197.
56. Stengers, *Another Science*, 81.
57. Anna Lowenhaupt Tsing, "On Nonscalability: The Living World Is Not Amenable to Precision-Nested Scales," *Common Knowledge* 18, no. 3 (2012): 507.
58. Bergthaller et al., "Mapping Common Ground," 265.
59. Stengers, *Another Science*, 123–4.
60. On reciprocal relations with plant life, see also Robin Wall Kimmerer, *Braiding Sweetgrass: Indigenous Wisdom, Scientific Knowledge and the Teachings of Plants* (Minneapolis, MN: Milkweed, 2013).
61. Anna Lowenhaupt Tsing, *The Mushroom at the End of the World: On the Possibility of Life in Capitalist Ruins* (Princeton, NJ: Princeton University Press, 2012), 37.
62. Stengers, *Another Science*, 42.
63. Rose and van Dooren, "Encountering," 124. See also Kristine Steenbergh, "Contemporary Compassions: Interrelating in the Anthropocene," in *Compassion in Early Modern Literature and Culture: Feeling and Practice*, ed. Kristine Steenbergh and Katherine Ibbett (Cambridge: Cambridge University Press, 2021), 293–301.
64. Stengers, *Another Science*, 123.

16

Humanities across Time and Space: Four Challenges for a New Discipline[1]

Rens Bod

Introduction

While histories within the context of a single humanities discipline have been written for more than a century, it is only over the last few decades that we have witnessed histories that go beyond individual humanities disciplines and that bring together different fields, periods, or regions.[2] There is an increasing number of historians who are interested in cross-links between fields and regions, or in questions that cannot be meaningfully confined to one discipline. It is therefore surprising that virtually no study to date has addressed the methodological problems of the new métier. Questions abound: What do we mean by "bringing together" different humanities fields across time and space? Should we study their shared concepts, methods, virtues, research practices, historical actors, pedagogical practices, personal interactions, institutions, or yet something else? And when in history can we speak of the "humanities" as a group of disciplines? And how can we compare the humanities from different parts of the world?

In this essay, I will discuss four methodological challenges which I believe to be constitutive for the history of the humanities as a field. These are the challenges of demarcation, anachronism, Eurocentrism, and incommensurability. Any history of the humanities that goes beyond the scope of a single discipline, period, or region must address at least one of these challenges. While none of my challenges has a definite solution, I will provide reasoned choices for each of them. I will argue that my solutions offer a viable way to write a comparative history of the humanities, and that we can therefore speak of them as maxims. Although the preferred solutions will differ among historians, the challenges remain the same. At the end of my essay, I will discuss other possible solutions to the challenges, as well as other possible challenges for the history of the humanities, such as the challenge of forgotten scholars, non-academic humanities, and colonial humanities. Finally, I will go into the relation between the history of the humanities and the history of science and knowledge.

Challenge 1: The Problem of Demarcation

The first question to get to grips with is: what are the humanities? While most of us will have an intuitive idea of what the humanities are, we are often left empty-handed if we are asked for a definition or for criteria for demarcation. We thus need to further specify our question by asking whether the humanities are characterized by their objects or by their methods. A well-known definition by the German philosopher Wilhelm Dilthey (1833–1911) focuses on the objects of the humanities: according to Dilthey the humanities are *the disciplines that study the products of the human mind*, such as texts, art, language, music, and theater.[3] However, this nineteenth-century definition does not do justice to new humanities fields such as environmental humanities and medical humanities whose objects are the ecosystem and human health respectively. Evidently, the humanities not only study the products of the human mind, but also nature and life. Another well-known definition takes the humanities as *the disciplines that study human culture*,[4] but such a definition would also include the social sciences such as sociology, economics, and political science. Perhaps we might better attempt to define the humanities by its method(s), such as the hermeneutic method, the grammatical method, the stemmatological method, and the source-critical method.[5]

If we follow this path, we find that these methods are used not only by "core humanities" disciplines, such as history, philology, linguistics, and art history, but also by (sub)disciplines that are often seen as boundary cases. For example, the hermeneutic method is used in cultural psychology and historical sociology.⁶ The source-critical method is employed in forensic science, legal studies, and governmental studies to distinguish false from reliable sources,⁷ and it is also employed by botanists, physiologists, and physicists.⁸ The stemmatological method (from "stemmatic" philology) has been appropriated by the field of cladistics which uses history trees for classifications based on common ancestry, and the grammatical method is used in computational linguistics to create natural language processing systems.⁹

While this expansion of humanistic methods to other fields may serve as an argument for the impact of the humanities, these methods alone do still not provide us with a demarcation criterion for the humanities. Unless we go for a definition that is more inclusive than attempted before and that *includes all fields that incorporate humanistic methods* but no more than that. According to this view, fields employing humanistic approaches are partly humanistic, just as some of the core humanities disciplines can be viewed as partly scientific when they use methods from the exact sciences, such as archeology and linguistics. In this way, our definition goes beyond the core disciplines of the humanities and acknowledges that there is a set of methods that originate (or "begin," if one prefers)¹⁰ in the study of the products of the human mind but that have also profoundly shaped subdisciplines from the social sciences, life sciences, and exact sciences.

Thus we can extend Dilthey's definition by stating that *the humanities are the disciplines that use methods that originate in the study of the products of the human mind*. This way we include both the core humanities disciplines and the newer fields, such as environmental, digital, public, and medical humanities, as well as fields that are partly humanistic because they use methods transferred from the studies of the products of the human mind. Our definition is inclusive in that it does not exclude any discipline that could possibly be humanistic with regard to methodology. On the other hand, the definition implies that methods that have a strong "scientific" flavor but that come from a field that studies the productions of the human mind—such as the method of topic modeling used in digital humanities and computational linguistics—are also attributed to the humanities. As a consequence the distinction between the humanities and the sciences may get blurred, at least for some (sub)disciplines. Yet I believe that it is historically important to know where methods start or come from, whatever flavor they have. And if we can ascertain that a method originates both in the study of the products of the human mind and in the study of nature, then a discipline using that method is part of both the humanities and the sciences.

All in all this leads to my first maxim:

Maxim 1: *Be inclusive with respect to the boundaries of the humanities: fields outside the core humanistic disciplines that employ methods that originate or begin in the study of the expressions of the human mind are part of (the history of) the humanities.*

Challenge 2: The Problem of Anachronism

My solution to the demarcation problem relies heavily on current disciplinary categories. What about fields before the modern period when the term *humanities* did not exist (I will deal with the *studia humanitatis* and notions of the humanities in other cultures under challenge 3)?[11] This touches upon one of the central themes in intellectual history, namely the issue of anachronism. That is, how can we write about a concept in a certain period if that concept did not exist in that period?[12] For example, can we use the term "humanities" to designate scholarly practices in the premodern period, or would this result in a misleading form of anachronism?[13] If we squeeze past intellectual activities into a straightjacket of present-day expressions, we run the risk of descending into an undesirable kind of presentism in which the past is interpreted in terms of current concepts and perspectives.[14] So what do we gain if we anachronistically assign precursors of the humanities to the "humanities"? According to Nicholas Jardine, anachronisms are not necessarily harmful or misleading. The application of modern disciplinary categories to past practices can result in an enlightening use of anachronism.[15] In this essay, I will go one step further and argue that there are cases for which the application of modern categories to past practices is not only enlightening but even a prerequisite for a proper understanding of the history of the humanities. Without an anachronistic application of modern disciplinary categories to the past we may run the risk of overlooking how humanistic concepts and methods came into being. And we may even run the risk of giving credit where credit is *not* due.

Take philology, in particular the work by the nineteenth-century philologist Karl Lachmann (1793–1851) who has been referred to as "one of the most important figures in the development of modern European theory and practice of textual editions."[16] Lachmann's major contribution is to the field of stemmatic philology for which he (further) developed the notion of a genealogical tree—or stemma—that represents the relations between variants of an original text so as to ascertain which texts have been copied from which other ones. This allowed Lachmann to derive a series of mechanical rules that can reconstruct the archetype from extant copies.[17] Lachmann's method had an unprecedented success in the nineteenth-century humanities: he succeeded in reconstructing dozens of Latin, Greek, and medieval works, the accuracy of which were unparalleled.

As successful as his method was, most concepts and techniques proposed by Lachmann had already been in use for decades and in some cases for centuries. Examples are the concept of archetype, genealogical tree, and some of the rules for reconstructing the original text.[18] For example, the rule known as *eliminatio codicum descriptorum*, which regulates the elimination of sources that entirely depend on earlier sources, was already introduced as early as in the fifteenth century by the Italian humanist Angelo Poliziano.[19] Subsequent philologists elaborated on Poliziano's work, including Desiderius Erasmus and Joseph Scaliger in the sixteenth century, Jean Mabillon in the seventeenth century, and Richard Bentley in the eighteenth century. The major addition by Lachmann was that he integrated the previous methods and techniques into a systematic whole.

Clearly we cannot understand the development of stemmatic philology if we leave out its predecessors. And since philology is part of the humanities, it follows that we can neither understand the development of the humanities if we do not face the fact that several modern humanistic concepts and methods were already in existence in premodern disciplines.

Similar stories can be told for other disciplines, too. Take the art-historical method of Heinrich Wölfflin (1864–1945), whose work has shaped generations of art historians. Wölfflin proposed to analyse paintings in terms of hierarchically layered structures in which the smallest elements are combined so as to create ever greater parts that make up a coherent organization of the whole art work.[20] Similar to Lachmann's stemmatology, Wölfflin's art-historical method made use of the work of predecessors, for example Leon Battista Alberti's fifteenth-century concept of *compositio*, which also proposed a hierarchical analysis in describing the composition of a painting.[21] Alberti, in turn, is believed to have built on rhetorical methods that go back to Cicero: a text is analysed by hierarchically dividing it up into paragraphs, sentences, clauses, and constituents all the way down to words.[22] This part-whole analysis turned out to be fertile in many fields, varying from linguistic and art-historical to musicological and poetical analysis. Many of these methods go back to ancient rhetoric that was intensively studied by early modern humanists. Thus, as with philology, for a proper understanding of the development of art history, and thus of the modern humanities, we must take into consideration early modern and even ancient concepts and methods.

The history of the humanities of the nineteenth and twentieth centuries can almost never be considered in isolation from the early modern period. This does not mean that there are no breaks in the humanities during the transition from the early modern to the modern period. What is new in the nineteenth century, for example, is the institutional embedding of disciplines into universities, together with specialized journals, conferences, educational curricula, and specialized professorial chairs. A major pedagogical innovation of the nineteenth century was the research seminar,[23] in particular Leopold von Ranke's *historische Übungen* (historical exercises), which ran from 1825 to 1870 and served as a model for history teaching in many other universities.[24] Ranke's exercises were held in his private library, so that students could consult the vast collection of manuscripts he had acquired (see Chapter 12).[25] As innovative as Ranke's *Übungen* and the research seminars were at the time, there are still significant precursors. In the late sixteenth century, Leiden professor Joseph Scaliger organized research meetings with his students in his private home, where he trained them in the finesses of philology and chronology with his own library at hand.[26] Of course, the institutional, social, and intellectual contexts of Scaliger's research meetings differ greatly from those of Ranke's, but the notion of seminary meetings is older than the nineteenth century.

This is not to say that studies in the history of the humanities need always go back to the earliest mention of a particular concept—this would make no sense for specific case studies. But we have to face the fact that many modern humanistic concepts and methods already existed in premodern humanistic practices. The anachronistic application of present-day concepts to past intellectual activities, then, is not misleading but enlightening, and even necessary if we want to understand how modern concepts and methods came into being.

This brings me to my second maxim:

> **Maxim 2**: *Be inclusive with respect to time: premodern practices need to be taken into account if we want to understand the history of modern concepts and methods in the humanities.*

Challenge 3: The Problem of Eurocentrism (and Ethnocentrism)

It is often taken for granted that the humanities start in the West. Almost all monographs that, for whatever reason, present an overview of the history of the humanities (be it bird's-eye or in-depth) either begin with classical Greece or with the European *artes liberales* (i.e., the *trivium* thereof). They usually continue with the first humanistic curriculum of the *studia humanitatis* in Renaissance Italy, and they reach a pinnacle with the nineteenth-century German and other European universities of which the humanities programs spread over the rest of the world.[27]

These monographs thus place the history of the humanities within an exclusively European framework, as if there is no other history than a Western one. To some extent, one could claim that the historiography of the humanities is even more Eurocentric than the historiography of science. Long-term histories of science at least include the Islamic contributions, and often more.[28] Instead, the long-term historiography of the humanities has almost entirely remained European. This is surprising, since it is rather uncontroversial that the European humanities incorporated insights from the Islamic disciplines such as philosophy, history, and linguistics. Well-known examples are the philosophical works of Averroes and Avicenna, the historical work of Ibn Khaldun, and the linguistic work of Sibawayh.

Perhaps the strongest Islamic impact is found in the curriculum of the *studia humanitatis* itself. This educational program is commonly attributed to the fourteenth-century humanist Coluccio Salutati,[29] while we see the identification of the term with the five disciplines of *grammar, rhetoric, poetry, history, and moral philosophy* for the first time in 1438 by Tommaso Parentucelli.[30] Yet, these five disciplines exactly correspond to the disciplines of the ninth-century Islamic curriculum known as the *studia adabiya* (or *adab* disciplines).[31] We do not know whether Salutati or Parentucelli were aware of the *studia adabiya*,[32] and neither do we know whether the two *studia*'s rely on an even older curriculum. Cicero used the term *studia humanitatis* in his *Pro Archia*, but he meant something different by it, as he mentioned geometry, music, poetry, and dialectic as the disciplines in which young boys had to be formed. As far as we know, the Islamic *studia adabiya* is the oldest curriculum that contains the five disciplines of grammar, rhetoric, poetry, history, and moral philosophy. Thus a widely acclaimed conception of the European humanities was already in existence in the Islamic humanities five centuries earlier. And even if both curricula go back to an older one (which is not currently known), the *studia adabiya* forms the missing link.

The absence of the *studia adabiya* in the historiography of the humanities is an example of a more serious pattern: not only are the Islamic humanities neglected, the Asian, African, pre-Columbian, and Polynesian humanities are conspicuous by their absence, too. A fascinating example is provided by the Indian linguist Pāṇini (c. 500 BCE), who developed a highly complex grammar of Sanskrit consisting of almost 4,000 rules for all aspects of language—from phonology, morphology, syntax, and semantics to pragmatics.[33] According to the historian of linguistics Paul Kiparsky, "modern linguistics acknowledges it as the most complete generative grammar of any language yet written, and continues to adopt technical ideas from it."[34] It took about a millennium before Pāṇini's work started to circulate outside of India, first in China (among Buddhist monks in the seventh century CE),[35] then in the Islamic world (as shown by the example of Al-Biruni, who wrote a chapter on Pāṇini's grammar in his *Kitab al-Hind* in the eleventh century),[36] and only much later in Europe (where it was taken up by nineteenth-century linguists such as Franz Bopp and twentieth-century linguists like Leonard Bloomfield).[37] Pāṇini's ideas thus circulated widely—yet most histories of the humanities neglect his work.[38]

Pāṇini's case is a wonderful example of the flowering of the humanities outside the "West." It has become clear that the humanities have flourished earlier and more intensively outside Europe, not only in India but also in China and elsewhere.[39] The study of art, literature, music, language, and the past were practiced basically everywhere in world: from the genealogies produced on the Polynesian island of Tonga, and the historical-mythological narratives *Popol Vuh* in the Maya civilization, to the famous manuscripts from Timbuktu that include historical, logical, philological, and musicological studies. The history of humanistic practices from different parts of the world can of course be studied in their own right, but in order to understand how humanistic concepts and ideas moved across regions (as we have seen with Pāṇini's case), these practices should also be studied in terms of their circulation. Instead of a *monocentric* approach to the history of the humanities, we thus need a *polycentric* perspective where every place can be viewed as a center.[40]

A polycentric approach treats the histories of the humanities from different places on a par; it studies these histories both from the perspective of each place itself as well as from the perspective of any other place to which knowledge transfer may have taken place. In this way we can explore how ideas, concepts, metaphors, methods, virtues, and practices—which we have called "cognitive goods" elsewhere—flowed from one place to the other, if at all, be it from Timbuktu, Xian, Amsterdam, or Totonicapán.[41]

Hence my third maxim:

> **Maxim 3:** *Be polycentric with respect to space: aim for a history of the humanities which treats the humanities from different places in the world on a par.*

Challenge 4: The Problem of Incommensurability

My solution to the problem of Eurocentrism and ethnocentrism triggers another challenge: the problem of incommensurable concepts. How can we compare humanities practices from different parts of the world when they use words or concepts that diverge so greatly that any comparison gets muddled by confusions about their cultural contexts?[42] I will argue that despite the existence of incommensurable concepts, we can often discern higher-level intercultural concepts that allow for meaningful comparison (of similarities as well as of differences). Intercultural or universal concepts have been criticized by anthropologists,[43] but in fields such as comparative literature or comparative history it is common to search for levels of analysis that involve comparable concepts. I will argue that two candidates for intercultural concepts in the history of the humanities are (1) the notion of *rule/pattern,* and (2) the notion of *principle*.[44] In all cultures, humans seem to have searched for patterns in their surrounding world (natural and cultural), and for deeper principles that try to explain these rules or patterns.[45]

Take the ancient Chinese concept of *qi* (氣), which in English is translated alternatively with "vital force," "material energy," "life force," "energy flow," and even with "air."[46] The concept plays a fundamental role in the history of Chinese medicine as well as in the Chinese humanities.[47] In Chinese art theory, for example, *qi* is used in Xie He's seminal text "Classification of Painters" (*Gu huapin lu*) from the fifth century CE.[48] According to Xie He, a prerequisite for a good painting is that it has a resonance of *qi*. This concept is not commensurable with any of the Greek or Roman concepts on good art. In the few art-theoretical works that survived from European antiquity, such as (parts of) Pliny's *Naturalis historia* (Natural History), we find descriptions of how to achieve an illusion of reality, but nowhere in Pliny or elsewhere do we find a concept that comes anywhere close to vital force or energy flow. Perhaps the "closest" comes Pliny's discussion of the capacity to depict the "spirit" of (a portrait) of Alexander the Great by the painter Apelles.[49] But any comparison between Pliny's temperamental notion of "spirit" and Xie He's mystic notion of *qi* becomes close to meaningless.

And yet, there are other levels of analysis that do allow for meaningful comparison of these art-theoretical works, for instance at the level of the concept of *rule*. We find this concept not only in Pliny and Xie He, but also in the Indian art-theoretical text *Sadanga* (Six Limbs).[50] The rules in these texts describe regularities for bodily proportions, for different forms of (parallel and geometric) perspective and for foreshortening. These rules are specified to such an extent that we can delineate both their commonalities and their mutual differences.

The concept of rule is also widespread in linguistics where the notion of grammar is used to describe the regularities of word forms and word orders. Although grammars have served different purposes in different regions and periods, the grammatical rules themselves are well comparable—from the so-called *context-sensitive* rules used in Pāṇini's grammar to the *dependency* rules used in Sibawayh's grammar from the eighth century CE.[51] The same holds for philology where rules for reconstructing the original text from extant copies have been developed, from early modern Europe to Ming-Qing China. And in the field of history writing, historians all over the world have tried to formulate rules for assessing the trustworthiness of a historical source—such as the *isnad* method in Islamic historiography and the method of historical source-criticism in Europe.[52]

Also, the principles that have been proposed to underlie the various rules can be compared. In rhetoric and logic, the search for general principles of reasoning can be found in different places. In both the Chinese *Mohist Canons* and Aristotle's *Metaphysics* we find formulations of the well-known *laws of non-contradiction* and *excluded middle* that can be properly compared.[53] These "laws" are taken as the criteria to which all reasoning patterns must comply. And in musicology we find a search for different harmonic principles underlying the observed regularities in consonant intervals (in particular the tonic, octave, and fifth) both in Greece (Pythagoras, Aristoxenus), India (Bharata Muni), and China (Liu An).

Thus the problem of incommensurable concepts can be rephrased as the *problem of finding the appropriate level of analysis,* such as the level of rule, pattern, or principle. Not everything can be meaningfully compared, but once we start searching for comparative levels of historical analysis across cultures, then the door is opened to an immense enrichment of the history of the humanities.[54]

>**Maxim 4:** *Not everything can be compared directly, but there are commensurable levels of analysis—such as rules, patterns, and principles—that are comparable across cultures.*

General Discussion

Other Solutions

The solutions to the four challenges given in this chapter represent only one end of the spectrum. My choices have been quite inclusive. Less inclusive or more exclusive choices are also possible. The other end of the spectrum would correspond, for example, to:

>**Challenge 1** (Demarcation): Only disciplines that study the products of the human mind should be included.
>**Challenge 2** (Anachronism): The history of the humanities should be limited to the period in which "humanities" existed as a term so as to avoid anachronism.
>**Challenge 3** (Eurocentrism): The history of the humanities should be limited to those disciplines that were established as humanities disciplines in the West.
>**Challenge 4** (Incommensurability): Humanities disciplines can only be compared if they use the same concepts.

Some of these exclusive choices may seem reasonable alternatives to the inclusive ones; yet if they are applied consistently, they reduce the history of the humanities not only to the period in which the term humanities is actually used, but to the anglophone world only. This is because the terms used in other languages and regions, such as *Geisteswissenschaften* in German, are not exactly translatable with "humanities."[55] Moreover, since the English notion of humanities gained traction in the first half of the twentieth century only, the history of the nineteenth-century "humanities" in the anglophone world would have to be excluded as well (for reasons of anachronism). The exclusive choices above would thus lead to an unparalleled barrenness and parochialism. This being said, there may be solutions that lie between the inclusive and exclusive ones. Whatever choices one makes, they need to be carefully argued for.

Other Challenges

While our four challenges are constitutive for the field of history of the humanities, they are far from exhaustive. An important challenge we have not discussed so far is the problem of forgotten or disregarded scholars, in particular women scholars. While women scholars have, for centuries, played a marginal role compared to male scholars, their contributions have been unjustly downplayed. One of the earliest women scholars, the Chinese historian Ban Zhao (45–116 CE), has only been accorded the honor of finishing the "Book of Han" (*Hanshu*), where her brother Ban Gu allegedly left off. But it has turned out that her share was far greater than was long admitted.[56] The Byzantine historian Anna Comnena, author of the famous *Alexiad*, received a reputation of having produced a "strongly colored" history, as if her twelfth-century male colleagues were not writing colored history.[57] And take the many early modern women humanists, such as Isotta Nogarola, Alessandra Scala, and Cornelia Vossius, who had little opportunity to develop their exceptional talent. Their fate was either seclusion or marriage; other paths would have met with scorn.[58] The philologists Anne Dacier and Anna Maria van Schurman may seem exceptions to this pattern, but an academic career was ruled out for them, too. There is currently a mounting interest in the history of women scholars from Europe and China as well as from Africa, such as the nineteenth-century Fula scholar Nana Asma'u who wrote a stunning narrative history of the Fulani wars: *Wakar Gewaye* (The Journey).[59]

This brings me also to the problem of the *non-academic* (or *non-professional*) humanities, which deals with the works of scholars who had no humanistic training. Examples include merchants writing grammars for practical, often commercial purposes such as Joan Ketelaar's first grammar of Hindustani from the seventeenth century.[60] Or non-academic historians who wrote about the history of a city, such as the *Ta'rikh al-fattash* recounting the rise and fall of Timbuktu.[61] Or artists and artisans who wrote handbooks with technical descriptions of the visual arts. Or musicians and actors who possessed embodied and tacit knowledge of music and theater. The latter is also relevant to the problem of oral traditions, involving historical, musicological, and art-theoretical knowledge that was never written down. Many of these non-academic productions in the humanities have been forgotten or even obscured.[62] Yet they form an essential part of the history of the humanities. Focusing on embodied and tacit knowledge shifts the attention from scholarly institutions to amateurs and practitioners in non-academic professions, including women and minorities.

The same counts for what has been referred to as the "colonial humanities." While it is increasingly recognized that European scholars took part actively in colonization and suppression, the contribution of the *colonized* scholars is still vastly understudied. Of particular interest are the joint productions of colonizing and colonized scholars, the study of which has only very recently begun.[63] The challenge to come to terms with the colonial heritage of the humanities is more important than ever and should be part of the history of the humanities.

Relation with the History of Science and Knowledge

To what extent do our challenges also hold for the history of science and the history of knowledge more generally? The relation between the history of the humanities and the history of science has become a vivid strand of research, in particular since the focus section in *Isis* on this topic.[64] Yet rather than dealing with the constitutive challenges, most of these studies go into the entangled histories of specific humanities and scientific disciplines, such as between philology and biology, linguistics and computer science, or history and physics.[65]

We believe that the four challenges discussed in this essay are directly relevant for the history of science and the history of knowledge. The problems of demarcation, anachronism, Eurocentrism, and incommensurability carry over to these fields, especially to histories that go beyond single disciplines, periods, or regions.[66] As far as our solutions and maxims are concerned, these can almost be literally applied to the history of science and knowledge. Only the maxim of demarcation is specifically geared to the humanities. Yet, what holds for the term "humanities" also holds for the terms "science" and "knowledge": we must come to grips with the questions as to what fields and practices are included, and how their histories can be written across time and space.

Notes

1. I am grateful for the excellent comments and suggestions on previous versions of this chapter. A first version was commented on by Herman Paul, Christoph Harbsmeier, Daniela Merolla, and Thijs Weststeijn. Given the global scope of this essay, I made a second version available on academia.edu ("open to comments"), on which I received valuable suggestions from Helene G. Albrecht, Remco Breuker, Lesley Johnson, Sjang ten Hagen, Floris Solleveld, William M. Barton, and Tim Markey.
2. See, e.g., *The Making of the Humanities*, 3 vols, ed. Rens Bod, Jaap Maat, and Thijs Weststeijn (Amsterdam: Amsterdam University Press, 2010–4); Jan Eckel, *Geist der Zeit: Deutsche Geisteswissenschaften seit 1870* (Göttingen: Vandenhoeck & Ruprecht, 2008); Rens Bod, *De vergeten wetenschappen: een geschiedenis van de humaniora* (Amsterdam: Prometheus, 2010), translated as *A New History of the Humanities: The Search for Principles and Patterns from Antiquity to the Present*, trans. Lynn Richards (Oxford: Oxford University Press, 2013); James Turner, *Philology: The Forgotten Origins of the Humanities* (Princeton, NJ: Princeton University Press, 2014). See also the journal *History of Humanities*.
3. Wilhelm Dilthey, *Einleitung in die Geisteswissenschaften: Versuch einer Grundlegung für das Studium der Gesellschaft und der Geschichte* (Leipzig: B. G. Teubner, 1959 [1883]). Note that the English notion of "mind" is not exactly equivalent to Dilthey's notion of "Geist," but in this chapter I will leave this as is.
4. See Rens Bod and Julia Kursell, "Introduction: The Humanities and the Sciences," *Isis* 106, no. 2 (2015): 337–440.
5. For these and other methods, see Bod, *New History*.
6. For an historical overview of the social sciences, see, e.g., Roger Smith, *The Norton History of the Human Sciences* (New York: Norton, 1997); Scott Gordon, *The History and Philosophy of Social Science: An Introduction* (New York: Routledge, 1993); Theodore Porter and Dorothy Ross, *The Cambridge History of Science*, vol. 7 (Cambridge: Cambridge University Press, 2003).
7. Fredrik Bertilsson, "Source Criticism as a Technology of Government in the Swedish Psychological Defence: The Impact of Humanistic Knowledge on Contemporary Security Policy," *Humanities* 10, no. 2 (2021): 13. See also Charles Bazerman, *The Informed Writer: Using Sources in the Disciplines* (Boston, MA: Houghton Mifflin, 1995).
8. Marianne Klemun, "Historismus/Historismen – Geschichtliches und Naturkundliches: Identität – Episteme – Praktiken," in *Wissenschaftliche Forschung in Österreich 1800–1900: Spezialisierung, Organisation, Praxis*, ed. Christine Ottner, Gerhard Holzer, and Petra Svatek (Göttingen: V&R Unipress,

2015), 33–4; Julia Kursell, "Fine-Tuning Philology: Helmholtz's Investigation into Ancient Greek and Persian Scales," *History of Humanities* 2, no. 2 (2017): 345–59; Sjang ten Hagen, "History and Physics Entangled: Disciplinary Intersections in the Long Nineteenth Century" (PhD thesis University of Amsterdam, 2021).

9. See Rens Bod, "A Comparative Framework for Studying the Histories of the Humanities and Science," *Isis* 106, no. 2 (2015): 367–77.

10. For a discussion on the distinction between origin and beginning, see Edward Said, *Beginnings: Intention and Method* (New York: Columbia University Press, 1985).

11. For a brief history of the term "humanities," see Floris Solleveld, "The Transformation of the Humanities: Ideals and Practices of Scholarship between Enlightenment and Romanticism, 1750-1850" (PhD thesis Radboud University Nijmegen, 2018), 14–16.

12. For a typology of anachronisms, see Quentin Skinner, "Meaning and Understanding in the History of Ideas," *History and Theory* 8, no. 1 (1969): 3–53. For a more recent overview, see Carlos Spoerhase, "Zwischen den Zeiten: Anachronismus und Präsentismus in der Methodologie der historischen Wissenschaften," *Scientia Poetica* 8 (2004): 169–240.

13. The anachronistic use of the term "humanities" has been noted by several authors, including Thomas Greene, *The Light in Troy: Limitation and Discovery in Renaissance Poetry* (New Haven, CT: Yale University Press, 1982), 30; Robert Proctor, *Defining the Humanities: How Rediscovering a Tradition Can Improve our Schools*, 2nd edn (Bloomington, IN: Indiana University Press, 1998), 8; Bod, *New History*, 8–11. Yet these authors use the term humanities to describe past activities in a period when the term was not used by the historical actors.

14. For a discussion, see David L. Hull, "In Defense of Presentism," *History and Theory* 18, no. 1 (1979): 1–15.

15. Nick Jardine, "Uses and Abuses of Anachronism in the History of the Sciences," *History of Science* 38, no. 3 (2000): 251–70.

16. Glenn W. Most, "Karl Lachmann (1793–1851): Reconstructing the Transmission of a Classical Latin Author," *History of Humanities* 4, no. 2 (2019): 269–73, at 269.

17. For a translation of Lachmann's original publication, see Glenn W. Most, "Translation of the Introduction of Caroli Lachmanni in T. Lucretii Cari De Rerum Natura Libros Commentarius," *History of Humanities* 4, no. 2 (2019): 275–86.

18. For a critical view on Lachmann, see Sebastiano Timpanaro, *The Genesis of Lachmann's Method*, trans. and ed. Glenn W. Most (Chicago, IL: University of Chicago Press, 2005).

19. See Anthony Grafton, *Defenders of the Text: The Traditions of Scholarship in an Age of Science, 1450–1800* (Cambridge, MA: Harvard University Press, 1991), 56.

20. Heinrich Wölfflin, *Kunstgeschichtliche Grundbegriffe: Das Problem der Stilentwicklung in der neueren Kunst*, (Munich: Hugo Bruckmann, 1915).
21. Leon Battista Alberti, *De pictura*, 1435. There are several translations of Alberti's work, e.g., Leon Battista Alberti, *On Painting*, trans. by Cecil Grayson (London: Penguin Classics, 1991).
22. See the discussion in Michael Baxandall, *Giotto and the Orators: Humanist Observers of Painting in Italy and the Discovery of Pictorial Composition 1350–1450* (Oxford: Oxford University Press, 1971), 130.
23. See Chad Wellmon, *Organizing Enlightenment: Information Overload and the Invention of the Modern Research University* (Baltimore, MD: Johns Hopkins University Press, 2015), 235–48.
24. See, e.g., *How to Be a Historian: Scholarly Personae in Historical Studies, 1800–2000*, ed. Herman Paul (Manchester: Manchester University Press, 2019).
25. Kasper Risbjerg Eskildsen, "Leopold Von Ranke (1795–1886): Criticizing an Early Modern Historian," *History of Humanities* 4, no. 2 (2019): 257–62.
26. Anthony Grafton, *Joseph Scaliger: A Study in the History of Classical Scholarship*, 2 vols (Oxford: Oxford University Press, 1983, 1993). See also Dirk van Miert, *The Emancipation of Biblical Philology in the Dutch Republic, 1590–1670* (Oxford: Oxford University Press, 2018).
27. See Proctor, *Defining the Humanities*, Ch. 1–4; Michiel Leezenberg and Gerard de Vries, *History and Philosophy of the Humanities* (Amsterdam: Amsterdam University Press, 2019); Søren Kjørup, *Humanities, Geisteswissenschaften, sciences humaines: Eine Einführung*, trans. Elisabeth Bense (Stuttgart: J. B. Metzler, 2001); Eric Adler, *The Battle of the Classics: How a Nineteenth-Century Debate Can Save the Humanities* (Oxford: Oxford University Press, 2020), Ch. 2. An exception is Bod, *New History*. Global approaches are used more often in histories of single humanities disciplines, such as Esa Itkonen, *Universal History of Linguistics* (Amsterdam: John Benjamins, 1991); *World Philology*, ed. Sheldon Pollock, Benjamin Elman and Ku-ming Chang (Cambridge, MA: Harvard University Press, 2015); Daniel Woolf, *A Global History of History* (Cambridge: Cambridge University Press, 2011); Christopher Wood, *A History of Art History* (Princeton, NJ: Princeton University Press, 2019).
28. E.g., James McClellan and Harold Dorn, *Science and Technology in World History: An Introduction* (Baltimore: Johns Hopkins University Press, 1999); Patricia Fara, *Science: A Four Thousand Year History* (Oxford: Oxford University Press, 2009); H. Floris Cohen, *How Modern Science Came into the World: Four Civilizations, One 17th-Century Breakthrough* (Amsterdam: Amsterdam University Press, 2010).
29. Coluccio Salutati, *Epistolario*, vol. 4, ed. Francesco Novati (Rome: Instituto Storico Italiano, 1911), 216. See the discussion in Paul Oskar Kristeller,

"Humanism and Scholasticism in the Italian Renaissance," *Byzantion* 17 (1944): 346–74.

30. See Benjamin G. Kohl, "The Changing Concept of the 'studia humanitatis' in the Early Renaissance," *Renaissance Studies* 6, no. 2 (1992): 185–209; Christopher S. Celenza, *The Intellectual World of the Italian Renaissance* (Cambridge: Cambridge University Press, 2017), 129.
31. See George Makdisi, *The Rise of Humanism in Classical Islam and the Christian West* (Edinburgh: Edinburgh University Press, 1990); Sonja Brentjes, *Teaching and Learning the Sciences in Islamicate Societies (800–1700)* (Turnhout: Brepols, 2018); Rens Bod, *World of Patterns: A Global History of Knowledge*, trans. Leston Buell (Baltimore, MD: Johns Hopkins University Press, 2022), 133, 197.
32. Even if these humanists had been aware of the *studia adabiya,* they would probably not have referred to it, since their goal, like that of so many an Italian humanist, was to revive the Roman classical world in a Christian context in opposition to both the Islamic and the medieval Christian world.
33. Pāṇini, *The Ashtadhyayi*, trans. Srisa Chandra Vasu (Charleston: Nabu Press, 2011 [1923]).
34. Paul Kiparsky, "Pāṇinian Linguistics," in *Encyclopedia of Language and Linguistics* (Amsterdam: Elsevier, 1993), 2918–23.
35. Sally Wriggins, *Xuanzang: A Buddhist Pilgrim on the Silk Road* (Boulder: Westview Press, 2003).
36. Edward Sachau, *Alberuni's India*, Vol. I (London: Trübner & Co., 1888).
37. Itkonen, *Universal History*.
38. Studies on the history of Western linguistics that do mention Pāṇini, typically underexpose his work. In Pieter Seuren, *Western Linguistics: An Historical Introduction*, Blackwell Publishers, 1998, only one sentence is dedicated to Pāṇini's work, and only with regard to his influence on Leonard Bloomfield (191).
39. See Bod, *New History*, Ch. 1. See also Rens Bod et al., "A New Field: History of Humanities," *History of Humanities* 1, no. 1 (2016): 1–8.
40. See Bod, *World of Patterns*, 4–9.
41. The term "cognitive goods" was introduced in Rens Bod et al., "The Flow of Cognitive Goods: A Historiographical Framework for the Study of Epistemic Transfer," *Isis* 110, no. 3 (2019): 483–96.
42. Note that incommensurable concepts may not only occur between different cultures but also between different periods within a single culture. In discussing Challenge 2 on anachronism I assumed that concepts are at least mutually commensurable. In case they are not, Maxim 4 below must be followed first. For the notion of incommensurability, see Ludwik Fleck, "Zur Krise der 'Wirklichkeit,'" *Die Naturwissenschaften* 17 (1929): 425–30. For

"comparing the incomparable," see Marcel Detienne, *Comparer l'incomparable: oser expérimenter et construire* (Paris: Points, 2009).
43. The anthropologist Mary Douglas referred to her colleagues' obsession with exceptions to intercultural concepts ("this does not apply to my tribe") as "Bongo-bongo-ism." See Paul Richards, "Mary Tew Douglas (1921–2007)," *American Anthropologist* 110, no. 3 (2008): 407–10. For a plea for making comparisons across cultures, see Mineke Schipper, *Imagining Insiders: Africa and the Question of Belonging* (New York: Cassell, 1999).
44. See also Bod, *New History*.
45. For the search of patterns and principles in different cultures, see, e.g., Gary Tomlinson, *Culture and the Course of Human Evolution* (Chicago, IL: University of Chicago Press, 2018), 4–18. See also Clifford Geertz, *The Interpretation of Cultures* (New York: Basic Books, 1973), 89. For a history of patterns and principles across knowledge disciplines, see Bod, *World of Patterns*.
46. For a discussion on the problem of translation, see the special issue "On Other Terms: Interfering in Social Science English," ed. Annemarie Mol and John Law, *The Sociological Review* 68, no. 2 (2020).
47. See David Pollard, "Ch'i in Chinese Literary Theory," in *Chinese Approaches to Literature from Confucius to Liang Ch'i-Ch'ao*, ed. Adele Austin Rickett (Princeton, NJ: Princeton University Press, 1978), 43–66. See also Huan Zhang and Ken Rose, *A Brief History of qi* (Boston, MA: Paradigm Publications, 2001).
48. Osvald Sirén, *The Chinese on the Art of Painting: Texts by the Painter-Critics, from the Han through the Ch'ing Dynasties* (Mineola, NY: Dover, 1936), 219.
49. Pliny, *Naturalis historia* 35, 79–97.
50. Prithvi Agrawala, *On the Sadanga Canons of Painting* (Varanasi: Prithivi Prakashan, 1981).
51. See Itkonen, *Universal History*, for a comparison of these rules.
52. For a comparison between the Islamic *isnad* method and the European source-critical method, see Rens Bod, "How to Open Pandora's Box: A Tractable Notion of the History of Knowledge," *Journal for the History of Knowledge* 1, no. 1 (2020).
53. See Jialong Zhang and Fenrong Liu, "Some Thoughts on Mohist Logic," in *A Meeting of the Minds: Proceedings of the Workshop on Logic, Rationality and Interaction*, ed. Johan van Benthem, Shier Ju, and Frank Veltman (London: College Publications, 2007), 85–102.
54. This is forcefully defended in Chris Lorenz, "Comparative Historiography: Problems and Perspectives," *History and Theory* 38, no. 1 (1999): 25–39. For an illustration of comparison with respect to the humanities, see Devin Griffiths, "The Comparative Method and the History of the Modern Humanities," *History of Humanities* 2, no. 2 (2017): 473–505.

55. For example, until *c.* 1950, the term *Geisteswetenschaften* typically included the social sciences, whilst the term *humanities* did not or did much less so. See also Herman Paul's introduction to this volume, in which other subtle differences between *humanities* and *Geisteswissenschaften* are discussed.
56. Anthony Clark, *Ban Gu's History of Early China* (Amherst, NY: Cambria Press, 2008).
57. See, e.g., Carolyn Connor, *Women of Byzantium* (New Haven, CT: Yale University Press, 2004).
58. *Women Classical Scholars: Unsealing the Fountain from the Renaissance to Jacqueline de Romilly*, ed. Rosie Wyles and Edith Hall (Oxford: Oxford University Press, 2016), 35.
59. *The Collected Works of Nana Asma'u, Daughter of Usman dan Fodiyo 1793–1864*, ed. Jean Boyd and Beverly B. Mack (East Lansing, MI: Michigan State University Press, 1997).
60. Anna Pytlowany, *Ketelaar Rediscovered: The first Dutch Grammar of Persian and Hindustani (1698)* (Utrecht: LOT Publications, 2018).
61. *Ta'rikh al-fattash: The Timbuktu Chronicles 1493–1599*, trans. Christopher Wise and Haba Abu Taleb (Lawrenceville, NJ: Africa World Press, 2011).
62. See Han Lamers, Toon Van Hal, and Sebastiaan Clercx, "How to Deal with Scholarly Forgetting in the History of the Humanities: Starting Points for Discussion," *History of Humanities* 5, no. 1 (2020): 5–29.
63. See the forum section "The Rise and Decline of 'Colonial Humanities,'" ed. Daniela Merolla et al., *History of Humanities* 6, no. 1 (2021). See also Kapil Raj, "Beyond Postcolonialism. . . and Postpositivism: Circulation and the Global History of Science," *Isis* 104, no. 2 (2013): 337–47; Will Bridges, "A Brief history of the Inhumanities," *History of Humanities* 4, no. 1 (2019): 1–26.
64. See the focus section "The History of Humanities and the History of Science," ed. Rens Bod and Julia Kursell, *Isis* 106, no. 2 (2015).
65. See, e.g., Josephine Musil-Gutsch, "On the Same Page: Paper Technology Practices in the Humanities and the Sciences," *History of Humanities* 5, no. 2 (2020): 355–81; Sjang ten Hagen, "How 'Facts' Shaped Modern Disciplines: The Fluid Concept of Fact and the Common Origins of German Physics and Historiography," *Historical Studies in the Natural Sciences* 49, no. 3 (2019): 300–37.
66. For further discussion on the foundations of the history of knowledge, see Peter Burke, *What is the History of Knowledge?* (Cambridge: Polity Press, 2016); the forum section "What is the History of Knowledge?" ed. Sven Dupré and Geert Somsen, *Journal for the History of Knowledge* 1, no. 1 (2020); Lorraine Daston, "The History of Science and the History of Knowledge," *KNOW* 1, no. 1 (2017): 131–54.

Glossary

Big science A loose label for large, government-funded research projects like the Manhattan Project and, more recently, the Human Genome Project. Although the English term became popular only during the Cold War, *Großwissenschaft* was a common German phrase already by the early twentieth century. Nineteenth-century humanities projects such as multi-volume historical dictionaries and source editions are sometimes referred to as "big humanities."

Boundary work The activity of drawing, defending, or challenging boundaries between fields of knowledge (e.g., between science and non-science, between the sciences and the humanities, or between one discipline and another). Sociologist Thomas F. Gieryn coined the term in the early 1980s to draw attention to scientists justifying claims to knowledge and power by means of value-laden lines of demarcation.

Colligatory concepts W. H. Walsh's term for concepts that bring together a heterogenous mass of material under a single heading. Typical examples are "Renaissance" and "Industrial Revolution": two historiographical concepts that simultaneously summarize and interpret a great deal of historical information about fifteenth-century Italy and eighteenth-century England, respectively. Many colligatory concepts are also essentially contested concepts (see below).

Comparative history A type of history writing to which comparisons between countries, traditions, or fields of study are central. It is premised on the assumption that only comparisons can reveal what is distinct, or not so distinct, about a particular case study.

Comparative method Although all comparative history uses comparative methods, the phrase "comparative method" as used in this volume refers more specifically to the nineteenth-century project of mapping similarities and differences between, say, languages or plant specimens with the aim of identifying patterns of development.

Critique An activity that many regard as central to the humanities, even if it comes in very different forms. Examples include *philological critique* (a careful reading of texts or images in their original contexts, focused on issues of reliability and meaning), *philosophical critique* (a Kantian sensitivity to the boundaries of what can be known), and *ideology critique* (the Marxist-inspired project of unmasking the ideological underpinnings of cultural products).

Demarcation problem The issue as to where to draw a line between, in this case, the humanities and other fields of scholarship, such as the sciences. In the absence of simple answers, it is a "problem" that returns time and again, causing scholars to engage in "boundary work" (see above).

Entanglement Literally meaning enmeshment in a complicated situation, the term is used in the humanities mainly to draw attention to dependency relations (i.e., between the sciences and the humanities, between the North and the South, or between humankind and the environment) that have historically not received the attention they deserve.

Essentially contested concepts Concepts like justice, fairness, humanities, and critique, which everyone recognizes as important, but no one is able to define once and for all. According to W. B. Gallie, concepts are essentially contested if their proper use "inevitably involves endless disputes about their proper uses on the part of their users."

Eurocentrism A shorthand label for ways of looking at the world that privilege Europe, or the so-called "Western" world more broadly, at the cost of especially the global South. In the humanities, the persistence of Eurocentric perspectives is often interpreted as testifying to the continuing legacies of colonialism.

Geisteswissenschaften A German equivalent to what is known in English as humanities, even if the term is perhaps more accurately translated as "human sciences." Nineteenth-century German philosophers like Wilhelm Dilthey, Wilhelm Windelband, and Heinrich Rickert famously distinguished the *Geisteswissenschaften* from the *Naturwissenschaften* (thereby engaging in "boundary work"—see above).

Humanities A term of American origin, in wide usage since the 1920s. On the one hand, it denotes a cluster of fields like English, philosophy, history, and media studies. On the other, it invokes connotations of human self-understanding, self-transformation, cultural capital, and wisdom as distinguished from knowledge. As such, the humanities resemble the *Geisteswissenschaften*, especially in their nineteenth-century incarnations (see above).

Human sciences A possible translation of *Geisteswissenschaften*, even if the term nowadays serves primarily as an umbrella category for disciplines that study human life in its biological, social, and cultural aspects. As the human sciences encompass field like biology, sociology, anthropology, psychology, and the neurosciences, they overlap only partly with the humanities or *Geisteswissenschaften*.

Interdisciplinarity An umbrella term for all sorts of cooperation across disciplinary boundaries and the knowledge, theories, methods, or tools that such collaboration may yield. Interdisciplinarity (integration of disciplinary perspectives) is often seen as more ambitious than multidisciplinarity (a mere aggregation of disciplinary perspectives).

Masculinities Socially constructed ideals of manhood ("this is how a real man looks like") that matter to historians of the humanities insofar as they affected expectations that scholars had to meet. Objectivity, for instance, was often gendered as a masculine virtue, which implied not only that it was inaccessible to women, but also that objectivity for men served as a marker of masculinity.

Personae Models of how to be a scholar (a scientist, a historian, a philologist), embodying habits, dispositions, attitudes, virtues, or skills that are deemed relevant for the pursuit of scholarly work. *Personae* (*persona* in the singular) may vary across time, space, and disciplines, but also—think of the "activist" or the "grant hunter"—appeal to scholars from very different areas.

Philology The study of texts broadly defined. By the early nineteenth century, philology encompassed three kinds of research: (1) the study of textual traditions and variants, as in Biblical studies, (2) inquiries into the nature and origins of language, and (3) comparative study of language families in their historical development (with help of the "comparative method"—see above).

Practices A notoriously slippery concept central to various forms of "practice theory" and "praxeology," but used in this volume simply to denote such recognizable professional activities as teaching a class, organizing a conference, writing a paper, and supervising students' work. Historians speak about practices in discussing the everyday realities of scholarly research and teaching.

Studia humanitatis The rubric under which Renaissance humanists like Coluccio Salutati placed the study of grammar, rhetoric, poetry, history, and moral philosophy. Distinguished from the *studia divinitatis* (theology), these "studies of humanity" or "humanistic studies" are often interpreted as forerunners of the modern humanities.

Virtues Personal qualities, habits of mind, or traits of character that enable their possessors to pursue a desired good like justice or knowledge. In the history of the humanities, "scholarly virtues" denote character traits that scholars expected each other to display, just as "epistemic virtues" refers to qualities that scholars saw as indispensable for acquiring epistemic goods (knowledge, understanding).

Index

Adams, Herbert Baxter 61
Adelung, Johann Christoph 113–16
Adler, Emanuel 223
Adler, Eric 7, 9
Adorno, Theodor 306
Ahmed, Siraj 12–13
Althusser, Louis 103
An, Liu 354
Anderson, Amanda 312
Anker, Elizabeth 312–13, 317–18
Appiah, Kwame Anthony 316
Appleby, Joyce 317
Aquinas, Thomas 89, 159
Arcenas, Claire Rydell 8, 15–16
Aristotle 76, 88–9, 200, 354
Åsberg, Cecilia 328, 335
Asma'u, Nana 356
Augustine 89

Babbitt, Irving 68
Baedeker, Karl 207
Ba Konaré, Adame 252–3
Balbi, Adriano 114–15, 122
Ban Zhao 356
Banks, Joseph 121
Banzan, Kumazawa 176
Barad, Karen 331
Barth, Heinrich 114, 117, 120, 122
Barth, Karl 307
Barthes, Roland 308
Bary, Theodore de 175–6
Bate, Jonathan 336
Battista Alberti, Leon 349
Baudrillard, Jean 309
Baumgarten, Hermann 199
Bayle, Pierre 232
Becker, Carl Heinrich 272, 276
Bendemann, Eduard 228, 230
Benjamin, Walter 308, 311
Bennett, Judith 247
Bentham, James 36

Bentham, Jeremy 36
Bentley, Richard 48, 51, 349
Berendt, Karl 113
Berger, Heike 220
Berger, Stefan 245
Bergthaller, Hannes 329, 332, 336, 338
Bernheim, Ernst 203, 206, 275
Best, Stephen 309
Bismarck, Otto von 195, 205
Bleek, Wilhelm 111, 113, 115, 117, 120–1, 125
Bloomfield, Leonard 352
Blumenbach, Johann Friedrich 91
Boahen, Adu 248, 250–1, 253, 255–8, 260
Boas, Franz 96, 112–13, 119, 122–3, 125
Bod, Rens 17, 89, 336–7
Bogumil, Jewsiewicki 253
Bonaparte, Napoleon 225, 230, 305
Bonpland, Aimé 329
Bopp, Franz 96, 352
Bosch, Mineke 246
Bourdieu, Pierre 309
Boyle, Robert 10
Brecht, Bertolt 308, 311
Bryce, James 291
Buckle, Henry Thomas 34–5, 184
Budge, Gavin 100
Buell, Lawrence 328
Burnham, Jack 325
Busa, Roberto 154–5, 158–9, 161, 164–6
Buschmann, Eduard 113
Butler, Judith 306, 314

Cage, John 312
Callard, Agnes 76
Callard, Felicity 331
Capshew, James 133
Carson, Rachel 331, 335
Castiglia, Christopher 312
Celenza, Christopher xii, 6–7, 9

Chateaubriand, François-René de 39
Chaucer, Geoffrey 59, 200
Chūshū, Mishima 185
Cicero 89, 136, 349, 351
Clavigero, Francesco 110
Code, Lorraine 334–5, 337
Coen, Deborah 133
Collard, François 199
Comnena, Anna 356
Comte, Auguste 35–6
Conant, James Bryant 296
Condorcet, Nicolas de 36
Connell, Raewyn 228
Cook, Thomas 121
Coquery-Vidrovitch, Catherine 253
Crane, Ronald S. 5, 70
Cronon, William 325, 328
Crowther, Samuel Ajahi 119
Cust, Robert Needham 115
Cuvier, George 94, 96, 121

Dacier, Anne 356
Dahlberg, Julia 246
Darwin, Charles 96–7, 99–103
Darwin, Erasmus 88, 90–3, 100
Daston, Lorraine 10–11, 122, 139, 145, 193, 197, 246, 274
Dawkins, Richard 103
Dehio, Georg 200, 205
Dehrmann, Mark-Georg 270
Derrida, Jacques 308, 312, 314
Diels, Hermann 137, 143–4
Dilthey, Wilhelm 31–2, 34–5, 37–40, 69, 195, 336–7, 346–7
Dodds, Harold W. 292, 294
Dooren, Thom van 339
Dove, Alfred 199
Dowden, Edward 61
Droysen, Johann Gustav 228, 230
Duignan, Peter 255
Dulk, Friedrich 273
Dümichen, Johannes 206–7
Dunlop, John Colin 59
During, Simon 3, 6–7, 288

Eagleton, Terry 74
Eckel, Jan 32
Eilderts, Luke 225
Eliot, Charles W. 290

Elman, Benjamin 177
Emmett, Robert S. 328
Erasmus, Desiderius 349
Eskildsen, Kasper Risbjerg 15
Eusebius of Caesarea 58

Facius, Michael 15–16
Fackenthal, Frank D. 296–8
Fage, John 251
Falola, Toyin 255
Felski, Rita 306, 309–10, 312–14, 317
Felton, Cornelius 53
Feuerhahn, Wolf 36
Ficino, Marsilio 268
Fiorillo, Johann Dominik 226–7
Fischer, Bonifatius 160
Fitzgerald, Des 331
Fitzpatrick, Kathleen 288
Flinn, Andrew 15–16
Flow, Christian 15–16
Forgan, Sophie 224
Förster, Eckart 92
Forster, Reinhold 121
Foster, Hal 311
Foucault, Michel 309, 314
Frei, Hans 307
Freire, Paulo 308
Freud, Sigmund 314

Galison, Peter 122, 193, 197
Gann, Lewis Henry 255
Garrison Brinton, Daniel 113
Gehmacher, Johanna 222
Gessner, Conrad 116
Gibbon, Edward 58
Gierl, Martin 135
Gieryn, Thomas F. 27
Gilij, Felipe 110
Glickman, Robert J. 159, 164, 166
Goeje, Michael Jan de 203
Goethe, Johann Wolfgang von 9, 88, 90–3, 95–7, 99–100
Goldschmidt, Siegfried 200
Golly, Frank B. 333
Grabenweger, Elizabeth 219
Graepler, Daniel 229
Grafton, Anthony 89
Gröber, Gustav 200
Grove, Richard 331

Grey, George 113, 115
Grierson, George 112, 113, 114, 116, 120
Griffiths, Devin 15
Grimm, Jacob 94–5, 120–1
Guizot, François 184

Habermas, Jürgen 314
Haeckel, Ernst 96, 123
Hale, Horatio 121–2
Halmann, Martin M. 163
Haraway, Donna 103, 326, 328
Harpham, Geoffrey Galt 3
Hassan, Ihab 308
He, Xie 353–4
Hedrén, Johan 328, 335
Hegel, Georg Wilhelm Friedrich 34, 92–3, 97
Heise, Ursula K. 328
Helmholtz, Hermann von 142–3
Herder, Johann Gottfried 59
Hervás y Panduro, Lorenzo 109–10, 112–15
Hill Burton, John 184
Hoenigswald, Henry 93
Hoffmann, Petra 141
Hofmann, August Wilhelm von 274
Hofstadter, Richard 297
Holtzmann, Heinrich Julius 204–5
Hopkins, Ernest Martin 290–1
Hübner, Emil 145
Humboldt, Alexander von 94, 100, 121, 232, 329
Humboldt, Wilhelm von 66, 113, 120–1, 275–6
Hunt, Richard 119
Huxley, Thomas 120
Hyakusen, Yoda 183

Ibn Khaldun 12, 351

Jacobsthal, Gustav 200
Jameson, Fredric 102, 306, 314, 319
Jameson, John Franklin 268
Janković de Mirievo, Teodor 110
Jardine, Nicholas 348
Jarrett, James 1
Jewett, Andrew 73
Jodl, Friedrich 203
Johnson, Samuel 59

Jones, William 93, 120, 155
Jordanova, Ludmilla 219, 221, 226

Kaibel, Georg 200
Kant, Immanuel 69, 121, 200, 232, 269, 307
Kauffmann, R. Lane 308
Kekulé, Augustus 274
Kelly, Kevin 163
Kepes, György 325
Kepler, Johannes 9
Kessel, Martina 231
Ketelaar, Joan 356
Kilham, Hannah 120
Kinjō, Ōta 177
Kirchhoff, Arthur 235
Ki-Zerbo, Joseph 252–3, 260
Klaproth, Julius 113, 115–16
Klein, Julia Thompson 330
Knaus, Ludwig 228–9
Knighton, Andrew Lyndon 313
Koelle, Sigismund 114, 116–17, 125
Koerner, Ernst Fridryk Konrad 94
Kōhei, Kanda 182
Koselleck, Reinhart 66, 68
Kraemer, Fabian 3, 14–15
Krajewski, Markus 139
Kwaschik, Anne 271

Lachmann, Karl 348–9
Lamarck, Jean Baptiste 94, 96
Lamprecht, Karl 203
Lange, Helene 218, 235
Latham, Rob 309
Lather, Patti 308, 311
Latour, Bruno 309, 328, 336
Lauth, Bernhard 4
Lavisse, Ernest 225
Leibniz, Gottfried Wilhelm 232, 268
Lepsius, Richard 116–17, 123
Lester, Elizabeth 308
Levi-Strauss, Claude 95
Liebig, Justus von 33, 273–4
Liebmann, Otto 203
Lindbeck, George 307
Lloyd, Lucy 111, 113, 119, 125
Locke, John 298
Lucae, Karl 272
Lyotard, Jean-François 309

Maat, Jaap 336
Mabillon, Jean 349
McArthur, Tom 166
McLaughlin, Andrew 58
McLuhan, Marshall 312
Magnus, Heinrich August 31
Makreel, Rudolf 35
Malm, Andreas 103
Malthus, Thomas 102
Man, Paul de 308
Mandler, Peter 66
Marcus, Sharon 309
Marsden, William 113
Martius, Carl von 121
Marx, Karl 88, 96–100, 102–3, 297, 305, 314
Mazrui, Ali 257
Merchant, Carolyn 326, 328
Merves, Uwe 272
Mill, John Stuart 33–7, 40
Miller, J. Hillis 308
Milton, John 59
Mitchell, Samuel 184
Mohl, Julius von 274
Mokichi, Fujita 184
Mommsen, Theodor 135, 137, 140–5, 229, 231–2
Moore, Jason 103
Moore, Rob 7
Moran, Joe 330
Moretti, Franco 11, 312
Müller, Friedrich Max 95, 122, 196–9, 209
Müller, Karl Otfried 226–9
Müller, Martin 115
Muni, Bharata 354

Neimanis, Astrida 328, 335
Neumann, Franz 271, 273
Newton, Isaac 9–10
Nicolai, Friedrich 110
Niebuhr, Barthold Georg 197
Niemeyer, Max 161
Noblit, George 311
Nogarola, Isotta 356
Nöldeke, Theodor 198, 203–4, 206
Norden, Eduard 162
Nye, David E. 328–9
Nyhan, Julianne 15–16, 161–3

Oesterley, Carl 226–7, 229
Olesko, Kathryn M. 271
Oliver, Roland 251
d'Orbigny, Alcide 121
Ortner, Sherry 328
Östh Gustafsson, Hampus 8, 15
Otfried Müller, Karl 226
Ott, Wilhelm 154, 160–6
Owen, Richard 91, 96

Paine, Thomas 294
Paletschek, Sylvia 271
Paley, William 89, 100
Pallas, Peter Simon 110, 112, 115
Pāṇini 352
Parentucelli, Tommaso 351
Parikka, Jussi 155
Paul, Herman 15, 188, 246, 250, 338
Peacham, Henry 89
Peiresc, Nicolas-Claude Fabri de 268
Perham, Margery 255
Perry, Matthew 180
Petermann, Ernst 114
Petrarch, Francesco 2, 7, 200, 268
Pickering, John 113
Plato 9
Pliny 354
Plumb, John 8, 67, 73–4
Plumwood, Val 326, 328
Polanyi, Michael 307–8, 318
Poliziano, Angelo 349
Ponceau, Peter Stephen du 113
Popper, Karl R. 307
Pouliot, Vincent 223
Proctor, Robert 2, 9
Provencher, Denis 225

Quintilian 89

Rader, Karen 133
Ramsay, Stephen 153
Ranger, Terence 256–7, 260
Ranke, Leopold von 35, 218–19, 230–5, 273–4, 350
Rao, D. Venkat 5
Rask, Rasmus 94–5
Rebenich, Stefan 141
Reitter, Paul xii, 7–8
Rickert, Heinrich 4, 69

Ricoeur, Paul 307, 314, 318
Ritter, Joachim 5
Robbins, Bruce 313
Robin, Libby 333
Rockwell, Geoffrey 154–5, 159–61, 164–5
Rose, Deborah Bird 339
Rueckert, William 325

Said, Edward 65
Saint-Hilaire, Étienne Geoffroy 91, 123
Salutati, Coluccio 351
Sartre, Jean-Paul 71
Saussure, Fernand de 1, 95
Scala, Alessandra 356
Scaliger, Joseph 349–50
Scheffer-Boichorst, Paul 206–7, 2
Schelling, Friedrich von 34, 121
Scherer, Wilhelm 202
Schiel, Jacob Heinrich Wilhelm 32–5
Schirmacher, Käthe 235
Schlegel, Friedrich 94, 121
Schleicher, August 95–6, 121
Schlosser, Julius 229
Schmoller, Gustav 207–9, 218
Schnicke, Falko 15
Schöll, Rudolf 198, 200
Schönbach, Anton 269, 275
Schroeder-Gudehus, Brigitte 135
Schulte Nordholt, Larissa 15–16
Schultz, Franz 201
Schurman, Anna Maria van 356
Scott, Daniel 314
Scott, Joan 219, 221
Scott, Walter 100
Sedgwick, Eve 309, 312
Selden, John 48
Sessions, David 317
Seyffert, Oskar 201
Shakespeare, William 59
Sheldrake, Merlin 332
Shōnan, Yokoi 179, 180
Sibawayh 351, 354
Sibum, H. Otto 246
Sima Qian 12
Sinclair, Stéfan 154–5, 159–61, 164–5
Slovic, Scott 329
Small, Helen 287
Smith, Adam 98
Smith, Bonnie 226

Smith, John B. 159, 165–6
Smith, Robert W. 136
Snow, C. P. 336
Solleveld, Floris 15
Sorai, Ogyū 177
Spoerhase, Carlos 136, 270
Steenbergh, Kristine 15
Stengers, Isabel 334, 338
Stichweh, Rudolf 272
Stover, Justin 57
Studemund, Wilhelm 198–9, 201, 203, 207, 209
Surkis, Judith 317
Sybel, Heinrich von 218, 231

Tacitus 83
Tasman, Paul 159
Thalmann, Marianne 220
Thomas, Sari 308–9, 312
Thoreau, Henry 328
Threlkeld, Lancelot 111, 120
Thucydides 57
Ticknor, George 59–60
Tocqueville, Alexis de 298
Tōju, Nakae 176
Tollebeek, Jo 12–13
Toshiakira, Kawaji 181
Touaillon, Christine 220, 223
Tredelenburg, Friedrich 35
Treitschke, Heinrich von 203
Trevor-Roper, Hugh 251, 260
Truman, Harry 296
Tsing, Anna 103, 338
Turner, James xii, 6, 14–15, 277
Turner, R. Steven 273

Uekötter, Frank 333
Ulmer, Gregory 308–12

Valla, Lorenzo 7, 9
Van Doren, Mark 293–5
Vansina, Jan 257–8
Vasari, Giorgio 226–7
Vater, Johann Severin 113, 116
Voltaire 58
Vossius, Cornelia 356

Waitz, Georg 273
Ward, Humphry 60

Wedgwood, Hensleigh 100
Weizsäcker, Julius 197, 200, 203, 274–5
Wellmon, Chad xii, 7–8
Weststeijn, Thijs 336
Whewell, William 36–7
White, Lynn 325, 332
Wiedemann, Theodor 218–19, 231–5
Williams, Raymond 37, 325
Wilson, Robert R. 131–3, 138
Winckelmann, Johann 268
Windelband, Wilhelm 4, 69
Winter, Thomas Nelson 160
Wolf, Friedrich August 52, 270

Wolff, Janet 309
Wölfflin, Eduard 133–40, 142–4, 268
Wölfflin, Heinrich 349
Worster, Donald 325, 328
Wriston, Henry W. 293

Yasutsugu, Shigeno 186–7
Yorck von Wartenburg, Ludwig 230
Yukichi, Fukuzawa 184

Zedler, Johann Heinrich 38
Zhu Xi 175–7
Ziegler, Theobald 202–3

www.ingramcontent.com/pod-product-compliance
Lightning Source LLC
Chambersburg PA
CBHW050134240426
43673CB00043B/1659